A HISTORY OF SPURS
ON THE PITCH & OFF THE DRAWING BOARD

Art by
PAUL TREVILLION
"The Master of Movement"

Foreword by
GLENN HODDLE
Spurs Legend

Words by
HARRY HARRIS
Multi Award-Winning Journalist

This book is copyright under the Berne Convention. All rights are reserved. Apart from any fair dealing for the purpose of private study, research, criticism or review, as permitted under the Copyright Act, 1956, no part of this publication may be reproduced, stored in a retrieval system, or transmitted, in any form or by any means, electronic, electrical, chemical, mechanical, optical, photocopying, recording or otherwise, without the prior permission of the copyright owner. Enquiries should be sent to the under mentioned address:

EMPIRE PUBLICATIONS
1 Newton St., Manchester M1 1HW
© Harry Harris & Paul Trevillion 2024

ISBN: 9781915616135

Dedications

With Harry Redknapp was in charge, Spurs fans began to feel more optimistic for the future, and I hoped that soon my son, Simon, would see a Spurs team he could be proud of in the way I had been in the past. It is with great pride that Simon took on the inheritance of being a Spurs fan. There was a stage, though, that I worried about my son's judgement. Well, he was only small, and at that time all the kids supported Liverpool, they were the most dominant team in the country for such a long time and Simon followed them. I took him to meet Kenny Dalglish and Irving Scholar arranged, through his close friends at Anfield, for me to take Simon into the director's box for a match - he loved it. There was little to nothing I could do to change his mind, so I made no effort to persuade him to follow Spurs, a club then in the doldrums. However it all changed when Simon grew up and I've no idea why. Perhaps, because his best friend was a Spurs fan. Maybe because it was a touch too far to go to watch Liverpool. Whatever the reason, he was converted, and I did nothing to convince him; he found his way to supporting Tottenham all on his own. But now it was his turn to suffer the way I had. Hey, at least we could both suffer the pains and anguish of being a Spurs fan as father and son.

This book is dedicated to the memory of Simon who passed away a few years ago.

HARRY HARRIS

I am proud to dedicate this book to my eldest son Mark who grew up with us both watching Jimmy Greaves score goal after goal. Today's it's Son…

Come On You Spurs!

PAUL TREVILLION

Contents

Dedications	3
About the Artist	9
About the Author	9
Foreword by Glenn Hoddle	11
Me, My Mad Mum & Spurs	13
My First Game	17
Push and Run	22
League Champions 1950-51	26
Arthur Rowe and I	30
The End of the Road for Arthur Rowe	32
Duncan Edwards	34
From Push and Run to 'Glory, Glory'	40
The Double 1960-61	42
Dave Mackay	45
Cliff Jones	46
John White	50
Jimmy Greaves	54
Bill Nicholson	58
A Nicholson 'No' Means a Revie 'Yes'	62
Alan Mullery	64
Mr Tottenham	70
Pat Jennings	72
Alan Gilzean	78
Nicholson Resigns!	81
Replacing The Irreplaceable	86
Life on the Tottenham *Weekly Herald*	91
Harry Harris by Steve Perryman	104
John Grimsdell	107
D J Bear, Gazza, Vinny and Fergie	109
Derek Kelly	111
Keith Burkinshaw	113
Peter Shreeves	116
Gerry Armstrong	119
Osvaldo Ardiles	120
Tottenham's '81 Wembley Triumph	125
The day Maradona played for Spurs!	127
My Friend Diego by Ossie Ardiles	131
Glenn Hoddle	138
Gary Mabbutt	143
John Ferguson	147
You Are The Ref	151
Irving Scholar	153
The Gazza Phenomenon	167
A Gazza Semi-Final Memory	173
Gary Lineker	177
My Footballing Friend Gary Lineker	181
Lineker's Low Down On Shooting	183
Grant Curran	184
Terry Venables	186
David Buchler	193
Alan Sugar	196
Ossie Returns	200
Jürgen Klinsmann	202
Gerry Francis	204
Christian Gross	207
George Graham	208
Daniel Levy	211
Juande Ramos	213
When 'Arry Met Harry	221
Jermain Defoe	231
Andre Vilas-Boas, Tim Sherwood, and (almost) the return of Glenn Hoddle	234
Mauricio Pochettino	237
The Tottenham Hotspur Stadium	241
The Bedi Family	244
Jose Mourinho	250
"He's One Of Our Own"	254
Ange Postecoglou	266
Jacqui Hall	271
Spurs All-Time Greatest Teams - Harry Harris; Paul Trevillion; Glenn Hoddle; Paul Miller; John Gorman; Tony Galvin; Lord Sugar; Ramon Vega; David Pleat; Teddy Sheringham	278
Acknowledgements	283

About the Author

HARRY HARRIS has written numerous books on Spurs including *Down Memory Lane* and the best-selling life stories of Spurs icons such as Bill Nicholson, Terry Neill, Glenn Hoddle, Gary Mabbutt, Terry Venables and Martin Jol. He has also written *Glory, Glory Nights - Spurs in Europe*, and *The Boss*, a history of Spurs modern managers.

As a young journalist at the *Tottenham Weekly Herald* he lived the dream of reporting on his club full-time, with no need to be dispassionate in his views! This gave him the background to move into a Fleet Street where he went onto become chief sports writer at the *Daily Mirror* and later a columnist on the *Express*.

Harry went on to become a double winner of the British Sports Journalist of the Year award and was presented with the British Variety Club of Great Britain Silver Heart for 'Contribution to Sports Journalism' and is the only journalist ever to win the Sports Story of the Year accolade twice. Harry has a total of 24 industry awards.

One of the most influential football columnists for three decades, Harry is one of the most acclaimed investigative journalists and news gatherers of his generation, he has also directed numerous documentaries including the life of Ossie Ardiles. He is currently Sports Development Director for SmartFrame Technologies.

About the Artist

PAUL TREVILLION has devised and drawn thousands of sporting features since the early 1950's and over his eight decades in sport, has become known as the 'Master of Movement' for his unique ability to convey dynamic movement in a static image and bring the personality of a subject to life.

His extraordinary artistic talent was discovered at a very young age and he was drawing for *Eagle*, *Tiger* and the Spurs supporters magazine, *The Lilywhite*, while still a school boy. In 1952, he met and sketched HRH the Duke of Edinburgh at an awards ceremony at Mansion House, which resulted in a letter from His Royal Highness in praise of the young artist being published in the national press, launching his career in sporting art. In 1955 he met Sir Winston Churchill who signed a smiling portrait painting of the great war leader, which is still today the only signed smiling portrait of Churchill in existence.

Paul then created the iconic refereeing feature 'You Are The Ref' which began in 1957 as 'Hey Ref!' in the *Sunday People*, and went on to appear in *Shoot!* Magazine in the 1970's and 1980's and from 2006 in *The Observer*. In 1963 he revolutionised *Roy of the Rovers* with his 'Comic Art Realism' style and within weeks children were writing in for Roy Race's autograph convinced he was real! Thanks to 'Comic Art Realism' – Roy Race, a footballer who never existed, lived FOREVER!

An acclaimed sports artist, author, inventor and motivator he has worked with the likes of Pele, George Best, Paul Gascoigne, Gary Player, Lee Trevino and Sugar Ray Robinson… to name just a few. His work has appeared in major London exhibitions and at the FIFA Museum and the National Football Museum. A lifelong Spurs fan, one of Paul's first memories is being taken to see a cup tie between Spurs and Everton and in the process developing a childhood obsession with Dixie Dean.

Foreword

The first thing that struck me about this new book is that it is unique. The one thing I have had in common with Harry, is that we are both Spurs fans, who coincidently first went to watch the team at the same age of eight. He has written many books, around ninety I think, which is some feat, but I don't think there has been a book quite like this one.

I really love it because it is so original, and that's because the drawings from Paul Trevillion bring the pages to life. Paul has a unique style and has been for many years the best of his kind, his work is more than caricature, he brings football athleticism to life and his accuracy of drawing faces and balance distinguishes his art.

I'm so pleased that Harry and Paul have chosen Spurs for this kind of book project and I wish them well, as I know they are both steeped in the traditions of the club as much as I am.

The first game I attended was a reserve match at the Lane against Leicester, when I went with a friend and his dad, and then my dad took me to my first big game, Spurs v Forest. I was hooked. I don't know why I was hooked it was just the whole experience: the smell of the grass, the whole event of such a big stadium packed with fans, the noise, the atmosphere, and watching such talents as Jimmy Greaves.

I lived in Harlow and that was a huge catchment area for Spurs supporters, even more so then than it is now. I remember turning up at Harlow Town station to catch the train with my dad to White Hart Lane station, and Harlow was just as packed as White Hart Lane, the trains were full and it was a journey I was soon to take every Tuesday and Thursday evening once I signed schoolboy forms for the club at the age of 11.

In those days the schoolboys and apprentices were given tickets for the game, and we sat on these little benches in the front of the stand where we had the most incredible pitch side view watching immense talents such as Martin Chivers, Alan Mullery, Martin Peters, Phil Beal and Mike England. We sat so close to the action, no more than a couple of yards from the white line, that you could almost touch the players, and you could even smell the liniment on their muscles. You could hear the players' verbal exchanges with each other, and feel the crunching tackles, aspects of the game you never appreciated in the stands.

I was a skilful player who wanted to do the right things, but I was also quite small as a 10- and 11-year old, very thin, and one game watching Mike England and Peter Osgood kicking lumps out of each other gave me quite a different perspective of a profession I was determined to follow. The centre-forward and centre-half were giants who were elbowing and kicking to such an extent I could hear and almost feel the thumps against each player's shin pads. It made me appreciate that this game was not just all about scoring goals and making goals, but also about the physical pain that you would need to experience. For a creative player, this made an enormous impact on me at such an early age. It was a rude awakening.

My favourite player? Funnily enough, even though I was and I am still a huge Spurs fan, my favourite player was George Best. He was the greatest individual I saw as a kid. It was such a great pleasure when Manchester United came to town and I could see

Best. I loved to watch Best, Law and Charlton. I remember sitting behind the goal at the Lane when all three played against Spurs, it was a wonderful experience.

Bill Nicholson signed me as a youth player, and he even picked me once to sit on the bench for a European Cup tie in Belgrade against Red Star ,and I can remember Harry, when he was on the local paper, the *Weekly Herald*, writing about me when I scored a hat-trick in the youth team.

Terry Neill was the manager when I first got selected for the first team, and Harry wrote an article about my emergence into the senior side coming through the ranks. When I made my debut coming on against Norwich, the headline in the *Herald* was one I shall never forget... "And You Ain't Seen Nothing Yet..." There was a smash hit record in the charts at the time, from Bachman Turner Overdrive, and that was the chorus. It was typical of Harry's kind of journalism to try to jazz things up. I loved it, but my mum loved it even more and cut it out and stuck it in a scrap book.

I felt I had a lot in common with Harry at the time as his writing emphasised the Spurs tradition of playing stylish football and that is why he pushed for me to be in the team. I've no idea how much he influenced Terry Neill's decision to pick me, but he keeps telling me it was his idea!

As for the 'new' Spurs under Big Ange, well they had a fantastic start, but I always felt they would be tested to the hilt if they had a few injuries and suspensions and I am afraid I was proven right. The squad was never deep enough to maintain that phenomenal start. Much depends if they can recruit more quality players as good as the handful they brought in who have done so well from the start.

None more so than Maddison, someone who I'd have loved to have seen at the club earlier as I was impressed with him at Norwich in his early days and indeed at Leicester. I would have loved for him to have played in the same team as Harry Kane. You can tell he loves playing for Tottenham and he feels at home straight away with the fans taking to his style of play, something I don't feel he has yet in an England shirt, but I am sure it will come good once he gets a run of a couple of games, something that is not always that easy for creative players, as I found out when I first broke into the England team.

The fans need to play their part, and I am sure that they will, they can see something developing, whereas last season they wanted the manager out, the owners out, and were totally disillusioned, it all felt a bit toxic. Son is another world class player but he has had his share of injuries and I was worried about him, particularly as he plays every minute for both club and country.

But now the arrival of James Maddison has meant he has a telepathic player to get the best out of him Now there is a lot of room for optimism in my opinion, although they do need a deeper squad, with more quality players so the next couple of transfer windows are so important to achieve that. There have been mistakes in the past, such as when the Gareth Bale money was spent on a batch of ordinary payers with few exceptions.

Maddison is mature and experienced and hit the ground running, it was such a shame he was injured as indeed were a couple more and that great run at the start came to an end, but I still believe they are good enough to get the club in the Champions League. Maddison is exceptionally gifted but he does need quality players around him to fulfil his vast potential.

I felt from the start that if Big Ange can select his best eleven they could go toe-to-toe with anyone but if they lost key players they might struggle and that's they way it has panned out. The squad is decent but not, as yet, top notch.

Yet, Big Ange, with his all out attacking style, has turned it around and the fans feel optimistic, there is a buzz about the place again.

Glenn Hoddle
Tottenham Hotspur (1975-87): 377 appearances, 88 goals

Me, My Mad Mum & Spurs

PAUL AND I HAVE almost 150 years between us supporting Spurs! Could there be any pair better qualified to write this history of the club in such a unique form? Paul and I last collaborated back in 1998, on a book called *World Cup Masterpieces* so it's been a long time between collaborations. However, this is book number 90 for me, and many of them have been about Spurs, and, having supported the club and watched my first game in the 60s, I have been waiting for a trophy, like all Spurs fans, patiently and frustratingly for some time.

The club's last trophy was the Carling Cup in 2008 when they defeated Arsenal in the semi-finals and Chelsea in the final; that was their first trophy for nine years and only their second in 17. The manager? Juande Ramos. Not a name now regarded as one of the club's greatest ever, and, judging by the rankings of Spurs top 20 managers based on win percentage, he doesn't figure anywhere among the best.

Looking at that appalling record of failure for such a so-called big club, who now play home games in a £1 billion super stadium and have a state-of-the-art training ground, it beggars belief. Yet despite Mauricio Pochettino taking us to the Champions League Final for the first time in the club's history and multiple near misses with glory over the past decade, we are still waiting!

The arrival of serial winner Jose Mourinho brought fresh hope, and hope is sometimes the worst thing in the world. Having led the club back to Wembley, Jose was sacked a few days before the League Cup Final, which Spurs duly lost to Manchester City. We went for the same again when Daniel Levy, having quickly realised his error in hiring Nuno Espirito Santo, appointed Antonio Conte to the role, and yet another serial winner of trophies went pot-less at Spurs, so last summer he sold our highest ever goalscorer Harry Kane and brought in a little known Aussie who had enjoyed fantastic success in Australian domestic football and at Celtic. Ange's start at Spurs has been sensational and it's not so much the results he produced early in his reign (which will wax and wane along with injuries, suspensions and a bounce of the ball) but the style with which Tottenham bounced to the top of the Premier League in September that got Spurs fans like Paul and I excited. Gone was the safety first approach of the previous few seasons to be replaced with a gung-ho attack first policy that chimed with Spurs fans. It also sparked sufficient excitement in the pair of us to embark on this new history of the club in art and words.

The arrival of James Maddison and a risk-laden approach from Big Ange had us all smiling for the first time in years – here we had a direct descendant of Arthur Rowe and Bill Nicholson playing the type of football associated with likes of Blanchflower, Greaves, Hoddle and Ardiles. In defeating Manchester United, Liverpool and coming from behind to draw at Arsenal, Ange's Spurs didn't alter their tactics once – not even when they went down to nine men against Chelsea!

There have been many books on the history of Spurs, but never one like this - a personal roam around the glory days and some of the dark days through the eyes of two pairs of rose-tinted glasses. This is a club laden with history. The first British club to win a major European trophy, Spurs were the first club to win the Double in the 20th century, and became a club synonymous with The Beautiful Game; there is no shame in rejoicing in Spurs' glorious past. It is a rich heritage of all that is good in football; the style, the attacking ethos, the philosophy of Danny Blanchflower, the grace of Alan Gilzean, the goal scoring phenomenon of Jimmy Greaves, the genius of Paul Gascoigne, the precision passes of Glenn Hoddle, the start of the foreign revolution (Argentinian to be precise) with Ossie Ardiles and Ricky Villa. How Ossie's knees went all "trembley" on the way to a wonderful and exhilarating FA Cup win with the greatest Wembley goal of all-time from Ricky, to 'Walking in a Jürgen Wonderland'. Yes, even a German could become a hero in a club steeped in Jewish traditions.

On a personal note I have spent more than half a century loving Spurs teams through thick and thin. At times it seems more thin than thick, but the memory often deceives; there have been some great times along the way, and we have seen many great players wearing those famous Lilywhite shirts. That makes the tears of joy at winning trophies, and winning in style, all the more pleasurable.

It is the perfect time to relive some wonderful memories of

Spurs' glorious past going back to the 1960s. Isolated cup triumphs have proved little more than a mirage. The reality is that the best time to be a Spurs fan was during the "Glory Glory" days, now a blur of black and white memories on television. Then, the big named 'foreign stars' came from Scotland, Ireland and Wales! And what great "imports" they were, with players such as Scottish tornado Dave Mackay, the elusive John White, who died far too young, flying Welsh winger Cliff Jones and the Irish anchor at the heart of the 1961 Double team, Danny Blanchflower.

Managers kept on coming in and moving out of the revolving door at the Lane in the wake of our beloved Bill Nick, the plain-speaking Yorkshireman who led us to all those triumphs, as the club sought the magic formula to bring back the Glory, Glory days. As each year goes by the memory tells you how much more wonderful the likes of Mackay, Greaves, Smith, Jones, Blanchflower - I could go on - really were - treasures of the golden past in a warm sea of nostalgia. Some things, though, never change though ... the hurt. The hurt of being a fan of a 'nearly club', or a 'never club', or seeing Leicester City buck the trend at the expense of your club. The hurt never ends!

I have been so fortunate that my job as a football reporter has given me enviable access to the team I love. There has been so much to marvel at on the pitch through the decades but I have also been privy to many developments off it as well.

As a boy growing up kicking a ball around the streets of east London, trying desperately to emulate my heroes, I never thought for a second that one day I would be sitting in a famous Fleet Street haunt discussing death threats with Irving Scholar and trying to talk him out of selling the club, or being invited to Alan Sugar's home when he first took over to receive advice on dealing with Terry Venables or discussing with Daniel Levy his buyout of the club. I have been in the thick of it and been privy to information from the horse's mouth. Not many fans get that close to the heart of their clubs. I have gone from a youngster getting in through the Boys' Entrance to watching from the press box where I got to meet, know and befriend chairmen, managers, players and staff and even being invited into the inner sanctum: the director's box. There can't be many accounts of following football where a fan has been catapulted inside the club to discover the truths other fans never see. So where did it all begin?

*

There is a public bench outside the library opposite where the famous Cockerel Clock used to be on Tottenham High Road where my mad mum would wait patiently for me throughout the match before collecting me for the long bus journey back home. Together we would make the pilgrimage to White Hart Lane from our home in east London, where the two of us lived at No. 13 Pauline House, on the third floor of a 17-storey block of council flats which housed the overflow from the already packed Jewish community in Brick Lane. It was a short walk to the bus stop, but it was imperative to set off several hours before kick-off, to allow for the hour ride to Tottenham High Road on board the crowded old 149 Routemaster. It was essential to arrive by around 1pm to join the queues at the time the gates were about to open. The queues got pretty long, pretty quickly! By the mid 60s White Hart Lane had become a popular venue. I loved every minute of that bus ride; I became familiar with virtually every inch of road, each landmark, every building. The closer we got to the Tottenham ground, the more excited I became. There was a spring in my step when I leapt off the bus right outside the ground. You were straight into the ambience of the whole football-spectator experience, there's nothing like it today. There were a profusion of stalls selling collections of small tin badges representing all the clubs. There were programme sellers on every corner, the air was alive with the raucous sound of rattles, 'graggers' my old mum called them, that made such a din at home, but could hardly be heard above the noise of all the other rattles.

Match day attire was simple enough, a coveted Spurs scarf, there were no replica shirts with names of the stars and their numbers on the back. I did collect shirts, but they were purchased without even the club's badge, let alone a name or number, and who would have thought of shirt sponsorship or billboard advertising? My dear old mum had to buy the badge separately and sew it on by hand or with the Singer sewing machine she used for the fur remnants but no one thought of wearing those shirts to a game - it was far too cold.

One of my greatest match day pleasures was to visit the Spurs Supporters Club whose head offices were in Warmington House, adjacent to the ground. The club sold all sorts of memorabilia, but my favourite was the upstairs section where they sold action pictures of the matches, with a wait of around a month before the most up-to-date games were available. I spent all of my pocket money on those pictures, and as a special treat my mum would often buy an extra one. They took pride of place on my bedroom wall, with a Spurs rug by the side of the bed as a Christmas present. The dedicated Spurs fans who manned the shop got to know my mum quite well and even gave her some discounts on any extra pictures she bought for me, they knew she couldn't really afford them. A Spurs pencil or pen was a treasure in those days, which is crazy in comparison with the lavish items on sale in the club store today. Back then it still felt like a sport rather than a business. The players were stars with their feet on the ground back then rather than walking advertisements for multi-national companies of dubious intent aimed at maximising club profits, as they often are today.

After the thrill of the game, came the enjoyment of getting back home, waiting outside the corner shop for the "pink" editions of the evening paper, a football special with the first match reports and pictures. I would immediately cut these out upon returning home and stick them in the scrap book. I had dozens of scrap books filled with the match reports of journalists such as Steve Curry and Nigel Clarke, both of whom I ended up working with.

However by far the biggest thrill was soaking up the atmosphere for the two hours before kick-off, while taking in the smell of fried onions to accompany the hot dogs from the multitude of unofficial stands. Now, of course, it's smoked salmon bagels at Tottenham's lavish new ground at a price that would equate to a week's wages back then! Yet such were our financial straits that my mum never thought about wasting money on hot dogs; she packed sandwiches for me instead. I don't think it was the fact they weren't Kosher that put her off; it was the fact that it was cheaper to bring your own food.

At first I would pay the minimum entrance fee at the Boys' Enclosure, and kept on going through that turnstile even when I was a year, maybe even two years, too old. But it reached the stage, particularly as I was quite tall for my age, when there was no more fooling the gate-man, or no longer could my mum persuade him to let me in for the cut price entrance fee. So my mum then came up with seats for the games. Sometimes, as I recall, she even managed to get herself into the ground without a ticket to keep a wary eye on me.

I was hooked and wanted to go to every game so it seemed a season ticket was more cost effective. However, there was a waiting list and it was highly unlikely that I would be able to get my hands on one of those coveted tickets so how my widowed mum managed to acquire one despite a 10-year long waiting list, let alone afford it, I shall never know, yet my mum often performed acts bordering on the miraculous to ensure her one and only son got what he wanted, which was a ticket to watch Spurs. When she failed to beg, borrow or steal a Cup Final ticket in 1962, after Spurs returned to Wembley following their formidable Double triumph the year before, I could tell she was never going to let me experience such disappointment again. She could tell how much it meant to me, even though she knew that I was perhaps too

FOLLOW THAT BALL

A good striker like JIMMY GREAVES of Spurs, follows every shot in towards goal, even when he knows there is no chance of getting to it before the goalkeeper. By following the ball in you make the goalkeeper act quickly, and the quicker you can make a player react, the more you increase the chances of error. Then should he fumble—and mistakes do happen — you are on hand to tap it in.

I've been fortunate in being able to continue my journey as a fan and a journalist mostly centred around Spurs for all of my working life. I've not missed a Cup final since, mostly viewed from the Wembley press box, and more lately in the privileged seats, none more so than at the 2008 Carling Cup final when Spurs beat Chelsea, the first League Cup final in the new £800m stadium where my wife, Linda, and I were guests of the Football League and sponsors Carling. My thanks for that marvellous experience goes to Steve Bradley of Hill and Knowlton, the public relations company charged with organising our five-star lunch and prime location seats in the corporate sector.

So, from childhood beginnings standing for hours waiting to go into the boys' entrance, to the Football League's own hospitality section, it's been an unforgettable and eye-opening journey. Yet I have never forgotten how my love of Spurs began, although sipping champagne with the movers and shakers who fashion the game always gives me a thrill and reminds me of how far one can go with sufficient will power, luck, and no doubt some degree of aptitude for the profession. Most of all, though, a passion for the sport. It's been a long and tough journey supporting Spurs, with many bizarre experiences along the way which I'll document in this book. Throughout that journey my mad mum has never been far away, perhaps not in body, but definitely in spirit. Even when I hit the dizzy heights of travelling around the world covering matches for the *Daily Mirror* and winning numerous awards along the way, my mum would send me small food parcels by post! The jiffy bags that arrived at the office with cooked chicken in them became a source of much amusement to my *Mirror* colleagues. Never mind the fact that, at the peak of the paper's powers, expenses were virtually limitless, and the opportunities for fine dining immense, I knew it meant an awful lot to her to know that her son was being well fed. For a good Jewish mother this was her lifelong duty.

young to be going off to join such a crush on my own, or be alone inside the stadium, so she made sure she got her hands on a Cup Final ticket in 1967 for the all-London final between Spurs and Chelsea; it might have been on the cheap old benches at the front without the best view in the world, but it was a ticket for my first final nonetheless.

Heaven.

Thankfully Spurs won with Joe Kinnear and Terry Venables in their side, a couple of players with whom I would cross swords in later life when they became managers. While I got on well enough with Venables when I first got to know him as manager of Crystal Palace, our relationship was cemented when he worked for Irving Scholar, but deteriorated during his bitter conflict with Alan Sugar. By contrast Kinnear and I enjoyed a very sound working relationship, once or twice even meeting at social events and hitting it off. So it was as a fan that I idolised the likes of Kinnear, the young glamour boy of that team, and yes, even Venables, despite the fact that he had a torrid time from most Spurs supporters who took an instant dislike to him following his move from Chelsea in 1966.

I am now in my 64th year supporting Spurs. It's time to look back with pride at a club that has all the right credentials to be successful once more in the near future. It's been too long without a league title and another crack at the elusive European Cup but we continue to dream. I hope you enjoy reading the inside track on Spurs' glorious past as much as I have enjoyed writing it!

HH

My First Game

EVERY SMALL CHILD gets excited when looking forward to their next birthday and I was no different. In 1937, the year of my third birthday, my father, a bus conductor, switched his working day shift to a night one in order to be able to take me to see Tottenham play Everton in an FA Cup replay as one of my very special birthday presents. My father, as was the case with my two elder brothers, believed three years of age was old enough to be able to enjoy and understand a 90 minute match.

On match day my mother gave me another birthday present, an enormous blue and white scarf which she had knitted and which I proudly wore as I stood for the very first time on the White Hart Lane terraces waiting for the game to begin. I was convinced nobody roared louder than me when the Tottenham team in their white shirts ran out but then an even bigger noise filled the stadium. Everyone was shouting 'GOOD OLD DIXIE'!

I had heard my dad and older brothers talk about Dixie Dean, the Everton and England centre-forward. I had seen lots of photographs of Dixie in newspapers and magazines, but none of this had prepared me for the sight of this blue-shirted muscular giant of a man with thick, black wavy hair, waving as he acknowledged the fans deafening welcome.

And what a game! Tottenham, after being 3-1 down, won the replay beating Everton 4-3 but I did not remember any of the match apart from the exciting, explosive heading power of Dixie Dean and the two goals he scored. When I came home I asked my mum to sew the name 'Dixie Dean' into my Tottenham scarf. From then on Dixie was my football hero and I wasted no time learning everything I could about him and went on to draw him a hundred times, possibly even more.

When I failed my 11 plus exam my teacher gave me my school report to take home and to soften the blow when my parents read a very bad report, my teacher put inside the large brown envelope my drawing of Dixie Dean which had been hanging on the classroom wall adding the note "Paul lacks concentration with his school work, but if Paul works very hard and with a bit of luck, it is possible he might have a career in the field of art."

I am sure my old school teacher would have smiled when, in 1960, I sent two drawings of Dixie to the *Liverpool Echo* suggesting I illustrate the life story of Dixie for the paper. The Editor liked the drawings and invited me up to Liverpool and when I walked into his office who was sitting in the chair next to his desk by my idol, Dixie Dean! I was thrilled that he liked my drawings and he was very impressed at how much I knew about his playing career and his life off the field.

I asked Dixie - obviously the Editor was all ears - about the motorcycle accident that fractured his skull - "It also fractured my jaw bone and busted my knee" said Dixie, "they thought I would never play again." We recalled how just two years later, in only 39 games in the 1927/28 season, Dixie set the First Division all-time scoring record of 60 goals! "I scored the goal that achieved the record with my head" Dixie confirmed but he was just as proud of that record as he was of being the first footballer ever to wear the No.9 shirt. It was in the 1933 FA Cup Final, Everton v Manchester City. The FA had decided to allow numbered shirts for the very first time; Everton wore numbers 1 to 11 and Manchester City wore numbers 12 to 22. Everton won 3-0 and Dixie scored one of the goals.

Before we had finished reminiscing on his career, the great man agreed to the Trevillion illustrated Dixie Dean strip to appear in the *Liverpool Echo* and I was over the moon. Being cheeky I asked Dixie one big favour. Would he take me to Goodison Park and head a ball for me to catch? Dixie agreed. When we arrived he picked up a ball and told me to get between the goalposts and stand on the line adding, "Don't move, just hold your two hands out". Dixie then stood on the penalty spot, threw the ball in the air and headed it upwards so it dropped gently into my hands.

"You never lose it, son" said Dixie, adding, "you can now say you saved a Dixie Dean header". "Not true, Dixie," I replied "you handed that ball to me with your head!"

I still believe Dixie Dean stands unchallenged as the greatest to wear

> "Paul lacks concentration with his school work, but if he works very hard and with a bit of luck, it is possible he might have a career in the field of art."

a No 9 shirt. You might argue with me... but I don't think you can argue with Bill Shankly who claimed, "Dixie was the greatest centre forward there will ever be. He belongs in the company of the supremely great, along with the likes of Beethoven, Shakespeare and Rembrandt".

TURPIN v ROBINSON

THE YEAR WAS 1951. I was 17 years old and gaining something of a reputation as an artist with the Trevillion drawings appearing In the *Tottenham Weekly Herald* Sport pages, the Spurs *Lilywhite* magazine and Fleetway comics. I always laughed when my school chums called me 'The Toulouse Lautrec of Tottenham Tech'!

I was meeting the sports stars of the day. and collecting their autographs on my drawings: Stanley Matthews, Stirling Moss, Denis Compton and many others made up a very long list of the stars who had signed my drawings, which meant I did not have the best attendance record at Tottenham Technical College but I did have a very enviable autograph collection! So, when Sugar Ray Robinson signed to fight Englishman Randolph Turpin on July 10th 1951 for the World Middleweight Championship, I started to draw both fighters. I was determined, no matter what, to get the finished artwork to the two of them.

Sugar Ray Robinson had lost only one fight (to the 'Bronx Bull" Jake LaMotta) in his 130 fight career. Robinson avenged the loss to LaMotta three weeks later and now Robinson had won his next 90 fights in a row. Turpin, we feared, was the next name to be added to the list.

The weigh-in for the title fight took place at Jack Solomon's gymnasium at Great Windmill Street, London. On the day mounted police were necessary to control the thousands of well wishers shouting 'Good Luck Randy' and blocking the roads in and around Great Windmill Street. I had always made my way to the front in the days when it was all standing at White Hart Lane and there were over 70,000 in the ground, so it presented no problem making my way through the crowd to the front of the gym. Then, when the opportunity presented itself, I was INSIDE before I heard a voice... "Sorry son, you're not allowed in here. OUT!"

I had already thought up a reply if I was stopped. The fight promoter Jack Solomons was a fanatical Spurs fan and the President of the *Lilywhite* magazine. So I LIED! "I won the Jack Solomons Spurs *Lilywhite* Magazine drawing competition" I told the imposing doorman and I showed him my drawings of Sugar Ray Robinson and Randolph Turpin. "I know nothing about that, son" replied the doorman but he was impressed enough by the drawings to say, "Give me those. I'll have a word with Jack. Don't worry. you'll get your drawings back...".

I was hoping Jack Solomons, in that crazy madhouse of activity with press reporters and photographers fighting for pole position, would swallow my story. After what seemed an eternity my drawings were handed back with a warning - "you can stay, you can look and that's it." From that moment on I did not take my eyes off Robinson or Turpin. When the formalities of the weigh-in were over the two disappeared into a room followed by a crowd of press men, photographers, and some hanger-ons. This was my chance. I made sure I was in that mass of bodies.

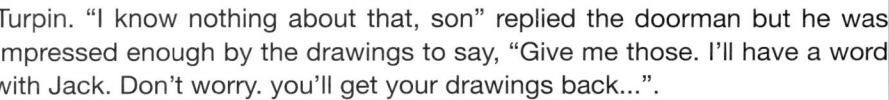

I may have been badly crushed, but I made sure my drawings weren't by the time I was inside the room with Robinson and Turpin. When Sugar Ray Robinson signed my drawing he looked up and said "When I was half your age I was tap dancing on the sidewalks of New York and I was doing pretty good. From the way you walked up to me I can see you're no dancer - stick to the drawing!" Good advice. I wasted no time getting to Randolph Turpin but as he took my drawing to sign, the legendary *Daily Mirror* sports writer Peter Wilson stepped in and pushed me to one side and Turpin handed my drawing unsigned to his manager.

who said, "That's it, son. OUT!". It was the same man I met when first entering the gym. "I'm waiting to get Turpin's autograph" I protested but I was wasting my breath. This time the "OUT" was accompanied by a strong pull on my arm. Turpin's manager George Middleton then intervened, "Put your name and address on the back of your drawing, son, I'll get Randy to sign it and get it sent straight back". I did just that, adding 'Good Luck Randy'. Then, like the man ordered, I was OUT and on my way back to the Technical College thinking I had about as much chance of seeing my Randolph Turpin drawing again, as Turpin had of beating Robinson.

No one gave 'The Leamington Licker' a chance. Robinson was 7/2 favourite with odds of 20-1 against Turpin winning on points. We were all wrong on both counts! Randolph Turpin, in what still remains the biggest upset in British boxing, beat Sugar Ray Robinson on points in front of a sell out crowd of 18.000 at Earls Court. Then, almost a *year* later, I received a letter with my signed Randolph Turpin drawing inside. At the top of the letter Turpin had added in his own hand 'Ex' to the printed words 'Middleweight Champion of the World'. The letter was a wake up call! Almost twelve months had passed and I had not thanked Jack Solomons for the part he unknowingly played in the two priceless autographs I had collected. I immediately put it right and my drawing of Jack Solomons appeared in the next issue of the *Lilywhite* Magazine. Solomons was pleased, he asked for the original and I sent it knowing this was one drawing which was not coming back!

To this day I wonder if Turpin signed my drawing when he *was* world champion and then it was mislaid or much later and sent on?

I will never know!

PT

LW LAITHWAITES

I would like to thank Laithwaites and Spurs fan Paul Dyer for supporting me at my recent book launches for 'The Greatest Goalscorers' at Kiki Bar in Sunningdale and 'Down Memory Lane' at their Virginia Water branch.

HARRY HARRIS

Push and Run

How Tottenham Hotspur changed the course of football history

Spurs' chequered record in the immediate pre- and post-war period had seen the club yo-yo between the top two divisions while watching neighbours Arsenal rise to become the dominant force in English football. Yet, despite a lack of success, there was always something a little bit different about Tottenham...

The point of difference between the clubs can be traced back to the 1925 change in the Offside Law, which decreased the number of players required to play someone onside to just two (from three) following several seasons of increasingly defensive football and falling attendances. The immediate effect was the phenomena of the prolific centre-forward with the likes of Paul's hero Dixie Dean setting goalscoring records that remain unbeaten to this day. This in turn brought a tactical change by managers who sacrificed a creative midfielder for another defender. The chief architect of this tactical change was Arsenal's Herbert Chapman who, having led Huddersfield to successive league titles was poached by the Highbury club and repeated the feat, setting the blueprint for their domination of 1930s football, even after Chapman's untimely death in 1934 at the age of just 55.

Inevitably other clubs quickly adopted Chapman's W-M formation but they could not afford the same quality of player and so matches became long-ball hit-and-hope affairs that relied on brawn and speed rather than skill and tactics.

British football at this time was still regarded as the dominant force in the game and England wins over the Austrian 'wunderteam', and World Champions Italy appeared to confirm that 'we' were still the best in the world (despite a self-imposed exile from the World Cup) but it was clear that the continentals had already caught up, and in some cases surpassed, English skill and these wins relied on muscle rather than brains.

One man who saw the writing on the wall was Tottenham captain Arthur Rowe who made his debut for the club in 1931 and would go on to have a huge and lasting impact on not just his club but the national game. Rowe was a deep thinker about the game and had long-criticised the new Offside Law for promoting the 'kick and rush' style which, while exciting for the huge crowds attracted to the game after the first war, was ultimately always going to be overtaken by a more thoughtful approach once continental players adapted to the physical side of the game.

Under manager Percy Smith, Spurs' 1931-32 team were labelled 'the greyhounds' by the press for their rapid close passing style in front of a defence ably commanded by Rowe and goalkeeper Joe Nicholls. According to Norman Turpin, author of the acclaimed biography *Arthur 'Push and Run' Rowe*, one moment in particular changed the course of Tottenham history:

Scoreless late-on at Bradford City on November 26th 1932 Spurs players feared the loss of their £2 win bonus when suddenly, just outside his own area, Rowe executed a sharp one-two exchange of passes with Felton. A further four quick, short passes followed before the ball was crossed from the right for Hunt to score, salvaging that bonus. On the train journey back this smooth, rapid-fire passing move became a classic 'Eureka' moment for Rowe, who recalled: 'I spread a load of sugar cubes on the table and tried to trace the passes that led to that goal… I argued that if we could ever plan that kind of move instead of just *hoping* for it to happen we'd score more goals that way.' But his colleagues were not convinced such moves could be planned. Furthermore, as Rowe pointed out, those in charge of running teams in those days '…wanted long, brave balls with forwards chasing and hoping.' Nevertheless Rowe wanted the Bradford incident repeated. As acclaimed Fleet Street football correspondent David Miller would write, Rowe '…was conscious of the haphazard nature of much of the game, the lack of organized thought. He began to realize that it must be possible to play in a manner that reduced, if only marginally, the element of chance and the unnecessary squandering of possession.'

An idea was born.

That idea would come to be known as 'push-and-run' and its architect would be Spurs captain Rowe who, having won just a single cap for his country (against France in 1933) and led the club to two promotions and a relegation was forced to retire in 1938 due to a knee injury. Yet a measure of his standing in the game can be gauged by him being hand-picked by the FA to spread the FA Gospel beyond English shores and he was packed off to Hungary where he would assist in the undermining of the Chapman style and ultimately the traditional English game.

While he was in Budapest to spread the gospel on the English approach to tactics and their more liberal approach to tackling, Arthur soon went 'off-piste', straying from the official tenets of the *FA Coaching Manual* to lay-out his nascent ideas on push and run. In seminars he would promote his ideas to key figures in the development of the game in Hungary such as Dr Károly Dietz who had managed Hungary to a narrow and controversial defeat to Italy in the 1938 World Cup final; Béla Guttmann, then manager of Hungarian champions Újpest, who later became the most famous of the Hungarian coaches best known for taking Benfica to successive European Cup triumphs in the 1960s; as well as players such as Ferenc Puskás and József Bozsik, who would star in Hungary's demolition of England in 1953, and Gusztáv Sebes, the manager of the team known all over the world as the 'Mighty Magyars' who followed up that 6-3 Wembley triumph with a 7-1 evisceration of what remained of English pride in Budapest in 1954.

Such was Arthur's popularity in Hungary that he was offered the job of national team coach for the 1940 Olympic tournament. Unfortunately war intervened and that opportunity was missed, yet following a war-time during which he coached teams of football stars who entertained the troops all over Europe, Arthur returned home to manage Chelmsford City where success in the Southern League quickly brought him to the attention of Second Division Spurs.

Tottenham were still stuck in a rut when Arthur took the reins in the summer of 1949. Previous manager Joe Hulme had looked to be heading in the right direction but a cathartic 3-0 cup defeat to his former club Arsenal did for him. The only player Rowe brought with him was centre-forward Len Duquemin who had guested for Chelmsford while Alf Ramsey was signed from Southampton for a modest fee, otherwise Arthur was left with a squad that had languished in Division Two for over a decade.

It was against this background that Arthur Rowe made a silk purse from a sow's ear, drilling his ideas on a game based on short, sharp passes into a squad brought up on the muck and nettles approach that had dominated the English game for over two decades.

So what was 'Push and Run'?

The quick answer is that it was against everything that the *FA Coaching Manual* espoused! Direct football was out, although long balls were not forbidden when the opportunity arose. Instead a premium was placed on short passing and movement off the ball. Players were drilled to think in terms of the time a ball takes to get from player A to player B and then player C - the shorter the time, the harder for the defence to react. Yet by passing only a few yards at a time, rather than wellying the ball down the field, the chances of the attacking team maintaining possession were massively increased. In Arthur's own words it was, "bleedin' obvious, mate" yet for the time it seemed radical and it took the Second Division by storm, Tottenham romping to the 1949-50 title by an eight-point margin ahead of runners-up Sheffield Wednesday.

Many commentators claimed that this new style would fail in the top division against international footballers and wily coaches but Arthur proved them all wrong yet again as his pass and move tactics — encapsulated in the maxim 'make it simple, make it quick' — bamboozled the First Division as well to give Tottenham their first league title.

The best example of Rowe's football that season came in a match against Newcastle United in November 1950. The Geordies were hot favourites for the title having raced to the top of the table on the back of the phenomenal strike partnership of Jackie Milburn and Chile international George Robledo. Yet what happened next would astound reporters and supporters up and down the land. Again this report comes from Turpin's excellent book...

*

TOTTENHAM 7-0 NEWCASTLE UNITED

On the sound of the whistle Spurs and Newcastle flew at each other, the home side proving the more threatening with their intense, short-passing game while Newcastle utilised more conventional English tactics, showcasing solo dribbling skills and long passes. Newcastle's tendency to run with the ball allowed Tottenham to drop back and snuff-out many of their attacks. With just five minutes on the clock the ball passed rapidly from Spurs' Colin Brittan to Les Medley, then to creator-in-chief Eddie Baily, before stocky home centre-forward Len Duquemin took possession in midfield, beat a man and passed back to Baily who spotted his left-winger Medley cutting inside and found him with a pass before accelerating outside to collect a return ball. Baily's cross was then struck waist-high, on the run, for inside-right Les Bennett to arrive at speed, diving to nod past 'keeper Fairbrother's right-hand at the near post. It was a goal described by *The Times* as '…glorious, even extravagant, and it took one's breath away.'

Joe Harvey and his men were already battling desperately to keep Spurs out but could not prevent Spurs increasing their lead after 21 minutes. The swift combination this time was between Baily, Medley, Bennett, Duquemin and then Baily again, who this time collected the ball before beating full-back McMichael and picking his spot. On the half-hour Medley, nominally stationed on the left but now in the inside-right position, took a forward pass from Bennett and, from the edge of the area, sent a shot screaming into the roof of the net. 3-0. Bravely the visitors nearly struck back, Spurs' goalkeeper Ted Ditchburn making a superb goal-line save from Taylor, who stopped to applaud before Spurs headed for the dressing-room with a three-goal advantage. In 45 minutes, White Hart Lane had become 'Red Hot' Lane, with the promise of more fast, inspirational football to come. Spurs' supporters had never had it so good.

Without doubt Newcastle will have discussed striking back early in the second-half so as to regain a foothold in the contest, but instead they were rocked on their heels when Medley scored his second (Spurs' fourth) just three minutes in. On the hour outside-right Sonny Walters picked up number five before coming close again when striking the crossbar, but there was Medley, on hand to complete his hat-trick for number six. With two minutes' remaining Alf Ramsey completed the scoring with Spurs' seventh, this time from the penalty spot. In between Newcastle had emphasised their own strengths, Milburn and Mitchell both striking the woodwork **but** that afternoon Spurs had carried out one of Arthur Rowe's foremost dictums in perfect fashion: 'Put good football before results,' to which **he would add:** 'Do this and the results will come.'

And how! The reporter from the *Times* could not contain his admiration and excitement: 'It is hard to imagine a more brilliant exposition of the game than was shown to that vast, swaying assembly, over 70,000 strong, held

Following a typical, seven-pass sequence, Spurs' first of seven goals enters the Newcastle net via the head of Les Bennett (left and below).

there spellbound in the rain of a grey November afternoon,' adding, 'This was vintage champagne, something to savour and remember.'

He continued: 'Tottenham, indeed, to use the language of the golfer, were deadly on and around the greens, and that is what counts. But even beyond the important matter of scoring, the quality of their football was sheer joy, demanding an immoderate use of superlatives.' As for Spurs' unfortunate victims that afternoon, the *Times* had every sympathy: '[Newcastle] kept playing football to the bitter end and died like heroes in the cause of something quite out of the ordinary…'.

The majesty of this Spurs performance, especially as it came from a novice First Division side, was emphasised by Newcastle United director Stan Seymour's comments after the game: 'If a film had been taken of the sensational 7-0 victory of Spurs over Newcastle United it could have been used as a world model of how football should be played.'

The sporting Seymour heaped further praise on Rowe's side: 'The greatest team since the war. No team in the world could live with them in this form. It's tough to watch your side being beaten, but this was football at its best. I'd pick the lot for England.'

Newcastle's Milburn thought Spurs were 'dynamite' while centre-half Frank Brennan said: 'I have always wanted to see football played like this. Spurs are a wonder team.' Bewildered captain Joe Harvey, who at one point in the midst of the action could be seen wearing a baffled grin, came out with a classic comment on the afternoon he had just endured: 'I always got to the ball when it wasn't there.'

An ecstatic *Tottenham & Edmonton Weekly Herald* reporter rhapsodised: 'Spurs have proved beyond all doubt the vast superiority of their new-style soccer… successful application of this style will, I predict, create a revolution in British soccer.' He added: 'Just as clubs found it necessary to discover an answer to [Herbert Chapman's] third-back game, so they will have to remould their ideas to counter Spurs' system. That this will produce a vast improvement in soccer standards is without question. It should give British football the boost it needs to put us back on top of the soccer world.'

Even sidelined Spurs' captain [Ron] Burgess was overwhelmed. He was easily able to overcome the disappointment of sitting out the game, saying: 'It was the finest exhibition of football I had ever seen, and although I was the Spurs' skipper and thought I knew everything about the team, I sat enthralled, for I realised for the first time why we had won so many matches with our push-and-run style of play. I was as excited as our most partisan supporters as I watched the close harmony of all departments of the team, the speed and perfection of movement, with the ball always on the move, and even the great Newcastle team were running around almost aimlessly in their efforts to prevent that spate of goals.' Burgess added: 'It was only by becoming a spectator that I realized just how special this side was.'

The *Daily Telegraph* poetically described how Spurs' attacks '…carried on right through the side, with each man taking the ball in his stride at top pace, for all the world like a wave gathering momentum as it races to the far distant shore.' The architect himself, Arthur Rowe, asked by Jack Milligan of *The Daily Graphic* for his own impressions of his side's performance, replied in typically understated fashion, 'Yes, I think we have a good side.'

Four years' later Hungary would also score seven goals, this time against England in Budapest. When reading the *Times'* football correspondent Geoffrey Green's lyrical summing-up of that superb Hungarian side of 1954 (see below), one can't help but ponder two things, firstly that Green's words might just as well have been applied to Spurs' hammering of Newcastle three years earlier and secondly that Rowe's work inspiring Hungary's own trainee coaches in 1939, most of whom would have 'come of age' in coaching terms by the time their national side was taking 1950s Europe by storm, was no coincidence.

'Here was football one could sit and watch until old age finally overcame one. Here was a cultural expression, a game which, even if it was not on this occasion hurtling with sharp conflict, was yet passionate and beautiful in its art. The Hungarian attack, in all its imaginative conception, was like light passing through a prism. It had all the colours of the rainbow and constantly the combination of those colours were changed.'

League Champions 1950-51

Arthur Rowe's remarkable 'team of no stars' confounded the critics to win the First Division at the first attempt with the same team that had struggled in the Second Division under his predecessor.

Alf Ramsey — Tottenham's worthy successor to Ronnie Burgess

Billy Nicholson

Ron Burgess says "Good-bye!"

The key players in Rowe's system were goalkeeper Ted Ditchburn (far left), who the manager later compared to Pat Jennings. He was the team's first line of attack; full back Alf Ramsey, who arrived from Southampton and became a quick convert to Rowe's ideas; right-half Bill Nicholson, who was always on the move and covering for his team-mates, and captain Ron Burgess had been a coalminer and would have returned to Wales were it not for him standing in for an injured player in a reserve team game and scoring twice. Burgess, only 11 years younger than Rowe, was a threat in both boxes and was the manager's eyes and ears on the pitch.

Of right winger Sonny Walters, Bill Nicholson said he was an 'up and down grafter who excelled at stealing into positions behind defenders'. His link up play with Ramsey and Nicholson was key to the success of Rowe's system as the manager instilled in his team the value of team-work within sections of the pitch.

Despite joining Spurs as a youngster and debuting in 1939, Eddie Baily, nicknamed The Cheeky Chappie, was assumed MIA during the Second World War and the player himself, having heard nothing from the club, signed for Chelsea upon demob but the Blues were forced to cancel his contract. Rowe said he had 'never seen a man play a moving ball with either foot as quickly or as accurately as Baily' - he was ideally suited to Rowe's system and was even more proficient at working positions on the left alongside Ron Burgess and Les Medley.

Channel Islander Len Duquemin, inevitably nicknamed 'The Duke', was the spearhead of Rowe's attack. Not blessed with huge pace, his skill was quickness of movement and a knack of knowing where the ball will come to him, a prize asset in a striker.

Tasked to mark Stanley Matthews on Spurs' first game back in the top flight, right back Charlie Withers (left) ended up with 'twisted blood', as the legendary Blackpool winger preyed on Withers' tendency to dive into challenges.

The visitors won 4-1 but afterwards Arthur Rowe preached calm, telling the press that "It wasn't that we played badly but Stanley Matthews had one of those days when a Sherman tank wouldn't stop him". Both he and his full back would be smiling by the end of the season.

Arthur Rowe and I

"Paul, I've just seen this weeks' Cup Final issue of the *Weekly Sporting Review*." I was on the phone listening to Ralph L. Finn, the editor of the Tottenham Hotspur *Lilywhite* Magazine, "and you are on the front cover".

"Yes Ralph," I cut in, "I went up to West Brom, talked to Len Millard and then on to Preston to talk to Tom Finney." It was then the turn of Ralph to interrupt. "I want your drawing of Arthur Rowe on the front cover of the *Lilywhite* to kick off the 1954-55 season."

West Brom went on to win the Cup and it was now the second week back for Spurs pre-season training, and I was sitting in the office of the Tottenham Manager Arthur Rowe, "Ralph showed me the drawing you did of the FA Cup final captains on the front of the *Weekly Sporting Review*." I listened as Rowe continued, "And he said he would like me on the front cover of the *Lilywhite* Magazine. That's the reason you are sitting on that chair with your sketch book on your lap and a pencil in your hand – how would you like to draw me, Paul? Standing at my desk or sitting behind it?" With no hesitation I replied "Behind the desk please". As Mr Rowe sat down he said, "apart from the West Bromwich Albion fans I believe we all wanted Finney to collect a Cup winners medal, but two goals from Ronnie Allen and the Frank Griffin's late decider meant it was not to be."

As I started drawing Rowe continued talking "Football's a team game, Paul. You play with your head up, looking to see a player ready in space to receive a pass. Give him the ball then race forward into space to receive a return pass. The wall pass played quickly is give and go to perfection and it's the way to win games. All the forwards in the side that won the 2nd Division then the 1st Division titles could finish off a push and run move and, with the exception of Baily, they all reached double figures." I continued to draw and Rowe continued to talk. Then, when the pencil stopped moving, Rowe got out of his chair and walked over. "I noticed you'd finished sketching" I lifted up the drawing for Rowe to see. "In football terms" smiled Rowe "you have hit the back of the net. Tell Ralph I want more than one copy!"

I walked out of Mr Rowe's office and at the end of that season he had walked away from Tottenham but his influence remained and his captain Bill Nicholson went on to manage the '60-61 Double side and full-back Alf Ramsey managed the England team that won the '66 World Cup.

I visited Arthur just once when he was manager of Crystal Palace. It was in the 1960/61 season when he guided Palace to promotion to Division 3. As always Mr Rowe had a big smile on his face when he said to me how pleased he was Tottenham were doing so well. But in truth on that visit I spoke more to Johnny

'Budgie' Byrne who had become the first outfield player from the 3rd Division to be capped by England. As I left, Rowe stopped me and said "Never forget Paul, it's football not headball. The ball played on the ground. It's the teams that give and go the Tottenham way that win trophies. TEAMS THAT PLAY THE LONG BALL, PLAY HOPE FOOTBALL."

At the end of that season Johnny Byrne moved to West Ham and the Upton Park club paid a record fee of £65,000, the highest figure between two English clubs. It was four years later I received a phone call from Eric Butler, who was the editor of the magazine *Sport Express* of which I was a regular weekly contributor. "It's a done deal, Paul", was the excited voice of Eric Butler, "Johnny Byrne has agreed to come aboard with the book, titled *The Strategy of Soccer*' and he is delighted you are going to do all the illustrations." I was amazed at the skill Johnny

demonstrated with the ball making my job easy with the pencil and Johnny would often mention Arthur Rowe, who Johnny said was a very sincere and kind man and how much he owed Arthur on his emphasis on the skill part of football.

When the book was published it was great to receive a phone call from Arthur who was pleased with Johnny's mention of his name in the book, but even more pleased how Johnny had passed on the skill part of the game.

When I became involved with Don Revie and Leeds United in 1972 I was for the very first time on the end of an exchange of very angry words from Arthur. "You've lost it Paul," he shouted down the phone. "All those years of exciting, skilful, entertaining football down at Tottenham – WASTED!" I tried to defend myself by saying Don Revie had become a very good friend, since I was commissioned by the *Weekly Sporting Review* to draw the front cover for the 1955 Newcastle v Manchester City FA Cup Final. That day I had spent most of my time talking to Revie on his deep lying centre forward role, which proved very successful at City. "We always talk football Arthur," I pleaded, "skilful football and Revie still says today your push and run team, Arthur, your give and go team, would have beaten Nicholson's Double winning team." But I was talking to myself, Arthur had long ago put the phone down!

Revie was upset that Leeds had, to his mind unfairly, earned the label 'DIRTY LEEDS', and Revie admitted the Norman Hunter nickname 'Bite Yer Legs' didn't help. But Revie defended this by saying every team has a hard man, a no nonsense player. Peter Storey at Arsenal, Chopper Harris at Chelsea, Tommy Smith for Liverpool, and insisted his team were all internationals saying, "you don't get picked to represent your country by simply kicking players up in the air". It was my role, with the help of Leeds trainer Les Cocker, to orchestrate a routine showing how fit the players are and for them to run out fifteen minutes before kick off. I also introduced sock tags, target balls to kick into the crowds, plus skill routines which helped considerably the following season which saw Don Revie's team win the 1st Division title and the nickname 'SUPER LEEDS'.

I continued to receive the odd phone call from Arthur and he begrudgingly admitted that the Leeds 1973/74 title winning team did play exciting, skilful, quick passing football but then added "Leeds should have changed much sooner and shown how the game should be played and it's the only way to play football Paul. SKILFUL AND ENTERTAINING."

PT

The End of the Road for Arthur Rowe

Having led Spurs to back-to-back titles, the following seasons saw Tottenham challenge for major honours without quite getting over the line, although they did add the Charity Shield to the trophy cabinet in September 1951. They would finish just four points adrift of champions Manchester United that season and 11th and 16th in the following two seasons as opposition managers adjusted to Spurs' style.

The biggest problem facing Arthur Rowe however came from within, as criticism of his style of play from certain directors and prominent reporters undermined his position. Furthermore, despite Spurs showing a healthy profit from the record crowds pouring through the gates (Tottenham were the best supported club in the country under Rowe) they were reluctant to part with cash for players. Deals for the likes of George Robledo of Newcastle and Nat Lofthouse of Bolton floundered on the parsimony of the Spurs board — these were players that would have improved Tottenham enormously.

An FA Cup run to the semi-finals in 1953 had been the highlight after those first two seasons but Spurs lost the semi-final after Alf Ramsey scored an unfortunate own goal to give Stan Matthews and Blackpool the chance to make history at Wembley in Coronation Year.

By 1954 the stress proved too much and, after a helter-skelter 3-3 FA Cup draw at Elland Road, Arthur had a mental breakdown and was hospitalised. Assistant Jimmy Anderson took temporary charge and quickly reverted to the 'hit and hope' tactics demanded by the directors before Arthur returned for the start of the 1954-55 campaign to reinstate 'Push and Run'.

That season saw the White Hart Lane debut of a player who is now synonymous with Tottenham when 14 year-old Jimmy Greaves appeared for London schoolboys against their Manchester counterparts. Arthur and Jimmy's father agreed that the young phenomenon would join Tottenham as soon as he left school...

In October 1954 the directors finally prised open the White Hart Lane safe to part with £28,500 for the services of Aston Villa's cerebral 28 year-old midfielder Danny Blanchflower following a protracted transfer battle with Arsenal. The Irishman joining, he said, because he admired Arthur Rowe's football - he would go on to make 382 appearances for the club and captain them to their greatest glories. Other members of that double side were added that season — Ron Henry (having signed professional forms in January 1955 following his demob) and Peter Baker forming a partnership in the reserves, while Terry Dyson made his first team bow later that season.

Solace appeared to come in the cup as Spurs set off on a stirring run that saw them march confidently to a tie at minnows York City but disaster followed as the hosts triumphed 3-1 on a frozen pitch. This proved the cue for more 'push and run' bashing and Arthur was said to have suffered a relapse in the days that followed and he stepped down at the end of the season.

The impact of Arthur Rowe's approach to the game can still be seen at the club today - Bill Nicholson's 'Glory Glory' team of the following decade was a direct descendent of 'Push and Run' and it is criminal that it is so often overlooked by football historians. The main difference between the sides is that Bill Nicholson was allowed to spend while Arthur Rowe (having won the title with a team composed of players who had struggled to get out of the Second Division) was forced to make do and mend!

Arthur's influence can still be seen in modern football, which is said to have stemmed from the movement, tactics and skills of that magnificent Hungarian team of the 1950s whose style he influenced. This was later imitated by Ajax and later moved with Johann Cruyff to Barcelona. 'Push and Run' represents the first rung on that ladder of development.

On a domestic level Rowe was at least half a century ahead of his time. The national game was still debating 'brawn versus brain' well into the 1990s with successive England managers dismissive of the likes of Glenn Hoddle because they 'didn't get stuck in' or were 'reluctant to track back'.

Arthur Rowe returned to football in 1960 at Fourth Division Crystal Palace promising fans that they'd be in the top flight before the end of the decade — a promise kept by his successors after he took the bottom flight by storm with the same football with which he had confounded the critics in the top flight a decade earlier.

Duncan Edwards and the Danny Blanchflower Interception

'The date will always be etched in my mind 30th November 1957'

I invariably travelled to Tottenham's away games with the hope, sometimes a wish, that Spurs would win, but it was different on 30th November 1957. This time I set off on my journey to Old Trafford to see the champions, Manchester United, nicknamed the BUSBY BABES, assuming they would easily defeat Spurs.

No London club had beaten the champions at home for nineteen

years and Tottenham were not having the best of seasons, sitting 18th in the First Division table but what happened that afternoon was nothing short of sensational.

Just 17 minutes after kick off David Pegg put United one up but to my surprise five minutes later Bobby Smith equalised. Then Danny Blanchflower flighted over a centre to Smith who collected, then lobbed the ball over Roger Byrne's head and put the ball past United's teenage 'keeper David Gaskell - Tottenham were ahead. Danny Blanchflower went forward again looking for Smith but saw his pass intercepted by his brother Jackie who, in attempting to pass the ball back to Gaskell instead put it through his own goal. Then it was George Robb's turn to knock over a centre for Smith to leap and head the ball into the United net – a hat-trick for Bobby Smith and when the whistle ended the first half, Tottenham were leading 4-1!

But the second half saw the full power of the champions. Attack followed United attack driven on by the unstoppable

Duncan Edwards. This was the first time I had seen Duncan up close, as corner after corner threatened the Spurs goal. I was able to see the young powerhouse of a player and I realised he looked nothing like my full page drawing of him which was in that day's *Sport Express*! From that moment on I could not take my eyes off of him. Without exception he was FAIR when he tackled, but invariably he left a Spurs player lying on his back. Twice he almost knocked the Spurs goalkeeper Ted Ditchburn into the net as he pulled off a save from an Edwards' thunderbolt, but even Ditchburn, who was having an inspired second half, saw Pegg beat him again to make it 2-4. Five minutes later Liam Whelan fastened onto an Eddie Colman free-kick to blast the ball past Ditchburn, 3-4. Right up until the final whistle it was onslaught after onslaught on the Spurs goal, and I'm sure everybody in the ground that day will never forget when the unstoppable Duncan Edwards, on a thrilling solo run, was only halted when Danny Blanchflower dived full length to take the ball off Edwards foot with his HAND. A free-kick was awarded for United and a big let off for Spurs!

At the whistle, as I left my place behind the goal, I was thrilled Tottenham had won, especially with a Bobby Smith hat-trick, but haunted by my full page drawing of Edwards in *Sport Express*. I decided to wait for Duncan and apologise.

When he emerged to a throng of fans waving copies of my picture, Duncan just laughed adding, 'We always have our bad days!' then winked as he signed for the many kids waiting to see their hero. He added his signature to the white shorts on that Trevillion drawing in *Sport Express*.

I did finally manage to capture the Duncan Edwards I saw that day, but unfortunately it was too late. Duncan, the greatest player I ever saw on a football pitch, had passed on to play his football in the sky.

Planet Hollywood in London was delighted to host so many Tottenham Hotspur events down the years with numerous great Spurs legends and other legends of the game in attendance for book signings, press launches, charity events and auctions as well as giving fans the chance to watch England matches along with their heroes.

We have some great memories and it's been a lot of fun. We hope to continue the tradition in the future.

ALEX GARLAND
Managing Director, Planet Hollywood
(And Lifelong Spurs Fan)

TREVILLION

From Push and Run to 'Glory, Glory'

Arthur Rowe's immediate successor, his former assistant Jimmy Anderson, tore up his 'Push and Run' blueprint and returned to the orthodoxy of the period and on the face of it his reign was a success with second- and third-place finishes in successive seasons and another FA Cup semi-final appearance. Yet a very public falling out with his captain, Danny Blanchflower, and the resulting stress put on him once more by directors and the media, forced him into early retirement in 1958. In reality Anderson was always regarded as no more than a stop-gap while Rowe's preferred successor, Bill Nicholson, gained experience as first team coach.

Scarborough-born Nicholson had joined the Tottenham ground-staff on £2 a week in 1936 and signed as a professional two years later. While the war cost him his playing career, his experiences during the conflict gave him invaluable managerial insight. Having been a vital cog in the 'Push and Run' team he won his only England cap in May 1951 and scored with his first touch. He remains the only player to have scored with his first touch for England and subsequently never play at that level again.

After retiring as a player Nicholson took an FA coaching course and was appointed first team coach in 1955. He also assisted Walter Winterbottom during the 1958 World Cup.

At the time of his appointment as Spurs boss, the club sat just six places off the bottom of the league but Nicholson's regime got off to an incredible start with a 10-4 victory over Everton and the Yorkshireman never looked back.

That first season the club finished 18th, however by 1959-60 most of what would form the Double team were in place and they shot up to third, just two points behind champions Burnley.

The following season Tottenham won 11 games in a row from the start of the season, which is still a top flight record, and never looked back - this is the team that did it... the greatest in Tottenham Hotspur history.

BILL BROWN was a very unflashy goalkeeper who just got on with the business of playing football. Born in 1931, he had played his first football for junior teams in Scotland before joining Dundee before Nicholson signed him for what was then regarded as an enormous amount. Brown brought confidence to the defence for the first time since the heyday of Ted Ditchburn.

PETER BAKER was first spotted playing for Enfield Town and turned professional with Spurs in 1952. He had to wait for the departure of Alf Ramsey before he got his chance and was a very underrated player. He was one of three players (Allen and Dyson were the other two) who never received a full international cap. Baker only missed one game during 1960-61, through injury.

RON HENRY was signed by Spurs in 1955 and figured regularly in the Reserves until Mel Hopkins broke his nose whilst playing for Wales in 1959. Henry took his chance so well that Hopkins could not regain his place. He played in all 49 League and Cup matches in '60-61 and was one of the few Spurs players to play as well as he normally did in the Cup Final against Leicester City.

DANNY BLANCHFLOWER (Capt) never saw eye to eye with Rowe's successor Jimmy Anderson and fell out with Bill Nicholson in the early days. But by March 1959 the cerebral Northern Irishman was restored to the team and appointed captain and was thereafter only absent through injury until he retired during the 1963-64 season.

MAURICE NORMAN signed for Spurs from Norwich City in November 1955. His early games were played at right-back but eventually he converted to centre-half where he went on to win international honours. Tottenham were the first team to send a tall centre-half up-field at corner kicks. In fact it was an argument about this ploy which cost Danny Blanchflower the captaincy under manager Anderson. A common sight today, it was regarded as a risk in the 1950s.

DAVE MACKAY played in 40 Cup Finals during his career and was never once on the losing side. Nicholson was widely expected to sign Mel Charles but persuaded Mackay to come to Tottenham and, while the Scot performed great deeds for Spurs, Charles flopped at Arsenal. It was Mackay who adjusted the balance of the side. Whilst he enjoyed rampaging forward, he was careful to defend when Blanchflower went forward so there were never great gaps in defence. Mackay twice broke his left leg, the second time during a come-back game in the Reserves at Tottenham. As he left in the ambulance his first thoughts were for Nicholson. "Don't tell him until they've finished playing at Upton Park!" he barked.

Spurs had CLIFF JONES under surveillance for quite a long time before they signed him in February 1958. Known for bravery bordering on recklessness, Cliff played for Tottenham for 10 years and broke practically every bone in his body during that time. The dentist was kept busy repairing his teeth after most games because he insisted on risking being kicked in the mouth to head home a goal. In 1960-61, injury restricted his League appearances to 29 games, from which he scored 15 goals.

After JOHN WHITE starred in Scotland's 4-0 win over Northern Ireland in 1959, Bill Nicholson snapped him up for £22,000. The Scot soon ousted Tommy Harmer as an inside-right and earned the nickname of The Ghost for his ability to move into scoring positions unmarked. John was tragically struck by lightning while sheltering under a tree on a golf course on 21st July 1964, he was just 27.

Spurs signed BOBBY SMITH from Chelsea for £55,000. Although he was just 5 feet 9 inches tall, Smith was prodigious in the air and deadly with his right foot. The Middlesbrough born striker was prolific for the club, breaking the club goalscoring record early in the Double season. He was capped 15 times for his country.

LES ALLEN had been part of Chelsea's all-conquering youth team and arrived at Spurs in a swap deal for Johnny Brooks in December 1959. He made an immediate impact scoring twice against Newcastle on his debut. Prone to bouts of self-doubt, he was ever present in 1960-61, forming a lethal partnership with the more bullish Smith.

TERRY DYSON joined Spurs from Scarborough in 1955 after completing his national service. He was the smallest player in the squad but made up for this with boundless enthusiasm.

The Double 1960-61

Aug	20	Division 1	Everton	Home	W	2-0
Aug	22	Division 1	Blackpool	Away	W	3-1
Aug	27	Division 1	Blackburn Rovers	Away	W	4-1
Aug	31	Division 1	Blackpool	Home	W	3-1
Sep	3	Division 1	Manchester United	Home	W	4-1
Sep	7	Division 1	Bolton Wanderers	Away	W	2-1
Sep	10	Division 1	Arsenal	Away	W	3-2
Sep	14	Division 1	Bolton Wanderers	Home	W	3-1
Sep	17	Division 1	Leicester City	Away	W	2-1
Sep	24	Division 1	Aston Villa	Home	W	6-2
Oct	1	Division 1	Wolverhampton Wanderers	Away	W	4-0
Oct	10	Division 1	Manchester City	Home	D	1-1
Oct	15	Division 1	Nottingham Forest	Away	W	4-0
Oct	29	Division 1	Newcastle United	Away	W	4-3
Nov	2	Division 1	Cardiff City	Home	W	3-2
Nov	5	Division 1	Fulham	Home	W	5-1
Nov	12	Division 1	Sheffield Wednesday	Away	L	1-2
Nov	19	Division 1	Birmingham City	Home	W	6-0
Nov	26	Division 1	West Bromwich Albion	Away	W	3-1
Dec	3	Division 1	Burnley	Home	D	4-4
Dec	10	Division 1	Preston North End	Away	W	1-0
Dec	17	Division 1	Everton	Away	W	3-1
Dec	24	Division 1	West Ham United	Home	W	2-0
Dec	26	Division 1	West Ham United	Away	W	3-0

Dec	31	Division 1	Blackburn Rovers	Home	W	5-2
Jan	7	FAC 3	Charlton Athletic	Home	W	3-2
Jan	16	Division 1	Manchester United	Away	L	0-2
Jan	21	Division 1	Arsenal	Home	W	4-2
Jan	28	FAC 4	Crewe Alexandra	Home	W	5-1
Feb	4	Division 1	Leicester City	Home	L	2-3
Feb	11	Division 1	Aston Villa	Away	W	2-1
Feb	18	FAC 5	Aston Villa	Away	W	2-0
Feb	22	Division 1	Wolverhampton Wanderers	Home	D	1-1
Feb	25	Division 1	Manchester City	Away	W	1-0
Mar	4	FAC 6	Sunderland	Away	D	1-1
Mar	8	FAC 6 replay	Sunderland	Home	W	5-0
Mar	11	Division 1	Cardiff City	Away	L	2-3
Mar	18	FAC Semi	Burnley	Villa Park	W	3-0
Mar	22	Division 1	Newcastle United	Home	L	1-2
Mar	25	Division 1	Fulham	Away	D	0-0
Mar	31	Division 1	Chelsea	Home	W	4-2
Apr	1	Division 1	Preston North End	Home	W	5-0
Apr	3	Division 1	Chelsea	Away	W	3-2
Apr	8	Division 1	Birmingham City	Away	W	3-2
Apr	17	Division 1	Sheffield Wednesday	Home	W	2-1
Apr	22	Division 1	Burnley	Away	L	2-4
Apr	26	Division 1	Nottingham Forest	Home	W	1-0
Apr	29	Division 1	West Bromwich Albion	Home	L	1-2
May	6	FAC Final	Leicester City	Wembley	W	2-0

BILL BROWN
41 League apps, 7 FA Cup apps

PETER BAKER
41 League apps no goals
7 FA Cup apps, no goals

MAURICE NORMAN
41 League apps 4 goals
7 FA Cup apps, no goals

RON HENRY
41 League apps 1 goal
7 FA Cup apps, no goals

DANNY BLANCHFLOWER
42 League apps 6 goals
7 FA Cup apps, no goals

DAVE MACKAY
37 League apps, 4 goals
7 FA Cup apps, 2 goals

TERRY DYSON
40 League apps 12 goals
7 FA Cup apps, 5 goals

JOHN WHITE
42 League apps 13 goals
7 FA Cup apps, no goals

LES ALLEN
42 League apps 22 goals
7 FA Cup apps, 4 goals

CLIFF JONES
28 League apps 15 goals
7 FA Cup apps, 5 goals

BOBBY SMITH
36 League apps 27 goals
7 FA Cup apps, 5 goals

FRANK SAUL
6 League apps, 3 goals

TONY MARCHI
6 League apps, 0 goals

John Hollowbread, Ken Barton and John Smith each made one league appearance without scoring.

Dave Mackay

David Craig Mackay, born on 14th November 1934, was once described by Manchester United's George Best as the "hardest man I ever played against". He was a complete player in every sense and one of my all time favourites from the 60s. A key part of Spurs' famous 1961 double-winning team – Dave passed away at a hospital in Nottingham aged 80 in March 2015. Paying tribute, Spurs described the Scot as "one of our greatest ever players and a man who never failed to inspire those around him."

Having started his career with Hearts in 1953, captaining the Edinburgh side to the Scottish League title during the 1957-58 season, Mackay moved south to join Tottenham in 1959 and helped the north London club become the first English side to win the League and FA Cup double during the 1960-61 campaign. The Edinburgh-born player helped Spurs retain the FA Cup the following season and was captain when Spurs lifted the trophy again in 1967.

A superb, brave, no-nonsense competitor, he also possessed all the technique, passing ability and talent to be the complete player, the heartbeat of the 1961 double side, a key member of the team that retained the FA Cup the following season and, although injury kept him out of the 1963 European Cup Winners' Cup final triumph, he had played a vital role in getting Spurs there. He formed a marvellous midfield combination with Danny Blanchflower and, when the Northern Ireland international left in 1964, Mackay took over as Spurs captain and led the team to triumph in 1967. He twice broke the same leg but, each time, came back stronger than ever.

Mackay left Tottenham to join Derby in 1968 and helped Brian Clough's side win promotion to the First Division the following year before taking up a player-manager role at Swindon Town in 1971. He left the Robins a year later to manage Nottingham Forest for a brief spell before succeeding Clough as Derby manager in 1973, helping the Rams win the First Division.

Mackay won 10 major honours as a player in British and European football. Spurs described him as "the heartbeat" of their Double-winning side and said he played a "vital role" in their 1963 European Cup Winners' Cup success despite missing the final through injury.

Former Tottenham manager David Pleat, speaking to BBC Radio 5 live commented: "He was a great man, inspirational. He was as tough as teak, led by example and was a wonderful leader of men. He represented everything that was wonderful about football in those days. He was a very polite, decent, humble and down-to-earth guy."

Former Derby captain Roy McFarland, talking to BBC Radio Derby added: "The majority of pictures you see of Dave Mackay, he had his chest stuck out. That is how he played and that is how he lived his life. He had a tough legacy taking over as manager from Brian Clough, in terms of the atmosphere at the club, but he calmed and settled everyone down."

Former Scotland manager Craig Brown, speaking to BBC Radio Scotland said: "Dave Mackay was the perfect midfield player and he would have been worth an absolute fortune today. When you see players like Gareth Bale going to Real Madrid you wonder what Dave Mackay would've been worth in the present market."

Mackay's first club, Hearts described him as, "A fearless defender regarded as the club's greatest-ever player."

1958: Captains Hearts to Scottish league title.

1959: Joins Tottenham from Hearts for £32,000.

1961: Wins the league and FA Cup Double with Tottenham. He won two further FA Cups, in 1962 and 1967.

1968: Sold to Derby County for £5,000, helping them gain promotion to the First Division in his first season.

1969: Named joint winner of the Football Writers' Association Footballer of the Year award.

1971: Appointed player-manager of Swindon Town.

1972: Becomes Nottingham Forest manager.

1973: Succeeds Brian Clough as manager of Derby County.

1975: Leads Derby County to the league title.

1977-1995: Manages Walsall, Birmingham City and Doncaster, and a number of clubs in the Middle East

2002: Made an inaugural inductee of the English Football Hall of Fame

2015: Dies aged 80

Cliff Jones

I owe my 'mad' mother an eternal apology. I am sure she was not mad. Obsessed? Most definitely. A typical Jewish mother? Yes. But she went beyond even that archetypal figure. After the death of my father, Jack, at the age of 45, following a painful and surprisingly rapid decline riddled with lung cancer, my mother became more than just a mum. Sara was a one-off. She gave up the chance to re-marry even though she became engaged to the lead violinist in the Dorchester Hotel orchestra, when she found out that my prospective step-father had clipped me around the ear for being a pest in his West London flat, she refused to have anything more to do with him. Considering we were banned from a Brighton hotel after I smashed a glass table top - by accident - it was clear she had a boisterous boy.

She was an overbearing burden, yet I do miss her eccentricities. She made many personal sacrifices. The East End was the traditional catchment area for West Ham United support, and even more centrally, Leyton Orient. Heroes such as Bobby Moore were the lure for the Hammers, but there had been a sudden shift in the early 60s towards North London and Spurs. The Double winning side of Bill Nicholson was my inspiration, the beautiful game played the way it should be, and later that year the arrival of Jimmy Greaves cemented my commitment to the cause. Jimmy was my No. 1 hero, and remains so. His goals were works of art, with grace and speed around the penalty area, a master of the goal scoring trade, he was a true match winner.

My mum's black Singer (a sewing machine not an entertainer!) was our only source of income after my dad passed away when I was five. I had pictures of my heroes on the wall, would use up my pocket money buying photographs they would sell in the Spurs Supporters Club adjacent to the ground in Tottenham High Road, and my mum's presents usually had a Spurs flavour, such as a deep blue Spurs rug for the foot of my bed.

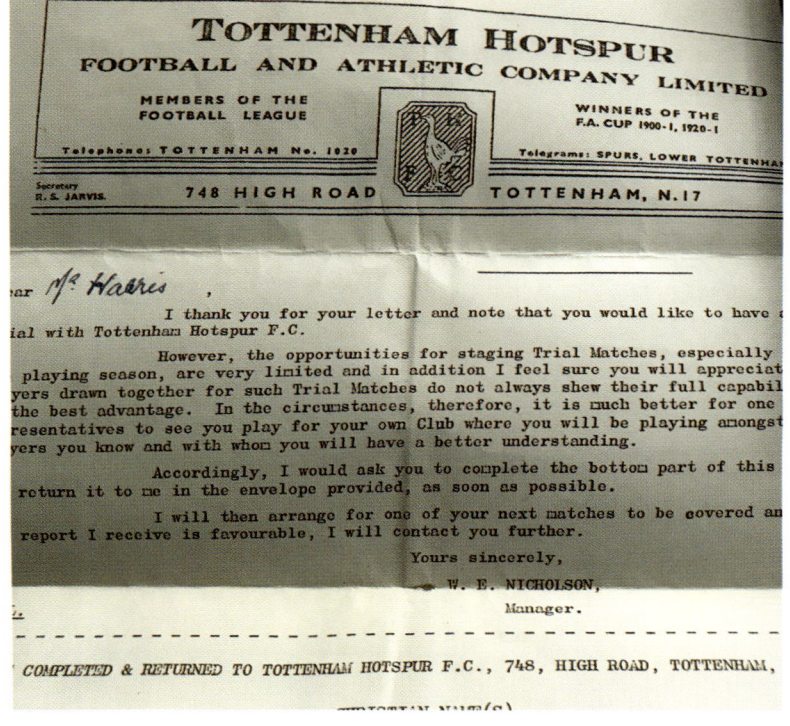

There were precious few green areas so the streets were our football pitch, as was the concrete school playground. Less than a quarter of a mile away lived Barry Silkman and his family. "Silky" went on to play for Orient, QPR and Manchester City, I enjoyed kicking a football around with him.

My first choice career was to be a professional footballer. Regrettably I wasn't quite good enough. Yet my 'mad' mum somehow wangled me a trial with Spurs. She actually wrote to Bill Nicholson and got a reply! When she showed me the forms, I was shocked. I filled them in, and sent them off. They requested dates of up and coming games, and I provided the club with the forthcoming Davenant Foundation Grammar School's senior fixtures.

I was a goalkeeper who had made the senior side a year early, and played alongside Terry Brisley and Dennis Rolfe. I am convinced a scout watched me in a game against an England Grammar School XI which Davenant lost 6-1, although I did save a late penalty (which was struck straight at me). After that "trial", the gossip was that Orient were keen on Brisley and Rolfe, and the East End club signed both of them as juniors.

True to her word, when it came to the first all-London FA Cup final between Spurs and Chelsea, Sara made sure I had a ticket. My mum took me and a friend to Wembley and waited outside while I sat there with my pal from school who also supported Spurs and from our semi-obscured vantage point loved every minute of a game all the pundits branded boring and one of the worst Wembley finals of all time.

But it didn't stop me rushing around to the local newsagents when I got back from Wembley to queue up for a copy of the evening paper's "Pink" edition for the match report and early pictures. As I was to discover later, the intensity of putting together a match report virtually as the game is still in progress, meant that there was no time for real analysis, so the evening paper report passed little comment on the quality of the game. However the Sunday papers and the Monday editions were scathing about the lack of quality and excitement as both teams cancelled each other out in their determination not to lose the final which meant so much to both sets of fans.

As a boy I had dozens of scrap books filled with the programmes of each game, and the newspaper cuttings. I loved the *Daily Express* reports which carried a little star with a number in from one to five as a rating for the match and its entertainment value. Incredibly some of the names that would appear on those reports, such as Steve Curry from the *Express* and Nigel Clarke in the *Mirror*, were still around when I finally broke into Fleet Street. And, some of the players in that final became more than heroes on the pitch but people I grew to know extremely well. One of them was Joe Kinnear who went on to become manager at Wimbledon and Nottingham Forest then Newcastle. Joe was the pin-up boy of the Spurs team that year. He then became an outstanding manager with the Crazy Gang and he was a nice bloke. I liked him a lot.

I set out to hone my journalistic skills, while still at school, by working on the school magazine, and taking school reports to the local paper, which they started to publish. My school report dated July 24th 1968, had this to say from the headmaster, "Gave most useful help in preparing the school magazine." I became a well known face at the local paper, bombarding them with visits, and with reports of school events from sports days to open days, and organising photographers. I managed to wangle some work experience during the summer holidays. The school report the following year, dated July 16th 1969, gave this assessment from the headmaster, "I appreciate his enthusiastic reporting of school events for local newspapers and I hope that his holiday job will help him."

I managed to get a job as the most junior of junior reporters in the smallest of branch offices in Loughton High Road for The Independent Group of newspapers. At first, it was the weekly round of local police station, fire brigade, local church and funeral parlour for any bits and pieces that might make some kind of interesting article. On a quiet week, I was told to take a ladder, place it outside the offices and conduct a survey of how superstitious the local population might be, by seeing who walked around it, rather than under it.

Naturally, when the chance cropped up to cover local football teams, such as Harlow Town, I jumped at it. I liked the assignment so much that I ended up training with the club occasionally, and even dreamed of playing for the team. But a five-a-side game was about as close as I came. I still fancied myself as a goalkeeper, and took part in a five-a-side tournament at Haringey Sports Centre. One of my

boyhood idols was Cliff Jones of the Double team. I was in awe of his courage and enthusiasm, his incredible ability to climb so high for a small man and score spectacular goals with his head at the far post. That enthusiasm for the game continued to shine through when I met him when he was working as a fitness instructor and coach at Haringey and I actually played against him in that five-a-side tournament. His feet were still lightning fast, and when he attacked my goal, it was impossible for me to judge which direction the ball was going. He scored five past me; he would chip it over me if I came flying out, or take the ball round me if I hesitated, or simply slot the ball into the corner with uncanny precision. Yes, it was time to give up the dream!

The best part was getting the opportunity to chat with him and to discover that he was such an endearing guy, totally unassuming, anything but the superstar one would associate with such a high profile and hugely successful international. Perhaps it was the era? The players still had some sort of affinity with the fans. Although they were highly paid, the differential was far less than it is now. Cliff was a modest man of modest means, and a truly nice guy.

If Cliff was playing today he would be worth £160m and command £400,000-a-week. He would be a multi-millionaire who wouldn't needed to have been a fitness instructor in the local sports centre to supplement his income after finishing an illustrious career laden with medals and plaudits.

Cliff is such a well-mannered individual, he suppresses a burst of laughter whenever I remind him of that time I tried to prevent him scoring a bag full of goals in that tournament!

HH

John White

Legacy of 'The Ghost' lives on through unique artwork

It was an emotional occasion for two lifelong fans as they visited the stadium recently. For one, it meant seeing the legacy of his late father live on in our new home. The other is the man who admitted being brought to tears when he first drew the image that now has a special place within the stadium and ensures an all-time great is never forgotten.

John White - affectionately known as 'The Ghost' for the way he used to appear within an opponent's box seemingly without defenders knowing - was a key member of our greatest ever team, the 1960/61 Double-winning side.

Tragically, aged just 27, the Scotland international lost his life when he was struck by lightning on a golf course at the peak of his career, leaving a widow, Sandra, a two-year-old daughter, Mandy, and a six-month old son, Rob. Now a Season Ticket Holder and somebody who has dedicated his life to building memories of the father he never got to know, Rob was accompanied on this special visit to the stadium by Paul Trevillion - a renowned artist famed for his long-running 'You Are The Ref' illustrated series.

It was Paul, a close friend of the club, who was asked to produce a piece of artwork that he describes as "the hardest thing I've ever had to do" just months after John's untimely death.

His iconic illustration of John formed the front cover of the match day programme for what was to be the John White Memorial Match as Spurs took on a Scotland XI at The Lane in November, 1964.

And it is that front cover that now takes pride of place within the stadium's South Stand Market Place within one of two match day programme collage feature walls that reside there - a popular attraction for fans visiting our new

> "When I drew that front cover [in 1964]. it was the hardest thing I'd ever had to do, because every time I started drawing my tears would keep hitting the paper and I couldn't finish, but I was on a tight deadline."

Rob White and artist Paul Trevillion meet in front of the famous sketch of Rob's dad John White

home.

Rob said: "Somebody had sent me a picture of the programme cover on the wall from the South Stand familiarisation event the Club held in December and I was really excited.

"People go to the stadium to feel at home - it's about more than just football. I was so pleased to see that my Dad would be remembered in the new stadium and that people would still continue to talk about him.

"The reaction from fans on a match day to the programme wall is brilliant because all the front covers evoke special memories that fans may have.

"As somebody whose Dad played for the Club and whose grandfather (Harry Evans) was Assistant Manager, I'm so pleased that such a fitting tribute has been paid to our heritage".

For Paul, this was his first visit to our new home and the experience was a particularly poignant one - upon seeing his artwork immortalised in the stadium, the memories came flooding back.

"When I first saw the artwork on the wall. I broke down in tears" revealed Paul. "When I drew that front cover [in 1964]. it was the hardest thing I'd ever had to do, because every time I started drawing my tears would keep hitting the paper and I couldn't finish, but I was on a tight deadline.

"At games I used to get as near as I could to the players so I could draw them. I used to stand behind Ted Ditchbum's goal at the Paxton Road end and I used to study the players' faces. That's how I learnt to draw. Players like John White were my heroes.

"The players even used to give me advice on my drawings -Alf Ramsey used to tell me that I drew him leaning too far back if he was kicking the ball! The best advice I ever got was from Bill Nicholson, who told me I could always do better. I was not the best at school and struggled to read and write - I considered the players to be like my teachers."

On the stadium itself, he continued: "It is unbelievable - it's more than a football stadium ... it's home. The result of the match is important - but what's more important is how you feel as a fan when you enter the ground. You wouldn't just come here to see the match - it would be a day out. When I walked out into the bowl for the first time, it was as though I could see all the players of years gone by out on that pitch… it was all too much for me."

Courtesy of Spurs Official Programme

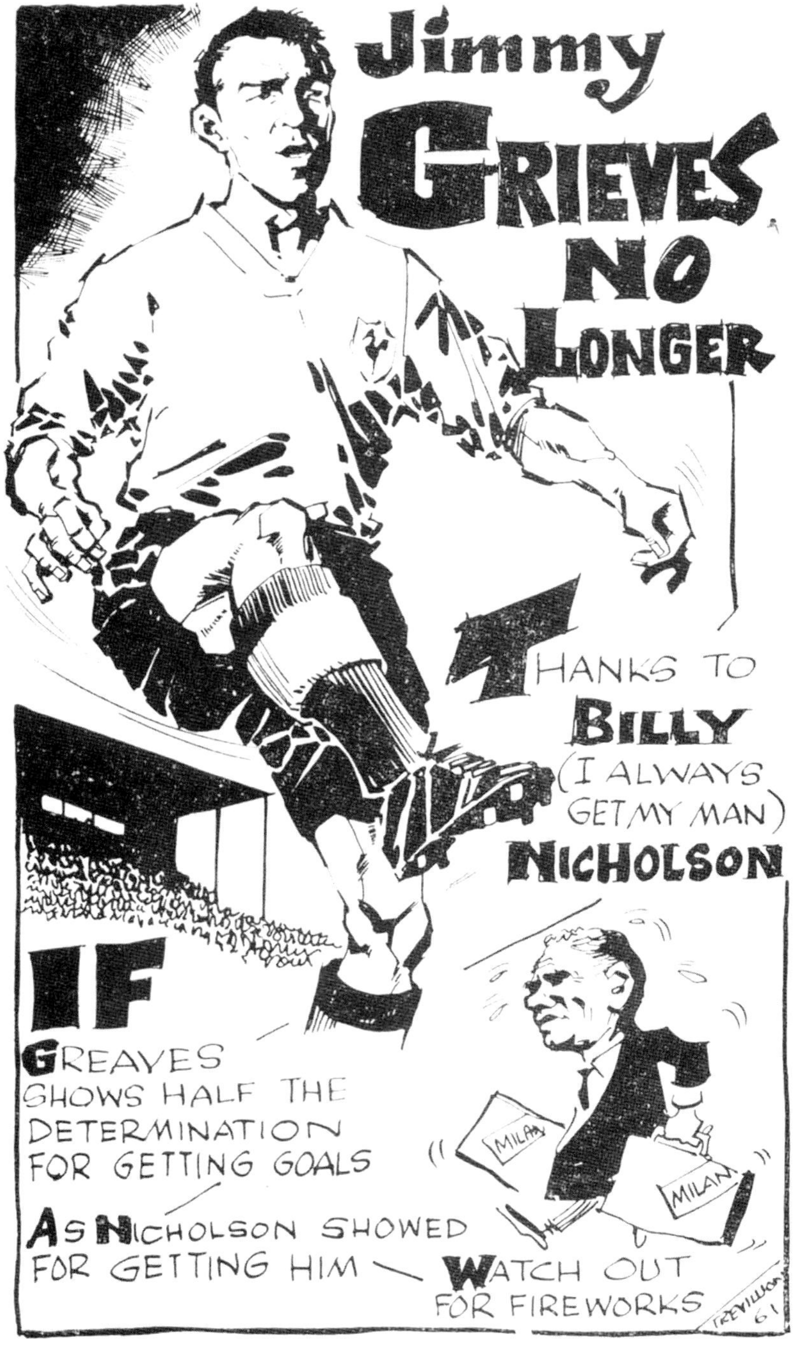
Jimmy
GRIEVES
NO
LONGER
THANKS TO
BILLY
(I ALWAYS
GET MY MAN)
NICHOLSON
IF
GREAVES
SHOWS HALF THE
DETERMINATION
FOR GETTING GOALS
AS NICHOLSON SHOWED
FOR GETTING HIM —
WATCH OUT
FOR FIREWORKS
MILAN
MILAN
TREVILLION 61

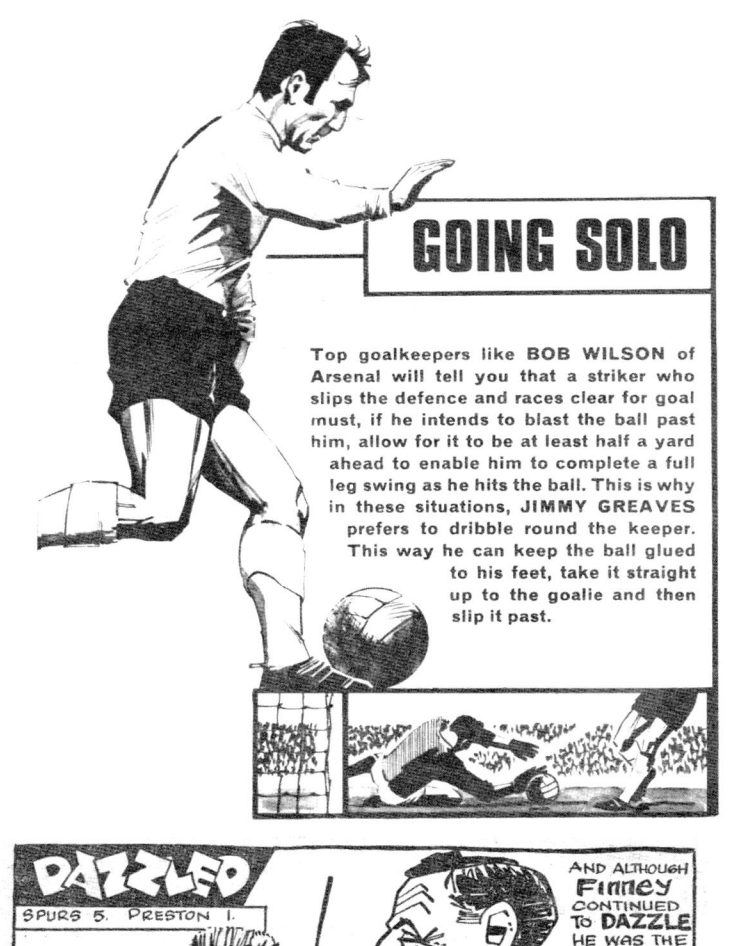

GOING SOLO

Top goalkeepers like **BOB WILSON** of Arsenal will tell you that a striker who slips the defence and races clear for goal must, if he intends to blast the ball past him, allow for it to be at least half a yard ahead to enable him to complete a full leg swing as he hits the ball. This is why in these situations, **JIMMY GREAVES** prefers to dribble round the keeper. This way he can keep the ball glued to his feet, take it straight up to the goalie and then slip it past.

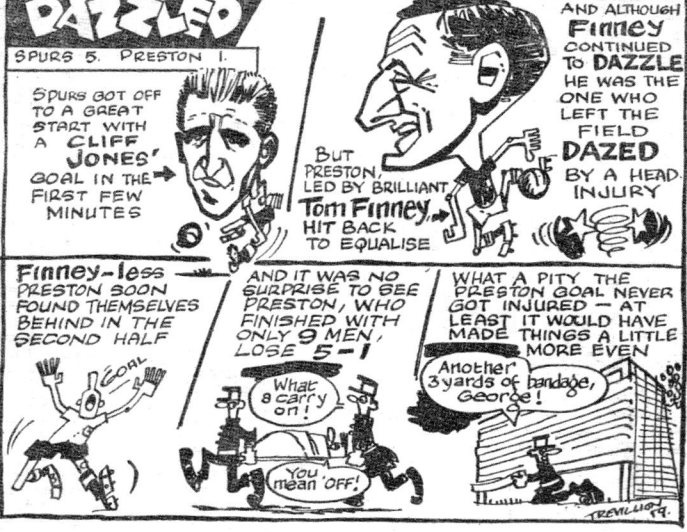

DAZZLED
SPURS 5. PRESTON 1.
SPURS GOT OFF TO A GREAT START WITH A CLIFF JONES' GOAL IN THE FIRST FEW MINUTES
BUT PRESTON, LED BY BRILLIANT Tom Finney, HIT BACK TO EQUALISE
AND ALTHOUGH Finney CONTINUED TO DAZZLE HE WAS THE ONE WHO LEFT THE FIELD DAZED BY A HEAD INJURY
Finney-less PRESTON SOON FOUND THEMSELVES BEHIND IN THE SECOND HALF
GOAL
AND IT WAS NO SURPRISE TO SEE PRESTON, WHO FINISHED WITH ONLY 9 MEN, LOSE 5-1
What a carry on!
You mean 'OFF'!
WHAT A PITY THE PRESTON GOAL NEVER GOT INJURED — AT LEAST IT WOULD HAVE MADE THINGS A LITTLE MORE EVEN
Another 3 yards of bandage, George!
TREVILLION 59.

A selection of Paul's art that appeared in Spurs' official magazine 'The Lilywhite'

Jimmy Greaves

A Master Craftsman in front of goal, Jimmy is one of the greats.

Jimmy Greaves remains my all-time favourite. I watched him from the stands at the Lane when I was a very young lad, and he was the player I used to buy pictures of from the Spurs Supporters Club to stick on my wall. What a goalscorer! It is still hard to believe he didn't fulfil his destiny and play for England in the 1966 World Cup final after starting the tournament in Alf Ramsey's side. We all know why — he was injured in the group stage against France and with England winning without him, Ramsey would not change his winning team. Still, half a century on, it still rankles. So does the fact he was never knighted.

Greaves scored 44 goals in 57 England games, and is now fifth-highest scorer behind Harry Kane, Wayne Rooney, Sir Bobby Charlton and ex-Spur Gary Lineker. He spent nine glorious goal-filled seasons at White Hart Lane during one of the most successful periods in the club's history. He scored the opening goal in Tottenham's FA Cup final victory over Burnley in 1962 and found the net in the European Cup Winners' Cup final against Atletico Madrid in 1963, which Spurs won 5-1.

Having been scouted by Spurs manager Arthur Rowe as a boy, Greaves started his career at Chelsea and broke into the first-team in 1957 after scoring 114 goals for the youth team in his final season at that level. He scored 132 goals in 169 games for Chelsea including a goal for them on his League debut against Spurs at the Lane in August 1957. After leaving Chelsea in 1961 he then spent an unhappy six months at AC Milan, where he scored on his debut, before returning to London to join Spurs in December 1961, scoring a hat-trick on his debut in a 5-2 win over Blackpool at the Lane. After Tottenham, he moved across the capital to West Ham, scoring on his debut at Maine Road, before quitting Upton Park at the age of 31 and seeing out his career lower down the leagues following a battle with alcoholism. After retiring, Jim co-hosted the popular and hilarious Saturday lunchtime football show *Saint and Greavsie* alongside former Liverpool forward Ian St John.

The record books might now downgrade Greaves goalscoring feats with England, but Kane has played far more games, and so many more against inferior opponents that they really are not comparable. Former Spurs manager Harry Redknapp picks Greaves as his personal favourite in a Three Lions shirt, "It's a tough one but I have to go with Greaves. I'm one of his biggest fans and the best striker I've played against. When he had the ball in the opposition area the world would stop. He'd have a defender come in and he'd feint one way then go the other, then the keeper would rush out towards him and he'd fake to shoot in one corner sending the keeper that way only to put it in the other corner. He was such an incredible finisher. I remember when he scored five at the age of 17 for Chelsea against a Wolves side that basically had the England back three. He was a special talent."

The modern game has lone strikers, or no strikers, but Greaves' partnership with Scotsman Alan Gilzean was a sight to behold, full of inventiveness and guile.

Here are some selected stats from Jimmy's brilliant career:

516 - Appearances in the First Division 1957-71

420 - Appearances for Spurs in all competitions between 1961-70.

402 - Club goals for Chelsea, AC Milan, Spurs, West Ham, Chelmsford City and Barnet.

357 - First Division goals for Spurs, Chelsea and West Ham, making him the highest top flight goalscorer of all time.

268 - Goals for Spurs in all competitions..

220 - League goals for Spurs - a club record

132 - Goals for Chelsea in just 169 matches

114 - Goals for Chelsea's youth team in the 1956-57 season.

100 - League goals by the age of 20 years and 290 days, the youngest ever to reach the milestone.

57 - England caps between 1959 and 1967

44 - Goals for England.

41 - Chelsea goals to become their record league scorer in one season (1960-61)

37 - Spurs goals to become their record league scorer in one season (1962-63)

9 - Serie A goals for AC Milan (in only 10 matches)

6 - Hat-tricks for England (a record), including four in a game twice.

6 - times Division One top scorer - a record: Chelsea (1958-59, 1960-61) and Spurs (1962-63, 1963-64, 1964-65, 1968-69)

5 - He scored on his debut on five occasions for every senior team he played for: Chelsea, England, AC Milan, Spurs (hat-trick) and West Ham (a brace).

The 'cockney cool' of Jimmy Greaves

A - Greaves like to take the ball right up to a defender before beating him. By doing this he forces the defender to jockey back on his heels, so catching him flat-footed as he accelerates past. This means Greaves is a yard ahead before the defender has had time to turn and pursue. The less-confident forward who pushes the ball wide of the defender too soon allows him the time to turn and get in another tackle.

B - Instead of challenging for the ball in a packed goalmouth, Greaves will leave it to a team mate and make for a spot where, if he receives the ball, he will be in a perfect position for a crack at goal. Greaves times his run - usually on the blind side - arriving in the open space at the same time as the ball. The less gifted striker will run into the space too soon causing defenders to follow and so plug the gap. Unfortunately in some matches Greaves will make as many as 30 such runs and never receive the ball. It is on these occasions that he is wrongly accused of contributing nothing to a match.

C - The Greaves genius is seen at its best when he runs on to a fast-travelling through ball. Without checking his speed, Greaves will, simply by dipping his shoulders, either to the right or to the left, race past two or three bewildered defenders without once touching the ball. So he is unlike George Best who prefers to kill the pace of the ball as he feints, then dummies his way past defenders with the ball at times glued to his feet.

D - When Greaves bursts through, he rarely has to make the vital decision of when to shoot. He takes the ball so close to the goalkeeper that he forces him to commit himself and this is the signal for Greaves to jab it home. This jabbing action, withdrawing the foot as soon as the ball is kicked, allows Greaves to kick the ball without any check in his running stride, and denies the goalkeeper the opportunity of anticipating the shot.

SUNDAY TIMES

BARE FACTS

JIMMY GREAVES WHO'S SO QUICK **OFF** THE MARK

AND BANG **ON** THE TARGET HAS A PROBLEM

His LIGHTNING SPEED HAS REFEREES AND LINESMEN GIVING HIM OFF-SIDE WHEN HE'S NOT

Something's GOT TO BE DONE AND I SUGGEST LITTLE **JIMMY** STOPS HIDING IN THOSE TOO LONG SHORTS

AND MAKES HIMSELF MORE **NOTICEABLE** TO OFFICIALS BY WEARING JUST A **SMILE** —

THEN AT LEAST THEY'LL BE ABLE TO SPOT HIM BEFORE HE STARTS HIS **RUN** INSTEAD OF AFTER

—TREVILLION

THREE CHEERS For JIM'S 300

Bill Nicholson

The Greatest Spur

David Leggett was the outgoing Spurs full-time reporter for the North London *Weekly Herald* group of newspapers. His primary task was to follow Spurs, although the paper included reports on the reserves and youth team. The broadsheet also carried the Arsenal match reports and news. David had been enticed away by a good offer to cover football in Scotland for a national and I was the only one left within the small local paper group with any kind of football knowledge, but more importantly with a burning ambition to cover Spurs. So when someone asked, "does anyone fancy being Sports Editor?" I put my hand up! This wasn't a job, it was like winning the lottery. Wow, I couldn't wait.

It was the summer close season break and Bill Nicholson hadn't been away for much of a holiday, he loved his work and preferred to be at work, so he was the first back, eager to prepare for the new season. David had made arrangements to say his farewells to Bill and to introduce me to him as his successor. Just the thought of meeting the great "Billy Nick", manager of the first Double winning side of the 20th century, filled me with apprehension and excitement all at the same time.

I took my usual route to the Herald offices in Tottenham High Road from Gants Hill via the Green Line bus that stopped at the top of my long road of terraced houses. Gants Hill was the posh annex to the East End, the first overspill from that Brick Lane Jewish community that wanted to better themselves, and had got a decent job and could raise their first mortgage. My mum helped finance that first mortgage and my newly promoted position of sports editor underpinned the repayments. My mum, though, had been reluctant to move from the East End and that's an understatement. Sara completely blocked it out of her mind that I had gone ahead and purchased my first property and that the we would be leaving our tiny third floor flat in Valence Road, the hub of the East End and not far from where the Krays were brought up. I packed all my worldly belongings into two suitcases but Mum just sat in her favourite armchair and remained there until the removals men rang the doorbell! The movers took what little furniture we possessed; including that sewing machine from which she used every day to scrape a meagre living with bits of fur throw aways from the nearby furriers which she meticulously sewed into, at first fur coats, but as the material ran out, into hats and shawls. Sara's argument for staying put was that it would become even tougher to beg for fur scraps from her old contacts and friends if she moved out of the East End where she was also top of the list for charitable handouts of food and clothing. In desperation I put down a bed sheet (I can recall to this day, that it had a hideous yellow, white and red striped pattern) in the middle of the living room floor and just shoved her clothes and bits and pieces into it, tied it in a knot and loaded it, and her, on to the removal van.

So we'd moved up in the world and my daily routine had been

to catch the bus from Gants Hill to Tottenham, then to walk down the three quarters of a mile to the offices. But that day the journey was vastly different. It seemed to take three times as long, even though I wanted it to take half the time. I wanted to be there to meet Bill Nicholson, and yet it was the most frightening prospect of my entire life. It was a relief to finally arrive outside Billy Nick's office waiting to go in. Once through that door, David did the customary "hand over" and left me alone with Bill for a quick chat and brief starting the process of "getting to know you".

"Now then", enquired Bill, trying, no doubt, to be kind to the local boy who looked rather nervous. In fact, I was so anxious it was hard to prevent myself from trembling but Bill's tone was kind and considerate. Suddenly I grew in confidence. He clearly perceived that here was a boy starting out in his career, and he genuinely wanted to help. I could sense it.

"When would you like to see me?" he continued.

"As I have to write about the team each week with a Wednesday deadline and early Thursday morning for any midweek game, could I see you every Monday morning?" I replied There followed a few seconds silence. Just enough to add the rider... "I feel it is vitally important to get your perspective, to find out what the club is thinking, which means what you are thinking and for the local paper to reflect that, and to support the club where ever possible." I had never rehearsed that. I had thought and thought about what I should say, and nothing I could think of in advance seemed the least bit appropriate, but once in front of Bill, it just came to me. I am sure I struck a chord with him.

Bill smiled and he leaned towards me in his chair, in a way you can imagine if you were one of his players and he was about to give out an important instruction, or piece of invaluable advice, where you had better make sure you listened to every word. "Your predecessor saw me once a season. That was it". There were a few seconds silence. It seemed like half an hour. Then he smiled again. "Come and see me Monday morning before training, here in my office, and we shall see how we go, but remember, once a season your predecessor saw me."

So every Monday morning before training for the next seven years Bill Nicholson saw me and we spoke for around 15 to 20 minutes as he gave me a fully comprehensive run down on everything that went on inside the club except, of course, those issues he wanted to keep to himself. As the years went by he began to trust me and confided in me.

It wasn't long before the daily national newspapers had my number and would call for inside information. Naturally they paid me for tips, or in the case of Victor Railton on the *Evening News*, sometimes for actually writing

some material, mainly gleaned from the editons of the *Weekly Herald*. In truth I was hard;y giving away any state secrets, just re-writing the information that I had already made public in my local newspaper columns. I never parted with any information I knew Bill would not want me to. No amount of money would have persuaded me to break faith with Bill Nicholson. No way. I looked upon him as a father figure and there were times when I think he almost treated me like a son.

As I became increasingly more useful to the national media, Victor would take the trouble to pop into my house in Gants Hill to pick up my stories from copies of what would be appearing the next day in my weekly column. On occasions Vic would tell me that the next morning he had arranged for a taxi to collect me at 6am to take me from Gants Hill to the Lane to make sure I was there for 7am as at 7.30am Spurs new signing would be arriving. I was to interview him, nip into the nearest phone box and dictate word for word what had been said, and back at the *News* Vic would put an intro to my words and it would be all over the back pages within hours as a major exclusive interview by Vic!

The papers weren't the only ones itching for the inside track; there was one guy I did confide in, an avid Arsenal fan called Laurence Marks. He was a news reporter on the *Weekly Herald*. At the time he was writing a book about Ruth Ellis, the last woman to be hanged in Britain, and asked for my help and he caught me by surprise by mentioning me in the credits to that book. Laurence and I would go out to lunch most days, to a nearby greasy spoon, whose owners were avid Spurs fans. They were also part of the big Greek community in the area. We loved their home made moussaka, and even when it wasn't on the menu the dear old mama would come out of the kitchen to say hello and ask us if we would like some of the moussaka which she had made for the family - and invariably we accepted. Over lunch Laurence was always hungry for football gossip, particularly if it had any connection to his beloved Arsenal. Laurence went on to become one of the world's most successful comedy writers, alongside his writing partner Maurice Gran with hit shows such as *Birds of a Feather* and *Goodnight Sweetheart*. In later years I met up with Laurence again and got to know Mo & Lo well. We came close to collaborating on a football book, but it never quite worked out.

One of my greatest achievements was to persuade Bill

Nicholson to write his memoirs. Oddly enough, it was another Arsenal fan who helped. Alan Samson was Commissioning Editor at Macmillan and, together with my good friend and *Daily Mail* colleague Brian Scovell, we collaborated on *Glory, Glory - My Life With Spurs*. Nicholson was initially reluctant but I nagged him for so long he finally relented. I went round to his modest semi-detached within walking distance of the Spurs stadium for a cup of tea and spent hours and hours chatting about Spurs.

I now have only two copies left of his book, one of them signed by Bill and all the Double team who turned up for the launch of the book in 1984. Among my prized souvenirs are three pictures of Bill in faded black and white. It is with great fondness that I look back on the help that Bill Nicholson gave me in my career, yet despite this father/son relationship he could be quick to admonish me for my over-enthusiasm on occasions...

After one European tie the press gathered around the manager outside of the stadium in a Swiss car park, which was the way most press interviews were conducted in those days. It

Billy Nick stayed on after announcing his resignation to supposedly help pick his successor. Bill wanted Johnny Giles and lined up Terry Butcher. They chose Terry Neill and the chairman told me later he didn't know he played for Arsenal! Billy waved to the crowd at the next game after his announcement. I'm in the press box just behind him

was September 1973 and Spurs had beaten Grasshoppers of Zurich 5-1 in the first leg of the first round of the UEFA Cup but in reality, Nicholson's team had actually been outplayed! Spurs had about seven breakaways from which they scored five times, and the man of the match was Pat Jennings for a string of world class saves.

Of course, I was always buzzing with questions and came up with the line "Are you convinced Spurs will get through after the way Grasshoppers played?" Nicholson looked at me as if I had just arrived from Mars and didn't have a clue what I was talking about and, of course, he was dead right. A man of such vast experience and knowledge knew that such a result away from home guaranteed your path to the next round, and that it would be a vastly different proposition when Grasshoppers came to fortress White Hart Lane, one of the most feared venues in European football at that time. He just laughed and said "Are you mad?" and moved on to the next question. For the record, Spurs won the second leg 4-1 going through 9-2 on aggregate.

It was a good lesson for the local newspaper boy. Think before you ask a question and don't make yourself out look like an idiot!

A Nicholson 'No' Means a Revie 'Yes'

In 1970 I was working in America for Mark McCormack and golf's big three: Jack Nicklaus, Arnold Palmer and Gary Player. I was based in Cleveland, Ohio, and I never missed watching baseball and the Cleveland Indians team, witnessing first-hand the Americans colourful razzmatazz at sporting events. Cheerleaders dancing in unison waving pom-poms and fireworks fired off with every spectacular baseball hit.

I realised British sporting presentation was light years behind and if I could introduce just some of these ideas into football it would revolutionise the game. Upon my return and bursting with enthusiasm, my first port of call was Bill Nicholson at Tottenham Hotspur, it was in July just before the start of the 1971/72 season. As always Bill's first words were 'Why are you here? You should be in your studio sharpening pencils.' I smiled and said 'Bill, let me explain. I've got some exciting ideas for Spurs. I've just come back from America. I've been watching their Baseball games. They've got cheerleader girls dancing in unison with pom-poms, fireworks and…'

Bill cut me short.

'It's not for Tottenham, we entertain the crowd with fast, exciting goal scoring football. But my friend Don Revie at Leeds might listen to you. Leeds have a team of internationals, they play great football and they are hard to beat, but their nickname, 'DIRTY LEEDS', needs changing. I'll give Don a ring.' It was Don's chance to make good the hospital visits to see Revie I made with Ron Burgess. I remember it well, it was the 1945-46 season. It was a straight forward tackle between Burgess and Revie. They both fell to the ground. Ron got up, but 19 year-old Revie stayed on the ground - his ankle was broken in THREE places! When Ron and I visited Revie in hospital we insisted anything we could do, he just had to ask. Thankfully Revie recovered…

'Leave it to me Paul. I'll phone Revie and fix a visit' Bill said and he was as good as his word and the Revie meeting took place in Revie's office at Elland Road. As I talked, Revie listened. He was a good listener. 'You need to do more than just win. You must entertain the Leeds fans. You need to work on the DIRTY LEEDS image and change it to SUPER LEEDS. Let's get the Leeds team to wear long sleeves, then when they go a goal down they push their sleeves up above the elbow. PSYCHOLOGICALLY you get your opponents on the back foot.

'Let's get the players wearing on the outside of each stocking top, a SOCK TAG with their numbers on. They can sign the front or backs and then hand them out to the young kids in the ground. I promise, the youngsters who get the Sock Tags will take them to school, tell their mates, and every kid will be asking to be taken to a match to get one. You'll SHUT THE GATES.'

As I continued talking, Don was still listening, 'I've been

watching the Leeds players train, and Les Cocker gets them to work and work, then work even harder. They are the fittest, most athletic team I have ever seen. I watched as they vaulted a wooden horse, they went so high I was sure some would need a parachute to land! Let's get the players to come out 15 minutes early and run in a 'formation' to the far corner of the pitch, and in unison start high kicking, jumping and bending, all perfectly timed. It will show how SUPER fit they are and it will send the Leeds fans wild.'

Don agreed to do it and so did the players, and it was then fate played a hand…Leeds United in the 6th Round of the FA Cup were drawn at home to TOTTENHAM HOTSPUR.

This was the match when Leeds were to become the first team in English football to come out 15 minutes early, wearing gleaming white track suit tops with their names on the back, sock tags tied at the top of their socks, waving to the crowd and performing a fitness routine to send the crowd crazy. Everything went to plan. The crowd greeted the fitness routine with a continued roar that shook the stadium, so much so that Bill Nicholson thought his watch had stopped, he stopped his pre-match talk and left the Spurs dressing room to check what all the cheering was about! The Press gave back page headlines saying Leeds were the new football entertainers. The Leeds United team did their part. They beat Tottenham Hotspur and then went on to win the FA Cup for the first and only time in their history.

The next time I saw Bill Nic he said 'You didn't tell me about the fitness routine.' I replied 'Sorry Bill, but it wasn't until I saw Leeds training that I came up with the idea, but if I had suggested the fitness routine – would you have said YES?' Bill put both hands on my shoulders, looked me straight in the eyes and said 'NO!' Then walked away….!

PT

Alan Mullery

The fact Alan Mullery is rated as one of Spurs' greatest midfield players is testimony to his wonderful ability and competitive instincts, because there has been such a wonderful profusion of world class creative players down the years to have worn the Cockerel, but few did so with quite so much pride and distinction.

He is probably best remembered for man-marking Pele out of the game in a World Cup tie but he was also involved in the infamous moment when he wrote his name in the football history books, when one of the most cultured midfielders of his generation became the answer to the quiz question: 'who was the first man to be sent off for England?' It is a burden that the man himself feels overshadowed his career. "I can never get rid of it," Alan told me, who started out at Fulham before winning three trophies with Tottenham in the 1960s and 70s. "I played more than 700 games in my career between the age of 15 and 34. People always remember that game, or another one when I scored a volley against Leicester in the cup and it was on *Match of the Day* every Saturday night for a year. People just remember those two games, they don't remember the other 698!"

Mullery's moment of madness occurred in the semi-finals of the 1968 European Championship as Alf Ramsey's world champions took on Yugoslavia in Florence. Incensed by strong arm tactics, and trailing 1-0 in the dying stages, Mullery retaliated after a bad tackle and kicked Dobrivoje Trivic where it hurts. "Bobby Moore rolled me a ball to the halfway line and I had my back towards their goal. I knocked it back to him but this fella came in and caught me on the left calf. Whatever he had on his studs it wasn't very nice and as I looked round the back of my sock it was red, the blood was pouring out and my heart was beating really fast. In sheer anger I turned round and kicked him in the groin, and down he went like a sack of spuds. The referee was about three yards away and just told me to get off. Frustration had set in with such little time left, and the referee had not protected any of the English players at all."

With England's exit from the tournament, Mullery headed for the dressing-room expecting a backlash from his team-mates and manager. "I apologised to the players, but Alf was very good to me. He came in, looked at me with a stern face and said: 'I'm glad somebody retaliated against those b******s.' He was very angry about it. When I got back, the Football Association fined me £50 and Alf paid the fine, which was absolutely unbelievable. Fifty quid was a lot of money in 1968." England had qualified for the final stages by drawing 1-1 with Scotland in front of 130,000 fans at Hampden Park to top a group of the Home Nations, before defeating Spain home and away in the quarter-finals. "I felt stupid when it happened but some of the tackles they were putting in were horrendous," says Mullery, who went on to represent England in the 1970 World Cup. "In those days there were no extra cameras in the grounds to pick up off-the ball incidents. If that game was played now it would have been abandoned after 20 minutes because they would have had six players on their side and we would have had about nine."

In the 1970 World Cup finals defending champions England progressed to the quarter-finals where they met West Germany and Mullery scored his only goal for his country to give England the lead before fellow Spur Martin Peters made it 2-0 just after half-time before the Germans fought back to win 3-2 in extra time.

Alan had made one shy of 200 appearances for Fulham before joining Tottenham in 1964 for a fee of £72,500. He followed in the footsteps of Danny Blanchflower in Spurs' midfield after the retirement of the club captain in April that year. He won the FA Cup in 1967, League Cup in 1971 and, a year later, the UEFA Cup, following a 3-2 aggregate win over Wolves in which Mullery scored the decisive goal.

Alan has particularly fond memories of the San Siro after skippering the Spurs side that travelled to Italy in the 1972 UEFA Cup, en route to lifting the trophy. He scored the Tottenham goal in a 1-1 draw against AC Milan in the semi-final second leg, which took the Lilywhites through to the final and, ultimately, glory at White Hart Lane. "We'd beaten AC Milan 2-1 at home in the first leg of the semi-final, so that result, the 1-1 draw, was enough to put us through to the final. Only a few weeks earlier I had been recovering from a pelvic injury and playing on loan at Fulham in the old Division Two. So for me personally, it felt a lifetime in just one month and for the club it was an incredible achievement. I can remember the excitement in the dressing room after the result in Milan. It was fantastic." Mullery left Tottenham soon after lifting the UEFA Cup, having made more than 312 appearances for the Lilywhites in eight years, scoring 25 goals. After returning to Fulham he won the BBC's goal of the season in 1973-74 and in 1975, appeared in a second FA Cup final, which this time ended in defeat to West Ham.

A flamboyant character, he was volatile as a player and manager and was a big personality in the dressing room. Mullery recalled an incident when he and his wife, June, as well as his dad, were approached by a supporter outside White Hart Lane. They were making their way through the car park when "this yob opened the door and pushed my wife and said I was fucking useless. I got out [of the car], took me jacket off, and knocked him out. The police were rushing round trying to calm me down, and I began fighting the police!" It took three of them to eventually send him on his way. "I must have been mad" he says but his evening only got worse when a couple of reporters arrived at his front door soon after. "They said they'd interviewed the boy and got a full statement," and the journalists told him the 'kid' was prepared to prosecute as they read his statement to Mullery. "It

> **Mullery recalled an incident when he and his wife, June, as well as his dad, were approached by a supporter outside White Hart Lane. They were making their way through the car park when "this yob opened the door and pushed my wife and said I was fucking useless. I got out [of the car], took me jacket off, and knocked him out. The police were rushing round trying to calm me down, and I began fighting the police," It took three of them to eventually send him on his way. "I must have been mad."**

was right, word for word," he admitted. "I let them finish and said if one word was printed I'd sue them for everything they've got." Nothing made it into the papers the following day and when he turned up on Monday for work, Nicholson called him in where the young lad he had floored was waiting. Mullery apologised and the yob – a Spurs 'fan' – agreed not to sue. "Luckily nothing came out in the papers about it."

After ending his playing career in 1976, Mullery went into management where I got to know him much on a more personal level. His first job was at Brighton and Hove Albion and in five years he achieved two promotions and kept the Seagulls in the First Division. Alan left an even more indelible mark on the club as he is often cited as the personality who ignited the rivalry between Brighton and Crystal Palace. The real acrimony came at the end of a 1976 FA Cup first-round second replay at Stamford Bridge, a neutral venue. Mullery's Brighton and Palace, then managed by Terry Venables, could not be separated over two matches but at the final whistle of the third meeting it descended into pandemonium which Palace had won 1-0 but an incensed Mullery felt referee Ron Challis had disallowed a perfectly good equaliser when Brian Horton was forced to retake a penalty and missed. "I've been accused of fanning the flames of a rivalry between the two clubs," Mullery writes in his autobiography. "Trouble flared with Palace when a controversial penalty incident knocked Brighton out of the FA Cup. I was furious and at the final whistle I remonstrated with the referee. As I walked back down

Palace folklore has it that Mullery ripped five £1 notes from his pocket in front of Palace's baying mob, tore them up and hurled the pieces on to the floor, declaring the club was not even worth that. Some accounts claim boiling coffee was thrown over Brighton's manager. Whatever happened, it ignited a derby rivalry that is baffling to outsiders as the clubs are 46 miles apart!

the tunnel, Palace fans spat all over me. I gave them two fingers, then did an awful interview bad-mouthing their supporters and saying I wouldn't give a fiver for any of the Palace players. I could have handled things better, but I just totally lost it. It didn't go down too well at Selhurst Park and I knew the fans there still held a grudge."

Palace folklore has it that Mullery took five £1 notes from his pocket and ripped them up in front of Palace's baying mob, hurling the pieces on to the floor as he declared that the club was not even worth that. Some accounts claim boiling coffee was thrown over Brighton's manager. Whatever happened, it ignited a derby rivalry that is baffling to outsiders as the clubs are 46 miles apart!

Alan later managed Charlton, Crystal Palace and QPR before returning for a second spell with Brighton. Mullery was hated by Palace fans after he became their manager in 1982. "I regularly received abusive phone calls and anonymous letters at Palace," he remembers. "Okay, we had two disappointing seasons, finishing 15th and 18th in the Second Division, but nothing could justify some of the filth directed at me. I found the constant abuse very difficult to deal with. Threats eventually turned to violence. As I walked to my car after a humiliating home defeat, a gang of Palace supporters attacked me. A friend helped to keep them at bay until the police arrived, but it was a nasty incident. It really scared me."

When QPR played in a European tie in Reykjavik the club opted to stay overnight after the game. After the match Alan invited the handful of football writers covering the tie, who had travelled on the same plane and stayed in the same hotel, to an after match meal and drink in an English-style pub. Alcohol was very much limited by law and spirits were strictly prohibited after a certain time. 'Mullers' had opted for this pub because he had heard that, to circumvent the no spirits rule, the beetroot was spiked with vodka. This was still a time when the unwritten rule that 'whatever happens on tour, stays on tour' was in force because there wasn't the media circus you have now with just one writer per paper. Some of the players invited a few of the football writers to join them at a night club called Hollywood, where we all enjoyed a very merry night out on the tiles.

The next morning I got a call in my room to come to the room of one of the big stars in that QPR team. He had been with us at Hollywood, where the local women were delighted to see some foreigners at a time when Reykjavik was not known as a tourist destination. He sounded a little distraught and needed to talk to me. When I knocked on his door, he shouted 'who is it?' When I announced myself he said 'come in quick'. When I entered the room, I found the player hiding under the bed!

A few moments later there was banging on the door, and the player told me to keep quiet. Apparently, after far too much drink, he had proposed to the girl he had been dancing with, and the girl had clearly said yes! But with a wife and couple of kids at home, there was no staying in Iceland. Eventually the coast was clear, we dashed off to the airport. On the plane I sat next to the player as he gazed out of the plane window, and looking at the girl he left behind - she was a stunner!

HH

JIMMY PEARCE might find even his spectacular benders useless when it comes to eluding Keelan's elastic leaps.

RALPH COATES'S hard rising shots hit on the run will have to be measured to the inch if they are to find a way past Keelan's cat-like agility.

...the Leeds side who took two FA Cup... the Keelan ghost. Cooper said ...between the posts this lad is a ...have h... has no right to, yet funnily ...gainst... were usually the worst hit ...

...ill do the bulk of the attacking in the ...a la... half chances on inside the ...

...hese ... was the old Spurs genius ...r seemed to hit the ball with power ...d there ... s the sort of shots to which ...ves were playing for Tottenham in ...idency tip him to score a couple

Why Coates costs £190,000

● RALPH COATES cost £190,000 when he moved from Burnley to Spurs in mid-week. Is he worth that much?

● Here's the team who can best answer that one — Ian Hutchinson, Chelsea striker, and Paul Trevillion, the finest writer-artist in sport journalism.

● Together they provide a fascinating insight into football.

● And "Hutch" has no doubts that Spurs have landed a winner with this signing. "He's a terrific reader of the game and extremely difficult to stop — a great football brain."

● "Hutch" does not get his theories off a blackboard — but from fiercely-won experience on the field. And he mainly remembers Coates for the chasing he gave Chelsea in the first half of a Cup replay at Burnley last season.

● "That was our hardest Cup game of the season — tougher even than the two Finals," says Hutchinson. "And the reason for it was this great little player, Ralph Coates."

RALPH COATES WAS THE PERFECT MIDFIELD LINK-MAN AT BURNLEY. HE WAS FOREVER CARRYING THE BALL OUT OF DEFENCE TO FEED HIS FORWARDS OR SHOOT AT GOAL HIMSELF.

AT ALL TIMES, COATES'S SHARP FOOTBALLING BRAIN HAS HIM ONE PASS AHEAD OF THE PLAY. THIS IS WHY HE'S SO QUICK TO SPOT THEN PENETRATE A GAP IN AN OPPOSING DEFENCE.

IN MANY WAYS HE HAS MUCH IN COMMON WITH BOBBY CHARLTON OF TWO SEASONS AGO — TREMENDOUS ACCELERATION, BODY SWERVE AND THE ABILITY TO HIT THE BALL HARD ON THE RUN.

AS A FORMER WINGER HE LIKES NOTHING BETTER THAN TO GET TO THE DEAD-BALL LINE TO SQUARE THE BALL BACK TO HIS ADVANCING FORWARDS — NOBODY DOES THIS BETTER.

ALSO LIKE CHARLTON, HIS ONE WEAKNESS IS WHEN THE BALL'S IN THE AIR. IT'S LUCK MORE THAN JUDGMENT WHEN COATES HEADS ONE IN.

THE MOST COMMON CRITICISM LEVELLED AT COATES IS THAT HE SHIES AWAY FROM TOUGH TACKLING. THIS IS NONSENSE. IT'S THANKS TO HIS SKILL ON THE BALL THAT HE CAN EVADE A TACKLE RATHER THAN TAKE ONE.

Penalty? Give him an Oscar

"On average, 60 per cent. of penalty kicks are 'bought' by play-acting. Usually the more skilful the ball player, the better the actor — although I'm convinced that George Best, for all his faults, has never ONCE been guilty of 'buying' a foul."
— PAT JENNINGS, Spurs.

Mr Tottenham

The *Daily Telegraph* was due to serialise their *World Cup '82* book over each day of the championship and the England and Arsenal coach, Don Howe, was to add his knowledgeable and inspirational words to its success with me working alongside him adding the illustrations.

"Can you remember the day, Don, you first decided to become a coach after your playing days were over?" were my opening words when we sat down to work on the book.

"It was the World Cup of 1958," he replied, "I was the England Right Back and Bill Nicholson, then England coach, came over to me and said 'Don, have you ever played in a match where you have no left winger to mark?' I said – 'No Bill, never!' 'You will tomorrow when you line up against Brazil' came back Nicholson. 'Then Bill,' I replied, 'I'm in for a very easy afternoon, time to put my feet up!' Nicholson took a step closer, pushed his face close to mine and said eye to eye 'You're WRONG, Don. No time to put your feet up. You'll be doing TWICE the running. Perhaps even more. The Brazilian outside left Zagallo plays as a withdrawn winger, he drops back to the half way line, even deeper. He operates from around the midfield, but don't you follow him. If you go chasing after Zagallo, they'll race into the space you leave behind and Billy Wright will have to come out of the middle and cover. With you two now out of position, they'll be in.'

"I listened as Nicholson continued to drive his point home. 'I want you to stay up close to Billy Wright. Never be more than ten yards away. This means we now have an extra man in the midfield. There's now no space for the Brazilians to put the ball. But don't take your eyes of Zagallo. HE'S THE BRAINS OF THEIR ATTACK. Watch him, watch him, watch him, and if he should suddenly pop up on the left wing, make sure you're shoulder to shoulder. It's going to take a tremendous amount of running and a tremendous amount of concentration, but you can do it, Don.'

"Nicholson turned to walk then stopped, adding, 'Give them any of the space Zagallo creates and they'll hammer us. DO YOUR JOB DON!' Nicholson had certainly driven his point home as he continued to talk to the other England players.

"I thought describing Zagallo as 'the BRAINS of the Brazilian attack' was going way over the top, but Bill's point to not go looking for him was advice I was going to follow religiously. If that was what I had to do to please Bill, then that was what I was going to do. Let Zagallo come looking for me!

"Nicholson's plan worked to perfection. The Brazilian goal machine failed to score, so I expected a pat on the back from him. Instead Bill came up to me and said 'You gave the ball away four times'. I said 'Yes Bill, but I made over forty passes and I only missed with four'. Bill took a step closer 'I know, but four's four…

> "It took a tremendous amount to please Nicholson, but then, like the magnificent coach he was, he was always pushing you to raise the bar"

cut it down!' It took a tremendous amount to please Nicholson, but then, like the magnificent coach he was, he was always pushing you to raise the bar.

"I was pleased after the match, and I'm sure Bill was because it was the first ever GOALLESS draw in the history of the World Cup Finals and it was the only game in which Brazil's goal machine failed to score on their way to winning the World Cup, but I will always believe, and I was in the England side that had qualified scoring 15 goals in their matches, we could have won that World Cup in '58 but the Munich air disaster ripped the soul out of the team. The Manchester United trio of Roger Byrne, Duncan Edwards and Tommy Taylor were no longer with us."

As it proved, Nicholson was right; Zagallo was the BRAINS of the Brazilian team. He was the first to win the World Cup as both a manager and as a player. Winning the competition in 1958 and 1962 as a player, in 1970 as a manager and in 1994 as coach to manager Carlos Alberto Parreira.

In World Cup 1994 I was part of the World Cup Umbro Soccer Theatre Tour with Carlos Alberto Parriera – Manager of the Brazil National Team, Andy Roxburgh - Manager of the Scotland National Team and Michelle Akers-Stahl, then the greatest female soccer player in the world. I had the brief opportunity, and it was very brief, to talk to Zagallo and I asked him who was the most difficult team they played against in the 1958 World Cup. Zagallo smiled "England – no space – no space – no space". Then as he walked away, he turned his face and looked over his shoulder. "The next match – SPACE" he laughed.

Don was right, it took a tremendous amount to please Nicholson but he admitted he took a leaf out of Bill's book and always asked for MORE. Asking his players to RAISE the bar. That was the unchallengeable Bill Nicholson way and why he is STILL called 'MR TOTTENHAM'.

PT

Pat Jennings
Spurs' Greatest Keeper

Tottenham have been blessed with some phenomenal keepers, from a long standing captain and World Cup winner to Ted Ditchburn in the 50s and Bill Brown from the Double team, yet when it comes to selecting the best ever, every Spurs legend I contacted selected Big Pat, someone I have come to know well over the years form my days at the local Tottenham paper, The North London *Weekly Herald*, and still stay in touch with.

Steven Davis only recently surpassed the record appearance for Northern Ireland in October 2020, for so long held by Pat Jennings of 119 caps. Jennings said: "I spoke to him when he equalled the record. I'm going back to him to say well done for beating my record. He's a lovely lad and a great little player for Northern Ireland. He deserves it. Reaching this number of caps is about being lucky and being consistent. I was lucky with injuries and it's the same with Steven. I wish him and the team all the very best."

Steven Beacom, *Belfast Telegraph* journalist, commented: "For me he (Davis) is in the top three and I would rank him alongside George Best and Pat Jennings. He will tell you he shouldn't be anywhere near that company but believe me he deserves to be mentioned in the same breath as those greats. He wrote a column for the *Belfast Telegraph* during Euro 2016 and without any fuss or fanfare he said to me would you please give my fee to Myeloma UK which is a cancer charity."

In 2023 the legendary Northern Ireland goalkeeper was taken ill when attending Tottenham's game against Chelsea and taken to hospital for tests, which came back clear, and was later discharged so he was able to attend the unveiling of his statue in his home town of Newry. "I wish I knew what happened to me but I've had all the check-ups and everything came up good, so no worries about that," Pat said of his illness.

Jennings spoke of his pride at the honour. "I'm very proud to say I'm a Newry man," said the 78 year-old. It meant "everything" to him as Big Pat praised the statue as "unbelievable" and "fantastic". He said: "That's the first I've seen it. It's unbelievable, what a fantastic job." When asked what it meant, Jennings said: "Everything really. It's something I've never even dreamed of, [I] thought it was something that happened to other people but would never happen to me. It's just a brilliant occasion to have this back in my home city." The bronze statue, which depicts Jennings throwing the ball, was unveiled on Kildare Street, among those in attendance were former Northern Ireland players Billy Hamilton and Gerry Armstrong, ex-Tottenham captain Ledley King and former Arsenal and Republic of Ireland midfielder Liam Brady. "It's a fantastic turnout," he added. "I didn't really realise that I reached out to so many people."

The pitch he played on in Newry is named after him, as is a lounge at Windsor Park in Belfast. He returns home often for work with the Irish FA. There used to be a suite carrying his name at White Hart Lane with two glass cases containing his memorabilia, but not so at the new stadium.

Pat's club career included winning five trophies with Tottenham and Arsenal. He was named the Players' Player of the Year in 1976 and Football Writers' Player of the Year in 1973; he is the only goalkeeper to have achieved this double. He won his first cap in 1964 at the age of 18 against Wales alongside fellow debutant George Best. He played for Northern Ireland at the 1982 and 1986 World Cups, making the final appearance of his 22-year international career in a 3-0 defeat by Brazil in Mexico.

He became a CBE in the New Year Honours in 2022 for his contribution to football and charity having become an MBE in 1976. Irish FA chief executive Patrick Nelson said: "Pat is a global icon and one of the most revered players to pull on the Northern Ireland jersey. This award underlines his impact both on and off the pitch where he continues to use his profile to promote good causes across the island of Ireland and in England. On behalf of everyone at the Irish FA I send my warmest congratulations to him." Irish FA President Conrad Kirkwood added: "Pat is one of Northern Ireland's greatest ever players and a huge ambassador for Northern Ireland and its football. His statesmanship and gentlemanly nature have earned him the respect of everyone. He richly deserves recognition in the honours list and I add my congratulations to those of every Northern Ireland supporter."

"I am delighted and humbled to have been awarded this prestigious honour," said Jennings. "I have had a fantastic career and I have always supported charities and good causes along the way, something I feel all sports people should do." Charities that benefited included Cardiac Risk in the Young and Variety Golf, which endeavours to improve the lives of young people, as well as the Willow Foundation where he teamed up with fellow legendary keeper Bob Wilson to raise money for 'special days' for cancer sufferers. Jennings celebrated 27 years of golfing at Royal County Down in support of the work of Co-Operation Ireland in October 2022. He has also been a long-standing ambassador for McDonald's through its work supporting grassroots football with the Irish Football Association. Another charity close to Pat's heart is Co-Operation Ireland, an all-island peace-building organisation. He explained: "I worked closely with Derek Dougan during the early days of the charity in the mid-1980s. Derek was from the Protestant faith, and I represented the Catholic community, and we knew how important that was, particularly given the times we were living in. Religion was no barrier, and we went on to organise some fantastic initiatives to raise money, including bike rides and walks from Belfast to Dublin, vintage car rallies and sponsored swims." In 1986 he received an OBE as well as an honorary doctorate from the University of Ulster. In 1999 he received the Knight of Saint Gregory, a Papal honorary knighthood.

Jennings won the FA Cup with both Tottenham and Arsenal, and the UEFA Cup with Spurs in 1972, and few, if any, have been revered by fans of both Spurs and Arsenal and loved almost in equal measure, although Pat would be more of a Spurs legend for sure. He still spends two days a week coaching the young goalkeepers at the club's academy. "When I packed up football after the 1986 World Cup, I was not involved in the game. I would get up in the winter, pull the curtains back and if it was raining and I couldn't get out on the golf course I went back to bed. After a few weeks you realise you're just wasting. So when Ossie Ardiles asked me back in 1993, I went in to Tottenham one day a week. Then two, then three. I was here 14 years as a player." He's been with the club now for 44 years. "Who would have thought that? I didn't enjoy the summer lockdown. I am used to kicking and volleying balls. I was back in as soon as possible and immediately felt great. Then the next day I seized up! But I love it.'

Jennings played and worked under 18 Tottenham managers. "I introduced myself to Jose Mourinho and he said, 'You don't have to tell me who you are'. That was nice. But the young keepers here don't necessarily know me. I tell them their parents might know. Or their grandparents! I never even had a goalkeeping coach until Bob Wilson at Arsenal in my 30s. In my day you just looked after yourself. I learned by playing games and making mistakes. I did OK."

I used to watch Jennings catch the ball one handed on the stretch at the far post, and as a budding goalkeeper myself, was in awe of the way he had such command of crosses. It came from his days playing Gaelic football. "I left school at 15 and worked in a linen factory for £2.3s a week. I'd put the envelope on the table for my mother every Friday. I was second eldest. We had 11 in the house. The factory closed so my dad took me with him to work on the timber gang on the mountain. The sawyer would fell about 100 trees and it was my job to trim the branches with a hatchet. I loved it, apart from when the snow was coming over the top of my Wellington boots. I thought I would do that job for ever. I wouldn't have complained.'

Association football was not played in County Down's Catholic schools but he was proficient at Gaelic football. He had played in goal for an Under 19s street side when he was just 11 so when he filled in as an emergency goalkeeper for his brother's team, a huge leap set him apart. A switch through local club football to the Irish national youth team led to a match at Wembley against the English in front of 35,000 in 1963. Ireland lost but Jennings caught the eye of Watford in the Third Division. "I got £23 a week but I was 17 and would have played for nothing. The physical element didn't bother me because of Gaelic football where you had to look after yourself. Crosses were no bother. I could just reach up and pull the ball down with one hand. People said my hands were big. They aren't. I just knew how to use them."

Bill Nicholson bought Jennings from Watford manager Bill McGarry in 1964. 'Bill McGarry called me back from Ireland for early summer training but when I got there it wasn't about that at all. He said Bill Nicholson was waiting for me at Vicarage Road. I had only been at Watford a year. My head was spinning. Bill Nick was offering me £35 a week. I was already earning that with bonuses at Watford. He didn't believe me. So I went back to Ireland. He wrote to me a week later asking if I'd thought any more about it. Then he and Bill actually flew to Belfast. McGarry said if I dare come back to Watford I would be training morning, noon and night. They needed the money and wanted me out. So I signed."

On 12th August 1967, Tottenham and Manchester United contested the FA Charity Shield at Old Trafford. They shared the trophy after a 6-goal thriller with Jennings among the goal scorers! Spurs had finished the previous season third and expectations were high for an entertaining match. A week earlier, Tottenham had taken on Celtic, holders of the European Cup, in Glasgow, that ended in a six goal thriller. Tottenham fielded the same team that won the FA Cup in May when they defeated Chelsea 2–1 in the Final at Wembley, while United had Bobby Charlton, Denis Law and George Best, the Holy Trinity, as their formidable front three. Spurs took an early lead after two minutes with Jimmy Robertson putting them ahead from a cross by Greaves. Five minutes later, Jennings played a long clearance down field which bounced between Alan Gilzean and Alex Stepney, the ball sailed over the head of the stranded United goalkeeper to make it 2-0. Spurs should have added a third, as three minutes later Frank Saul hit the bar and Mike England's shot from the rebound hit a defender on the line, yet United were level by the twentieth minute, scoring twice in two minutes through Charlton. Early in the second half Saul put Spurs ahead again but with fifteen minutes remaining United drew level when Law tapped in after Jennings had parried another thunderbolt from Charlton. The clubs shared the trophy. Two of Tottenham's three were scored by the goalscorers in the Cup Final – Robertson and Saul. Then, in 1973, Jennings pulled off what is surely a unique feat when he saved two Liverpool penalties from two different players in the same match at Anfield, first from Kevin Keegan, then from Tommy Smith.

Keith Burkinshaw surprisingly sold Jennings in 1977 but the Spurs manager

figured that his goalkeeper was 32 and his deputy, Barry Daines, couldn't wait forever for his big breakthrough. Jennings played 590 times for Tottenham, but he was far from finished and went on to turn out 327 times for Arsenal and play in his final World Cup. "Burkinshaw just came to me in training one morning. He said they were selling me and Bobby Robson at Ipswich would call me at 6pm. I couldn't believe it. It was the worst day of my life." Jennings did not go to Ipswich, Manchester United or Aston Villa, who also enquired. He opted to keep his family where they had settled and moved to Arsenal instead. "Arsenal were a great club and 10 minutes down the road. My kids not being dragged up the country was important. I had literally lived for Tottenham for 13 years. Under Bill Nick it was 'Tottenham, Tottenham, Tottenham'. But they made it clear they didn't want me. "I went to say goodbye to the lads next morning. The directors blanked me. They were pushing out stories that I wanted to leave and was being greedy over a contract. It was rubbish. Everywhere I went people were asking me how on earth I could quit Tottenham for Arsenal. They were blaming me. Now, whenever I do a dinner, people can't believe the truth. I kept it to myself all those years."

Jennings left at the end of the season with a record 472 Football League appearances - 23 of them in a relegation campaign when he shared duties with the emerging Barry Daines but was still on top form. That team, that boasted Jennings, Peter Taylor, Steve Perryman and Glenn Hoddle, still finished bottom of the old Division One with just 33 points from 42 games. By New Year's Day, the danger was already clear as Spurs didn't earn their first win until they beat Manchester United in their fourth game of the season. It was at the start of October where the damage was really done, with the defence leaking 21 goals in six league games, the worst result being an 8-2 drubbing at Derby. By the end of the year Spurs had 13 points from 19 games although they increased that to 15 with a 2-1 win over West Ham on New Year's Day. Four successive defeats in February and a 5-0 hammering by Manchester City in their penultimate game left them down, despite a final day victory against Leicester. They crashed out of the FA Cup to Cardiff in the third round and Wrexham in the fourth round of the League Cup.

The full story his departure was covered up for years. In the summer of 1977 Pat was informed by the Tottenham Hotspur board that he was being offered a contract on reduced wages because they harboured doubts regarding how long he had left in him. Having believed an agreement was already in place, Jennings was of the view that a deal was being reneged on and, after 13 years of sterling service, felt he deserved better. He always felt it was a mystery why Spurs showed him the door, but at the time, I knew it was due to Barry Daines agitating, quite rightly, behind the scenes to become the first choice as he had waited patiently for so many years and the manager thought Daines was the future and Jennings the past. "I know now and it was explained in Bill Nick's book," Jennings says. "There was legislation due out that said if you'd been five years at a club you were due a free. They feared I could go and had better get some money. They got £40,000. Was it Keith's decision or the directors? Nobody has ever said." Whatever lay behind it, leaving remains a bitter experience but his bond with Spurs remains intact. "I couldn't ask for more in terms of a place to work," he says.

When Arsenal boss Terry Neill got wind of Jennings' availability, he moved quickly and from there on in there was only one place the Irishman wanted to go. He was 32 when he joined Arsenal, he lasted eight years, playing in three consecutive FA Cup finals, 1978-80 — winning one — and a European Cup-Winners' Cup final. His first visit to White Hart Lane as an Arsenal player sticks in his mind "Yes because we won, 5-0! I was motivated, of course. Listen, I have been at Tottenham for more than 40 years so there is no doubt where my loyalties lie. But I will never say a bad word about Arsenal. They were brilliant to me. I was on £15,000 a year at Spurs and Arsenal gave me £20,000. And they also played in two testimonial games for me at the end."

By the time the 1986 World Cup in Mexico tournament came round Jennings had finally lost his place in the Arsenal first team to John Lukic for good and had, in fact, returned to Tottenham to play for the reserves to keep fit for international duty. Jennings did turn out once for the Spurs first team in a 3-0 home defeat to Liverpool in the Screen Sport Super Cup and was then signed by Everton as cover for the rest of the season following a long-term injury to Neville Southall. His last appearance in English club football was on the Wembley bench as an unused Everton squad member for the 1986 FA Cup Final. That summer Pat bowed out of football for good when he played for Northern Ireland against

Brazil in the World Cup on his 41st birthday.

Sir Bobby Charlton described Jennings as 'one of the greatest of all time'. "Bobby was a great man. It's unbelievable to look at the numbers. Ex-players are three times more likely to get dementia. It's hard to believe there isn't a link. In my day everyone had big centre forwards up against big centre-halfs. They would spend hours in training heading balls. You look back now and wonder."

Of the late former Liverpool and Spurs keeper Ray Clemence, who ultimately succeeded Pat at Spurs, he remembers fondly, "Ray lived down the road and we had been working on Tottenham hospitality for years. Ossie lives nearby, too. We would drive in together. I was briefly back at Tottenham in 1985 as back-up. Ray was their only fit keeper and was an absolute gent, a great team-mate and a fabulous keeper. When you look at what he won — phenomenal."

HH

PAUL TREVILLION GLOVES – DESIGNED FOR PAT JENNINGS

In Hunter Davies's *The Glory Game*, there's a tantalising reference to gloves designed in the early '70s by *Roy of the Rovers* artist/Beaver Sports supremo Paul Trevillion. So we asked Paul about the gloves – and he only went and sent us his drawing of the prototypes!

"Pat wasn't impressed," Paul laughed. "He said it made his hands look even larger. Pat was not too enamoured by the media who used to call his hands 'shovels'. A *Sunday People* article mentioned that Pat could hold four oranges in one hand!

"Today the glove would be a multi-million seller, and goalkeepers would stop dropping the ball or palming it away. As in the '60s and '70s, they would go back to catching it cleanly as all goalkeepers did before those big MICKEY MOUSE gloves came into fashion. The Trevillion glove enabled TOUCH AND FEEL!

"The finger and palm cut-outs gave that secure, natural hand feel. In wet weather the cut-outs were a different material to the glove, like Velcro.

"The prototype gloves were originally for Gary Sprake but unfortunately the Liverpool nickname 'Careless Hands' meant I was forced to switch to Pat Jennings."

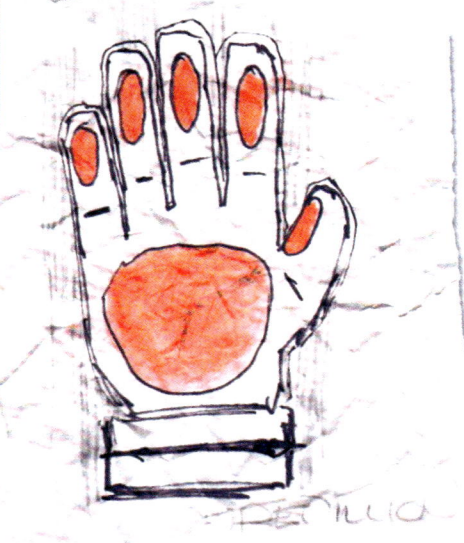

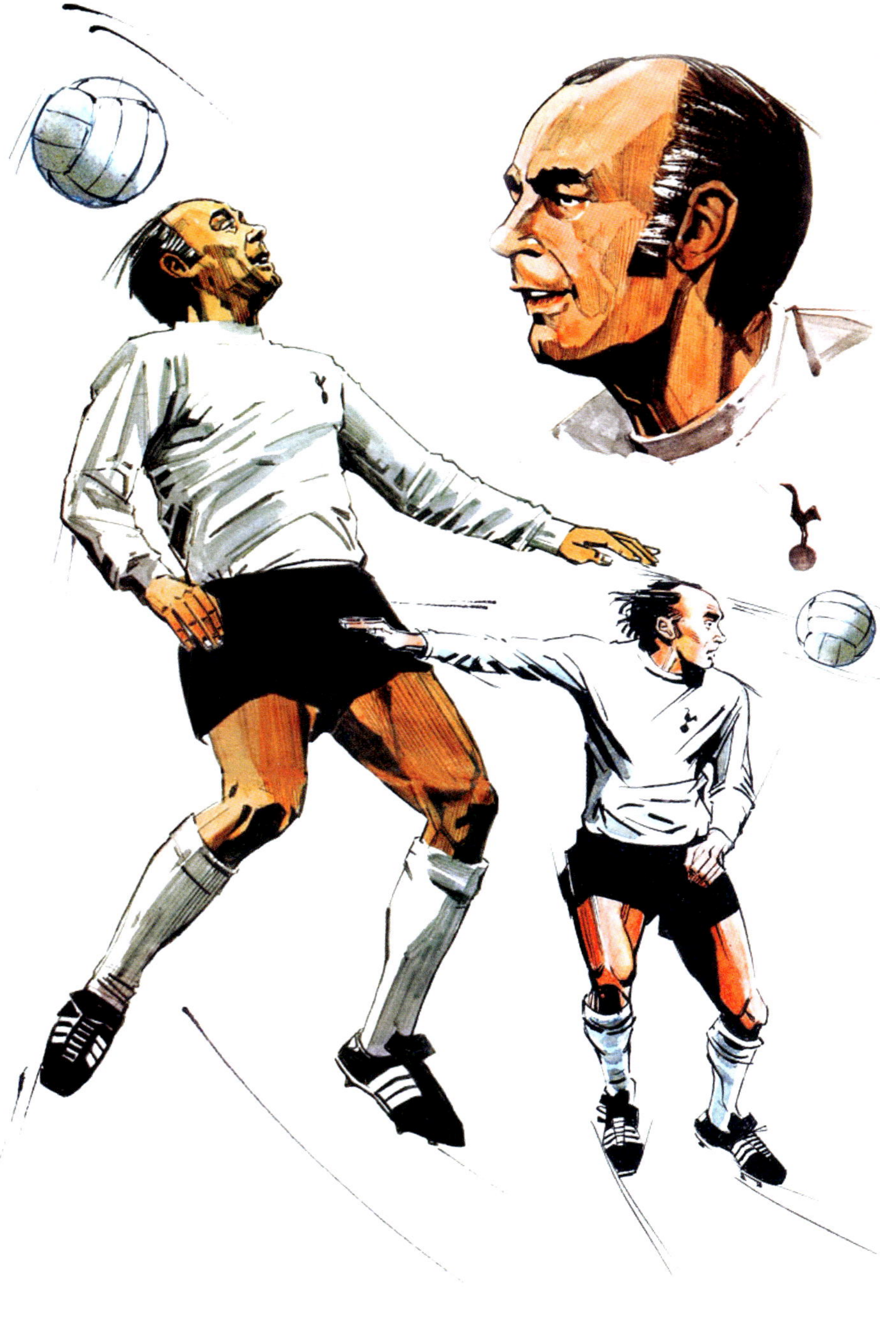

KING GILLIE

Alan Gilzean

I became very good friends with Alan Gilzean, dating back from my first *Weekly Herald* cartoon. It was when I was working with Dixie Dean for the *Liverpool Echo* that Dixie told me when he had the motorbike accident and fractured his skull he was told by the specialist he would never play football again. Dixie then told me he then took the bladder from inside the football and slowly gained the confidence to head the ball correctly, adding 'school boy's neck muscles have not developed so they should not head a ball but should practice with a soft ball until they are in their teens.' This was the story I told Alan Gilzean and we came up with the WORLD CUP HEADER TRAINING GAME for MUNCHMALLOWS. It proved a runaway success and every time I met Gilzean after that, he always greeted me with 'MUNCHMALLOW TREVILLION'.

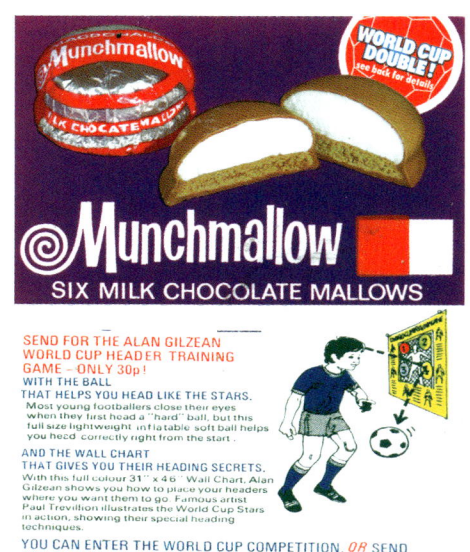

Munchmallow
MILK CHOCATE MALLOW
WORLD CUP DOUBLE!
see back for details
Munchmallow
SIX MILK CHOCOLATE MALLOWS
SEND FOR THE ALAN GILZEAN WORLD CUP HEADER TRAINING GAME – ONLY 30p!
WITH THE BALL
THAT HELPS YOU HEAD LIKE THE STARS.
Most young footballers close their eyes when they first head a "hard" ball, but this full size lightweight inflatable soft ball helps you head correctly right from the start.
AND THE WALL CHART
THAT GIVES YOU THEIR HEADING SECRETS.
With this full colour 31" x 46" Wall Chart, Alan Gilzean shows you how to place your headers where you want them to go. Famous artist Paul Trevillion illustrates the World Cup Stars in action, showing their special heading techniques.
YOU CAN ENTER THE WORLD CUP COMPETITION, OR SEND AWAY FOR THE HEADING GAME, OR BOTH IF YOU WISH.

DESPITE MY LATER renown for sniffing out stories, I literally missed one right under my nose when I was still very much a novice. I was so nervous about presenting a bag full of footballs for the lucky North London *Weekly Herald* prize winners on the White Hart Lane pitch before Alan Gilzean's testimonial match, that I didn't notice how one fan had run onto the pitch and kissed his feet! The first I knew of it was when I picked up the *Evening News* the next day and there was the picture on the back page. The young girl was one of the recipients of the prizes, and the long haired bearded guy in the background on the far right was the *Herald*'s resident photographer Nick Townsend, who went on to become a writer and columnist. There is another picture of me actually looking up to see what was going on and pulling out one of the footballs to hand out to the queue of prize winners.

'Gilly' was one of my all time heroes. His grace and artistry was awesome. His bald head belied his athleticism. Dimitar Berbatov was often likened to 'Gilly' but to me the Scot was pure magic, and very consistent, unlike the sulky Bulgarian.

'Gilly' was also more devastating the bigger the occasion. He developed a telepathic understanding with Jimmy Greaves, who was lightning fast over a short distance, and never seemed to miss when in front of goal. The G-men were mind-blowing, a joy to watch, they played glorious attacking football, out-playing the opposition.

I met Jimmy briefly in my privileged days as a journalist but never really had the chance to chat with 'Gilly' but I'll never forget his testimonial or the scoop right under my nose that I missed!

HH

Nicholson Resigns!

Spurs greatest manager resigned in the wake of a disastrous 4-0 League Cup defeat at Middlesbrough in September 1974, but promised to stay on while his successor was appointed. Yet the parting of the ways quickly turned acrimonious and Bill Nicholson left under a cloud. It was a sad end to the most glorious era in the club's history.

OFTEN, AS I MADE MY WAY HOME from the North London *Weekly Herald* offices late at night, particularly on edition times, I would walk past Bill Nicholson's office and I could see the light still on. He lived and breathed the club, spending more time in his office than he did at home in his own bed. He travelled the country watching games, scouring clubs for talent, even north of the border. Nowadays that would be done by scouts, but he always wanted to see the player for himself, especially the ones he was thinking of signing and he would insist on seeing them a few times.

When he gave me a detailed list of the reasons why he decided to quit when he did, one of them was the stress. Personally, I didn't set much store by this reason, although I think he preferred people to think that, rather than criticise others, which was never the way he went about his job.

He told me, though, the reasons behind his long hours and devotion to Spurs, "In all those 16 years I never had a long holiday, not even during the close season. I popped into the ground every Sunday to work, and kept my house in nearby Creighton Road so I could be minutes from the ground. We could have moved out to a bigger detached house in Hertfordshire, where many Tottenham players lived, but it would have meant spending more time travelling. Being nearby I was sometimes able to return home for lunch with Darkie (his wife), otherwise she would rarely have seen me. Most evenings I attended matches all over the country and sometimes in Scotland. Being in such a state through overwork was entirely my own fault. No one asked me to work all day and every day. But I ran the club and wouldn't trust the smallest job to anyone else. I wouldn't delegate, which perhaps was wrong, but it was my way of working and it had been successful.

"I had felt it was essential to have organisation and method, but now that wasn't enough. New thoughts and ideas were needed. I believed a new manager would provide them and also added motivation which I felt was no longer coming from me. After our humiliating loss to Middlesbrough I decided I could not remain any longer in my post. Not even Darkie knew of my decision. She heard about it on the radio the next morning."

I spoke with Bill about the appointment of his successor and he thought, after a lifetime at the club, that the board would have consulted him. They didn't. Yet, as we have seen at Old Trafford, there isn't necessarily a right or wrong way to go about things as the Glazers and United's board consulted Sir Alex Ferguson who nominated David Moyes to succeed him and from there it all went pear-shaped. Moyes didn't last long, and the fans soon fell out of love with his successor Louis Van Gaal, despite some encouraging results. However there is still a distinct possibility that even Sir Alex, with all his phenomenal influence inside Old Trafford, could yet be treated similarly to Bill Nicholson.

Bill, like Sir Alex, was sure he would do what was right for the club he loved. But any decision was quickly taken out of his hands despite an earlier suggestions that he would play a prominent role in choosing his successor. That hurt him, really hurt him, and no matter how much praise was heaped upon him for all of his successes, he left the club feeling that all his long service had really counted for little.

He confided in me, "I naturally assumed I would be allowed to nominate my successor as manager of the club. After all, I had virtually run Tottenham for 16 years. The directors had enjoyed a comparatively easy time in those years, enjoying the matches and the glory and leaving me to take the strain. At Liverpool, the best run club in Britain (at least it was in the 80s when Bill was telling me this story), Bill Shankly had attended the meeting of the directors who decided to appoint Bob Paisley to succeed him. And I have no doubt that Bob Paisley's recommendation about his own successor was heeded by the Liverpool directors and that led to the promotion of Joe Fagan to the No.1 job at Anfield.

"I did not know whether the Tottenham board had anyone in mind as the new manager. They did not confide in me. My guess is that they had no idea. The man I wanted was Danny Blanchflower. Even though he had been out of the game for some time, apart from writing a weekly column in the *Sunday Express*, it was my opinion that he would still have made an exceptional manager of the club. He had kept in close contact with people in the game, including me, and I thought he was the outstanding candidate. He had similar ideas to mine about how the game should be played. He knew the Tottenham set up and its traditions. He was a popular man with a sense of humour."

There can be no doubt that whatever the board of directors and their chairman, Sidney Wale, had in mind, Bill was convinced he would be given the respect he deserved and would have an enormous input. He was crestfallen to discover he had none. But, as you would expect from the man who ruled the club for 16 years without any interference, he went about the task of lining up what he thought was the best man for the job.

"I interviewed Danny for the job of manager of Tottenham. He knew his relationship with the players would be different and he accepted that. Typically he wanted to know all the details. He was very interested and after a long talk, decided he'd like the job. He said he wanted me to stay on in a background job and I was prepared to do that."

Nicholson made the point to me when I wrote his autobiography in the early 1980s when fellow Yorkshireman Keith Burkinshaw was manager of Spurs, how Liverpool had kept on Bob Paisley for his wisdom and experience. When we spoke, in the early 1980s, Nicholson said: "I believe that it is important to have experienced managers to call upon. I fulfil that role now at Tottenham and I think Keith was glad to be able to call on me when he needed to. It is a fallacy that a new manager should have his own men and his predecessor should be cut off completely. If the retiring manager has been successful, it is wasteful to discard all the knowledge and expertise he has built up over the years. Too many good men have been thrown out of the game, men with whom I shared the early FA coaching courses and who became outstanding managers.

"The idea that a clean break had to be made was fostered by directors who imagined that Sir Matt Busby had interfered with his numerous successors at Old Trafford. I spoke to Matt about this on a number of occasions and he assured me that he had not tried to interfere. He said his experience was available if anyone wanted it, but he did not push himself forward. I intended to be a general advisor to Danny when he took over. I would not have permitted players to seek advice from me behind his back. It would have been the ideal working relationship."

But Nicholson also thought there was another possible candidate to succeed him.

"There was another person I thought might be a good manager of Tottenham: Johnny Giles, captain of Leeds and Ireland. I rang him and asked him to travel down to be interviewed and he agreed. I spent an entire afternoon with him and was most impressed. He had all the requirements and I thought he would make a good manager. Even Danny approved. Had Danny been appointed manager, he would have wanted Johnny as his player/coach. Giles had experience of management with Ireland and had learned from his years working under Don Revie at Elland Road. I was sure at the time that he was capable of making the jump from player to manager. He subsequently proved that with West Bromwich Albion.

"I felt contented that I had done my best to ensure that the running of Tottenham Hotspur would remain in good hands. During my second week as temporary manager - the two weeks extra time I had agreed to serve - a board meeting was called at the club to discuss the applications for a new manager. To my great surprise I was not called to the meeting. I really couldn't believe this because I had previously told the chairman that I had interviewed Blanchflower and Giles and would like to submit a report on both of them for consideration as my successor.

"I said that I felt they both had the right qualifications and had my full support. I was shocked by the response from the board, chairman Sidney Wale in particular. He was upset that I had interviewed the two men without his knowledge or approval. The other directors appeared to share his indignation.

"I was angry too because they had asked me to continue as manager and all the time I had been in charge they had never queried any of my decisions. They knew my motives were sound. Everything I undertook was for the good of the club. No one worked harder or longer than me in its interests. I told them in no uncertain manner that what I had done was for the benefit of Tottenham. I was using my experience of my lifetime in the game to find a man capable of taking over a great club. I felt the directors must be interested in what I had to say. Instead, my recommendations were ignored.

"I believed I was doing Danny Blanchflower and Johnny Giles a service by interviewing them but, as it turned out, I was doing them a disservice. I had killed off any chance they had of being short-listed for the post. I found the attitude of the board very disappointing.

"The chairman said he wasn't really opposed to my taking the initiative, but was annoyed that I had done it without telling him. I countered by reflecting that I had never had to ask his permission before to do anything I thought was in the best interests of the club. Why he should have such strong objections I really do not know. I felt the directors were making excuses. Had Blanchflower taken over, there would have been a new look to the team and possibly even to the running of the club. Perhaps they felt their position had been threatened in some way.

"I also reported that I had been busy trying to line up transfer deals. I was in contact with Everton regarding their centre-half Mike Lyons. There was no commitment to let him go, but I had not received a straight refusal. I felt there was an

BLANCHFLOWER

THE MAN WHO MISSES TODAY'S MATCH — DANNY BLANCHFLOWER! AT 37, DANNY IS THE OLDEST PLAYER IN THE SPURS TEAM. HE WAS TWICE VOTED "FOOTBALLER OF THE YEAR" — A RECORD HE SHARES WITH TOM FINNEY. BORN IN BELFAST, THIS SLIGHTLY BUILT RIGHT-HALF RECEIVED ALL HIS EARLY FOOTBALL TRAINING FROM HIS MOTHER.

opportunity there for negotiations. There was also the possibility of an exchange deal with QPR over Martin Chivers. For some time Gordon Jago, the Rangers manager, had wanted Chivers. I might have been willing to agree to a swap for Stan Bowles who, I thought, was one of the outstanding players in the country at the time. But with hindsight I must admit that he was really like Chivers in that he had only two good seasons.

"Jago gave me the impression that he was prepared to let Bowles go as well as Gerry Francis and Don Givens. I had mentioned these proposed deals to Danny and he had been excited by them. He had also wanted Giles in his midfield but these plans were wrecked when the board decided to appoint their own man and ignore my advice."

Despite the obvious snub, Bill remained circumspect about Sidney Wale. It was typical of him as Bill told me, "Mr. Wale did not want me to leave. He asked me to stay and so did his charming wife Cynthia when I attended a private cocktail party at his house in Hadley Wood the following Sunday morning. But my mind was made up." However, Nicholson was indignant about the way appointing his successor was being handled, and at that point, his relationship with Wale deteriorated beyond repair. But Bill was touched by the actions of his players and while Wale had no chance of changing his mind, the players nearly did.

Nicholson told me, "One of the most touching moments was when the players asked me to reconsider. A delegation led by senior players Martin Peters and Pat Jennings was so persuasive that I wondered whether I was right to go. I was surprised and heartened about how the attitude of the players towards me had altered. I suppose it is true that people are vastly different when they are relaxed from when they are working under stress.

"It was said at the time that one of the chief reasons I resigned was that I had lost touch with the players. That was not the case. My relations with them were not much different from what they had been when I first took over. I had no favourites. I treated them all alike with firmness and, I hope, understanding.

"I think players respect discipline. If there are slack attitudes in a club, the team becomes slack and inefficient. We had a book of rules, which I insisted had to be observed. But just as I never put a soldier on a charge when I was in the army, I cannot remember having taken serious disciplinary action against any player.

"Though we had a set of rules, we were not intolerant. I treated the players as men and I think they respected that. In the dressing room I liked to discuss points with individuals in such a way that other players could either agree or disagree with me. I encouraged them to take part in the debates. I was not authoritarian."

One of the major reasons given for his decision to quit was because of what happened in Rotterdam in the second leg of the UEFA Cup final against Feyenoord in May 1974. Rotterdam, of course, was the city where Nicholson's Spurs became the first British winners of a European trophy when they won the Cup Winners' Cup there nine years previously. Now the city produced the catalyst that would lead to his eventual departure four months after Feyenoord ended Spurs' proud record of having never lost a major final.

After a 2-2 draw in the first leg at White Hart Lane, Feyenoord won the second leg 2-0. Nicholson's plea over the PA address for the Spurs fans to show restraint and calm went unheeded as the visiting fans were having their heads smashed in by baton-wielding Dutch police.

"The crowd trouble at the Feyenoord Stadium undoubtedly contributed to my decision to retire. The increase in soccer hooliganism sickened me, and the full horror of the problem confronted me in Rotterdam that night. Tottenham had a friendly relationship with the Dutch side. I had often visited the club and been entertained by the directors. We had developed a good understanding with them. While the hooligan problem was taking root, the attitude of the players was becoming more mercenary and that too, was one of the reasons why I was disillusioned about the game."

Here lies the crux of Bill Nicholson's decision to quit, listening to him intently and knowing what I did about what had been going on behind the scenes. My gut instinct was that Nicholson was fed up with the spiralling wage demands, more so from the ordinary players. He made the point that he felt he could freshen up the side, even after the bad start to his final season, by signing new players. But gone were the days when Bill Nicholson would come calling and players jumped at the opportunity of playing for Spurs and for a manager with such a wonderful reputation for the purist aspect of the game. Instead the "mercenary" instincts Nicholson hinted at became a barrier which this manager felt disgusted about. Players were looking as much, perhaps even more so, at the finances rather than their ambitions and goals in their career.

Which is why it was wrong to blame someone like Martin Chivers for Bill's departure. Even Bill picked up on this point when we sat down at length to go through all the finer points of his reasons for quitting. "At the start of my final season in charge, I was involved in a series of wearisome talks with the players over contracts and one of them was Chivers. But it was untrue, as some critics claimed, that I resigned over him. The fact that I told reporters little probably stirred the rumours, but that was my way. I mistrusted most newspaper reporters from the moment I became manager when I had sought advice from an official of the Football Writers Association when I took over about how I should handle the press. I was told I would be able to work in harmony with most reporters providing I trusted them and made sure that anything I did not want quoted was 'off the record' and not to be used. In one of my first dealings with a reporter I told him some information 'off the record' as I thought and he swore it would never be used. Two days later it was in the headlines and I vowed never to make the same mistake again."

Fortunately Bill trusted me, and as time went on he imparted some fascinating insights into the way he operated at the club. And, one of the reasons he might have been tempted to change his mind when the players made representations to him to stay was that he felt badly about letting down his back room staff, whom he knew would inevitably be kicked out.

That was another reason: I am sure he was trying to put into place a dynasty, just as Liverpool did with the Boot Room, involving Blanchflower and Giles, which could have meant the back room staff staying on.

Some years later, after he had stopped playing, I bumped into Martin Chivers prior to an England international at the old Wembley, where many people would gather across the road for a pre-match meal. Martin was eager for some inside information about Nicholson's reasons for quitting and how much a part he did actually play in that decision, or not as the case might be.

He was intrigued by my observation, based on long conversations with Bill, some that I was able to use in writing his life story, some that remain with me to this day, that I was able to reassure him that he was not, indeed the culprit.

Replacing The Irreplaceable

Sidney Wale was an 'old school' style of football chairman. He never gave interviews and was rarely even pictured, let alone heard making public statements. However, as the local reporter on the *Herald* I had known Sidney for long enough for him to trust me, well, as much as he trusted any journalist, and when I approached him in an empty Tottenham car park when he just happened to be on site during the week, I didn't miss my opportunity to ask him why he had chosen an ex-Arsenal man in Terry Neill to be the next Spurs manager in succession to Bill Nicholson.

"Did he play for Arsenal?" came Sidney's shock response accompanied by an incredulous look of horror. Did he play for Arsenal, indeed! Good grief, you would think the man appointing such an important employee would know his CV!

Sidney was one of the last of the amateur chairmen; men who were supporters through and through, and who took little to no active role inside the club other than chairing the annual meeting and signing off the audit for the annual accounts. Yet if I was shocked by Terry Neill's appointment, imagine how the fans felt. Then again I understood the fans' reaction because I was still very much a fan at heart.

All that was as nothing compared to the shock of the outgoing manager Bill Nicholson who received a mysterious call from his successor. Nicholson told me that the telephone call from Neill came just two days after the Spurs board had vetoed Nicholson's attempts to recruit Danny Blanchflower and Johnny Giles as manager and assistant manager. Nicholson confided, "I was surprised to have a telephone call at home from Terry Neill. At the time he was manager of Hull City and Northern Ireland. He wanted to know what was happening at Tottenham about a new manager. I told him what the directors had told me; that they would accept written applications only. He said he didn't have time to write. He was calling from a hotel near London airport. I said, 'Are you in your room? 'Yes' he replied. 'Well,' I said, 'there should be some writing paper and envelopes there. Get your application off as quickly as you can. It won't take you long to scribble out a note. Give it to the hall porter downstairs and he will drop it in the post box for you.'"

Nicholson was very curious about that call. Eventually Neill was appointed, and Nicholson remained surprised by their choice. He told me, "Terry was the man the board appointed. It caused a considerable stir among our supporters. I wonder whether Sidney Wale really knew Terry's background. It was unique, to say the least, to appoint an Arsenal man."

As it turns out it is not unique, there have been several former Gunners hired as manager before and since, yet even before he started Neill had the problem of winning over the Tottenham supporters. Given the choice, I could not imagine any of our fans welcoming as their manager a man who had played nearly all his career at Highbury.

"The appointment of Terry Neill meant that I would no longer be connected with the club in any way," Bill continued, "I did not blame him for that; I did not expect to be asked to stay on in any capacity. My guess was that the board took the view that as I had resigned it was better to start afresh rather than risk a 'Matt Busby situation'. I was sure it was in their minds that, had I remained, I would have tried to interfere in the running of the club, thereby undermining the authority of the new manager. I suspected if any of the directors thought that way it would have been Charles Cox, the vice-chairman, whose father George first became a director in 1907. A widower, he had worked for Car Mart, part of the Kenning car sales group and supplied the royal family with cars.

"When Terry Neill arrived he had his own advisor and assistant in Wilf Dixon. Had the club kept me on, there would have been the burden of an additional wage. Tottenham was never a club to skimp when it came to signing players, but on the administration side they had the reputation of being mean and it was well deserved."

The arrival of the Neill-Dixon regime meant that Bill's loyal assistant, Eddie Baily, was also out of a job, which distressed Bill no end. In fact the whole handling of Nicholson's departure had left a sour taste for the great man.

He told me, "It was not a pleasant way to leave White Hart Lane after such a long time. I can remember receiving a telephone

THE CUP'S COMING TO SPURS

"When I was 17, playing for Watford in the Third Division, Derek Dougan frightened the life out of me. He'd say 'I'm sticking four past you today, Jennings'—but he never did. In fact, I've played against Dougan 20 times and his only goal was a deflection off a defender."
PAT JENNINGS, Spurs.

"But I still treat Doog with respect. He's tremendous in the air, crafty, with all the skills. If he could tank a ball like Chivers he'd be the greatest centre-forward of all time."

"Because away goals count double, our 2—1 win at Molineux means Wolves have got to knock two past me to stand any chance of lifting the E.U.F.A. Cup. It's just not on if our defence play as well as they did up there."

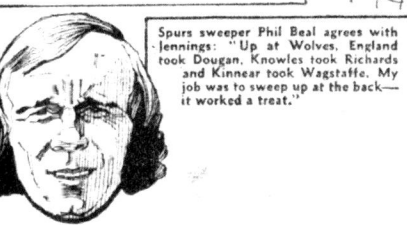

Spurs sweeper Phil Beal agrees with Jennings: "Up at Wolves, England took Dougan, Knowles took Richards and Kinnear took Wagstaffe. My job was to sweep up at the back—it worked a treat."

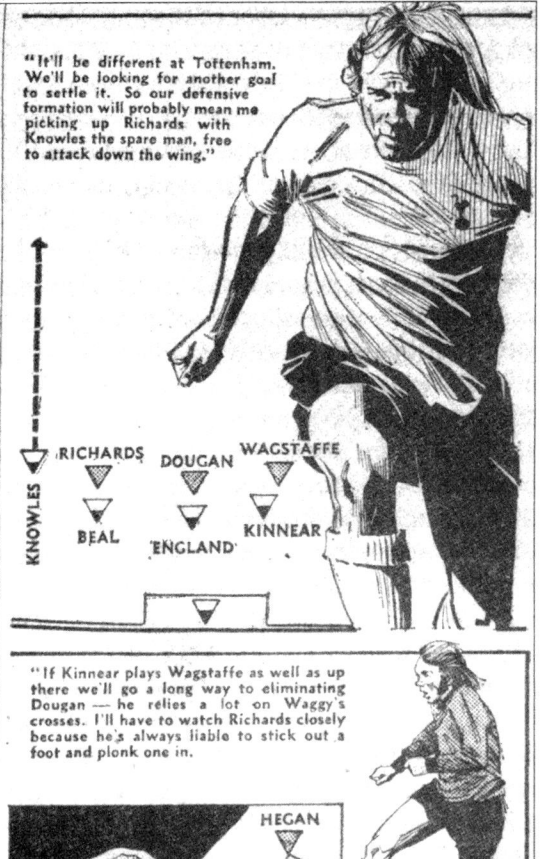

"It'll be different at Tottenham. We'll be looking for another goal to settle it. So our defensive formation will probably mean me picking up Richards with Knowles the spare man, free to attack down the wing."

"If Kinnear plays Wagstaffe as well as up there we'll go a long way to eliminating Dougan — he relies a lot on Waggy's crosses. I'll have to watch Richards closely because he's always liable to stick out a foot and plonk one in."

"It'll be danger when Hegan gets the ball — he's got a tremendous brain, always testing a defence with first-time balls into space and long accurate upfield punts to the strikers."

"But next Wednesday the best forward on the park will be ours — Chivers. And I'm sure he'll add one to the couple he got at Molineux. That can only mean one thing... the E.U.F.A. Cup for Spurs."

call from Terry Neill. He was inquiring about certain items he had discovered. It was obvious that he was in my office. I hurried round to clear my desk. I was given a certain sum by the club as a token for my years of service. All I am prepared to say was that I was far from satisfied with it."

Neill's reign at Spurs lasted just two years. Keith Burkinshaw, recruited by Neill as a coach, took over with Pat Welton as his assistant. Nicholson recalls, "I was glad of the break from football but a desire to get back into it soon made itself felt. When I attended pre-season training sessions at some of the London clubs I began to miss the involvement. I went to West Ham's training ground at Chadwell Heath and also to London Colney, Arsenal's training ground.

"For so many years coaches from all over the globe had come to Cheshunt to study my methods. Now I had time to take a look at others'. One day at Chadwell Heath, Ron Greenwood, then manager of West Ham, asked me what plans I had. I said I was doing nothing and had no plans. He asked me if I would like to help him at West Ham. That season they were in Europe, having won the FA Cup. He asked me to join the club for the season. He felt my experience of Europe would be useful. I was with West Ham for a year and I enjoyed it. I was grateful to Ron for giving me the opportunity to return to football. When Terry left and Keith took over he felt his staff needed strengthening and thought it was a good idea for me to return to the club.

"I realise there must have been a worry that I would interfere but that never materialised. Keith wanted to use my experience and when he sought advice I gave it. I did not volunteer it. Football is a matter of judgement about players. You can be sure in your own mind about a player, but it is valuable to have the backing of an older, more experienced person. Ever since I was back

at the club I kept my thoughts to myself unless asked for advice. Keith may have invited me to a meeting of the coaching staff for a chat or he may have talked things over with me in private. I did a lot of scouting, looking at players of all types to see if they could suit Tottenham."

I know from numerous conversations with Irving Scholar that the new owner was behind the recruitment of Bill Nicholson. It really didn't matter what Bill did, even if he did very little, but for Irving it was imperative for a man such as Nicholson, and what he meant to the club, that he was immediately brought back to the fold and never allowed to leave again.

But Nicholson could see that the arrival of Irving Scholar, which eventually led to Burkinshaw's departure, was the start of a new era in football. Nicholson told me: "The club going public created extra pressure for the manager. Each season a profit had to be made to satisfy the City and, football being what it is, that is not easy to achieve. Keith was disillusioned with the way the team played in his last season and attendance at league matches had fallen. The wealthy directors who had taken over the club were assuming more of the managerial responsibilities, following

the Continental system in which a managing director runs the administrative side and the team manager looks after the playing side only.

"I can see other clubs in England following this lead, so that they come more and more to resemble Italian clubs. This might well have advantages over our present system. Football's finances have changed so much for the worse that one man can no longer be in almost sole charge of a club as I was for 16 years.

"In Italy a new team manager or coach, with new ideas and methods, comes in every season, or every two years at most. He avoids disputes with players over pay and contracts, such as in which Keith was involved with Steve Perryman during his last close season and which affected their relationship for a while. In Italy the managing director deals with these problems, leaving the team manager to devote all his time to working with his players. When the players no longer respond to his ideas, it is time for him to move on to another club; there is little time for complacency among the players."

Remember Bill was telling me this for his life story which was penned in 1983! As ever he was spot on and nearly all clubs have Directors of Football now and managers change at the drop of a hat.

*

While Terry Neill could hardly be described as a Spurs man, Nicholson *was* Spurs, and Spurs *was* Nicholson and always will be. But there were some fun moments with Terry Neill in charge. If he had nothing else, he had a sense of humour, and a willingness to have some fun. As well as a picture of myself with Martin Chivers at a restaurant, I have also kept a picture of *that* race with Terry Neill. There was never a dull moment when Terry was manager of Spurs, believe me! Even though he wasn't around for too long. One sunny afternoon, for some reason, a challenge was thrown down and Terry and I found ourselves on the dirt track surrounding the White Hart Lane pitch, racing around it! I took the first bend ahead and that spurred Terry to kick in and he ended up the winner by some distance as the picture will testify.

Terry was never going to be a managerial norm, but my relationship with him continued when he became Arsenal boss,

One day I challenged Spurs manager Terry Neill to a race around White Hart Lane. It's safe to say it wasn't a close run thing!

and long after his managerial career came to an end, when he opened a wine bar and restaurant close to the *Daily Mirror* building in Holborn. That meant I actually saw much more of Terry than I had when he was in the game.

The publishers held a book launch at Terry's bar when I co-wrote an account of Terry Venables' life in football and his business affairs with Steve Curry. After a good few years Terry sold the wine bar and headed off back to Ireland. The fact that the Mirror Group sold off their traditional Holborn HQ and headed off to Canary Wharf sounded the death knell for Terry's bar, a watering hole for many of the football mad *Mirror* boys of the time.

I caught up with Terry at one of many launches at Planet Hollywood where Alex Garland runs the show for owner Robert Earl, another big Spurs fan. Terry also came along on the terrace of the House of Lords, where Ossie Ardiles many other big names turned out on my invitation. I reminded him how he missed out on signing Ossie for Arsenal. It was good to see him, and Terry hadn't changed much I can assure you! He told me about even bigger names he had been trying to sign for Arsenal, including Johan Cruyff. The game was poorer for his passing in 2002.

HH

Life on the Tottenham *Weekly Herald*

THE EAST END HAD a mystical atmosphere, a community spirit, where you seemed to know everyone, and everyone knew you. Brick Lane possessed a buzz all of its own, as there appeared to be vastly contrasting sections of the old East End. There was Whitechapel High Road, where I would walk down towards Aldgate, passing the jellied eel stalls, of which Tubby Issacs was the most famous, on the pavement. If I ever headed up towards Liverpool Street station, the smell of freshly baked bread would waft through the streets from Kossoffs, mixed with the odours of salt beef and tasty potato latkas. If I fancied more adventure as I got older, there was always a long Sunday stroll past the old Royal Mint to the Tower of London, the awe-inspiring back streets around Tower Bridge and the endless imaginative games by the Tower itself; naturally I couldn't afford the entrance fee to enter the Tower. The East End was home to my mum. She never wanted to leave, and she returned as soon as she could. It was in these streets and familiar venues that my mum was one of many disadvantaged widows who were treated with enormous kindness and sympathy and the hand outs were given with kind hearts by the Jewish community, especially at the Jewish New Year and Passover.

Yet while it was a big-hearted place it was also a tough neighbourhood. Not everyone worked within the law. There were those who owned stalls in Petticoat Lane where you knew that, at best, the goods were "seconds" and at worst had "fallen off the back of a lorry" from the Essex docks. My mum sewed together old bits of fur remnants, which her three sisters would sell from a stall in Hackney. They pushed the stall all the way from their terraced house in Shoreditch. It was at least a mile shifting that heavy stall, and I really have no idea how they managed it. Sheer will power, I suppose; it was their only chance of making any money on which to survive, apart from the handouts.

One sister was truly mad, I mean medically insane, but they refused to have Freda sectioned and instead kept her pacified with about two dozen cats that roamed the house freely creating a unique smell as you entered. It was always a "thrill" visiting my mum's three sisters. They idolised me and all wanted a kiss, including Freda. Believe me that was not a great experience!

Commercial Road had a reputation of being somewhere to avoid for the faint of heart. The Krays lived around there but Mrs. Kray was always a friendly face. There was a large area of green in front of her house, ideal for large scale football kick-abouts, and a regular haunt as I got older and ventured further.

On the outside, purely as a fan, it all seemed like a starry-eyed experience. Somehow that sense of occasion of going to a game, and the expectancy of wanting your team to succeed, didn't desert me when it became a means of earning a living. It was always something special to meet those heroes, from managers to players and of course, working for the local Tottenham paper, there was no need to disguise the biased reporting!

On the *Weekly Herald* I soon became friends with some of the young professionals just about breaking into the first team. One in particular was Danny Clapton, nephew of one of Arsenal's most famous ever footballer's of the same name. His father managed the local amateur side Haringey Borough, and I even ended up training there and playing in a practice match - naturally, it never went much further than that. I went to Danny's flat, a massive tower block in Hackney, one of three, all identical, and once went with him to the nearby Turkish Baths as he maintained his fitness regime during the summer, which also included tagging along on one of his runs around the local park.

Danny was a gifted midfielder who followed shortly after Graeme Souness left, and Danny made it as far as the Tottenham bench once but never came on. He grew impatient and soon moved on. Danny was slight of build, like John White, who could pick out a pass, and could dictate the midfield under the right circumstances. However, he could sometimes become easily discouraged, with pitches often heavy, laden with mud, it slowed down his ability to spread the play and gave defenders the chance to nail him in the tackle. It was such a shame, as he had all the ability, recognised by Bill Nicholson, but there was far too much competition, and a youngster had to have the right mentality and possibly even more physical presence than he might require now.

Danny and I remained close friends, he had become my best friend of that era, and we were chums with other developing players such as young centre-forward Chris Jones and Irish wingers Chris McGrath and Noel Brotherston, who made just one league appearance. Danny, though, had the sweetest of natures, and was a loyal and trustworthy friend. I never abused that friendship to find out from him anything that went on behind the scenes. However, to meet him for a drink would often be very useful as there were invariably some Spurs stars at the same location, such as the Lacy Lady in Ilford, or a couple of pubs in the Tottenham area. It was a vastly different era, and these days the players are VIPs in some of the trendiest and most exclusive night spots and restaurants in central London.

One summer I have this vague memory of going on holiday in a caravan with Danny and one of his close East End pals. I cannot recall, though, Ray Winstone being there. But much later, after I had made my name as a football writer and had organised a media game at Stamford Bridge, Ray approached me in the lounge and introduced himself. I am embarrassingly ignorant of anything other than football. Ray explained that he knew me when we were all youngsters in the caravan down at the coast, just outside of Hastings. Linda was appalled I didn't know who Ray Winstone was, but we kept in touch for some time after that, and so too did his uncle who rang for chats about football.

Of course the mind does play tricks, and sometimes I have to ask myself, "Did It All Really Happen?" So, with true journalist gusto I went in search of recollections from those who knew me at the time.

After three decades as the Spurs press officer John Fennelly was about to retire, he was appointed the club's historian following the sudden death of Andy Porter, the man who had every Spurs fact at his fingertips, aged just 54, in October 2014. John had succeeded me on the *Herald* as the "Spurs Man", the lovely job of covering all Spurs games and writing about them full time.

The temptation might be to doctor some of the things people of that era might have to say about me, but to resist such folly, I asked those concerned to email their entries, which I promised would be unedited. So here goes, the truth as they see it...

John Fennelly

I first met Harry when I turned up to replace him on my first day at the *Tottenham Weekly Herald*. I had just finished my newspaper apprenticeship on the *Enfield Gazette* and was there to take over from Harry as the paper's Spurs correspondent.

Typical Harry, not only did he hand Spurs over to me when they had just been relegated to the old Second Division but he also took advantage of my naivety to sell me two LPs to help him pay off a tax debt! I'm sure he had some decent stuff in his collection but by the time I got there they had all gone so I ended up with a Lulu album and *Crazy Horses* by The Osmonds! Who even buys that stuff? I didn't even play either apart from the title track on the Osmonds album but, looking back, even that was rubbish. They're probably worth a few bob now! No, even collectors wouldn't touch them!

Harry then took me over to meet Spurs manager Keith Burkinshaw to introduce me as I was to produce the back page on my own the following week. But from the minute we walked into Burkinshaw's office at White Hart Lane the manager launched into a tirade of abuse at Harry for something he'd written the week before and chucked us out! That was my preparation for taking over the most important page in the *Herald* because many of the readers only bought the paper for its Spurs news and in those pre-web, pre-magazine explosion days there was very little specialised coverage around.

I'd like to say that Harry stayed around to help and often called me to see if all was okay, but he didn't! In those days sports reporters on local papers were also expected to sub and lay-out their pages themselves but I had no experience of the production process. So the *Herald* editor, Peter Edwards, sent me to Newcastle on a course. On the first day the tutor held up the back page of a newspaper to show us how not to do it - it was one of Harry's!

Harry was a legend at the *Herald* – but so was his dear old mum who regularly phoned in the evenings to see how her little Harry was and was he wearing his vest etc. (Harry you can expand on this, PS apologies if it's not true, this came from Dave Gold at the time, remember him?).

Years later we worked together when I did a two-week reporting shift on the *Daily Mail* in Fleet Street. Harry had us walk miles to find the cheapest lunch in town, a small Austrian restaurant around the back of St Paul's. He ate his in two minutes flat and then went back to the office and phoned everyone he knew for the entire afternoon and went on doing so well into the evening as I finally set off for home. He never gave up.

Sometime further on I found out what it was like to be on the end of one of Harry's non-stop calls. Working at Spurs by now I met up with former West Ham manager John Lyall who was doing some coaching at White Hart Lane with his old pal Terry Venables. "Harry the Phone, we used to call him – he was never off it," moaned John as he recalled being consistently chased by hound dog Harry!

*

Well, you've guessed it. It was a wrong move to let loose people like "Fenners". As I told him in my reply. So, I am just going to flip through Memory Lane on what has actually happened in the near 60 years I have supported the team.

My imagination was stirred by the club winning the Football League title and the FA Cup in the same season. That was phenomenal at the time. I can recall reading how Danny Blanchflower had been convinced before the season started that such was the talent within the team that he just knew they would land the Double. Spurs became the first club to complete the Double since Preston North End in 1889 and Aston Villa in 1897, making Spurs the first team to win the Double in the 20th century. Little wonder my head was turned. More than that — I was hooked. I longed to see my first match and it had to be a Spurs game. The trophies and the glory-filled games came thick and fast, even though Spurs should have won the European Cup in 1962, they did hold onto the FA Cup, no mean feat in itself in those days and the following season Spurs were worthy winners of the European Cup Winners' Cup, to become the first British club to win a major European competition. Jimmy Greaves, who signed for the club six months after the historic Double, became Spurs' highest league scorer in one season with 37 goals in his 41 appearances.

By the time Spurs won the FA Cup in 1967 for the fifth time, I had become a regular at the Lane, and travelled to a few games within the London area but had not ventured too far afield. By the time Spurs won the League Cup in 1971, I was watching every single Spurs game, both home and abroad, thanks to my job with the *Herald*. The year after the League Cup triumph Spurs won the UEFA Cup. The following season they won the League Cup again, the first club to have won the trophy twice.

In 1974 Spurs became the first English club to have played in three major European finals but the glory days didn't last forever and on April 28th, 1975, the Lane staged one of the most bizarre games with Spurs having to at least draw against Leeds United to stay in the First Division. Leeds, who were the reigning champions, finished in a disappointing ninth spot in the First Division that season, but were in the final of the European Cup. Although they had nothing to play for, Jimmy Armfield's team were still a massive obstacle for survival. I can recall that the then-manager Terry Neill tried just about everything. Even employing all sorts of pre-match mind games, including a hypnotist, a man called Ronald Markham, whose stage name was Romark.

Terry had first met Romark when he was manager of Hull City. Ron told Neill that he could improve the team's attitudes and expectations through the power of positive thinking. So when Hull played a game at Bristol City he invited Ron to the team's hotel the night before the game. He got the players locking their fingers behind their heads, and for most, when asked to unlock, they couldn't do so. Ron had got them to believe they were interlocking steel bars. He even got a player with only a slight chance of being fit to accept the power of positive thinking. Now Neill turned once more to Ron in his hour of need. As I wrote in Terry Neill's life

> **On Monday April 28th, 1975, the Lane staged one of the most bizarre games with Spurs having to at least draw against Leeds United to stay in the First Division... Terry Neill tried just about everything. Even employing all sorts of pre-match mind games, including a hypnotist, a man called Ronald Markham, whose stage name was Romark.**

story *Revelations Of A Football Manager*, Neill told me "Tough wasn't the word to describe our task against the European Cup finalists." Neill booked the West Lodge Park Hotel in Hadley Wood from a telephone in the office of Arsenal's club secretary, Ken Friar. He wanted total concentration from his players in the final game. In reality, knowing Terry the way I did, it was the manager who was more nervous than his players. He told the players to report at lunch time on the Sunday.

Neill told me, "I decided to ring Ron Markham and invited him to help ease the tension. I was half inclined to think that this smacked of gimmickry and might have a detrimental effect on the players. We had, after all, lost the match to Bristol City the year before, but we didn't have anything to lose, and if Ron handled it properly it would be a diversion from all the pressures.

"I introduced Ron to the players, saying, 'This is Ronald Markham. There's no magic but he may have a few interesting things to say to you.' Ron then spoke to them collectively, telling them that he had no knowledge of the game and couldn't affect their technical performance. A lot of the players had given everything during the course of the season and had taken personal knocks in their confidence because of the club's troubles. Ron's jocular approach and party tricks made them feel better."

Cyril Knowles had a hard man reputation, but he had, apparently, succumbed to the hypnosis, and he was told to recall one of his greatest moments, which was scoring from a free-kick. He was told that if he got a similar free-kick, he must take it, and he would score.

And sure enough, the next day, the nerves of nearly 50,000 people crammed into White Hart Lane were settled after just five minutes when Cyril slammed home a free-kick from the edge of the area. When the home side were awarded a free-kick in a similar position to a wonder goal Cyril had scored against Manchester United, no one could stop the left-back storming through the field to demand that he took it!

Neill told me how it had all been down to the hypnosis, "Ron then said he would like to try a little hypnosis on a volunteer, and Cyril stepped forward. After hypnotising Cyril, Ron told him to put his hands by his side. 'You are now a rod of solid steel,' he said to Cyril. I was sure the players would not take it seriously, but when Ron pushed Cyril over he never flinched, keeping as straight as the said steel rod. There was no laughter from the players, who were certainly impressed. We picked up Cyril, a six-footer weighing over 12 stone, and on Ron's instructions laid him across two chairs, the tips of his shoulders and head on one chair and his feet on the other. He remained rigid.

"Now it came to individual sessions. Ron was going to bring out the power of positive thinking in the form of each player's successes on the field. He couldn't improve a player's fitness or ability, but he wanted to convince them that they were going to win the match. He asked the players to recall their finest moment in football - their best game, their best goal, or anything they would be proud of recalling." Only two players were too sceptical to join in, Pat Jennings and John Pratt, who later became assistant manager at the club under Peter Shreeves. They were both determined to succeed or fail without outside influence. As Pat Jennings joked later, some of the players must have been struggling to remember anything!

Ralph Coates selected a European game as his favourite moment of triumph. Cyril chose the free-kick against Manchester United when he curled the ball round the defensive wall into the top corner - a goal *Match of the Day* had featured it in their titles for a year.

Neill continues, "Champagne was brought in to celebrate Martin Chivers' birthday and some cake was provided by the hotel. The players were laughing and joking. If anyone had chanced by our hotel that night they would have found it very strange. The team that was under the most severe pressure was laughing and drinking and seemed to have no worries.

"As Ron left the hotel, he said to me, 'No problems. You are assured of the right result.' Certainly he helped to prevent the players from wasting nervous energy. They were relaxed and their confidence was restored. In a

> **Cyril Knowles had a hard man reputation, but he had, apparently, succumbed to the hypnosis, and he was told to recall one of his greatest moments, which was scoring from a free-kick. He was told that if he got a similar free-kick, he must take it, and he would score.**

very different way as the late Bill Shankly was superb at lifting the spirits of players with his powers of positive thinking.

"At the ground the next night, I noticed that some of the directors were looking extremely nervous. I noticed one taking a heart tablet, while another couldn't prevent his cup and saucer from shaking. I thought to myself that if I was similarly affected I would give up the game. I carried on to my office and poured myself a drink, laughing all the while. I couldn't prevent whatever was going to happen, so there was little point worrying about something I had no further control over."

As Terry Neill rightly told me afterwards, the game couldn't possibly have gone any better. Perhaps it was the magician Ron doing his work, or maybe, more down to earth reasons such as Leeds concentrating on their forthcoming European Cup final against Bayern Munich in Paris.

Spurs dominated the opening period once Cyril had scored from the free-kick but were unable to get the vital second despite a constant bombardment of the Leeds goal. The second half continued in a similar vein but Spurs finally got their reward when Martin Chivers, back in the starting line-up after a two-month lay-off, fired home from close range. The result was virtually made safe on the hour when Knowles converted a penalty after Trevor Cherry had brought down Perryman. Joe Jordan pulled a goal back for Leeds to silence the Spurs fans but the celebrations which followed Alfie Conn's strike to make it 4-1 were as loud and as long as any Championship winning season. An 81st minute Peter Lorimer goal for Leeds went largely unnoticed by the home supporters who swamped the pitch on the final whistle to mob their heroes on a memorable night.

Neill recalled, "It made me feel that bringing Ron to the hotel was worthwhile. Cyril scored two goals and after the final whistle, everyone at the club was delighted and relieved. There was a crowd of 49,886, the largest of the season, a great atmosphere, and the night was ours. They had flocked to the ground in case it was the club's last game in the First Division for a while. Fortunately it wasn't. Shortly after the final whistle, the local police chief came into the dressing room and said, 'You will have to come out and make a personal appearance. They won't go home until you do. They are all shouting for you.' My first reaction was to think how different this was from the early part of the season, when they were screaming abuse at me. It had been such a hostile atmosphere that some fans took to spitting at me while others shouted at me on the telephone.

"They yelled, 'You Arsenal bastard, what the hell are you doing messing up our Tottenham team?' I received abusive letters by the sack load. After one game two big fellows had come over and wanted to punch me. If it hadn't been for the prompt action of the police I might have been forced to fight both of them. I could understand everyone's concern, but I was concerned too and I was working a full day every day of the week trying to put things right.

"All this went through my mind as the police chief stood at the door, 'tell them to go and get stuffed,' I said. Perhaps in hindsight that was undiplomatic and ungracious, but at the time I meant it. I had a cup of tea and went home. It was not my intention to be abusive or abrupt to all the fans, but I was weary after the long campaign against relegation and rightly or wrongly didn't feel the need for congratulations. I was content that I had played my part in keeping Tottenham in the First Division."

I had got to know every member of that team. Relegation would have been heartbreaking as a fan, but also from a professional view point. For both reasons I didn't want "my" club relegated. But, like every Spurs fan, one couldn't help being concerned about how much it really meant to Terry Neill. Yes, of course, it meant a great deal as a professional football manager, but it confirmed the feeling that he was the wrong man for the job, and it didn't take long for the Spurs board to appreciate that the fans didn't trust his reign as manager.

The players became very dear to my heart too. Knowing them as a fan is to idolise them. Knowing them more intimately often results in disillusionment. For me, it intensified my admiration for my heroes. Pat Jennings

I had got to know every member of that team. Relegation would have been heartbreaking as a fan, but also from a professional view point. For both reasons I didn't want "my" club relegated. But, like every Spurs fan, one couldn't help being concerned about how much it really meant to Terry Neill.

McNab wins on speed

● EVERY WEEK Ian Hutchinson, Chelsea striker, teams up in The People with the top talent of artist Paul Trevillion to tell how he rates the men he plays against. It's a fascinating insight into big football.

● TODAY "Hutch" looks at two of the top defenders — Bob McNab of Arsenal and Cyril Knowles, of Tottenham. Both are excellent players — but one is a shade better and this is an expert telling why.

CYRIL KNOWLES, A VERY HARD PLAYER, HAS LITTLE TIME FOR FINESSE WHEN GOING INTO A TACKLE. HIS AIM IS TO KICK THE BALL AWAY FROM THE MAN IN POSSESSION.

BOTH DEFENDERS ARE QUICK TO MOVE UP IN SUPPORT OF THEIR ATTACK. McNAB, IN PARTICULAR, HAS A TREMENDOUS UNDERSTANDING WITH GEORGE ARMSTRONG, WHO BENEFITS FROM THE SPACE CREATED BY McNAB'S INTELLIGENT DECOY RUNNING.

McNAB, EVERY BIT AS HARD AS KNOWLES, SHOWS MORE SKILL — FREQUENTLY EMERGING FROM A TACKLE WITH THE BALL AT HIS FEET.

CENTREING WHEN RUNNING AT FULL SPEED IS NOT McNAB'S STRONG POINT — FAR TOO OFTEN HE WILL SEND THE BALL INTO THE CROWD.

KNOWLES IS McNAB'S SUPERIOR HERE — HIS VERY ACCURATE CENTRES HAVE LED TO MANY SPURS GOALS.

WHEN BEATEN IN A TACKLE, McNAB'S TREMENDOUS TURN OF SPEED ENABLES HIM TO GET BACK AND CHALLENGE AGAIN. KNOWLES, SLOWER IN RECOVERY, CANNOT COMPARE HERE AND SINCE I RATE SPEED ONE OF THE PRICELESS ASSETS OF A FULL-BACK I NAME McNAB THE MORE COMPLETE PLAYER.

in goal was such a soft spoken, likeable big Irishman, who you couldn't help but love, and everyone loved him. He had enormous hands, and when he first joined the club from Watford, it seemed like a huge gamble by Bill Nicholson. But when he caught the ball one handed on the stretch at the far post, it left fans like myself breathless. It was an awesome sight.

The full-backs were Joe Kinnear and Knowles, with the central defenders Phil Beal and Keith Osgood. Keith was one of the players who had come through the ranks, and I had got to know him very well. Phil Beal wore these ludicrously long side burns, very fashionable at the time, and he was a hugely likeable guy. He was one of those underrated players who came through the ranks when the fans wanted a big name signing to follow in the footsteps of some of the club's great central defenders, but whatever Phil Beal lacked in star quality he made up for in sheer consistency and effectiveness which made him a regular in the side.

Terry Naylor was as hard as nails, ruthless in the tackle, a typical cockney with a heart of gold. Alfie Conn had the charisma and was

BLIND SIDE RUN

A high ball centred into the goalmouth is the signal for MARTIN PETERS to sneak into the penalty box, find space and score. The spectators will often applaud the man who made the pass when, in fact, they should be applauding Peters for his imaginative run which enabled him to sneak in on the blind side of the defence.

all showman with those flowing blond locks, but he was also infuriatingly inconsistent. On his day he was the wizard of the dribble, but too often it wouldn't come off, and he could also be quite temperamental when things were not going his way. Steve Perryman was there to provide the all-energy leadership, his influence within the dressing room was total. With John Pratt, another selfless runner and tireless tackler, no team had more energy in midfield. But the entire team never seemed to get it together, and that's why they found themselves fighting off relegation, even though they possessed such enormous talents as Conn and the enigmatic Chivers. Martin Chivers often failed to punch his weight, but when he was in the mood he was virtually unstoppable. Alongside him was the hugely talented Chris Jones, a centre-forward who seemed destined never to be a great goalscorer, who seemed to miss chances through fate rather than inability.

Neill was highly ambitious and after the horrific brush with relegation wanted to achieve something special at Spurs, and tried to recruit, unsuccessfully, Johan Cruyff at a time when foreign signings were almost unknown in English football. Neill was an innovative thinker and his drive to recruit Cruyff was inspired, even if he was trying to convince a rather conservative board about the revolutionary capture. Neill failed with Cruyff, and also missed out on bringing Charlie George to the Lane, but did bring in Keith Burkinshaw and Peter Shreeves as coaches, fortuitously because when Neill left as manager, as always seemed inevitable, Burkinshaw and Shreeves were on hand to pick up the reigns.

And surely Spurs would never make the same mistake again and select an Arsenal man as their manager. Surely not? Oh well, no one told Alan Sugar but that's another story! Neill finished ninth in his second season, but on the pre-season tour there were all sorts of fall-outs with rumours he had been approached by Arsenal. With all his frustrations at the Lane, a quick switch across North London to his true love Arsenal was always going to be a big draw. So off he went.

Burkinshaw, who spent seven years at Liverpool as a player without really making the grade before ending his playing career at Workington and Scunthorpe, arrived at the Lane from Newcastle United in 1975 after working as a coach at St James' Park for seven years. Popular with the players, Burkinshaw had their full support when he applied for the manager's job and he

was appointed in 1976.

Although Spurs had survived relegation in 1975 and rallied to finish ninth in Terry Neill's only full season in charge in 1975-76, Burkinshaw inherited an unbalanced, under-achieving side and could not stop Spurs going down in 1977. But whereas the Board may have made mistakes in the past, they now made the right decision. Burkinshaw kept his job and led Spurs back into the First Division at the first attempt. Spurs were determined to make it straight back to the top flight and won five and drew three of their first eight games before a couple of defeats to Hull City and Charlton Athletic. But they soon put those setbacks out of their system when they achieved one of the biggest wins in their history when, on 22nd October 1977, they thrashed Bristol Rovers 9-0 at the Lane. That came a week after the 4-1 defeat at Charlton, prompting Burkinshaw to fork out £60,000 for little-known Torquay striker Colin Lee, a man who had only been playing as a forward for a season.

Lee had a dream debut putting four past a hapless Rovers side. It took him just 21 minutes to get on the score sheet when he swept home Glenn Hoddle's cross. Four minutes later he grabbed his second when he headed home John Pratt's corner. Hoddle was the provider once more a minute before the interval when his cross was met by Peter Taylor to make it 3-0. The second half saw Spurs simply overrun the Pirates and the bearded Ian Moores made it 4-0 on 56 minutes. The final quarter was simply an exhibition by Burkinshaw's side with Hoddle teasing Rovers with some sublime pieces of skill. Lee grabbed his hat-trick on 75 minutes and two goals in as many minutes from Moores saw him complete his first treble for the club to make it 7-0. Two minutes from time Lee capped off a memorable debut when he tapped home his fourth, but the best was

saved until last when Hoddle collected Moores' pass over the Rovers defence to score a magnificent goal which sealed Spurs' record league victory.

Barry Daines kept goal that day in front of a 26,311 crowd, with Don McAllister in defence, a young Neil McNab in midfield and Peter "Spud" Taylor on the wing. The attack was led by the most unlikely strike-force of Colin Lee and Ian Moores, two giant centre-forwards, hardly a traditional Spurs attack. The entire team was constructed of very "nice" guys. Even the accepted "ball-winner" in midfield John Pratt, was a lovely guy off the field. The two big men in attack were mild-mannered.

The only one with a touch of nastiness about his play was the slightest and lightest player of all, McNab. Yet off the field he was also a really nice guy. I can recall the very first day he turned up at the Lane as one of Nicholson's last signings as a tiny 16-year-old, one of the youngest players Nicholson had ever purchased, and who had such enormous gifts he was destined for the first team almost immediately after arriving south of the border. It was a tough job interviewing the new signing. I took him to one of the local, and very cheap, greasy spoons in the Tottenham High Road, and could hardly make out a word through his very broad Scottish accent but we became very good friends.

You just couldn't imagine that kind of access these days, turning up, via an introduction from the manager, and then taking a player off for a cup of tea. These days, it's the formality of a structured press conference, in front of a room full of newspaper journalists, TV cameras and crews, radio and even specialist internet providers.

Sir Alex Ferguson refused to allow David Beckham to be interviewed by any outlet for several years protecting his player from a media that had mushroomed beyond recognition from the time that young McNab turned up at Tottenham totally bewildered and looking lost and alone. Now a new recruit is accompanied by an agent, specialist house hunters and Mr. Fix-Its coming out from all directions to ensure every last detail is taken care of so the player can concentrate on his football.

Spurs never really looked back after crushing Rovers, losing only four more times the whole season, but because three of those defeats came in quick succession to Burnley, Brighton and Sunderland in the closing weeks, there was a nail-biting end to the campaign. Spurs finally had to settle for automatic promotion in third place ahead of Brighton on goal difference and behind Bolton and Southampton after a 0-0 draw at Southampton in their final match.

Once promoted, Burkinshaw knew he had to rebuild the team and pulled off one of the greatest transfer coups in the club's history by signing Argentinian World Cup stars Ossie Ardiles and Ricky Villa. The team built around the talents of Ardiles and Hoddle went on to win the FA Cup in 1981 and 1982 and the UEFA Cup in 1984. I had heard whispers from my contacts inside the game that Burkinshaw had signed Ossie and Ricky by default. The idea belonged to Terry Neill, who wanted Ardiles, but knew Ossie wouldn't go without Ricky and had "conned" his old mate Keith into taking Ricky. Burkinshaw was invited by Neill to tag along to Buenos Aires, who suddenly ditched his own plans of recruiting Ardiles, leaving the Spurs boss at the airport on his own. However he decided to go through with the travel plans and ended up signing Ardiles as well when he only went to get Villa.

Neill told me his side of the story, "I do not regret my decision not to buy Ardiles and Villa in the summer of 1978. The deal that brought them to Tottenham proved successful for our North London rivals, but it did not enable them to take over from Arsenal as London's top club! [Sheffield United manager] Harry Haslam first rang me to say Ardiles and Villa were available after the World Cup in Argentina in 1978. Oscar Arce, an Argentinian coach, and former Argentine World Cup captain Antonio Rattin, who was sent off at Wembley in 1966, were friends of Harry's and had helped him set up a proposed deal.

"I had seen Ardiles on television and admired his skill, but knew little about Villa, who had appeared briefly as substitute in a couple of matches. Harry said Ricky Villa might be more suited to English football than Ossie because he was bigger and stronger. The deal would cost $700,000 with 15 percent going to the players and 2 percent to the Argentine FA. By transfer standards at that time, it was not an exorbitant sum.

"I rang Ron Greenwood to seek his advice. Ron said he fancied Ardiles but was less keen on Villa. At the time I was having problems with Alan Hudson and perhaps needed a midfield player but I did not need two. We had appeared in the FA Cup final and finished fifth in the First Division, we already had a strong squad.

"But Tottenham, who came up from the Second Division on goal difference ahead of Brighton, needed new faces. Their need was greater than ours. Harry suggested that I fly to Buenos Aires to see Ardiles and Villa, but as there were no competitive matches left that season I did not see the point of travelling that far. Denis Hill-Wood (the Arsenal chairman) was not keen on signing foreign players, but he did not stand in my way. If I had decided to go to Buenos Aires, I am sure I could have signed them. Harry Haslam was naturally disappointed with my decision and asked me if I could recommend another club. I mentioned Tottenham.

"Burkinshaw had taken over at White Hart Lane and it would be a bold gamble on his part to take the Argentinians. I spoke to Keith, and though he was at first reluctant I told him if I was in his position I would consider the gamble worthwhile. He decided to investigate and the Tottenham board gave him permission to open negotiations. Keith wanted me to fly with him to Buenos Aires. 'At least we can enjoy the trip and have a few drinks,' he said. But I'd made my decision, and declined. He went alone, and within a couple of days had finalised the deal. Ossie Ardiles has adorned English football and has been a great asset to Spurs over the years, but I still maintain I made the right decision.

"Ricky Villa confirmed daydreaming at Highbury when the player he should have been picking up, David Price, scored a goal. He was that type of performer - brilliant in one game, infuriating in the next. He will be remembered, however, as the player who scored one of the truly great individual goals in the history of the FA Cup final at Wembley."

Well, all any Spurs fan can say to Terry is "thanks, and thanks again." Arsenal's loss was Spurs' gain! Although Terry got his revenge by taking Pat Jennings to Highbury when it was considered he might be past his sell-by date at the Lane. Pat was far from finished and ended up playing for many years still at his peak with the Gunners.

The arrival of Ossie and Ricky opened the floodgates for foreign stars, a trickle at first, but more recently a deluge. But Terry's prediction in his book, published in 1985, about the foreign influx was wide of the mark. He predicted at the time: "Even if there were no limit on the number of overseas players in the English Football League, I do not think there would be a significant change in the number of foreigners playing for our clubs. For a start, clubs wishing to buy them will find the same difficulties I encountered. The big name players will want salaries far in excess of what most players earn in England, and only a few clubs will be able to meet their demands. Then there are difficulties with acclimatisation, language, the style of football and everything else.

"Few foreigners have been successful here. Ossie Ardiles, Ivan Golac, Frans Thijssen and Arnold Muhren are exceptions. On the Continent many of the best players are mercenaries, going from country to country and being employed by clubs on short term contracts. I cannot see that happening here."

Well, Terry couldn't have foreseen the explosion of Rupert Murdoch's Sky TV cash and the advent of the Premier League. Dennis Bergkamp and Thierry Henry are examples of foreign superstars who were far from short term at Arsenal for a start, and none of them seemed to be put off by the

weather. Whatever Terry might boast about Spurs' Argentinians failing to elevate Spurs above Arsenal, it clearly reinstated Spurs as the great entertainers of English football.

*

Eddie Baily was an outstanding star for Spurs and England in the 50s, in the same team 'Push and Run' team as Bill Nicholson, and later became Bill's assistant manager. The players unkindly nicknamed Eddie 'strawberry nose', but it was hardly surprising as his nose did glow like a strawberry. I liked Eddie. As a young journalist on the local *Weekly Herald* paper I would often find Eddie in the back office having his morning meeting with Bill, before my audience with the manager. I was always given a warm and encouraging greeting by him.

In Bill's autobiography he described Eddie as "one of the many jokers within the club that helped to keep spirits up" but Eddie had his own unique style, and he could produce some colourful industrial language when dealing with players on the training ground and in the dressing room. According to Bill,

Eddie couldn't get on with certain players and sometimes the exchanges got heated, one notable case was that of the emerging and incredibly talented youth team midfielder Graeme Souness. Souness was a spiky personality even as a youngster and ran home back to Scotland at one point and Bill had to chase after him to persuade him to return. He was one of those players who made Eddie throw his coat across the dressing room floor in exasperation adding a curse or two along the way, and there is no doubt there would have been coaches at Anfield and Ayresome Park who would have known, how Eddie felt at times!

I can recall watching Souness when Spurs won the FA Youth Cup in 1970 and even then, you just knew he was going to be a star. Souness and Perryman were being groomed by Nicholson to play together in the first team. Souness had all the skills, Perryman the application. As a fan you wanted both to emerge into the senior side, but while Nicholson favoured Perryman to come through first, that left Souness disgruntled, and he went AWOL back to Scotland in a sulk. Nicholson knew he was a special talent and went after him and brought him back, but the relationship wasn't going to last with Souness remaining impatient while Perryman prospered.

I have since crossed swords with Souness when investigating his involvement with Lord Stevens and his Quest team looking into transfers at the behest of the Premier League. I clearly rattled his cage, and when he is angry he is not a nice person to be around, I can vouch for that.

While still at the *Weekly Herald*, I found Martin Chivers one of the more difficult characters to come to terms with. He seemed aloof and introverted. Yet, once he stopped playing I got to know a vastly different personality; charming and warm. I am not quite sure what triggered such a charismatic character change. Pressure maybe? Or perhaps he thought I was just after a story?

It was some years later after the big centre-forward stopped playing that I bumped into Martin prior to an England international at the old Wembley, where many people would

THEY CAN'T KICK HIM OUT OF IT

MANAGING a First Division side doesn't keep Jackie Charlton awake at night. He sends himself to sleep by counting the number of Scottish caps his Middlesbrough midfield star Graeme Souness will win.

Charlton says: "Tottenham would not be in the trouble they are now if they'd kept this lad. His midfield aggression and will to win would have provided the red blood the Tottenham side lack.

"Watching Souness reminds me of Billy Bremner. He hates to see the opposition with the ball and he goes in like a terrier, yet I've never seen the lad guilty of a dirty tackle. More important, I've never seen him pull out of one."

Charlton says that Souness lacks real pace, so when he gets in trouble he can't kick the ball past opponents and race them for it.

"His only way out is to play a bit of football —and when he turns that on you'll swear you're watching Bobby Moore," says Charlton.

"The other night I counted over 50 Scottish caps for Souness before falling asleep. I don't think I'll be far out."

DEVISED BY TREVILLION

gather across the road for a pre-match meal. Martin was eager for some inside information about Nicholson's reasons for quitting and how much a part he did actually play in that decision, or not as the case might be. He was intrigued by my observations based on long conversations with Bill, some that I was able to use in writing his life story, some that remain with me to this day, that I was able to reassure him that he was not, indeed the culprit.

*

When I started out, I took on an unpaid job on a charitable weekly show on hospital radio at Whipps Cross in Leytonstone where my co-host was the football writer from the rival local paper, *The Guardian*. Steve Tongue went on to become one of the country's most respected football correspondents for *The Independent on Sunday*.

I remember when Steve and I met the late Jimmy Neighbour, a promising young Spurs winger at that time, who became a very close and dear friend during our first flush of youth. Jimmy was one of the nicest people I have ever had the pleasure to meet in football in all these years. The Chingford-born winger broke into the Spurs team at an early age, and had enormous talent, but never seemed to be able to produce enough of it consistently to tie down a regular place, which at times he deserved, but maybe not all the time. His talent was worth persevering with and Bill Nicholson encouraged him a lot. As he developed as a player, he always had time for the young journalist making his way at the North London *Weekly Herald*, and it was a pleasure to have known him.

Jimmy died aged 58 of a heart attack following a hip replacement operation in the summer of 2009. In a tribute to him Brian Glanville, one of the all-time great football writers, described Jimmy as "a quintessential winger of his time. That is to say he was small (5ft 6½in) though sturdily built, fast, clever on the ball, and a maker, rather than a taker, of goal opportunities."

Jimmy joined his beloved Spurs as a junior in 1966 but it was not until the 1970-71 season that he gained a place in the first team. Though he started only a dozen league matches — and made five more appearances as a sub — in February 1971 he played on the left wing as Spurs beat Third Division Aston Villa 2-0 at Wembley in the League Cup final in front of 100,000 with Martin Chivers scoring both goals. In all Jimmy made 158 appearances for Spurs and scored 15 times before he left after only seven matches of the disastrous 1976-77 season which ended with Spurs relegated after 27 years in the First Division.

Jimmy moved to Norwich City for only £75,000 but he was so successful at Carrow Road that the Canaries doubled their money when they sold him to West Ham in September 1979. In 1981, a decade after winning the League Cup with Spurs, he was back in the League Cup final with the Hammers but only gained a runners-up medal this time after they lost a replay to Liverpool.

Going on loan to Bournemouth in December 1982 for just three League games, and another three for non-League Enfield, he then embarked on a coaching career, before opening a sports shop in Chingford, and working, like Cliff Jones, at a sports centre in Haringey. After a short spell coaching Wealdstone in January squad and stay in the same hotel, although the press would travel to the games in their own coach. A separate coach would also be provided for the excursions to and from the airport for European matches. But there were numerous opportunities to meet up with the players for private chats, at the airport waiting to check in, at the other end waiting to collect the luggage, and also bumping into them at the hotel.

Now it's vastly different. The media invariably travel independently. The media never share a team hotel, apart from in exceptional circumstances. Now it's all social media and dressing

A meal with Martin 'Cheers for' Chivers

1987, he returned, for two years as coach at his old club, Enfield. In October 1990 he began a four-year spell as youth development officer at West Ham, after which he went north to coach at Doncaster Rovers before managing non-League St Albans City for two years and finally returning "home" to coach Tottenham's under-17 squad. His early death in April 2009 robbed his wife Sheila of a husband and left son Ian and daughter Faye without a father but he is still remembered fondly wherever he played and coached.

When Jimmy was playing for Spurs, relationships between the club and the media were very different to today. Those were the days when the media had access to Spurs' Cheshunt training facilities, invited usually to watch one session of pre-season training before an interview with Bill Nicholson.

The next time such an invite might be forthcoming would be on the eve of a cup final. The media would also travel with the room selfies; have times changed for the better?

While at the *Tottenham Herald* I had the chance to interview one of my boyhood heroes, left-back Cyril Knowles, in the back of a cab during my days as a novice reporter. The fans would sing 'Nice One Cyril', as the mild mannered guy off the field would be a demon on it launching into rock hard tackles that would intimidate any winger in the world.

Tragedy struck Cyril when his young son was killed by a stray stone that flew through the front windscreen of his car, and hit his forehead. Cyril was unable to play for some time, and it was impossible to convey to him how sorry you felt. I would watch him wandering around the ground in a daze, before he was in a fit state of mind to resume his career.

My career was taking an unusual turn. The *Weekly Herald* was part of a chain of local newspapers owned by Thompson Newspapers, with their training school in the North East. I loved being the Spurs local reporter so much I never envisaged ever leaving, but for personal reasons I moved from the North London *Weekly Herald* to the *Newcastle Journal* and stayed in the North East for just over a year before returning south, moving to Croydon to begin work for the London *Evening News*.

At that time there were seven editions a day, the first was on the streets to greet everyone going to work in the capital. I would need to leave Croydon at 6am to be assured of being at my desk by 7am to prepare for the first edition.

My usual route was to take the fast train from East Croydon which was usually a short bus ride or a long walk from home, then from Victoria on the tube to Blackfriars, and from there it was walking distance to the old Associated News building. My first sports editor was Peter Watson, next up was Vic Wakeling who went on to a TV career and became Head of Sport for Sky.

I got to know Danny Blanchflower very well when he became manager of Chelsea. I always thought he was the right man for the wrong club. He was a perfect fit for Tottenham, but not so for Chelsea. And it showed.

Although not many people, including his own players and especially the media, understood him I found his bizarre conversations and thoughts absolutely enthralling. Perhaps it was because he was one of my all-time heroes as captain of the Double team, that I warmed to him more than most.

Maybe, it was because I liked to listen to him, because somewhere there was enormous insight, if you were able to decipher it. He didn't last too long in management; he was far too intelligent and years ahead of his time, but he did put up with me, which was something, as I was young, over-enthusiastic, and probably over the top, ringing Danny at 6am in order to check out national daily newspaper stories, mostly tittle tattle, for the first of the evening editions of the *Evening News*. The first edition "copy" deadline was something quite bizarre in itself, at 7.15am, which meant that I prepared the stories overnight at home, on one of those old fashioned typewriters, and brought them into the office to be immediately subbed and raced off for the extra early edition.

Eventually Danny's wife must have complained because he picked me up on it and told me that he couldn't take any more 6am phone calls. I was surprised that he hadn't done this after the first one! I suppose he understood my predicament. That was Danny all over.

He told me that he had actually had a plaque made which he hung over his bed, and it said, "Don't take any calls from Harry Harris before 7am".

I didn't believe him. But with Danny you just didn't know for sure!

Harry Harris
By Steve Perryman

Whatever I might think of Harry Harris, and I have some very strong opinions, there is no doubt that he changed the face of local and national journalism.

When he arrived on the local North London *Weekly Herald*, my first impression was this was a guy who livened up the match reports. As a player, you are always protective of your own professional performance, and as captain of the side I felt a responsibility towards the entire team. So, I did not like the way he sometimes reported our games, there was a sharp edge we had not been used to from the local paper before.

But Harry did make the local paper more professional, and you would have to say, why not? However, we didn't sometimes like the way he stirred the waters, but then it didn't do him any harm as he made his reputation and moved onto the bigger stage with national newspapers with papers such as the *Daily Mail*, the *Daily Mirror* for many years, and the *Daily Express*, I have read his columns with interest, as he does produce some thought provoking articles.

However, I cannot be honest unless I also state my opinion that I felt he wielded far too much influence with certain Spurs chairmen, namely Irving Scholar and Sir Alan Sugar.

I always felt he was in Scholar's camp when I was a player at the club, and I know they had a very close relationship so Harry had the inside track. I accept that Irving and Harry had the best interests of the club at heart as they are both Spurs fans but Irving was the first of the new breed of chairmen, and while his heart was in the right place as far as his love for Spurs is concerned, I did have my run ins with him over the 1984 UEFA Cup bonuses. Irving also drove his first manager, Keith Burkinshaw, potty with the amount of phone calls! That's not to say I didn't have my own dispute with the manager over a new contract!

As for Alan Sugar, I felt, from working on the inside as Ossie's assistant, that Harry was a tool for Sugar, and for that reason I took a dislike to the way Harry operated as an ally of Sugar's which no doubt suited his career. In fairness I did have, and probably still have, a jaundiced view of anything to do with Sugar, and I am not going to elaborate why. Perhaps Harry is a touch unfortunate that he has been dragged into it, because of my views on the then chairman.

Harry used Sugar as much as he thought he was using Harry. The result was that Harry had exclusive stories and an incredible "in" with one of the most powerful men in the country. But this was *my* club they were playing with, and so at times it all made me very angry.

I wouldn't describe Harry as one of the "suits" who were infiltrating the board rooms and having far too much influence on the management of the clubs, because he was a journalist doing his job and getting some damn good stories in his papers.

spurs art **no.23** Steve PERRYMAN

To Paul "THE ARTIST" — MY HONOUR TO BE DRAWN BY SUCH A MAN!

The reason I took an exception is that Harry never saw the real inside story of the Sugar regime with Sugar's appointed chief executive Claude Littner and the way he operated. The finer details of what really went on behind closed doors are for another day, when *my* book is published!

I was hopeful somewhere along the line that someone would stand up and disagree with Sugar but he had surrounded himself with too many yes men, such as Littner.

Equally, I am not saying I was pro- or anti- Terry Venables, nor am I saying I am pro- or anti- Sugar in their personal fight about what they got up to inside the club.

So, perhaps it is harsh to blame Harry for doing his job and finding out as much as he could. Sugar though, I am sure, used Harry to gain information about the wider game. Sugar loves the press when it suits him but hates things in the press when they are critical of him. If it doesn't suit Sugar than there can be big trouble.

Also, I felt the way he ran the club put extra pressure on his manager, and it became intolerable for Ossie and myself at times. Contrast that to the way Sir Alex Ferguson used to run Manchester United, there were no directors interfering, nobody telling him who to buy or sell. One season, he had five draws in as many games at the start of the season and it might have looked like a crisis time, but it wasn't. There was no panic and he went on to win the Premier League and the Champions League.

I had my run-ins with Sugar when I was Ossie's assistant to

the extent that I fell out of love with football and even Tottenham - that's how bad it got for me, anyway.

I am sure Harry will give his own unique insight into what he feels went on between Venables and Sugar in this book. And, if he's writing about 50 odd years as a Spurs fan, I am convinced it will be something no Spurs fan would want to miss. Equally, his take on the broader aspects of the game would be of immense interest to every fan of football. Even though I am sure it will be more subjective than objective!

John Grimsdell
Encounters with my heroes!

This picture (right) was taken the night after Spurs beat Wolves in the FA cup semi-final in 1981. Steve was opening an extension to a stand at my local football club, Beaconsfield United, with former Head of FIFA Sir Stanley Rouse. I was 19 and Steve is my all-time Spurs hero, I was so nervous when I asked him for this photo. I was in awe of the man and still am, as you can see in the other picture!

This photo was taken when myself and a mate managed to get into the players' bar area for the legend induction for Steve Perryman and Jimmy Greaves. Sadly, Jimmy wasn't well enough to attend, so me and my mate just worked ourselves around the room chatting to all the players.

The large photo of the players I took for Mickey Hazard (you can tell as he's the only one looking at his own camera!) as he was struggling with his phone for his social media page. At the end of the evening there was an auction for a signed Spurs legends shirt, the bid got up to about £1400 when I caught Steve Perryman's eye, he nodded and I waved and this was taken as a bid of £1500!

I was hoping someone else would bid and that pause lasted ages, fortunately someone else did bid! At the end we left to find my car blocked in, I wasn't impressed until John Pratt and Mark Falco came along and apologised. What a night!

There is a story behind this shirt. It was an evening fixture versus Aston Villa to celebrate 125 years of Tottenham Hotspur. I was walking along the High Road just past the West Stand when, about 20 yards ahead of me, a black cab pulled up and out got Dave Mackay and his wife. I asked him if he'd sign my shirt, he said he would but what did I want him to write. I asked him to put "To John, 100% Spurs, Dave Mackay" by the time he'd finished a small crowd had gathered asking him for autographs and he just turned around and said "that's the only autograph I'm giving" - I was walking on air!

Another story from a mate who was at the Chelsea/Spurs League cup final in 2008; my mate had a corporate invite and in the bar was Kenneth Branagh, award-winning actor, having a drink on his own and about ten yards away was Roger Lloyd-Pack, the actor who played Trigger in *Only Fools and Horses*, surrounded by people buying him drinks and having photos taken. My mate went over to Kenneth and said, "Fools & Horses, hey? One that got away maybe." He laughed and raised his glass.

I also recall a corporate occasion at Elland Road where Spurs were playing, the great 70's Leeds side were there and a couple of Spurs lads. As I left my table to go to the loo I saw the great John Charles sitting on his own having a beer and a cigarette, I went past and said hello, he stopped me and asked me to sit with him a while to chat, so I did, we talked football for about 15 minutes, meanwhile I was crossing my legs hoping not to let myself down! What a fantastic man to spend time with, when I got up to leave he shook my hand and thanked me for stopping to talk to him.

D J Bear, Gazza, Vinny and Fergie

The 1980's saw football terraces ringed with railings obstructing the fans' view of the game, in an attempt to maintain segregation between rival fans and stop hooligans invading the pitch. Watching football was now no longer FUN.

Then I had an idea and my good friend Peter Stewart, the editor of *Shoot!* Magazine to which I had been a contributor for 10 years, was the first one I turned to. I suggested a campaign for the magazine to promote SPORTSMANSHIP, FAIRPLAY AND FAMILY ENTERTAINMENT with the aid of a giant panda character. Peter Stewart agreed and after much thought I arranged a meeting at Lancaster Gate with the FA's media specialist Glen Kirton but, having failed to convince him, I decided to aim much higher – the government. I managed eventually to arrange a meeting with Prime Minister Maggie Thatcher who listened to my ideas and agreed it could work and Maggie set the wheels in motion, by giving it the THUMBS UP.

Peter Stewart was delighted and *Shoot!* Magazine heralded the news. But when I suggested a two-page spread for a Panda Bear club with art from the kids I could judge, with every child's birthday mentioned and a skills strip I would contribute – Peter Stewart shook his head, so I turned to *Match* Magazine and they AGREED.

I decided I would be the person inside the giant panda costume and I would call him D J BEAR – THE PANDA OF PEACE. Then, with the aid of five football mad youngsters from Dexters Football Club in Dorset, I arranged for each to have a newspaper bag slung across their shoulders with a different letter on each bag spelling out P – A – N – D – A. Each newspaper bag would be full of FREE football goodies and the five lads would hand out Panda Drinks, *Match* Magazines, Panini football stickers, and DJ BEAR would kick out lightweight plastic *Match* Magazine footballs into the crowd.

At every Football League club the players the opportunity to get involved especially Paul Gascoigne and Vinny Jones. Every Football League ground welcomed D J BEAR to their club with the free football goodies for the fans. The Football League

wasted no time in stepping in to join the campaign's success, by naming D J BEAR - The Panda of Peace, the Official Football League Mascot.

Then, just when it appeared the campaign was running out of steam, Alex Ferguson stepped in and walked to the centre circle to be photographed with D J BEAR to receive a SPORTSMANSHIP, FAIRPLAY AND FAMILY ENTERTAINMENT AWARD. Alex's gesture did the trick. The photograph made the national press and it was then onwards and upwards for the DJ BEAR Panda of Peace Campaign.

Finally, after a two year campaign THE RAILINGS CAME DOWN and I received a letter from the Football League thanking the D J BEAR campaign. I was especially happy that the DJ BEAR mascot had encouraged every football club to have their OWN MASCOT.

PT

Derek Kelly

I became a life time Tottenham Hotspur supporter through my father Alan Kelly who was born in Enfield and spoke fondly of watching players like Sir Alf Ramsey, Mel Hopkins, Tommy Harmer, Len Duquemin, Ted Ditchburn, George Robb and Ron Burgess of the great push and run team in the 1950's managed by Arthur Rowe. He then went on to watch the great double team in the 1960's managed by Bill Nicholson and spoke about watching John White and Cliff Jones flying up the wings, the G men Jimmy Greaves and Alan Gilzean scoring goals, Dave Mackay running the midfield, captained by Danny Blanchflower at the back with Bill Brown stopping the goals going in the net.

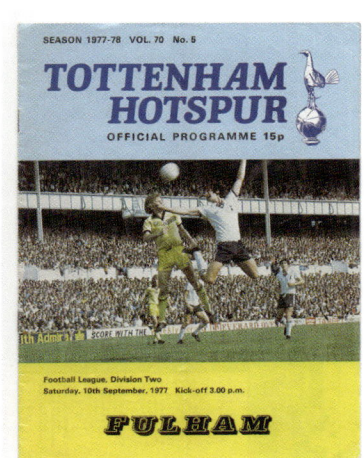

We watched numerous football matches over many years home and away, as far away as Newcastle. Here are a few matches that stand out from years gone by.

My first game I ever watched at White Hart Lane was Tottenham playing Fulham in League Division Two Saturday 10th September 1977 Kick Off 3.00pm. We all went as a family: Alan, Gwen, David and myself Derek. We had tickets for the East Stand in the middle tier better known as The Shelf and we stood at the front. There was a large crowd of 31,000 and we watched the players warming up before the kick off. My memory of the game was mostly of Tottenham being on the attack with Glenn Hoddle and Steve Perryman passing the ball in midfield to Peter Taylor flying down the wing and crossing to John Duncan and Chris Jones. Tottenham scored late in the second half when Chris Jones finished a cross from Peter Taylor and managed to beat Fulham 1 -0.

On another occasion, on 31st October 1984, my father had just got off duty from Oxfordshire fire station and said 'let's go up on the motorbike and watch Tottenham play Liverpool in the League Cup tonight'. We set off on the motorbike up the M40 and North Circular Road to White Hart Lane where we parked up just outside the ground. We went through the turnstiles and stood up in the Lower North Stand just to the side of the goal watching the players warm up with a large crowd of 38,000. The match kicked off and started well for Tottenham who went 1-0 up early on with Glenn Hoddle passing to Tony Galvin who raced through and shot at the goalie Bruce Grobbelaar which hit him on the chest

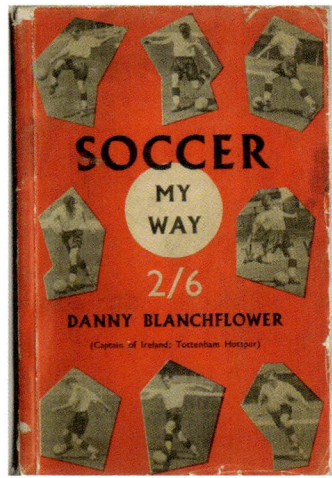

Derek lives a stone's throw away from Blenheim Palace – Sir Winston Churchill birth place - and the last time we met up he insisted on taking me for a visit to the very room where the great man was born, and to see his grave at St Martin's Church in Bladon just outside the Blenheim Palace grounds - PT

and rebounded out to Clive Allen who put the ball in the net. Mark Falco also had a header cleared off the line by Sammy Lee after it beat Bruce Grobbelaar. The game was evenly matched between both teams and the referee blew the final whistle for full time with a win for Tottenham 1-0.

We also went to the first live televised league football match on 2nd October 1983 Tottenham playing Nottingham Forest managed by Brian Clough. They had Chas and Dave playing music before the kick off in the South Stand and the atmosphere was electric with an attendance of 30,000. The game was exciting at both ends of the football pitch with Nottingham Forest scoring first through Colin Walsh after Tottenham gave it away in their own half. In the second half Garry Brooke came on for Alan Brazil and Tottenham had more of the game with Garry Brooke crossing twice, once for Gary Stevens to head in for the first goal and then the second time for Mark Falco heading towards the goal for Steve Archibald to tap in to the net at the end of the game making it a 2-1 win to Tottenham.

On my birthday my father and I went up to Goodison Park to see Tottenham play Everton on the 29th November 1997. There was 36,000 at the game and Tottenham didn't play well in the first half it was all in Everton's favour with ex Tottenham player Nicky Barmby shaving the crossbar. Tottenham came out in the second half and began to get on top and in the last quarter period Andy Sinton crossed from the left and Ramon Vega headed in from close range to put Tottenham in the lead. A few minutes later David Ginola picked the ball up in the centre of Everton's half and ran wide left into their box and shot with his left foot which beat Everton's goalie Neville Southall and made it 2-0 to Tottenham which was the final score.

Keith Burkinshaw

Taking over following the disastrous and brief reign of Terry Neill, Keith took Spurs down into the Second Division before storming to promotion, transforming the game by signing Ossie Ardiles and Ricky Villa and winning three major trophies in the early 80s with a superb team playing in the Spurs tradition.

KEITH BURKINSHAW ranks as one of Tottenham Hotspur's most successful managers. He served at White Hart Lane from 1976 to 1984, winning two FA Cups and the UEFA Cup. The FA Cup triumphs were in successive seasons, 1981 and 1982, in an era of Spurs greats which included Burkinshaw's key signings of Argentine World Cup winners Osvaldo Ardiles and Ricardo Villa. The UEFA Cup win came over R.S.C. Anderlecht in 1984 which proved to be Keith's final game in charge.

He had been a coach at Newcastle United from 1968 until 1975 when he was sacked as part of a cost-cutting exercise after which Terry Neill appointed him First Team Coach for Tottenham. When, in the summer of 1976, Neill resigned to become manager of Arsenal, the unassuming Burkinshaw was appointed in his place. Spurs were relegated that season but the board stood by him and they made a good start to their first season in Division Two since May 1950 with an emerging Glenn Hoddle, a young Neil McNab and Keith Osgood. Spurs lost the title but managed to get the vital point they needed at Southampton in the final game of the season for promotion; their goal average was superior to Brighton's solely because of a 9-0 thrashing of Bristol Rovers the previous October.

During that close season, the World Cup was held in Argentina. Within days of that competition concluding, Spurs had sensationally signed two members of the winning World Cup squad, Osvaldo Ardiles and Ricardo Villa, plus a centre-half from Fulham, John Lacy. Villa scored on his debut at Nottingham Forest, while Ardiles quickly forged a partnership in midfield with a maturing Glenn Hoddle. There was a spectacular 7-0 thrashing by Liverpool, where Tommy Smith was heard to dismiss Ardiles as a 'Fancy Dan' who would disappear when the winter months came, but Spurs enjoyed a good FA Cup run to the 6th Round, and finished the season in 11th place.

The following season saw them slip down the table but another good run in the Cup saw them reach the 6th Round again. Probably the high point of that season was winning at Old Trafford, when Glenn Hoddle was forced to replace Aleksic in goal and kept a clean sheet, and Ardiles scored the only goal of the match seconds from the end of extra time.

In the summer of 1980 Burkinshaw signed Steve Archibald and Garth Crooks to form a new strike partnership. The pair gelled from the start and they scored the majority of the goals over the season. That season Spurs returned to Wembley for the first time since 1971 for the Centenary Cup final against Manchester City. Ricky was awful in the first match and was substituted midway through the second half by which time Tommy Hutchison had put City ahead and it looked as though Spurs were about to lose a proud record of never having lost a Wembley final. But late on Spurs won a free-kick and Hoddle's shot took a wicked deflection off Hutchison, who thus scored for both teams!

In the replay, Villa fired them ahead after only five minutes and apart from a short spell where the Mancunians equalised and led, Spurs were the better team - Garth Crooks equalising midway through the second half. Then came the moment that has been replayed millions of times on TV. Tony Galvin was running lazily down the left wing, and slipped the ball to Villa, who dodged round one City defender, then another, drew City 'keeper Joe Corrigan and slipped the ball over him before turning and racing to where Burkinshaw sat applauding, like the rest of us, in sheer disbelief at what we'd just witnessed.

Burkinshaw, a typically taciturn Yorkshireman, was not entirely happy because Spurs had only finished 14th in the League. Just before the start of the 1981-82 season Spurs bought Gary Mabbutt from Bristol Rovers, despite the fact he was diabetic and needed regular injections of insulin. The side set off on what was to be a long, gruelling season with an appearance at Wembley against League Champions Aston Villa in the Charity Shield which was drawn 2-2, Mark Falco, deputising for the injured

The Two Bs, Bond and Burkinshaw, agree that the two Hs, Hoddle and Hutchinson, have the sort of class that no blackboard planning can cope with. They can decide a match in a split-second of sorcery.

Hoddle and Hutchinson have both been criticised for trying to do too much on the ball when directness might pay off.

Cesar Menotti, manager of the Argentine national team, defends Hoddle. "He's a world-class player who can perform delicately under pressure at breath-taking speed. A staggering fact of football is that the best Europeans rarely exceed 90 seconds of possession in an entire game.

"Franz Beckenbauer had a reputation for holding on to the ball yet seldom for longer than 10 seconds. He appeared to hold the ball longer than most because when it was hit to him, he'd control it without trapping it, turn and go past a player, covering something like 10 yards in the same time a typical English player took to bring the ball under control."

Ossie Ardiles of Spurs says, "Spurs play a typical Continental game. They play the ball from the back and work it through midfield. It's good to watch and a joy to play."

John Bond's City are different. Bond says: "I've always believed in direct football, knocking it up and getting into the box as quickly as possible. It's what Jack Charlton calls a 'sophisticated Third Division style.'"

Bond is proud of Hutchinson, who he claims adds width to his attack going past players and turning defences with the mazy runs that have earned him international honours but no medals ...yet.

Strikers Steve Archibald and Garth Crooks are the two that most people believe can win it for Spurs, but let skipper Steve Perryman have the last word: "Old-time Spurs supporters love telling me about great players they have seen at White Hart Lane, but I can't believe any of them had more skill than Hoddle. He's in a class of his own."

SUNDAY PEOPLE 5TH MAY 1981

Crooks, scoring two great goals. Back in the Cup Winners' Cup for the first time since 1967, Spurs made good progress until they were drawn against Barcelona in the semi-final. Graham Roberts scored a vital goal in the first leg at Tottenham, but they crashed in Spain, losing 1-0. In the League Cup they returned to Wembley, only to lose to Liverpool 3-1 in extra time, having come within four minutes of winning the final. The league slipped beyond their reach when they had to play 18 League matches between the beginning of March and the end of the season, Spurs eventually finished 4th but Spurs beat Arsenal, Leeds, Aston Villa, Chelsea and Leicester to return to Wembley again to face Queen's Park Rangers in the Cup Final.

After Terry Fenwick, then playing for QPR, had struck to force injury time, Hoddle having put Spurs ahead, the replay saw a Hoddle penalty give Spurs the win that gave them the Cup but Ardiles and Villa were not at Wembley with Tottenham as both had fled the country following the outbreak of war between the UK and Argentina over the Falklands. Ricky didn't return while Ossie went on loan to PSG for a season before returning in 1983-84.

Season 1982-83 saw Spurs set off on another four-pronged assault. They lost possession of the Charity Shield to Liverpool, who beat them 1-0 at Wembley and were knocked out of the League Cup by Burnley, who crushed them 4-1 and 2-0 at Everton in the FA Cup. Their interest in Europe ended when a Karl-Heinz Rummenigge inspired Bayern Munich side beat them 4-1 in Munich after a draw at Tottenham but changes were already afoot that would lead to Burkinshaw's departure. Paul Bobroff and Irving Scholar had engineered a hostile take-over of the club and sold a new tranche of shares to make Tottenham a publicly-owned company with a listing on the Stock Exchange, the first such football club to do so.

Burkinshaw, unhappy about the proposed changes, also fell out with striker Steve Archibald when he refused to allow the substitution of the Scot in the first home game of the season. Their relationship, never very strong, collapsed with the two protagonists completely ignoring each other. Despite the return of Ardiles from Paris St Germain, Spurs slipped to 8th in the League in 1983-84 and made early exits from both domestic Cup competitions but in Europe they got past Eire's Drogheda United and Feyenoord,

gained revenge over Bayern, before beating Austria Vienna and Hadjuk Split of Yugoslavia to reach the UEFA Cup Final where they would face Anderlecht. Unhappily, following a 1-1 draw in Belgium in the first leg, Steve Perryman was suspended for the home leg and missed out on the celebrations but Spurs won the Cup on penalties following a 1-1 draw, with goalkeeper Tony Parks making the vital save.

Keith Burkinshaw announced his resignation the next day. Looking at the new West Stand he made the withering observation, "There used to be a football club over there!" Keith rarely relives the ending of his time at Spurs as it brings back too many painful memories, but he told me, "the proudest, most memorable moment was winning our first trophy, the FA Cup. We had some great times with a great team back then, but the club hadn't won anything since Billy Nick's day and winning the FA Cup was a huge achievement, with some great players, playing good football, but a trophy to show for it all, so that would rank as the highlight of all my years as manager of Spurs.

"The saddest… well, leaving the club the way that I did. Regrets, yes, for sure, plenty. It was the saddest moment of my Spurs time, leaving the day after winning the UEFA Cup. I left straight away, it was awful. With the players we had, the players coming through the ranks, I was sure we would push on and have even more success, although of course, nothing is guaranteed in football, so I cannot be absolutely sure.

"The directors and owners thought they had Alex Ferguson wrapped up. There was a lot going on behind my back that you only get to realise after you've left. It was one of those things where the owners thought they knew better than the manager, and to be fair, times haven't changed too much in that respect generally in football.

"For me, one of the most important, if not the single most important aspects of football, should be man-management. Yet, man-management is one of the things most missing in the game, back then, and even now. It should be a big factor in football, man-management of directors and owners, man-management of the coach with their players.

"It was also sad knowing that there were so many talented young players we had been bringing through, and the club let about five or six of them go. Most of them went to Norwich and they reached the quarter-finals in Europe a few years on. Those kids had the potential to be really good players at Tottenham, but they didn't keep hold of them."

Keith is the second most successful manager in Tottenham's history after the legendary Bill Nicholson but left for a succession of jobs in the Middle East, including the Bahrain national team, then Zambia and Sporting Lisbon before returning to England to manage Gillingham. He was then appointed Chief Scout for Glenn Hoddle and Ossie Ardiles at Swindon Town and in May 1992 he became assistant to Ardiles at West Bromwich Albion. He also had a spell as Director of Football and caretaker manager at Aberdeen, before becoming the assistant manager of Watford, where he helped the club reach the Premier League in 2006.

Chairman Irving Scholar did indeed believe he had already lined up Sir Alex Ferguson to succeed Burkinshaw in May 1984, insisting that he had shaken hands with the Scot, and considered the deal to be done. Scholar said: "The truth was that I had been talking to and negotiating with Alex Ferguson about a deal. He and I had very long and detailed discussions. I told him that I was a very old-fashioned type of chap and that the most important thing was that once you agree something, once you shake someone's hand, it's in concrete. Once you do that, then you do not — under any circumstances whatsoever — you do not go back on it. It's over. I told him that, when I first met him. So we had this big thing about the handshake."

Scholar, a property tycoon who took control of Tottenham in 1982, knew that Burkinshaw planned to quit at the end of the season because of his dislike of the new business model. Ferguson, though, has his own version of events and claimed that Spurs were not prepared to give him the five-year contract he wanted to burn his bridges at Aberdeen at a time when he was dominating the game up in Scotland, having just secured the League and Cup double. Scholar also believed that when Manchester United came calling a few years later, Ferguson had a bigger incentive to leave Aberdeen.

Peter Shreeves

Peter Shreeves, who had been elevated through the ranks at Spurs by Burkinshaw, leaving the youth team to take charge of the reserves before he was appointed assistant manager in 1980. Shreeves enjoyed two spells as Tottenham boss, leading them to a third-place finish in 1985 and then from 1991-92 during the Venables/Sugar experiment. He brought a wealth of experience in the Spurs hot-seat.

It seems crazy now but Real Madrid were underdogs when they arrived at White Hart Lane for the first leg of their UEFA Cup quarter-final in March 1985. A recent run of just one win in 10 matches had taken them out of the race for La Liga, as Terry Venables' Barcelona were walking away with the title — Madrid would go on to finish fifth.

Shreeves could not have asked for a better start to his Tottenham reign after taking over from Keith Burkinshaw. Sitting second in the table behind Everton, the club were aiming to win their first league title since 1961. In contrast to Real, their run to the last eight of the UEFA Cup had been relatively stress-free; a 9-0 aggregate win over Braga was followed by a 4-2 win against Club Brugge. In the 3-1 victory over Bohemians Prague in the third round, Hoddle and Graham Roberts left the pitch with stitches during a bruising second leg in Prague, with Roberts also picking up a booking that kept him out of the first leg of the quarter-final at White Hart Lane. Given Real Madrid's European home record, Tottenham were desperate to take a sizeable advantage to the Bernabéu. Real were nothing like the teams of their notable brilliant past and nothing like the force of today. Yet with talent such as José Antonio Camacho, Uli Stielike, Ricardo Gallego, Emilio Butragueño, Santillana and Jorge Valdano, they had enough to threaten Tottenham's proud record of never losing a home match in Europe.

With Paul Miller and Tony Galvin fit, Gary Stevens moved to centre-back to fill in for Roberts and Mickey Hazard returned to the team, confidence was high in the Spurs camp but a determined Real left London with a slender lead. The only goal came after

14 minutes, a crucial away goal. For the first time in 44 ties in European competition, Spurs had failed to score at home.

"It doesn't please me to say that Real played some superb stuff at times," said Shreeves at the time. "This is a night when we must salute the victors. It will need a special performance in the return game if we are to get through." As the crowd of 39,914 filed out of White Hart Lane, the Tottenham PA announcer boldly pronounced, "This tie is far from over."

After Spurs first win at Anfield since 1912, confidence was high going to Madrid but Mark Falco had a goal disallowed and Steve Perryman was sent off three minutes later as Real progressed 1-0 on aggregate and went on to lift the trophy. Shreeves would never experience such highs again. Five defeats in Tottenham's remaining league fixtures — all suffered at White Hart Lane — left them third in the First Division.

Shreeves' debut season had been impressive. No debut Spurs manager since has improved on his third-place finish in 1984-85 until Mauricio Pochettino's Tottenham finished runners-up to Leicester City in 2016-17. Having been top on New Year's Day 1985 following a win at Arsenal, a poor run of home form in the second half of the season saw Spurs lose 6 out of 8 games and, but for a number of serious injuries, they would have been much closer to runaway champions Everton.

Throughout the following season Spurs were constantly in mid-table. It had started well with a 4-0 home win over Watford with new signings Paul Allen and Chris Waddle scoring. That put them as early leaders but it was downhill for the rest of the season. Following a win over West Ham on Boxing Day, Spurs went until late February without a league win, taking one point from six games. Spurs then lost at home to Liverpool and dropped to 13th.

Amid talk of unrest in the dressing room, it was clear Shreeves would be leaving White Hart Lane in the summer. From early March Spurs results showed a great improvement with only one defeat, at Upton Park, in 12 games. The sequence of results included eight wins with a number of high-scoring victories starting with a 5-0 home win over West Bromwich Albion. They also won 4-1 at Leicester City and finished the season by scoring 14 goals in their final three games; 5-2 at Queen's Park Rangers and 4-2 and 5-3 home wins over Aston Villa and Southampton respectively. The only blemish in Tottenham's record to the end of the 1985-86 season was a 2-1 defeat at Upton Park to a rampant West Ham team that would storm to a close third behind the Merseyside giants, the Hammers highest-ever league finish.

In the previous game they had defeated Arsenal at the Lane, but at Upton Park West Ham took a first half lead. Ossie Ardiles equalised within five minutes but West Ham regained the lead two minutes before the interval. Although Clive Allen hit the post in the second half after replacing Ardiles, Spurs suffered their first defeat in five games. Tottenham finished 10th and the late run of results came too late to save Shreeves. Having started life as a taxi driver, now it was time to call "taxi for Peter Shreeves" as he was replaced by David Pleat.

Peter remains well-liked by the Spurs players he managed and is held in high esteem by Spurs fans. I always enjoyed his company, and felt that his best role was "looking after" Keith Burkinshaw. He often needed to be Keith's minder, his punch bag with the players if the manager was being too strict or aloof. There was never a dull moment in those days, as you would often be privy to some of the more bizarre goings on.

A flight back from one of Spurs' European adventures provided one such bizarre episode: I watched a furtive Shreeves following Burkinshaw as he paced up and down at the check-in desk looking very grim. I was part of a small contingent of senior football writers who accompanied them on their big European excursions. Keith was a serious type, but his assistant had a much more affable streak, a contrast to the dour Yorkshireman. At this time the media would travel with the team, with the media companies lightening the financial load of the trips by footing part of the bill. So, on the morning of our return flight, it was not a surprise to see the managerial pair together, as they would invariably be side by side, but on this occasion it soon became apparent that all was not well by the pair's body language. Both were extremely agitated to say the least.

A conversation between them went on for some considerable time and was getting more heated by the minute. We were all wondering what was going on. Then it quickly became apparent the cause of the problem. Enter England goalkeeper Ray Clemence being supported by Spurs staff dragging him towards the departure lounge. One of the country's most respected players had a very stupid grin on his face, and he was bellowing out a

song at the top of his voice that ensured no one would miss his entrance! It should be pointed out at this juncture that he was no Harry Redknapp or Sam Allarydce - he couldn't sing! Yet that minor detail didn't stop Ray signing at the top of his voice, all the way up the stairs of the plane, as he was helped to his seat. Once seated he instantly feel asleep, and we were left in blissful silence. As he drifted off into a very deep sleep all was very peaceful again, except for Burkinshaw's mood; the manager was fuming, and it was easy to see why. Clemence had been out the night before and had got back to his hotel bedroom after all the Spurs party had left the hotel for the airport. Clearly, therefore, no one saw him returning. Worse still, no one missed him. Oblivious at the time to the entire Spurs staff and the players, he was still in his bed fast asleep when a couple of the Spurs staff were assigned to return to the hotel to find him while the charter flight was held up.

Peter asked the small group of journalists who were travelling with the team not to report this incident and we all agreed. It was a vastly different era in the early 80s. For a start, these days the media party no longer travel with a team or stay in the same hotel, unless it cannot be avoided. The barriers between press and players have gone up over the years, keeping pace with the way the media has mushroomed. Now there can be five or six representatives from one newspaper if a game is big enough and warrants blanket coverage, and even in routine games with the big clubs there might well be two reporters and a news man present. Whereas back then there would be just the one to file a match report and perhaps a bit of transfer gossip, so it was far easier for clubs to control the output, particularly if things went wrong as they did on that day. The press pack would often go out drinking with the players, I've even been to a nightclub with a group of players with a London club after a European tie abroad, and no one worried about anything being reported in the press, we would keep their minor indiscretions to ourselves if we were invited into their inner sanctum, which is why no one ever read bout Ray's boozy flight home - until now of course!

Naturally, both Spurs and Liverpool fans were distraught at the passing of Ray Clemence in November 2020 after a long cancer battle at the age of 72. Ray won five league titles and three European Cups with Liverpool between 1967 and 1981, but was diagnosed with advanced prostate cancer in 2005. As well as league and European Cup success, Clemence also won the FA Cup, League Cup and two UEFA Cups during his time at Anfield. He made 470 league appearances for them before joining Tottenham. During his seven-year spell at Spurs he helped the club retain the FA Cup in 1982 and clocked up 330 appearances. Capped by England 61 times, Ray also worked on the Spurs' coaching staff and was inducted into the club's Hall of Fame in November 2014. He made his England debut in 1972 and spent the majority of his 11-year international career in a battle with Peter Shilton for the number one shirt. He captained the Three Lions for the first and only time in a narrow defeat to Brazil at Wembley in 1981 and later took up the role of goalkeeper coach with the Football Association.

HH

Gerry Armstrong

From time to time "offending" journalists are placed in a manager's sin bin, banned from a press conference or two, kept out of the loop of any inside information the manager might have wanted made public, usually for his own ends and, of course, generally treated like a pariah for having the audacity to step out of line in some way.

Often the "offence" might be trivial; being ultra-critical of the team, or more importantly, critical of the manager and his tactics. Maybe there has been a misquote that he has taken the wrong way, perhaps an over the top headline that caused him some kind of embarrassment with his players or worse still with his chairman. It doesn't take an awful lot to trigger a fit of pique from a manager, particularly one under pressure, and the majority are always under some sort of pressure. Some deal with it with a deliberate hard-line approach designed to keep the media pack under control, and one of the best control freaks with the media was Sir Alex Ferguson who used effective punishments for anyone who stepped out of line by causing them as much grief as he could in preventing them from performing their job. In the case of the BBC, he refused to speak to them for years after an offending broadcast.

I was relatively new to the job of football reporting, still working for the North London *Weekly Herald* group of newspapers, when for some reason Keith Burkinshaw got the hump with me about something I had written, and I was shunned by him. Now, that was pretty damn tricky for me, as I was covering just about everything that moved in relation to the club, and it was tough if you were being ostracised by the most important man there. In fact, he even told me that he would not cooperate with me for a full month; that was my punishment for upsetting him.

Players at any club like nothing better than to "wind up" their manager if they can, and at this time the Tottenham stars were expert at this irritating little game, and they liked nothing better than winding up Keith, who didn't see the funny side of their many practical jokes.

On this occasion several players were in the treatment room, and Gerry decided he would use me as a means of winding up the manager. He kept lookout at the door awaiting the manager's arrival, as Keith was always quite predictable about the time he would check out the injured players prior to the weekend's game. When he spotted him, Gerry rushed over to the phone and pretended to be deep in a meaningful conversation with me, while also pretending not to have noticed Keith entering the medical room.

"Sure Harry, no problem, we'll let you have the team for Saturday" he said loudly. It was hard for Gerry and the treatment room full of players to hide their sniggering, but Keith hadn't noticed the players mocking him, his blood pressure was quickly rising, as Gerry continued, "We've got some injury problems, Harry, so I will have to make a shrewd guess based on our training this morning what the team will be; Jennings..."

Keith was bright red by this time, according to Gerry, who loved telling me the entire story afterwards. Soon, Keith was shouting at Gerry, who told him that the players always gave this particular journalist the team every week. As it was intended to do, that only made Keith redder in the face and on the verge of exploding with rage. It went on for quite some time until the players couldn't restrain themselves any longer, and when, finally, Keith realised it was just an elaborate wind up, he stormed out.

The real funny side of it, of course, was that the players always fed me inside information, and Gerry would often help me out with team news without giving too many secrets away. Gerry liked a laugh, but he was a true professional, and would never damage the team's chances of success by giving away the kind of information that the opposition needed to know.

Gerry Armstrong would later score one of the great World Cup goals for his country and on the back of that strike against Spain bagged a lucrative move to Real Mallorca and, having mastered the language, remains to this day a highly respected and knowledgeable TV and radio pundit in Spain. At one time he was assistant manager to the Northern Ireland team under Lawrie Sanchez. Gerry and I remain firm friends to this day, and for all the thousands of people I have ever met in football, Gerry Armstrong is one of the guys I have become closest to over the years.

Osvaldo Ardiles

Ossie's Going to Wembley,
His Knees Have Gone all Trem-bley,
Come on you Spurs, Come on you Spurs...

Ossie's arrival at White Hart Lane with compatriot Ricky Villa was a landmark in English football history. It is credited with opening the floodgates for foreign footballing imports. Ossie and Ricky were one of the main reasons for a change of direction for me, as their arrival convinced me I needed to return to London to cover this momentous event, rather than remain in the North East. The call to return to the capital and back to the Lane was over-powering. The year was 1978: Spurs had been promoted and somehow recruited two of the world's best players from newly-crowned world champions Argentina. It was too much. I was mentally packing my bags as soon as the news of their signings broke in the press, with wall-to-wall TV coverage of the amazing events.

A switch to the *London Evening News* was the start of my journey through some of the major tabloid newspapers in Fleet Street. Upon my return home the football was breathtaking, not at first, but eventually there was a new dawn of exhilarating football with the Argentinians combining so beautifully with the flamboyance of Glenn Hoddle, culminating in a wonderful Cup final triumph. And who can forget the build up to that final with 'Ossie's Dream', suddenly Chas and Dave ruled the airways, it was magical. It was a good career move too. Four fabulous years on the *Daily Mail*, 18 on the *Daily Mirror* and nearly seven on the *Daily Express*.

The Spurs team of the 80s brought back all the old memories of stylish football, exhilarating goals, and mouth-wateringly good individuals. Up front Spurs boasted a lethal combination in Steve Archibald and Garth Crooks. I got to know Garth on a personal level after he had finished his playing career. Garth

is now with the BBC, and takes an awful amount of stick for his long-winded questions to managers and players after games, but he is a highly respected figure, who has been chairman of the Sports Institute. Garth regularly calls for some inside gossip on certain subjects he is featuring on *Football Focus*, and he has been around to my home a few times to conduct interviews for the Saturday lunch time programme.

Ossie Ardiles and Ricky Villa have been friends of mine for many years, and it was a great pleasure for me to 'direct' a 60-minute film documentary on the life and times Ossie. The

Legends Lives documentary was filmed with the World Cup at Wembley, in the Spurs dressing rooms beside the shirts of current heroes Kane and Alli, and striding out at the Lane for the very last time before the stadium redevelopment. A stellar cast were lined up to be interviewed to tell some enthralling inside stories about him: Mauricio Pochettino, Jürgen Klinsmann, Chris Hughton, Teddy Sheringham, Glenn Hoddle, Garth Crooks, Ricky Villa, Mario Kempes, and Gerry Armstrong, among them.

For the film, I obtained an exclusive interview with Jürgen Klinsmann, who set up the filming personally out in LA, such is the German superstar's admiration for Ossie. Jürgen said in the film that he will always be grateful to Ossie for bringing him to English football. Klinsmann's striker partner, Teddy Sheringham, told the story of how Ardiles wanted to sign Diego Maradona for Spurs but changed his mind and signed Klinsmann instead. But Klinsmann said that his footballing career was inspired by watching Ardiles win the World Cup. "When I think of Ossie Ardiles, many, many things come into my mind. One major point was that I was 14 when I watched him playing in the 1978 World Cup, watched Argentina win the World Cup and his performances were admirable. His style of playing, his creativity, he was an inspiration, a master of the game.

"Many years later he became my coach and probably made the biggest change in my life when he brought me to Tottenham. I got the experience of English football through his eyes, his vision, his character and for that I will always be grateful. What I liked most about him was that he was always open minded, open to taking risks, never satisfied, as he always wanted to explore things and try things. Sure, it was a little bit risky – five forwards all the time! But it was fun!

"His personality was admirable, he reached out to people, he reached out to see the world. South America, Japan for many years, Paraguay, was one station, Israel another station, he never stopped. You had to admire that his brain was always seeking out new horizons, constantly challenging himself. For that he was a role model with what he has done, what he has achieved in his life – simply amazing."

Such was the close relationship between the two Argentines, Ardiles and Pochettino, that Mauricio was more than willing to offer his personal tribute in my film. Talking in the film the then Spurs manager said, "He represents a legend, not only for Tottenham, but for world football, and for Argentina he is one of the most important players ever. It was very special for me especially as I was six years old and I listen and the names I hear were Ardiles, Passarella, Kempes, so for me he was one of the best in the world. He is forever in the history of world football and he will always be a legend in football."

Former Spurs manager Terry Neill also took part in the film and he revealed it was "the worst decision of my managerial career" that he didn't sign Ardiles and Villa for the Gunners! But Neill, an Arsenal man in his heart and soul, contacted then Spurs manager Keith Burkinshaw with the idea of signing Villa while he was signing Ardiles. Neill always denies this part of the story whenever I mentioned it. He would insist that the Arsenal board vetoed any foreign signings as he had also lined up Johan Cruyff.

Ossie still lives in England and, speaking from his home in the Hertfordshire town of Hoddesdon, he told of his sheer joy of having been associated with Spurs for so long, "It has been a brilliant 40 years, an extraordinary adventure and, of course, I am still here. White Hart Lane has been a second home, not just for me, but for all the friends I've made in that time. My team-mates and the supporters as well.

"I must say when I first arrived the food was pretty terrible, we were not used to it at the beginning and we both had steak every day. But little by little over the years it has improved and now of course London is the food capital of the world. As for the weather, well, very bad, very bad. Now though I am used to it. It makes you appreciate it a lot more when the sun shines – there's always a silver lining, even to the weather here.

"I was very lucky to have arrived here with Ricky in '78, because England now is much more different to the England then, nothing like it is today. We were the first two, and at the time, no I

didn't have a clue the impact it would make. Yes, I understand it now. Back then it was a great, great adventure, a big, big adventure, but it was good to be with Ricky."

Ricky Villa achieved Tottenham immortality for one of the best ever — if not the best ever — Wembley FA Cup Final goal. Yet it was Ossie's winning mentality that delivered important trophies to the Lane, but also arguably one of the most catchy Cup Final songs. "Ossie's Going To Wembley, His Knees Have Gone All Trembly. Come on You Spurs, Come On You Spurs", were the lyrics to the Chas & Dave song that has lingered longer than most Cup Final songs. It's still dusted off and sung with gusto by Spurs supporters at the merest hint of an FA Cup run. Ossie admits he hated it at first but the song grew on him! "It's a beautiful song, from when we won the FA Cup in 1981," he said "In the final, when Ricky scored such a wonderful goal. Although it all happened in 1981, it is still very much in the hearts of every Tottenham supporter. I didn't like it when I first heard it, but because the supporters remember the song it has become a beautiful song – but I am very, very surprised that the supporters still like it. I am very pleased when they now sing this song."

When asked about his greatest moment in English football he has little hesitation, "Well it was winning the 1981 FA Cup Final. We had a wonderful team, full of flair and quality, but up until that point we had won nothing. Winning the FA Cup gave us the confidence to be an even better team. Yes, there has been a lot of ups and downs, but I wouldn't change a thing. And to prove how much I love the country, and Spurs, I am still here, of course."

Ricky regularly comes to stay with Ossie, especially around Cup Final time, when he is much in demand. Ossie says: "When I first arrived I immediately felt that Tottenham was my second home and I always will. The more I stayed in this country, the more it felt like my second home."

A few years ago now Glenn Hoddle was voted as the greatest ever legend of the north London club by Spurs fans but Ossie was in the running. For the man himself, however, there was only one winner, "For me Glenn Hoddle was Spurs' greatest player of all time. I have heard that Bill Nicholson would have selected Ronnie Burgess, and many fans would go for Dave Mackay, but it is so hard when I have seen neither of these players. However I played with Glenn and I have seen him in training and in games, and he is the best as far as I am concerned. He was a genius."

Ardiles felt most honoured when former team-mate Paul Miller suggested that he would come out on top. The centre-half played alongside Ossie and Glenn in that memorable eighties Spurs team, and when asked to name his favourite Tottenham players he said, "this club has had some real greats and it is hard to examine the credentials of players you haven't seen, but Mackay is right up there, so too is Pat Jennings, and of course Glenn Hoddle, but I would vote for Ossie or Dave Mackay."

In January 2014, Ardiles and Villa were involved in a car crash in the Falklands during the filming of Camilo Antolini's documentary *White, Blue and White*. Ardiles sustained minor injuries in the accident, and required more than 20 stitches in his head. In April 2022, he underwent heart surgery. Thankfully he has made a full recovery and remains a Tottenham ambassador.

Tottenham's '81 Wembley Triumph

I was waiting for referee Clive Thomas to blow the final whistle. I believed the '81 Semi Final against Wolves had been won by goals from Archibald and Hoddle cancelling out the Wolves goal scored by Andy Gray, but instead of blowing up for full-time, Clive Thomas pointed to the penalty spot for what looked to me like a perfectly good tackle and Willie Carr scored. It went to extra-Time and with no goals scored, a REPLAY at Highbury.

At the time Clive Thomas was the featured referee in 'You Are The Ref', who would answer my many questions concerning the laws of the game. This popular feature had originally started as 'Hey Ref!' in 1957 in the *Sunday People* in which I was the 'referee' before moving on to *Shoot!* Magazine in which Stan Lover, chairman of the London Referees Society, answered the readers' questions before Clive 'The Book' Thomas took over. Somewhat peeved by the decision I phoned Clive for an explanation on the penalty for a foul on Kenny Hibbitt. "It was a penalty" said Clive, brooking no argument, "end of story." Fortunately Tottenham won the replay thanks to two goals from Garth Crooks and a Ricardo Villa rocket.

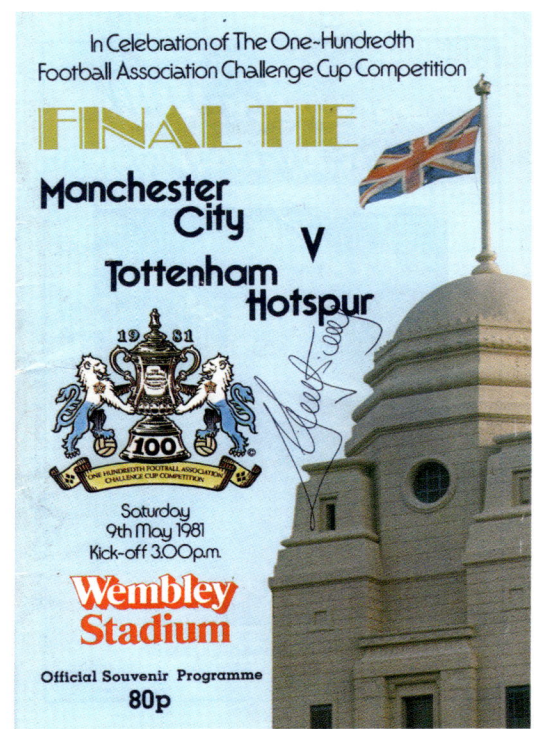

Tottenham were now to play Manchester City in the 100th FA Cup Final at Wembley. With just ten minutes remaining and with the Manchester City leading 1-0, Gerry Gow brought down Ossie Ardiles two yards outside the penalty box. Glenn Hoddle took the free-kick and the ball struck the shoulder of Tommy Hutchison and flew into the net for an own goal. Poor Tommy Hutchison had the distinction of having scored for both sides.

When Keith Hackett blew the final whistle after extra time, two very tired teams climbed the steps to be received by the Queen Mother, but neither side would receive the Cup. It was the first time in 58 years that the FA Cup Final was to be re-played at the home of football, Wembley and what a game! Ricky Villa opened the scoring for Spurs in the eighth minute but three minutes later Steve MacKenzie equalised for City with a spectacular volley. A Kevin Reeves penalty five minutes into the second half, which every Spurs fan felt was unfair, put City ahead. It was not until the 70th minute that Garth Crooks fired one home to draw Spurs level again. Then six minutes later Tony Galvin passed to Ricardo Villa who was thirty yards from

the City goal and the Argentinian proceeded to weave past four defenders before placing the ball passed Joe Corrigan in the City goal. This goal was voted Wembley Goal of the Century and it won Tottenham the FA Cup for the sixth time.

Like every Spurs fan in the ground that night I thought the City penalty was outrageous and unfair, I phoned referee Keith Hackett and asked for an explanation and funnily enough it was word perfect. "It was a penalty, Paul," said Keith. "The City player, Dave Bennett, was in the penalty area with a goalscoring chance when Paul Miller and Chris Hughton got Bennett caught up between the two of them. They were both to blame because Miller had his arm across him and Hughton caught his legs." Having watched replays closely I had to agree with Keith. I, along with all the other Spurs fans, had been caught up with the emotion of the Final.

Later I asked Keith if he would like to take over answering the YOU ARE THE REF readers' questions in *Shoot!* magazine and with no hesitation he said 'Yes' and we have remained firm friends ever since. Even now when I have a referee problem I will phone Keith, and as always I get the CORRECT EXPLANATION.

PT

The day Maradona played for Spurs!

Ossie was panicking. Diego was fast asleep and he was pacing up and down the hotel lobby. "Typical Diego" he moaned, shaking his head and fretting like I had never seen him before. Always super cool, this was the one time I saw Ossie Ardiles lose it. "Always asleep, sleep, sleep, sleep, he loves to sleep, and he's always late, late, late and he's late now…" for this was an important assignment. That night Diego Maradona was playing for Spurs in Ossie's testimonial against Inter Milan at White Hart Lane.

I was there to witness all the behind the scenes drama in getting Maradona to London in the first place, to get him and his substantial entourage from Heathrow to the airport, and then to awaken him from his slumbers so as not to miss the big kick off on what proved to be another memorable night at the Lane on May 1, 1986.

Because of my great friendship with Ossie, he had brought me with him to the hotel for a pre-arranged exclusive interview with Diego. What a coup! The *Mirror* were absolutely enthralled by the prospect, and the sports editor had put aside the back page and a two-page spread inside for the big interview with the world's greatest player.

Now I was beginning to catch the Ossie bug: the nerves, the fear, he would sleep through it all. Worse still, my interview was looking increasingly like it would be aborted. The plan, put into place meticulously by Ossie, was that as Diego would have arrived early that day, there would be plenty of time and opportunity long before Maradona left the central London hotel for North London, that I would be able to sit down for a relaxed interview. So, a chat with Diego, with Ossie interpreting, then I'd stay at the hotel to file the wad of copy to the office by phone, and then I could take my time getting to the game and watch it having already filed the story. There would even be time for the two Argentines to catch up on old times.

Not a chance.

When Diego eventually emerged from the lift with his entourage crammed in behind him, there was barely enough time to make it to the ground in time for kick off. Diego might have thought it was still early, but Ossie knew the peculiarities of the Seven Sisters Road.

Ossie suggested that I accompany them to the ground, and there was just enough time for a quick photograph with myself, Diego, his wife at the time, and Ossie outside the hotel, on the way to the car. At least it was worth the photographer's long and patient wait. He then hurried off with his precious picture to the office. The photograph of Maradona, Ardiles, and myself currently adorns my wall, alongside some signed shirts from Pelé, David Beckham, Ruud Gullit and a signed copy of George

Best's European Cup winning shirt - not a bad collection.

The day was still full of surprises, as Ossie said he would personally drive the three of us to the game, with me in the back seat, and Diego in the front passenger seat.

I sat there with my notebook and pen while Diego's entourage and wife followed in a couple of limos. I asked the questions and Ossie translated as he drove.

Diego was just a kid when he first got into the national side and Ossie looked after him, he was almost a father figure, giving him advice and helping him to settle in. Diego never forgot how much support he had from Ossie.

I also asked Diego if he would one day like to play in English football and he was very positive that he would, and if he did he would like to follow Ossie to Spurs. I know the club had made some attempt to see if that was possible, but it never really came close to happening. Still, it was headline news for me that Diego wanted to play in England.

I caught up with Ossie and Paul Miller in December 2008, for a Sky One show called *Off The Bar*, hosted by Matt Lorenzo at the Botanist on the Green pub in Kew. After recording the show, which just happened to coincide with the day Roy Keane quit as Sunderland manager, Ossie, Paul and myself enjoyed a quiet meal chewing over old times, and chatting about the day Maradona came to town to play in Ossie's big game.

Ossie recalled, "The game

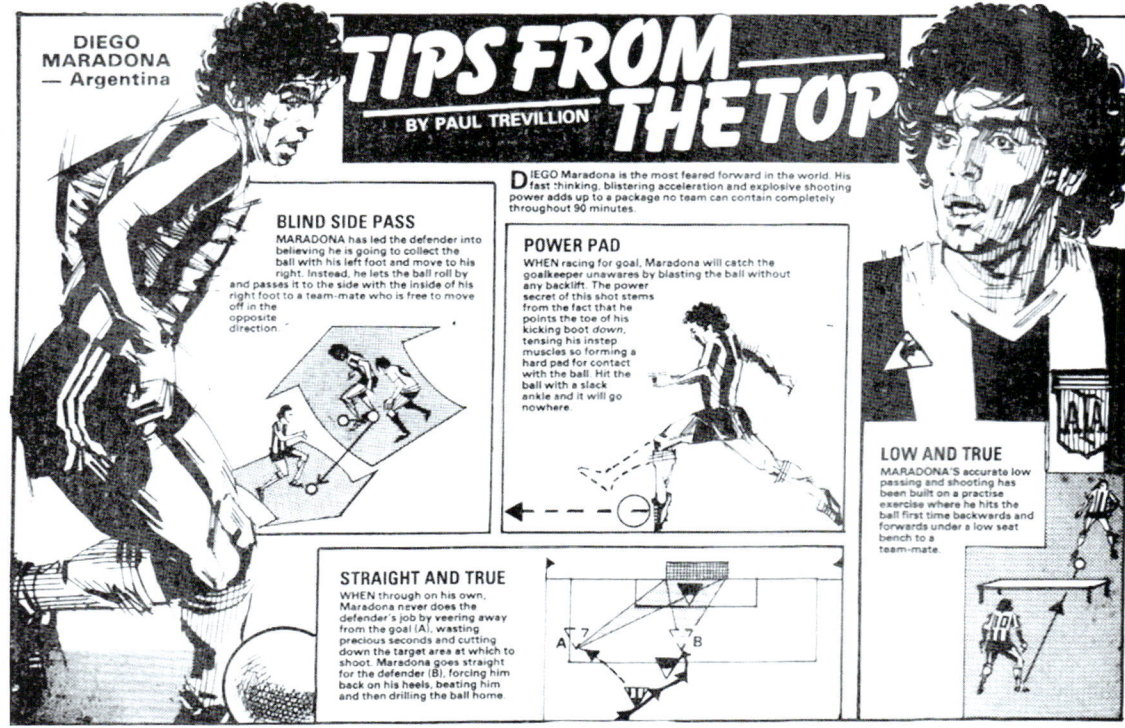

had to be delayed for 15 minutes because it took us so long to get there! Even so, it was worth waiting for. Everyone wanted to see Diego who was still then the best player in the world. That's why the ground was bursting to capacity."

Paul chipped in, "That was some game, Diego in a Spurs shirt playing for us and Liam Brady playing for Inter Milan. The brochure from Ossie's testimonial was some prize, particularly if it was signed by Diego. I sat in the dressing room and got Diego to sign a hundred copies! He was absolutely delighted to do so. My mum has got one somewhere, I gave a lot of them away. Here was the best player in our lifetime sitting next to us and signing our match programmes. He embraced us quite well I thought for someone so important in the game.

"And make no mistake, this was no testimonial. We were playing Inter, and we had Diego in our side. We wanted to win, and win badly. Me and Robbo (Graham Roberts) were kicking shit out of them, Pat Jennings came on for us in the second half and Chippie Brady scored against him, did him with 'the eyes' from a free-kick, but we won 2-1."

As you can see "Maxie" Miller took no prisoners as a player, and now he is just as uncompromising in his new life as an entrepreneur. With his City connections, he actually launched a bid to buy Spurs from Alan Sugar. He told me over lunch, "Backed by the Bank of Luxembourg and a consortium of four private investors I tried to buy Spurs from Sugar. I offered 85p a share at the time when they were trading at 80p a share but Sugar wouldn't entertain the bid. In fact he told me that I wasn't welcome at the club anymore. I bit my tongue but never said anything against him or the club. However I did tell Sugar, 'This will always be my club, it will never be your club.' No, I don't like him. But I have always kept my silence about what happened."

Ossie listened intently to his former team-mate, but declined to join in the anti-Sugar lobby – even though Sugar sacked him. Ossie explained, "I don't have a fucking problem with anybody! Managing Tottenham was my dream job of course it was, but I did a crap job, of course I did. I couldn't do the job the way I wanted to do and that is my deepest, biggest regret in football. I cannot blame Alan Sugar if I got it wrong. For me the circumstances are different to what happened to Paul. For many the dream job would be Real Madrid or Barcelona, but not for me, it was always Tottenham. I put so much into it…"

In those days the *Daily Mirror* had an awful lot of clout, particularly at a club such as Tottenham. The players knew I was close to the chairman and owners, and 'Max' added, "Monte Fresco was the photographer at the *Mirror* at that time, and he was a big Spurs fan and a lovely fellow. The Mirror was 'our' paper."

'Maxie' didn't score too many goals in his Spurs career but the header he powered into the Anderlecht net in the first leg of the 1984 UEFA Cup was pivotal in the club's history. He understandably looks back on that tie with great satisfaction having played such a major role in that triumph. But he had his doubts in that first leg as the team missed chance after chance. Miller praises the strength shown on the night by his co-defenders Graham Roberts, Chris Hughton and Danny Thomas which provided the platform for ultimate victory. "Looking back, it was a wonderful evening," said Maxie. "We had fantastic support from the Spurs fans behind the goal who made it feel like a home game for us... if we had won 3-0 Anderlecht could not have complained."

My Friend Diego
by Ossie Ardiles

Ossie was one of the first to pay tribute to his ex-team-mate following his death, tweeting: "Thank you dear Dieguito for your friendship, for your football, sublime, without comparison. Simply, the best football player in the history of football." He tweeted posted a photo of himself and his two sons along with Maradona at White Hart Lane: "Diego with my two sons... still in shock. Very very sad but I'm sure Dieguito will have peace now. Prayers and thoughts with his family and friends."

All our conversations would finish the same way... He would say it is very beautiful to be Maradona, but it is not easy to be Maradona.

First of all, it was a big, big shock when I heard the news of his passing. In many ways, it was news I had been expecting at some point but when it happened it was an incredible shock, whether I was prepared for it or not. A week earlier Ray Clemence passed away, and then Diego. It was a very sad time.

For me, Diego was one of the three I would always pick out as the very best in the history of the game. There are, of course, more players I could mention, but there are three when I ever mention the all-time greats — Pele, Maradona, and Messi. Of those three, Diego is the best.

Like Pele, Diego played at a time when it was much more difficult to play than now. Now nobody is allowed to touch you, but when Diego played there was always the chance of being injured, and it was always a question of when you would be hurt — and hurt by what I would call 'the bad boys', who were out to catch him.

It might have been incredibly difficult at the time he played, but he was extraordinarily skilful, tremendously gifted, an unbelievable talent. What would he be worth now? Even at that time he was the most expensive transfer of all time, and he would be the most expensive transfer now.

He will be remembered as a genius in football. You can see the extraordinary amount of interest that he generates. People like Ronaldo, or people like Messi, they couldn't even dream of having this kind of admiration. That was the Maradona phenomenon - all the time.

Diego came from Villa Fiorito on the outskirts of Buenos Aires. It's not quite a shanty town but it's very close to that. It was a poor background. In Argentinian football we have this myth about 'El Pibe' or the boy. It is the little, skilful boy footballer who succeeds against all the odds and makes it big, that is the legend behind 'El Pibe'. It's part of our culture. And Diego fulfilled that role absolutely. From where he was born, there was a sense of being against the law. It was a world where the police were the bad guys and the criminals were heroes, because you had to survive however you could. This is what Diego was. He had to survive and he would be prepared to do anything to do that. And survival for him was to win the game. And he would do anything to do it. Despite his background, money didn't really interest him. To be honest, he didn't need it. Wherever he went, everything was paid for him. Wherever he went they gave him a car or a watch… he would have one hundred watches at home, all better than the other. He never needed anything. He didn't carry cash. What for? But there were many people in his life who exploited that and cheated him but he never forgot his background and he felt at peace with the fans and poor people. He was a hero for them and they identified with them.

Presidents and kings would invite him and he would refuse. Or he would go and keep them waiting, arriving one hour late. He was always fighting with the powers that be: presidents of Argentina, the Pope, presidents of the USA, the FIFA president and people identified with him. I've seen this in India, in Jordan, in Japan. And in Latin America he was hugely popular because of what he represented. Only our former president, Juan Peron and his wife Eva Peron — Evita — have come close to his popularity with the poor. People wouldn't really appreciate the intelligence of Diego unless you shared a dressing room with him. He was incredibly sharp with the banter. There was no point getting into a verbal contest with him. You couldn't get the last word, he would always answer you back in a way that meant he won the argument. He was a graduate of the university of the street.

He always wanted to know things, especially about Europe. In Argentina at the time, they looked down on European football. The general feeling was 'they're strong, they run like mad but they can't play' but he wanted to know about Europe and at this time he was about to move to Barcelona, so he would ask me. He was humble despite being Diego. When we watched football on the TV in camp and someone made a mistake, he never joined in the laughter or mockery and he had an extraordinary respect for the guys of the 1978 team. He once picked his all-time Argentinian XI and six were from the 1978 team [Ossie was one of them].

My first memory of him was some time before this. Back in 1975, when we were playing with the national side at Boca Juniors stadium, La Bombonera, they would get a child to entertain the crowd before the game. This kid was at Argentinos Juniors, but he hadn't made his debut. He was 14 or 15 years old but he was

already a minor celebrity, juggling the ball before the games. And, to be honest, he was fantastic. We were national team players but we would go out to see him perform. He would be walking around the stadium with the ball, doing these extraordinary tricks as he talked to people and waved to the crowd. We were saying to each other: 'How can he even do this?' That was how I met my lifelong friend, Diego Maradona.

For the last few days I have been thinking about all the memories

"He was a sensation. But you know footballers. They can be very cynical… and we were saying: 'Well, of course, he's very good. But look at him! He's too small! He will never make it. We're talking about playing in the Argentinian first team'."

I have of him and thinking back to that time when he was a child. Within a year, we would meet him again at training for the national team. He was 15 or 16 by then. Cesar Menotti, our manager, would always bring a couple of young players to the sessions to make up the numbers, so that we could play 11 a side. The day came when Diego showed up, very humble, a bit nervous. To be honest, he was in awe of us. He was still a child, already a little bit stocky. You can imagine how sceptical we were. Of course, as soon as he played, we could see how good he was. He was a sensation. But you know footballers. They can be very cynical. We had seen so many young players who were extremely skilful but never made it. He was more skilful than any other but there was still this doubt. And we were saying: "Well, of course, he's very good. But look at him! He's too small! He will never make it. We're talking about playing in the Argentinian first team." This wasn't football for creative players. It was football for the baddies. Within a year, he had made his debut for the national team at the age of 16, when he came on for Leopoldo Luque against Hungary in 1977. And after that he was one of us.

The 1978 World Cup was approaching and it would be hosted in Argentina. Because of that, 25 players were taken out of club football and went to a training camp to work together for six months from January 1978. It was obvious he was brilliant. But I think it created a problem for Menotti. During difficult times in 1976-77, he had promised the squad of 22 that he would stick by us for the World Cup because we had stuck by him. And I don't think he felt he could break that promise.

And that is why, at the end of April 1978, Diego was one of the players left out. This has been on my mind ever since the news of his death came through. That day Diego was crying as he left the hotel. We couldn't comfort him. We were saying: "Diego you're young. You'll have other chances." But he carried on crying and crying. By the end, all of us were crying. For Diego, it was the biggest setback he suffered as a footballer. He had some wonderful moments and some bad moments in his career but that was the biggest shock of his footballing life.

When we played in the 1978 World Cup, the team that started the tournament was pretty much the team that played and won in the final apart from one position, where we struggled to find a solution: the No 10. We started with Jose Daniel Valencia, we had Norberto Alonso, we had Ricky Villa and we finished with Mario Kempes, a centre forward, playing there. What might we have been like with Diego? Soon after 1978 he was recognised as the best player in the world and when he was with the national team he would almost do the same as he had done as a 14-year-old boy before the matches. Only this time he was a player and it was part of his warm-up. He would stand in the middle of the pitch and start juggling the ball. Then he would kick the ball up in the air and begin chatting to you as though he had forgotten it. "Ossie, how are you today?" And then "Boom!" the ball would fall on to his foot again as though he knew exactly where it was all the time. It is impossible to do that! I haven't seen anyone do anything close to that! He would do that knowing that the other team was there. Most of the time, the opponents stopped their warm-up to watch, knowing that ten minutes later they would be playing this monster. He knew that and did it to give us the advantage. For the other team it was: "Blimey!" and for us playing with him, it was: "Hello! He's playing for us! No problems."

Diego was unique, that is the word. He was extraordinary, out of this world. He had feet like hands. I was blessed to play with the world's best players, but he was the greatest. What made him so special was his courage. It was always hostile for him, he was always a marked man but he always wanted the ball. When they kicked him, he wanted the ball even more. He was a winner. He just could not lose. And I should know, I played him at tennis!

There is one story I have never told about Diego. It happened in the 1982 World Cup in Spain and we travelled to a small town in Spain about 10 days before the tournament. I was sitting next to Diego at dinner, when he asked me what I was doing the next day. It was an unusual situation as we also had our wives, and in Diego's case, his girlfriend, staying in the next hotel. That never used to happen as we were happy just to concentrate on the tournament. It was a Saturday evening when he asked me about my plans for the next day. "Cordobes, what are you doing tomorrow?" he said. He called me that because I was from the town of Cordoba in Argentina. We woke the next morning and, after a quick breakfast, we slipped past all the security that was around us due to the war with England over the Falklands, pinched a car outside of the hotel, as there were so many there, and headed into town — about a 15-minute drive away to go to mass and have some lunch afterwards.

We went to this small cathedral and when we opened the door everybody looked at us, the priest had to stop the mass, as everybody wanted to touch Diego, or have a picture with him, as even then, he was so well known. The priest took us into a corner but Diego said it was no problem if anyone wanted a picture. During the mass, you would turn to the person next to you and say "Peace is with you", and put your hand in their hand — and sitting next to us was someone from England! Incredible. Back at the hotel, we heard later, there was panic. "Where are Diego and Ossie?" Back at the cathedral, before mass had finished, at the door were some big guards in sunglasses, "Oh, there they are!" We took our car back to the hotel accompanied by security.

For the 1982 World Cup we were favourites and we were confident. Basically we had the core of the '78 team which were world champions, and added Jorge Valdano, Ramon Diaz and Diego. We fancied ourselves very strongly but immediately things started to go wrong. And the main thing was the war with England over Las Malvinas/The Falkland Islands. Because of the way the news was reported in Argentina under the dictatorship, when we left Argentina everyone had the impression that we were winning the war. When we arrived in Spain, we had surrendered. That was an incredible shock. Some of us had family and friends in the war and I had a cousin who had died there. We had a team meeting and we said: "Boys, the best way to help the country is to win the World Cup." All the time, it was at the back of our minds. We lost against Belgium in the first game and we ended up

DAZZLING DIEGO!

WORLD-CLASS players such as Napoli and Argentine ace Diego Maradona learn to control the ball with the outside of their foot. The ball controlled with the inside of the foot is directed TOWARDS the defender; the ball controlled with the outside of the foot is directed AWAY from him.

in the Group of Death with eventual champions Italy and the Brazil team, which is the greatest Brazilian team not to win the World Cup.

Against Italy, they just lined up to kick Diego and we lost 2-1. Against Brazil he was also marked in a very physical way and, when he reacted, he was sent off - we lost that one 3-1. We had taken on all the pressure and responsibility for the nation from the war, Diego more than most, and it proved too much. Daniel Passarella may have been our captain but Diego was the leader. There was too much on his shoulders. But throughout his life, there was always too much on his shoulders. On the plane home, I told him, "Diego, they will destroy us. The criticism will be so big. And you will be the one who will be criticised more than anyone. Because you are the best player in the world and you didn't perform. And you were sent off." He knew that. And it was exactly as we said. It was very difficult to take.

After the World Cup he left Argentina for Barcelona and there he received similar treatment, with that infamous tackle from Andoni Goikoetxea. If he had done that on the street it would have been a crime, but in the context of football at the time, it was OK. This was a career-threatening injury and Diego was out for half a season and at the end of that season he would move to Napoli a year before the 1986 World Cup finals. Can you believe that Naples would win Serie A? People laughed. Football was dominated by the north, by Juventus, AC Milan, Inter, Roma. It had never happened that Napoli could win the title.

It was during his time at Napoli, at the 1986 World Cup, that he cemented his legend. It's the tournament for which we will always remember him. I was injured and for that England game I was an analyst for ITV. I saw the first goal and immediately I saw Glenn Hoddle, my team-mate at Spurs, and Steve Hodge protesting. I sensed something was wrong. It wasn't offside. I was puzzled. What could it be? I could see when Diego was celebrating, there was a quick look back in his eyes. And I thought: "Uh, oh!" Only when we got a different angle could you see the hand. I know people will say: "How could he do such a thing?" But these things happen in football all the time. As for the second goal, Diego has scored better goals than this but it is the occasion that makes that particular goal special. This was one of the most famous games in the history of the World Cup and that's why it is the goal of the century. And because of the burden he carried for Argentina for the defeat in the war. That's why he would never apologise for the handball. If it had been another opponent, maybe he would say sorry. But for him, it was personal.

"For him to come and wear a Spurs shirt and play that game for me, it was very special"

In the lead up to that World Cup Diego was Argentina's big hope, but there were two very important warm-up games in Denmark and then Israel but after the Denmark game, Diego announced that he was off to London to play a game for Tottenham. Diego said to Carlos Bilardo, the manager, "By the way, I'm going to London for Ossie". Bilardo said, "What? You are joking, you're not going!". "No, I'm Diego Maradona, I'm going". They couldn't believe it, and told him, "No, you are not going." He told them: "I am going." They insisted he was not going. But he had told me he would play in my testimonial, so he left the World Cup camp and headed off to London even though he was not allowed to.

I picked him up at the airport and took him to a hotel in central London where he insisted he wanted a sleep before the game. I told him we must leave early as there would be a big crowd wanting to see him, and that it was always a lot of traffic. I waited for hours, and as he had his phone off the hook, could not get through to his room. He finally emerged with little to no time to get to the ground.

We inevitably got stuck in traffic and the kick off had to be put back, there was a full house.

I was panicking as I drove him along Seven Sisters Road which had come to a standstill, but we had a police escort for the final stages to get us to the stadium. He wanted to wear his famous No. 10, so Glenn gave him his No.10 shirt. Diego had arrived without a thing, not even a bag, let alone any kit.

For him to come and wear a Spurs shirt and play that game for me, it was very special. He had a fantastic game, and after the game the team went to dinner with Diego, and then onto a private nightclub where I left him about three in the morning. He hardly had much sleep the night before travelling and not much sleep the next night but had to make it to the airport at 7am, and almost missed his flight to Israel, but I imagine he got some sleep on the flight.

I brought him to Wembley when Spurs played there and beat Liverpool 4-1 when Mauricio Pochettino was the manager, and all the players wanted to meet him. I introduced him to Harry Kane as he popped into the dressing room to say hello. He gave some advice to Harry, with me translating, "Harry, when you shoot, look one way with your eyes, but shoot the other". But the way Diego talks, so passionate, so funny. Harry loved it.

Diego was a guest speaker at the Oxford Union in 1995, when I was the interpreter. Here was Diego, on the same stage where Nelson Mandela and Ronald Reagan had stood. Suddenly, one guy shouts, "Can you do keepie-uppies with this?", and he throws a golf ball towards us. I'm thinking, "Oh no, he's wearing a suit and brand new shoes, this will be difficult". Diego pulls his trousers up and starts keeping the ball up. Boom, boom, boom. Easy. He then kicks it back to the guy with his heel. It was incredible. Only Diego. The Union erupted with cheers.

Obviously everyone talks about the Hand of God goal, but he did what he had to do, and for me it is blown out of all proportion. Here we have a unique talent, who scored a wonder goal against England, but the Hand of God goal is the one they talk about. He wanted to win at all costs, do anything to win, he was a winner, but he wasn't the only forward who handled a goal, there are many other examples, from Thierry Henry to Joe Jordan, it happens all the time. I can't judge him on that. In the intervening years I have talked to Diego regularly, sometimes for five minutes, sometimes half an hour; we would talk about football, but we would talk about everything. I always tried to help him as much as I could.

At the 1990 World Cup finals, when Argentina lost in the final, Diego was in incredibly bad shape physically and to play every game he had cortisone injections. In 1994 it was the same. He was taking drugs to get him through games. So drugs were always there. There was no control in his life at that stage. And the only part of his life that was happy was on the pitch. It was sad to see him. He couldn't continue to live like that. He would always say: "If I was a good boy and looked after myself, imagine the player I could be!" For him, a match was a show. At his best, he didn't need to warm up or concentrate. But before a game he would almost be in frenzy, using swear words to motivate himself and us. He would transmit just how much it meant to him. And the team would look at him and think: "We have to play so well for him today." He was our leader and that is how I will remember him.

All our conversations would finish in the same way… He would say "it is very beautiful to be Maradona, but it is not easy to be Maradona". I knew what he meant. He was loved wherever he went, no, more than loved, people wanted a part of him, a picture with him, just to touch him, and he was wonderful with the people. But he was mortal just like the rest of us, he never had a childhood because he was so famous so quickly. He came from a very poor background, but never forgot it, and the first thing he did when he could was to buy a house for his mother and father, and to make sure all his family were well looked after.

When you were with him, because he was such an icon, you were always surrounded by people. Things were

> "Drugs were always there. There was no control in his life at that stage. And the only part of his life that was happy was on the pitch. It was sad to see him. He couldn't continue to live like that. He would always say: 'If I was a good boy and looked after myself, imagine the player I could be!'"

always happened: exciting things. I loved him, absolutely loved him. He was incredibly sharp, very funny. He had an answer to whatever you said. But he had so many problems outside the pitch his entire life. Inside the pitch, he was the happiest person in the world.

Diego was an inspirational person. He had a magic around him, on the pitch and off it. Special, so special. I am blessed to have been his friend.

He didn't need to work, but the best thing for him was to be involved in football. When the pandemic happened, there has been no football in Argentina for six months. That did not help. He had been ill and he deteriorated badly. I am very sad, but now, he is in a place where he will find peace.

Glenn Hoddle

Glenn Hoddle epitomises everything about Spurs and provides the reason why anyone with love for the much-quoted "beautiful game" in their heart and soul should be a Spurs fan.

Ruud Gullit dubbed it "sexy football", Pelé coined it as "the beautiful game", but whatever phrase you use, a certain type of player can take your breath away. Whether a touch of magic from Diego Maradona or Ricky Villa's solo FA Cup final goal at Wembley, the genius of George Best, Johan Cruyff, Lionel Messi or Cristiano Ronaldo, you know it when you see one of the game's masters performing something that you thought you might never see.

So, how gratifying for me that my true claim to fame is not my big news exclusives and all the awards as a reward for them, but being (partly) responsible for Glenn Hoddle breaking into the Tottenham team!

On the *Tottenham Weekly Herald* it was my duty to cover the Spurs youth and reserve teams as well as the senior side and, having set the precedent with Bill Nicholson, I would attend a Monday morning briefing each week with the manager. On this occasion it was Terry Neill, who had succeeded Nicholson. Having spoken to the Spurs reserve manager week after week, and closely watched the team, it soon became apparent that a 17 year-old kid was already first team material.

I am convinced that Terry Neill had never seen him play. When, one Monday during my regular weekly briefing, I enquired when we could all expect to see the latest youngster from the Spurs conveyor belt of local talent to be playing in the first team, Terry looked at me blankly but, as he was never someone who was lost for words, he waltzed around my question with relative ease, talking about never rushing kids saying his time will come etc. It was clear to me he didn't know Glenn Hoddle from Adam!

The next week though, to my surprise and delight, Glenn was named as a substitute for the senior team for a Division One game against Norwich City at the Lane and came on for Cyril Knowles in a 2-2 draw.

He continued to impress for the reserves and the youth team and on 21st February 1976 he made his full debut against Stoke City at the Victoria Ground and beat Peter Shilton with a fabulous long-range left-footer that sealed a 2-1 victory for Spurs.

During the many lunches Glenn and I have shared over the years, I never tire of reminding him about that story, which always brings a chuckle. I keep repeating it in the hope that Glenn will one day actually believe it! I admit, it is hard to believe.

Of course Hoddle would have eventually made it to the first team with or without my prompting. He was just too good. Brian Clough tried to sign him for Nottingham Forest on multiple occasions. 'Old Big 'Ead' was a committed Hoddle fan. He once said, "You don't have to bare your false teeth to prove you're a real he-man in football. Some people are morally brave and Hoddle is one of them. I've heard him criticised for non-involvement, but I'm not sure what that means. If you can compensate with more skill in one foot than most players have in their whole body, then that is compensation enough."

Back in 1987, I "ghosted" Glenn's first autobiography *Spurred To Success*, in which he personally subscribed this touching note "To Harry - Thanks for your support - over many, many years." Not content with that, I got him to sign another copy at the book launch, in which he wrote "God bless. Great working with yer!"

Many Spurs fans have worked behind the scenes at White Hart Lane and one of those was Paul Barber, who was the club's executive director for a while and a man with wide experience in the game, including a spell as the FA's marketing director and chief executive at Brighton. Paul recalls his first Spurs game and the first time he saw Hoddle...

"It was August 1975. I was eight years old. I had spent the previous three nights unable to sleep as my dad, a lifelong Spurs fan, had told me we would be going to see Spurs play Norwich at White Hart Lane - my first ever game. I remember the day itself being warm and sunny - just as well as I wore full Spurs kit, shorts and all! The thrill of seeing the pitch for the first time was unforgettable as we secured a good spot in the Enclosure in the old West Stand. My dad's family, keen watchers of reserve team football too, had been raving about a curly-haired youngster called Glenn Hoddle.

"As luck would have it, the gangly youth also made his debut at the Lane that day coming on as substitute as we battled for a 2-2 draw. The player who was to become the most outstanding midfield player of his generation made an immediate impression rescuing a poor ball with exquisite chest control and spraying a 50 yard pass - later to become his trademark - cross-field to feet. The mood in the Enclosure audibly lifted. 'This boy will be a star', said dad, and murmurs of strong agreement spread from those long-time Spurs watchers all around us. The rest, as they say, is history!"

Glenn was capable of such magical moments; his chip against Watford, a spectacular sideways angled volley or an 80 yard pass of perfection. In the introduction to his autobiography I wrote at that time, "He has been described as the 'White Pelé'; he has Diego Maradona among his admirers; yet despite his rare gift for inspirational skills, he has remained English soccer's greatest enigma for more than a decade.

"Glenn Hoddle provokes almost violent debate among fans, managers and football journalists alike. Some say he is a genius – others condemn him as gutless. Managers at the highest level are divided on the question of whether they would choose Hoddle for their team. The 'Hoddle Argument' is more fundamental than a simple assessment of an individual performer - it highlights the deep and often disturbing morality of the English game. Are we too dependent on workers and runners? Should we develop the more complex artists? Can we afford to 'carry' the play-maker who does not bear the responsibility of defensive duty?"

I raised the point that those questions had haunted Glenn ever since he scored a wonder-goal by improvised an unorthodox side-foot drive from outside the box to score on his England debut against Bulgaria at Wembley in 1979 at the age of 22.

"Hod", as they affectionately called him in the Tottenham camp, won two FA Cup medals, a UEFA Cup medal and a Little World Cup medal with the England youth team. But a league title eluded him, and that hurt.

It is often cited that Hoddle should have won far more than his 53 England caps; that he should have been one of the elite England Centurions, and he would have been if more England managers had trusted in his skills. Instead, he was hardly given the chance of two successive internationals until Bobby Robson persevered with him a year before the World Cup finals in Mexico.

Never blessed with blistering pace, he made up for it with the kind of creativity that raised Spurs to a team you wouldn't want to miss watching. And at times, this was shown in his international games.

Again I can only call it a privilege to have been the chief football writer on the *Daily Mirror* covering the World Cup finals in Mexico. Ineffective, together with all of his team-mates, against Portugal, in a terrible and controversial opening game, Glenn began to shine against Poland when he was involved in all three Gary Lineker goals. Hoddle really turned on the magic against Paraguay, creating all three England goals, two more for Lineker and one for Peter Beardsley.

The turning point for Hoddle in the World Cup was a mixture of farce and fortune. Ray Wilkins managed to get himself sent off in a fit of pique and frustration shortly before half-time against Morocco and strangely that worked in Hoddle's favour, almost decreed by the fate upon which Glenn placed so much store in his personal beliefs.

Immediately England re-organised, Hoddle assuming his familiar central midfield role, and his flair for the creative long ball began to become evident in the second half against the African team hailed as the surprise of the World Cup. With Peter Reid installed as Wilkins' replacement against Poland, Hoddle had more freedom in the next two games, but unfortunately he was to be overshadowed by Maradona in the quarter-final tie at the Azteca Stadium in Mexico City.

This was to prove Maradona's match, not Hoddle's. Perhaps if Glenn had inspired England in the same way that Maradona inspired Argentina, he would have been spoken about in terms of one of the world's greatest ever. Instead it was Maradona who took the game by storm with his blistering second goal proving the winner after his cheating "Hand of God" opener.

In 1987, thanks to the generosity of Irving Scholar, Hoddle was promised that he could pursue his ambition to play on the Continent, and the Spurs chairman granted that wish when he allowed his star player to move on to Monaco where, under Arsene Wenger, Hoddle was allowed the kind of freedom he was never granted in English football. Glenn blossomed and also forged a close relationship with Wenger, and the pair remained close when they were rival managers.

Glenn's transfer was a tale in itself. I was in Toulon with a group of rival reporters covering the Under-20 tournament when we heard that he was being transferred from his beloved Spurs. Bob Harris from the *Today* newspaper told us all confidently that he was going to Paris St Germain, but I knew differently. Yes, Bob was right to an extent, it looked as though a deal with PSG had been fixed up, but there was a last minute change of heart and a dramatic change of direction. I had spoken to Glenn directly and knew he was on his way to Monte Carlo. I left the media hotel with a couple of other journalists to head there, while Bob and two others headed to Paris. When we reached our destination and checked into the Beach Plaza hotel, we bumped into Glenn and Mark Hateley who were both signing for Monaco with Dennis Roach, orchestrating the double signing. It might have been a journalistic coup to be at the right place at the right time, but in many ways it was sad that Hoddle was leaving Spurs at the age of 29.

One journalist, Rob Shepherd, was sure Bob Harris was right, and was planning to go with him to Paris, but as my taxi was pulling away from the hotel the following morning, "Shep" was rushing down the stairs to the lobby with his suitcase hastily packed, with a shirt or two hanging out the sides, to join us on the trek to Monte Carlo. It was a good change of mind for Shep.

I have known Pelé, Maradona, Cruyff and Best, not just from the stands as a fan mesmerised by their unique skills, but have met each one of those world icons, and have gone much further and become so close to them that I have been privileged to have written their life stories. I wrote George Best's last book, Pelé's life story, met Cruyff in the offices of Robert Maxwell in the Mirror building at Holborn, and written Glenn's autobiography. In fact, I've even played football with Hoddle! Well, I've got the pictures to prove I had a bit of a kick around with him. It was an invitation from the FA for a charity event when a few journalists challenged him in a test of accuracy.

Needless to say Glenn won with ease.

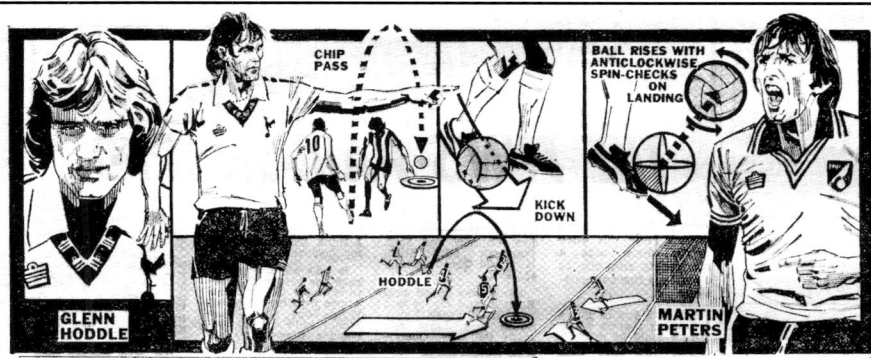

DAILY STAR - September 1979
SUPERKID Glenn Hoddle has modelled his game on three of Soccer's top players. They're George Best, Alan Hudson and Martin Peters.

Hoddle, Spurs' midfield star, says: "I was playing eight matches a week when I was 10. And when I wasn't kicking a ball around in a backyard I was trying to pick up tips by studying George Best.

"I was also a big fan of Hudson's. He was a fabulous lad and got my career off the ground. My first full League match was at Stoke where Hudson was having a brilliant season,

"I was only 17 and had to pick him up. I was sick with nerves. Top pros sometimes take the mickey out of a kid starting his career —but not Hudson.

"He gave nothing away but every time I did something special he'd say I'd done well. I scored our winner and Huddy said: 'That's done it. I'll get a rocket — I should have been on your toes stopping you.'

"How can you thank a player who says that?"

Hoddle also rates Norwich star Martin Peters. He says: "Bags of class— I can watch him all day chipping those lovely passes forward. It's those little lofted passes that have become such a part of my game. No defender can mark space in the AIR so a chipped pass can't be intercepted. Hit it right and the man on the receiving end is off and away.

"Last season I looked good on the ball but wasn't so hot at winning it back. I'm better now because I'm stronger. When I make a tackle now the other fellow knows about it."

Hoddle is getting in the tackles but is still playing the way he wants to play. Keith Burkinshaw, Spurs boss says: "There's no limit to what the lad can do. He's a one-off job in this country, I can't recall anyone as skilful. His ball-control is incredible and he can either go past a player or chip a pass. He uses both feet really well."

*

Glenn eventually became Spurs manager following a mixed spell as England boss during which he qualified for the 1998 World Cup from a difficult group that contained Italy following a memorable goalless draw in Rome and a difficult build up to the tournament itself which saw a spectacular fall-out with Paul Gascoigne before an exit at the hands of Argentina in St Etienne. Glenn emerged from that débâcle largely unscathed as the tabloid press firmly placed the blame on David Beckham for getting sent off. The scapegoating of Beckham in the press that followed, stoked up by the tabloids, and the manner of the United man's comeback the following season, during which he led his club to the treble, was in contrast to Glenn's rapid demise following an interview with Matt Dickinson of *The Times* that saw him sacked as England supremo and replaced by the hapless Kevin Keegan and, a year later, Sven Goran Eriksson.

Meanwhile Glenn had staged a successful comeback at Southampton so when George Graham was fired he was seen as the perfect antidote to the depression which had fallen over the club during the former Arsenal manager's time in the dug out.

The club appointed Glenn as manager on Friday March 30, 2001 just four days after resigning as boss of Southampton, agreeing a long-term contract appointing his long-time assistant, John Gorman, after the club dismissed Graham's number two Stewart Houston. Speaking at a media conference at White Hart Lane, Hoddle was delighted to have "returned home". "It's emotional and exciting," he said. "I've spent many years here and the supporters have given me a superb reception. I walked through the gates of this club at age eight as a supporter and left when I was 29. That's a huge part of my life."

There had been no doubts on his part. "I don't feel guilty," he said of his controversial departure from The Dell. "The timing was right to come back. It's a fantastic club. I'm very surprised to be here and when I was offered the chance to talk to Spurs it was something I wanted to pursue. There was only one club I would have left Southampton for and that was Tottenham Hotspur Football Club."

Hoddle had high hopes but it was important to plan for the long-term. "The potential is there to do well and there's lots of hard work to be done. The fact that the contract is five years means the club are looking to the future. We want to win the Premiership, of course we do, and that is my ultimate goal, but it's early doors to be talking about that. Spurs have always had a style. In an ideal world that is what we want but you must have a balance. The game has changed since the 1960s and you have to change with it. Tottenham didn't have to prove anything to me and there is talent in the squad, no doubt about it."

Glenn guided the club to a League Cup final against Blackburn a year later, which they lost 2-1 in Cardiff, and took Spurs to finishes of ninth and tenth in successive seasons before he was sacked in September 2003. Perhaps his most infamous game in charge took place in September 2001 when his Tottenham team surrendered a 3-0 lead to Manchester United.

After a poor start to the 2003-04 season and with no wins in four games, a 3-1 defeat to, of all teams Southampton, proved too much for new chairman Daniel Levy.

HH

Gary Mabbutt

When I first joined the Tottenham *Weekly Herald* I got to know the club's physiotherapist Mike Varney well and soon wrote my first book with him called *The Treatment of Football Injuries*. I have initiated other projects to do with Spurs because I wanted to write the life stories of the people I knew, liked or who had fascinated me for a variety of reasons. However, it is not always easy to convince publishers about your ideas, and even harder to win commissions from them, as they have such a wide selection of options.

So Irving Scholar came up with the novel idea of starting his own publishing company calling it, appropriately, Cockerel Books Ltd, the company's address listed at his own business premises in Maddox Street, off Oxford Street.

One of the first and, indeed, one of the few Cockerel Books, was *Against All Odds*, the Gary Mabbutt autobiography, published in 1989, which I had the privilege to write for one of the players I admired the most.

There were two forewords to the Mabbutt book, one from the player's consultant in diabetes at St Bartholomew's Hospital, E A M Gale MA, FRCP, in which he wrote, "I think the word that best sums up Gary Mabbutt is commitment. Everyone knows how hard it is to get to the top as a professional footballer. What only a few people know - or perhaps not so few, since diabetes affects one person in a hundred in this country - is the commitment it takes to make a success of a life with diabetes.

"To combine top class football with diabetes takes a very special sort of person. Gary's performance on the football pitch has given pleasure to fans all over the world, but I wonder how many have paused to think of the very special meaning it holds for those, particularly the young, who themselves have diabetes. Gary has provided hope and inspiration for countless thousands by showing in the most practical way possible that if you can learn how to live with diabetes, the sky really is the limit.

"I would not care to count the number of times I have turned to someone with diabetes and said 'if Gary Mabbutt can do it, so can you.' The message of this book is simple: you really can."

This was one of the least commercial books I have been involved in, but by far the most important, and I can only applaud Irving for insisting the project went ahead, and my admiration and respect for Gary multiplied after sifting through the inside story of his life with diabetes.

The England manager at the time, Bobby Robson, also put his name to a second foreword in the book, in which he wrote, "There is no doubt in my mind that I have never come across any player like Gary Mabbutt. Injury is an every day hazard for the professional footballer; diabetes is not.

"Any manager will tell you, there are certain players who use their injuries to escape responsibility. Because of it, some of them never reach their full potential - they simply will not deliver the goods when it matters. What do you say, then, about a 17-year-old who discovers he is diabetic but, instead of giving up, learns how to cope with it, gets back into training within two weeks, captains the England youth team, becomes a star with and captain of one of the country's top teams and goes on to represent his country at Under-21, "B" and full international levels? You have to say that he is something special and, as far as I am concerned, Gary Mabbutt certainly is.

"His adaptability, his skills, his athleticism and work-rate would be remarkable in a young man enjoying perfect health. In a lad who has to cope daily with the problems of a debilitating illness, these attributes are astounding. Yet I have never known Gary Mabbutt to look for sympathy or make a fuss about his diabetes. The nearest he gets to advertising the fact is the bottle of Lucozade that he brings with him to every training session.

"Also, from time to time, on a long flight, Gary will quietly get up from his seat, put on his jacket and stroll off to the toilet. Very few of his fellow passengers will realise that he has slipped quietly off to give himself one of the self-injections that he needs on a regular basis to keep his metabolism in balance. The thought of it fills me with horror - Gary takes it calmly in his stride.

"It is the same air of quiet authority which brought him the captaincy of Spurs and which led me to pick him for my very first Wembley international, when I became England manager in 1982."

Robson went on to talk about Gary in glowing terms about his commitment to the England cause, but his final paragraph summed up the player and the man the best, "For me, Gary is the original Bionic Man. I wish him every success with this book, which I am sure will prove an inspiration to many youngsters facing a setback in their lives, and with the rest of his career in football."

The book proved an inspiration, and to this day Gary remains a major figure in the campaign to help youngsters come to terms with diabetes.

The real shock for me was to hear the horrible truth about how Gary's life was often threatened by his condition. One of the most serious incidents occurred when Gary was preparing for a midweek Littlewoods Cup tie with Barnsley. He told me this story which appeared in his book.

"Part of my routine, and most footballers' come to that, is to sleep in the afternoon prior to the game. I had now switched from my earlier schedule of two injections a day to four and also had a compact blood testing machine. This machine accurately reads the blood sugar level. I would have six to eight tests a day to work out the exact amount of insulin I would need. We trained in the morning, then I had lunch - a gammon steak - taking a blood test before the meal. I was surprised that the test showed quite high levels of sugar in my blood; after all, I was about to eat, I hadn't just had my meal! It was pretty unusual. The reading on the machine was 18. A normal reading would show levels of between five and nine, so to compensate I injected twice the amount of insulin I would normally need for lunch. This sort of thing had happened before, I had worked out the right amounts and everything had been fine.

"I had my injection, then my lunch and went to bed at 1.30pm. All I know from my side is waking up in hospital at 2.00am the following morning. I'd missed the Cup tie. I hadn't a clue what had happened. Everything else is a complete blank.

"I have only managed to piece the rest of the story together accurately through information given to me by other people. I've been told that I did not wake up, I did not turn up for the match at White Hart Lane and that at 6.30pm, just an hour before kick off, the management, staff and players in the team began to worry about me.

"The team meeting went ahead as usual, but obviously without me. Everyone thought there must be a logical explanation. Was I held up in traffic? Generally, I'm a punctual sort of person; I'm hardly ever late for training, let alone for an important Cup tie. One or two people became frantic, knowing me well and knowing how unlike me it was to be so late. Some players are always late and they are continually being fined, but not usually me. As it got closer and closer to kick off time people started to wonder whether something really serious had happened. They knew that if there had been an accident I would have phoned in, or at least

the police would have notified the club.

"At 6.45pm Ossie Ardiles, one of my closest friends at the club, got really worried and thought it was about time to do something - to find out if I was okay. From the dressing rooms, with now just 35 minutes before he was due to trot out with the team in readiness for the Cup tie, Ossie rang up one of Tottenham's former players, centre-half John Lacy, who lived two doors away from me. 'Can you go and see if Gary is alright? Have a look if there is a light on or see if his car is there', Ossie asked.

"Big John Lacy was only too happy to help out and became concerned when he looked out of his window and couldn't see any lights on where I lived. He went round and looked in the garage, where my car was still parked. Fortunately, I had kept the back door open to let my Afghan Hound walk in and out to the garden. John came in through the back door and started calling my name. When he came through the door to my bedroom the sight that greeted him must have led him to think that I had been attacked. The entire room was turned upside down and I was lying naked on the floor, unconscious.

"There was blood all over my body, face, arms, legs - all over the bed, behind the bed, on the walls, on the curtains. I had cut myself all over. What had happened was that I had tried to give myself a blood test, and was so 'low' that I was unable to do so, and kept cutting myself.

"I was out cold. John could get no sense out of me but he noticed that I once opened my eyes, although all there was, was a glazed look. It must have been frightening for him, and he couldn't be sure what had happened. He snapped to his senses and remembered that among our neighbours there was a couple, both of whom were doctors. He rushed over and the wife was there, the husband was out on his calls.

"Knowing that I was a diabetic she tried to give me some sugar, but I was in no condition to take it. Her husband soon arrived on the scene. They decided to give me a glucose injection straight into my veins... I still didn't come round.

"That was the point where they both began to worry. It is normal to come round after the sugar level in the blood is restored. An ambulance was called and I was rushed to Queen Elizabeth Hospital in Welwyn Garden City. It was felt that once they got me to hospital I would be alright - although that was what they had thought once I was found and given the sugar! When I finally woke up there I had two drips in my arm feeding me glucose intravenously. Just imagine how I felt. I didn't know where I was or how I'd got there. I saw two nurses and asked them, 'What's happened?' They started to explain that I had fallen into a deep diabetic coma.

"The next thing I thought about was the game. I was supposed to have been playing against Barnsley. 'How did Spurs get on?' I asked the nurses. They didn't have a clue. Perhaps I should have been more concerned with the fact that I was lucky to be alive, rather than that I had missed the game. But my main reaction was sheer shock. What had happened? I just couldn't work out what had gone wrong. I had always gone for an afternoon nap before a game, and if ever I was going 'low' that would normally be a good wake up call!

"Remarkably, the next morning when John Lacy walked into the hospital to visit, I was fine, absolutely nothing wrong! I'd even got up out of bed. Of course I looked terrible, unshaven, no clothes, but I was ready to go. John had kindly brought me one of my tracksuits and drove me straight round to White Hart Lane. I began training! I was running round the track by myself as good as new.

"The manager, David Pleat, asked me how I felt and I said, 'Absolutely fine'. He looked unsure, was no doubt still concerned, and said he would take advice before considering whether to play me that weekend.

"As it turned out I got the all-clear, travelled up to Liverpool on the Friday with the team and played at Anfield - I was delighted that I had a good game. Thursday I was in hospital, Saturday I was playing. That shows you just how quickly it can all change."

It was, naturally, in the club's and Gary's best interest for the full gory facts of this incident to be kept out of media at the time, so little was given away about why Mabbutt missed the Cup tie.

Gary also told me how he had once lost consciousness at the wheel of his car, and ended up in a ditch, but that was one of the stories that we decided at the time would be best kept out of the book. Gary was still involved in the game as a player and it would not have helped his cause, so the episode remained confidential.

I experienced at first hand the kind of problems that Gary has suffered all of his life. It was frightening. Once, when I invited Gary to the *Mirror* and he was sitting with me in the sports editor's office, his blood sugar levels fell drastically. At first he rambled, then became incoherent and then virtually passed out before we called "medical". Fortunately we had a medical department within the building. A bar of chocolate was the miracle cure to raise the sugar content of his blood, and within seconds he was fine.

There was never a sign of any mood swings or anger at his condition. Gary is one of the nicest guys you are ever likely to meet. He is also one of only three men to score at both ends in the FA Cup final, a fate that befell him when he scored to put Spurs 2-1 up at Wembley against Coventry City in 1987, but then saw the ball spiral off his knee and over Ray Clemence in extra time to give Coventry their winner. That was the first FA Cup final the club had ever lost after victories in all their seven finals between 1901 and 1982 and was the first of two finals in five seasons to be settled by an own goal.

Ironically, when Spurs won the FA Cup for a then-record eighth time in 1991, Nottingham Forest's Des Walker headed into his own net in extra time to give Spurs the winner. He did that under pressure from the Spurs player closest to him - who else but Gary Mabbutt.

LILLYWHITE INTERNATIONAL

John Ferguson

Like many of my age, I fell in love with Spurs because of Glenn Hoddle. As a kid I only ever wanted to be Hoddle whenever I was in the playground kicking a ball around. Then in 1978, imagine my excitement when we signed Ossie and Ricky. It was brilliant for a 10 year-old who had just watched these superstars on TV win a World Cup - I was well and truly hooked. The 80's were the glory years for me as a teenager with the Cup Finals of 1981, 1982, and 1984 and then that FA Cup semi where Gazza beat Arsenal and the cup win of 1991.

I have been a season ticket holder for over 40 years. My company is called Lillywhite International, my daughter is named Lilly White Ferguson, and in 2016 we launched the Lillywhite Foundation to help disadvantaged kids get into sports and activity. The Foundation gets regular support and help from Spurs legends – Ossie Ardiles, Ricky Villa, Paul Miller, John Pratt and of course Glenn Hoddle.

Paul 'Maxi' Miller is a good friend and through Maxi I have become friends with Ossie and Glenn Hoddle and get to play golf with these guys on a regular basis – they say never meet your heroes, but I'm lucky to have not only met them but become friends and they are simply top guys.

I emigrated to Prague in 2007 but still make most home games. Although I grew up watching from The Shelf, I was fortunate to spend the last couple of seasons at the old Lane sitting in the Directors box and dining in Ossie's lounge. It was fascinating to see a little bit of what goes on "behind the scenes". This continued when we spent a couple of seasons playing at Wembley, watching from the Royal Box with all the legends. As a result I was invited to be a founder member of the Tunnel Club in the new stadium. I was able to make regular visits in a hard hat as the new stadium was built – what an amazing experience. The Tottenham Hotspur Stadium is without doubt the best in world right now and I'm privileged to be in the The Tunnel Club sat right behind the manager and substitutes getting to hear everything that is said - it's a real feeling of engagement with the match. The Tunnel Club means my partner and I get to meet the players and manager and of course share a glass or two with legends such as Ossie, Maxi, Big Pat Jennings and Ledley King each week.

For me, recent history peaked on that night in Amsterdam – that amazing come back and goals from Lucas Moura that sent us to the Champions League Final. It was so brilliant to then meet him several times in the Tunnel Club, get a shirt signed from that night and for him to find me on his last game to say goodbye.

My car number plate always raises a laugh – living in Prague I was able to get an unusual plate and on several trips back to the UK I have taken it to the stadium and the training ground where it always gets noticed. The training ground and Spurs Lodge is

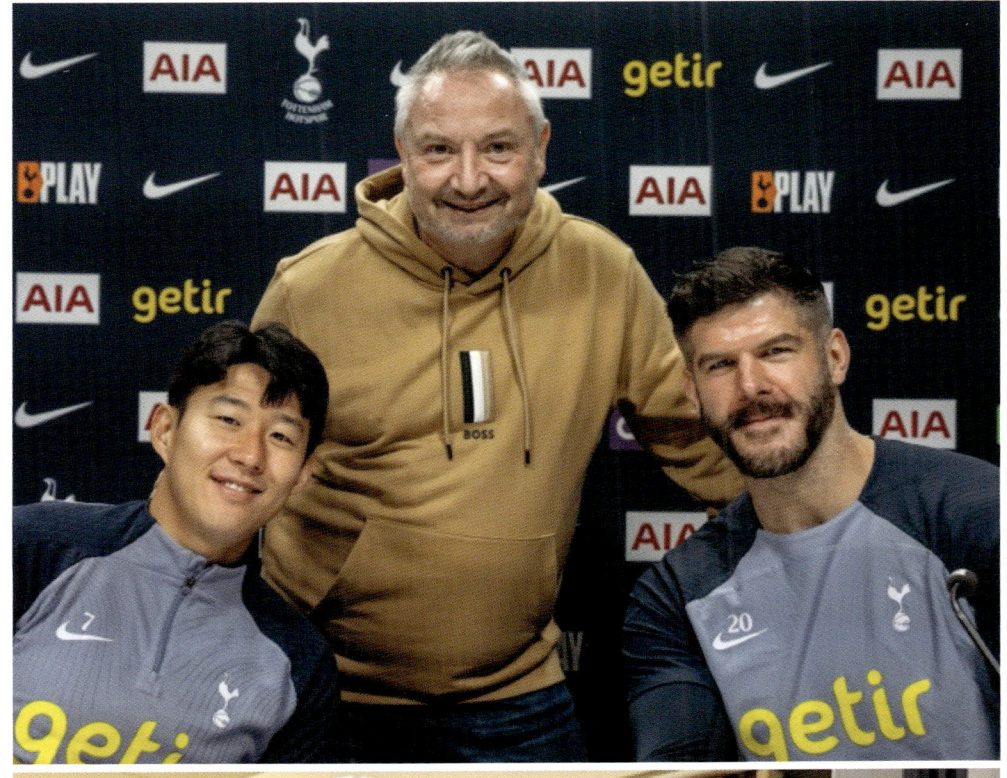

as impressive as the Stadium and I was fortunate to get to stay a night – staying in Eric Dier's room - and then train with some of the coaches on the training pitch.

Making new friends in the Tunnel Club has been great fun – travelling away with Spurs for European games is always brilliant as you get to meet new people all the time. Commuting from Prague has been difficult at times and often disappointing but the drug that is Tottenham keeps you coming back. I still get as excited waking up on a match day as the 10 year-old that used to go in 1978.

Highlights have been taking my daughter to both stadiums – where she has met Ossie and Ledley and various legends who have all been wonderful to her, and taking my Dad for his 80th to the Tunnel Club and letting him experience the new stadium.

As a Tunnel Club member I get to experience the behind the scenes views that most never get to see and it all fuels the Spurs drug. Now my partner joins me in the Tunnel Club and she has got the bug too, and enjoys the Spurs journey wherever it goes. She now understands the buzz, the sights, sounds and smells as you approach the stadium – albeit we now get there early and enjoy an unrivalled experience in the Tunnel. The journey now continues under Ange Postecoglou and who knows what the next chapter will be. COYS.

You Are The Ref

In all my years 80 and more watching football I have never once sat in the Press Box. Always, and I do mean ALWAYS, I would position myself with the fans as close as possible behind one of the goals in order to study the players of the opposition team. The Tottenham players I knew well, but not the visiting teams, so with a small sketch pad and pencil I would make the odd sketch of a visiting defender or forward, depending on which way they kicked off. Without exception it was never a player but always the REFEREE who would receive most of the verbals from the fans. In their eyes he was to put it politely, a "F***ING IDIOT!". The Tottenham manager Bill Nicholson, who was a qualified referee, would often laugh at some of the criticism of the man in the middle who Bill knew had in fact made an excellent decision, but not in the eyes of many of the fans whose team had been penalised.

SOCCER CHATTER... by Joe Hulme and Harry Peterson

DANNY COULD BE ON THE MOVE SOON

DANNY BLANCHFLOWER doesn't mind playing for the reserves; has no grouse against Tottenham for dropping him from the League team. But it could be that he'll be moving on soon....

Tottenham have no more time for him as an attacking wing-half. Danny, who is 32, refuses to change his style. It's a stale-mate. Only thing that could solve it is a move!

Spurs, we know, might let him go. Danny is prepared to play football for another two years. He could be a snip for a club wanting a wing-half.

● But sporting Danny makes one proviso. " It wouldn't be fair to ask a big fee for me."

A club which might be interested? We're putting our money on Fulham!

HEY, REF!

DANNY CAULIFLOWER is playing for the reserve team; but at half-time he hears that his first team, who are playing near by, have only ten men and are 2–0 down.

A real hero is Danny. He borrows a motor-scooter and dashes off to the aid of the first team. He plays a blinder ... until he tells his story to an opposing player who complains to the referee. What's the verdict?

Answer at foot of column 4

HEY, REF!

DANNY should have kept his mouth shut! He is ordered off under F.A. Law No. 3, which states that a player who leaves a match before it is completed must not take part in another game.

My 'Football Quiz' cartoon in the Spurs *Lilywhite* Magazine included a referee question, which resulted in Bill Nic (who was the answer to the question 'Name the present day Tottenham Player who is a qualified referee?') giving me an FA. Law book with the words "Read and learn about the rules of the game. Educate yourself!" As always Bill's words were valuable advice. I did read and learn and in 1957 the *Sunday People* 'HEY REF!' appeared. I never did receive a compliment from Bill apart from

"Good to see you read the book I gave you". During the *Sunday People* 'Hey Ref!' series the one on 'Danny Cauliflower' was inspired by Danny Blanchflower who at the time was playing in the Tottenham Reserves with a very strong rumour he was about to be transferred to Fulham. It amused Danny but not Bill Nic who, with a shake of his head, said to me "Concentrate on the rules and less on trying to be funny."

In the 1960's *Shoot!* Magazine stepped in, but believed 'Hey Ref!' was not the best title for their readers. So I suggested 'YOU ARE THE REF". They agreed and very soon, YOU ARE THE REF gained a cult following. I have lost count of the number of years it appeared in *Shoot!*. Next it was to appear in the *Sunday Observer* and *Guardian* Online, followed by a series of books. I have to thank YOU ARE THE REF for becoming very good friends of both Howard Webb, Chief Refereeing Officer of the PGMOL and Darren Cann who, when Howard Webb refereed the 2010 World Cup Final, was one of his line officials. Darren, who I call 'The Bobby Moore of Assistant Referees', deservedly still gets a regular name check when the game in which he acts as Assistant Referee - although many fans still insist on 'linesman'- is televised.

Keith Hackett and I worked together on YOU ARE THE REF in 'Shoot!' for years, and from 2006 continued with the weekly series in the Sunday Observer and Guardian Online, which spawned our very successful books that are still on the bookshelves today!

Whenever I have a query relating to referees, Keith is always the first to receive my phone call and unfailingly Keith unravels the referee scenario I'm struggling with!

PT

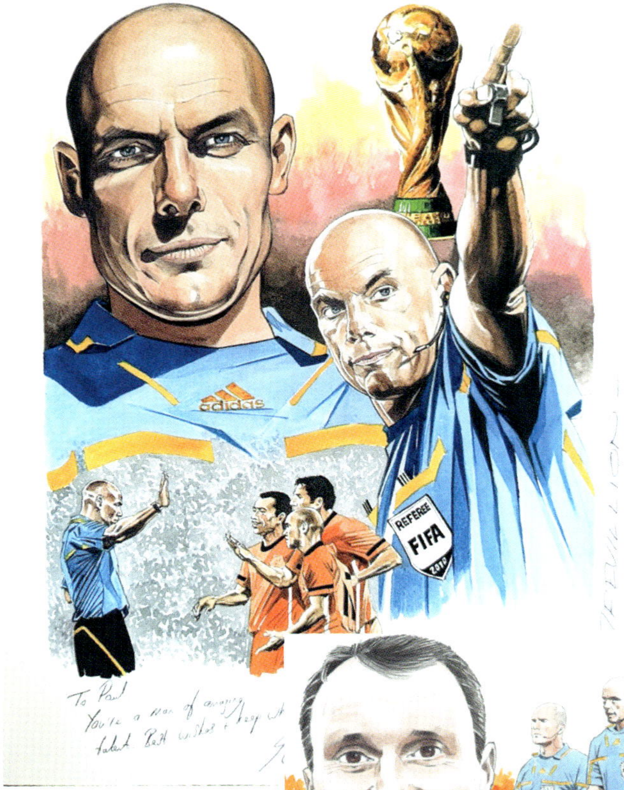

Irving Scholar

Irving Scholar and I shared a deep and meaningful relationship (a love affair) with Spurs. It was this common ground that bound us together to become great allies during his seven years as Spurs chairman and part-owner, and well beyond that point for many years. If there is ever a time when I needed a friend, needed advice, or just someone to talk to, Irving was always there, if you could track him down between his home in Monaco, his frequent holidays in the United States, and his roaming between London hotels, usually staying at the Millennium in Mayfair.

During Irving's seven years in charge I was in the privileged position of knowing so much of what was going on, with the then-chairman increasingly informing me of inside information as long as I assured him it would go no further - and certainly not into the *Daily Mirror* - unless he specifically gave the okay. It led to a string of blockbuster exclusives that left our rivals trailing. It also underlined my accurate reporting of events at the Lane. Spurs fans came to trust my stories, in fact regard them as gospel, and they had every reason to believe them. In some cases, I even helped create them!

For example, I broke the story in the *Mirror* in 1986 that David Pleat would be the new Spurs manager following Peter Shreeves' departure. Unfortunately for Pleat, I also knew that he was going to get the sack a few years later, something that hurt him very deeply, arguably more so than the run of the mill dismissals which are hard enough to take for any manager. On this occasion David was still very much the right man as Spurs manager. In fact he was being touted as the next England manager. It also hurt Irving to get rid of him, because it was due to non-footballing matters; David Pleat had been accused of kerb-crawling. It was also a very difficult period for me; I liked David, and no one wanted him to survive more than I did; I was the journalist putting Pleat forward as an outsider coming through rapidly on the rails as a contender to become England manager once Bobby Robson retired. I doubt whether he would ever have made it right to the top of the England pile, but he might have come very close. I have kept in touch with David, who is now a TV pundit and analyst. I know how bitter he feels at times because he never quite fulfilled his potential as a manager.

One of the more unusual episodes came when Irving called me to help him in his excruciatingly difficult quest to sign Chris Waddle from Newcastle United. There were other top clubs chasing the winger's signature, but Irving had set his heart on the Geordie star.

As I had lived and worked in the North East I had an insight into the Geordie psyche. Irving wanted to tap into this local knowledge as he had discovered that Waddle was reluctant to move to London. I could understand why. Certainly at that time there was still a great deal of subconscious mistrust of southerners and their lifestyle in the north.

Waddle had been selected to play for England at Wembley and his wife wanted to surprise him by leaving work early that Wednesday, travelling down to watch him play - without telling him. Irving was arranging the tickets at Wembley, and asked if I would forsake my usual place in the press box, covering the game, to sit in the stands with Mrs Waddle to keep her company, but more importantly, to subtly talk to her about my experiences living in Newcastle and then to convince her it would be the right

> "The truth is he did not want to sell Waddle to Marseilles in 1989"

move for Chris if he signed for Spurs. Then I had to convince my sports editor of the merits of forgoing the normal match report on the England game in pursuit of the big transfer story.

The whole escapade worked; I chatted to Mrs Waddle about life in Newcastle and how easy it would be for them to settle in the south and how wonderful Spurs would be and how supportive the chairman was. As a consequence Chris signed for Spurs and I got the exclusive. Job done. What a coup for the club and for the newspaper. More importantly, it gave me enormous pleasure in playing my role, however small, in securing one of the most talented individual players for my club.

As for Chris, he didn't forget the part I played in persuading him to move. Chris inscribed in his autobiography "To Harry, thanks for being around."

Irving was regularly accused of selling Spurs stars, but actually his only interest was buying them. He never interfered with the decisions of any of his managers to the extent that people believed. After all the trouble Irving went to in acquiring Chris Waddle, he hardly wanted to sell him, irrespective of how much profit he would make.

The truth is he did not want to sell Waddle to Marseilles in 1989. Spurs had been approached with an unbelievable offer from the reigning French champions who had established themselves as a major European force at the time, and he felt it was an obligation to a player he particularly admired and with whom he got on with, to at least inform him of this unique opportunity. Irving hoped Waddle would turn it down and he made it absolutely clear to him that he didn't want the England left-winger to go.

To help put the French club off, manager Terry Venables was mandated to put a ludicrously high valuation of £4.5million on the 29-year-old signature, and no one expected Marseilles to come up with that kind of money, which then would have been the third highest fee of all time. So when Marseilles came back and matched Spurs' valuation, it would have been financial madness not to take it. Don't forget Spurs bought him from Newcastle for only £600,000. The funny thing is that, following the sale, Spurs then came third in the League the following season and won the FA Cup a year after that.

On a personal level, Irving Scholar was, and remains, a true football enthusiast, who is still in love with Spurs, and I hate to say this, someone even more obsessed with the club than myself.

Irving also fancied himself as a footballer, and to be fair he wasn't bad. Eighteen months before he bought the club, Irving played in a Tottenham shirt on the White Hart Lane pitch and scored two goals in a charity match. That, no doubt, persuaded him to go off and buy the club! Just two weeks before the 1984 UEFA Cup final he played in the same team as Ossie Ardiles at Leyton Orient in another charity game but it didn't end in glory this time as he snapped his Achilles and ended up on crutches. He was, in turn, snapped hobbling out of the ground on those crutches with his lower leg encased in plaster with physio Mike Varney finding it extremely hard to suppress a grin. Irving saw the funny side of it, and he was also smiling as he hobbled out of the stadium. In fact when Spurs lifted the UEFA Cup trophy after their penalty shoot out victory over Anderlecht at White Hart Lane, Irving had to be wheeled around the stadium in a wheelchair and was determined to be in the dressing room to celebrate along with his players, despite his painful handicap.

*

Because of my close relationship with Irving Scholar I was aware of the financial problems within Spurs much earlier than any other journalist. It was with great reluctance that Scholar had to concede to me how it was going, but he had no choice when leaks within the City began to undermine him. Scholar needed a rescue plan in a hurry. My suggestion was Robert Maxwell. Scholar and Maxwell got together and the Spurs chairman was trying to negotiate a financial package with Maxwell that would have injected £13m into the club and averted the impending problems.

For Venables it was a double-edged sword. He feared that the arrival of Maxwell would take football, and more importantly Spurs, further down the line of becoming a corporate play thing, manipulated for the purpose of a new owner wanting more hands on control over the manager, as well as trying to turn a huge profit.

The big problem for Venables was that the attitude of the fans might be more powerfully in favour of someone,

anyone, who would inject new funds into buying players. Venables' fear has proved correct in the modern game, where supporters are prepared to turn a blind eye to where the funds are coming from because they are thrilled with their new signings; whether it is a former Thai Prime Minister with a history of human rights issues with his assets frozen and his wife charged, or a Middle East consortium buying Robinho, a £32m flop during the earliest days of the Abu Dhabi ownership of Manchester City.

So Spurs became the battle ground for one of the first contentious football takeovers between global big-hitters, and in the case of Maxwell, someone who turned out to be as colourful and dubious as Thaksin Shinawatra.

Venables said at the time, "The role of the manager in English football is being diminished by amateur directors who want to play at professional football and if we had Maxwell as well as Scholar we could all move one step down towards the boot room, myself included."

While Scholar was trying to save the club, Venables was giving the fans what they wanted - success on the pitch. Venables' team began the 1990-91 season going ten league games unbeaten with a goal tally of 17-4 before their first setback, a 3-1 loss at Liverpool in early November. Venables had given David Howells a role just in front of his back four and this allowed Paul Gascoigne the freedom to make forward runs; matching Lineker for goals, 19 apiece that season. The club were full of optimism on the field, but off it Scholar was in a panic about the £900,000 outstanding to Barcelona on the Gary Lineker deal.

The master plan when Scholar had taken Spurs public was to invest in a diversity of areas outside of football and to utilise the profits to re-invest in the team. The chairman allayed any fears about the possible failure of these subsidiaries with the assurance that it would never affect team matters.

Most of the subsidiary companies did not initially perform particularly well, but this had been buried in the accounts so that when the parent company showed a profit in 1987-88, it was mainly due to profit on football operations and the sale of the club's Cheshunt training facility, which brought in £4.5m. Two other companies, Synchro Systems, a computer-ticket operation, and the Hummel sportswear franchise, deteriorated dramatically during 1989. It was a mistake to inject £3m of football club money to support it.

This contradicted Scholar's belief that it was the subsidiary that should support the club. Paul Bobroff, who had been Scholar's long-time partner, took the opposite view, as he argued that Tottenham were now a public company with a responsibility to shareholders. This difference led to Bobroff's failed attempt to oust Scholar. When Bobroff discovered that the third major shareholder, Tony Berry, backed Scholar, he resigned and offered his 10 percent stake in the company up for sale. Scholar and Berry realised they could not buy this stake without having to make a similar bid to all shareholders, in accordance with Stock Exchange regulations. But then the club's merchant bankers insisted on Bobroff's reinstatement. By the summer of 1990, it was clear that two more of the Spurs subsidiaries, clothing companies Martex and Stumps, were also in serious financial difficulty.

With the problems mounting, another cash injection was urgently needed to write off the debts of the subsidiaries and to service the Midland Bank debt, which had touched £10m and was still rising. On the day of the World Cup final in Rome, Scholar spotted Robert Maxwell being driven through the streets of the Eternal City and felt it might have been an omen.

For some time he had in mind that the Mirror Group Newspapers owner might yet be the man to rescue his ailing club from bankruptcy. He phoned Maxwell with whom he had sat on a Football League television committee in 1984, and the two men met on a Sunday morning, 25th July, in Maxwell's office.

Scholar outlined his plan to create a new share issue for the parent company while accepting that in the current financial climate the chances of City investment were small. He felt the help of a major investor would do the trick and wondered if Maxwell would underwrite a rights issue at £1.30 a share. The shares would be offered to existing shareholders on a one-for-one basis. Scholar and some of his colleagues would not take up all their offer and Maxwell would be left with a guaranteed 26 percent of the company, possibly a good deal more if the new shares were not bought. This would have the effect of injecting £13.2m into the company, thus clearing the £12m that Scholar now assessed to be the debt. In return for an assurance that he would not sell his shares and would remain to run the club, Scholar had Maxwell's provisional agreement, providing the whole deal was kept strictly secret.

In addition there was also the outstanding debt to Barcelona, which Scholar knew would not be forthcoming from the bank. Scholar turned to Maxwell again. He asked Maxwell to loan Scholar's company, The Holborn Property Company, a sum of £1.1m which Holborn would then re-loan to Tottenham to pay out on the Lineker deal. That way, Maxwell's involvement in paying off the outstanding amount would remain secret. Maxwell, in turn, supplied the money from a private company, Headington Investments. Scholar offered a block of shops he owned in the Kings Road as security for the loan.

Scholar had to place his rescue share package before the club's directors without being able to identify the man who would underwrite it. Scholar and the club's financial director, Derek Peter, were given the go-ahead at a board meeting from which the chairman, Bobroff, was missing, having taken a holiday.

Although he was unaware at the time, Scholar was now in uncharted waters and was not receiving the soundest counsel about the rules governing the conduct of public companies. The Stock Exchange would look with distaste on a company that negotiates a rights issue and loan without its chairman being present or its shareholders informed. When Bobroff discovered the plan, he felt it smacked of desperation and he immediately attempted to slow down the deal. Most of the club's shareholders were the fans who stood on the terraces and who would not normally be consulted on the running of the football club. But a public ownership should have obliged the board to inform and consult. This was to have serious repercussions on Scholar and Tottenham within weeks.

Maxwell reached agreement with Scholar on the rights issue, but was for the moment unable to proceed because of the rules of the Football League. These stated quite clearly that no individual could have a financial interest in more than one football club and had been introduced when Maxwell had tried to purchase Elton John's shares in Watford while he was still involved with Oxford United and Derby County. To proceed with the Spurs agreement, he would have to sell his interest in Derby County and when the directors there refused to buy his shares, he put the club on the market, blaming the sale on what he described as "a lamentable lack of support". He added, "They (the supporters) must realise that I do not have a license to print £50 notes". His asking price for the Baseball Ground was £8m, but he was not bowled over by the rush to buy as this was not the climate where buying a football club was seen as a common-sense investment. It was while Maxwell was waiting for a buyer that *The Sunday Times* revealed his identity as the man who would underwrite the share issue. This story, by the paper's City editor Jeff Randall, was to send shock waves through the game.

When I spoke with Irving about the leak which effectively scuppered the Maxwell bid for Spurs, Scholar suspected that Maxwell might have tipped off Randall himself, because he was getting cold feet about investing in Spurs and didn't want to let Scholar down, so thought of a clever ruse of forcing him to pull out. Scholar is now re-thinking this theory. In a weak moment of anxiety he told me that he confided in someone he thought would maintain discretion and keep the faith he showed in him. He now suspects he was the man who leaked the story to Randall. It may or may not be right, but Scholar has his suspicions. At the time, it appeared only Maxwell and I knew about it. Now Scholar has confessed that he also told someone else!

The Football League were still adamant that any such deal

could only proceed if Maxwell sold his shares in Derby County, and that his son Kevin would need to relinquish his chairmanship of Oxford United. The PFA made comments about people who chose to use football clubs like Monopoly pieces.

Maxwell advised Scholar that the deal was off because he felt he had not been given the full details of the scale of the trouble at Spurs. Scholar refused to accept he had lost his, and the club's, potential saviour. Yet, it was the secrecy surrounding the deal with Maxwell that was to cause as much of a furore as the arrangement itself. Had Scholar kept his shareholders fully informed of the dire straits into which the company was sinking, he might well have evoked more sympathy and certainly prevented official action from the Stock Exchange, who launched an enquiry into the £1.1m loan from Maxwell which paid off the Lineker transfer. In legal terms, that deal should have been presented to a meeting of shareholders for their approval.

Venables was managing to shield his side from the worst of the behind the scenes manoeuvres as they embarked on a very successful early season run of results, knowing little about how perilously close they were to seeing the club's finances crumble beneath them.

A board meeting on 14th September, squeezed between victories over Derby County and Leeds, had Scholar seeking Bobroff's resignation since their destructive squabbles were threatening the Maxwell rescue package. A vote of no confidence in the company chairman was passed by four votes to one, after Bobroff refused to resign, though he could not be kicked off the board without a full shareholders vote. He insisted that he would stay to protect the interests of the smaller shareholders. Scholar threatened to call an EGM to have him removed while, in the meantime, the club's financial advisor and broker both resigned in protest at Bobroff's sacking.

At this stage, Maxwell went on David Frost's Breakfast TV programme to say that once the bickering was over he would re-start negotiations. "I am flashing a yellow card at those involved in the squabbles," Maxwell proclaimed in typical authoritarian mode, as he used his *Mirror* sports pages to try to get across his message, led by yours truly. It was riveting news coverage, almost on a daily basis, creating mayhem and animosity among our rivals, and, naturally, exclusive to our sports pages, egged on by me in the background. "It is inconceivable that I or anybody else would entertain a rights issue, or become in any way involved in a club, while some of the board are behaving like children," Maxwell declared. Privately, though, he told me, "I want Bobroff to accept me or I want him out of the way."

On 19th October, the Stock Exchange suspended shares in Tottenham Hotspur pc and would also censure Scholar for the way he had conducted his negotiations with Maxwell. When the board finally tried to explain their intentions in a letter to shareholders, several of Scholar's actions were described as "ill-conceived and inappropriate". Within two weeks of the share suspension Scholar had bowed to advice that he should resign from the PLC while maintaining his position as chairman of the football club.

Venables may have been shielding his players from the turmoil, but he himself was keeping a sharp eye on the various developments and sensing that this might be his own opportunity to throw his hat in the ring as the man who could lead a move to rescue Tottenham. He had made no secret from back in his QPR days that one of his ultimate ambitions was to own a football club. Here, it seemed, opportunity was beckoning, and in a big way.

Perhaps, given these extraordinary off the field problems, it was not surprising that, after such a good start, results began to deteriorate. In November, Venables pointed to a squad depleted because of the shortage of money, which meant he could not rest key men and had to select others with niggling injuries. But results were not the only thing occupying Venables' mind at this time. He had been linked to a vacancy at Real Madrid following the departure of John Toshack, even though it always seemed unlikely the Spaniards would allow one British manager to follow another, even if he had once won the La Liga title with Barcelona. Venables was not unhappy that the story was being floated, because his own contract was due for renewal at the end of the season and he had found the new offer insulting.

Venables had clearly spotted an opening, an opportunity, and Scholar discovered, through another *Sunday Times* exclusive, that Frank Warren was trying to mount a takeover bid, with Venables as his chief executive and funds from overseas investors, including pension funds. Warren's profile had been high following the trial, for attempted murder, of Terry Marsh, the former boxing world champion, following Warren's shooting in Barking, Essex. Marsh was found not guilty.

It was all going wrong for Scholar. An indication of the financial plight came with the announcement of an increase in admission prices halfway through the season, which outraged fans, quite naturally, coupled with a slump in results. Since the beginning of November they had dropped 19 points out of 30. As the team prepared for the FA Cup third round tie at Blackpool at the beginning of January, there were humiliating revelations as Southampton threatened court action over a £20,000 sum they claimed was outstanding on items for the club shop under the old Hummel agreement while Chelsea were seeking £45,000 over a ticket bill.

Scholar went to see businessman Ted Bull, whose company was called Landhurst Leasing. Scholar had talked to Bull previously about a scheme to raise money by creating a leasehold investment out of the boxes at Tottenham. Warren had been involved in some of those discussions. Bull was opposed to Maxwell. Chairman Nat Solomon had to find the finances to avert the crisis and the bank wanted a sale of assets. There was no bigger asset than Paul Gascoigne. Scholar was unaware that the Midland Bank had made the sale of Gascoigne one of their conditions of continuing to service the £12m debt. In one of his first public statements Solomon made it clear that the sale of Gascoigne was a possibility.

That news broke on the day of the Rumbelows Cup quarter-final against Chelsea. No longer could Venables protect his team and players from the boardroom machinations. Relations between Scholar and Venables were frosty over the Warren link, and now the impending sale of Gascoigne was the subject of red-hot daily newspaper gossip, claim and counter claim.

Behind the scenes the bank were pressuring the directors over this issue, and co-director Douglas Alexiou warned Scholar that unless he complied he would have to go. Alexiou, like Scholar, wanted to find an alternative to selling Gascoigne.

Scholar said at the time, "I attended the board meeting but made it very clear I would be prepared to discuss the sale of Gascoigne only on the basis that the alternative would be putting Tottenham into administration or receivership. If it was a choice of Tottenham going broke or Gascoigne going, then I was prepared to discuss his transfer, although I was still opposed to it and would do everything to stop it."

Dennis Roach was Scholar's choice to tout Gascoigne abroad, even though he had fallen

> **As he drove, Irving explained that he had received a death threat that the police were treating seriously. I had never seen him so shaken up. I knew from that moment that Irving would consider a potential sale of his shares, although, knowing him as well as I did, he would want to ensure the future security of "his" club.**

out with Mel Stein over the sale of Chris Waddle to Marseille. Scholar warned Roach that even if he found a suitable Italian club, there was no guarantee that the club would sanction the move — if they could avoid it, that is.

However Scholar was happy to sanction the sale of Vinny Samways to Aston Villa for £800,000, even though the "deal" was put on ice for a couple of days so the midfielder could play against Chelsea in the Cup tie. But with Villa manager Josef Venglos and his chairman Doug Ellis at the game, and after a poor display by Samways, Villa wanted to pull out of the deal. Scholar knew that Venables objected to the Villa deal as he valued Samways at £1.5m and when the manager substituted the player Scholar suspected it was to scupper the deal! Such was the paranoia behind the scenes at the time!

Venables was, indeed, plotting. He was linked with an offer of a huge salary to manage the US World Cup squad, and, with his connections and popularity with the press, there seemed a campaign mounted to "sort out this mess".

In the event, Spurs lost their Rumbelows League Cup replay going down 3-0 at the Lane to Chelsea. I was covering the game for the *Daily Mirror*. It was a tough report to write. It was clear all the boardroom shenanigans had finally reached the dressing room, and that was hardly surprising. With the momentum growing towards the sale of their hero, Paul Gascoigne, the mood was turning nasty and Irving had become the focal point of the supporters' anger.

I sat in my seat in the press box and called "copy", and filed my report. But during my work, I received a message from one of the press box stewards. "Don't leave the ground, go to the main reception and wait in the foyer for the chairman, Mr Irving Scholar".

It was all rather unusual. Even though I was a close friend of the chairman's, I never abused that position, never hung around him after the game, never accepted an invite to go to the boardroom. Strange, then, that he needed to speak to me urgently. I thought he was depressed at the result, and that he wanted someone to talk to.

When White Hart Lane was virtually deserted he emerged from the private director's only executive lift into the foyer and looked genuinely delighted and relieved to see me. Then I noticed he was surrounded by police, some of them armed. Irving thanked me for hanging around, and began to tell me that he needed a police guard and that he would appreciate it if I would accompany him home in his car. Three policemen escorted the two of us to Irving's car, parked quite nearby in the director's car park. Two police cars chaperoned Irving's 4 x 4 out of the ground through the streets of North London, and all the way to his West London home.

As he drove, Irving explained that he had received a death threat that the police were treating seriously. I had never seen him so shaken up. I knew from that moment that Irving would consider a potential sale of his shares, although, knowing him as well as I did, he would want to ensure the future security of "his" club.

*

The night before Irving finally sold his shares to Alan Sugar and Terry Venables, I sat with a very depressed and harassed Spurs chairman in the intimate surroundings of the up-market Bleeding Heart wine bar restaurant, down a side alley off the jewellery outlets and gold merchants, in Holborn. My wife Linda was there with me, and we did our best to console someone who was clearly distraught at the prospect of selling his beloved Tottenham. We told him over and over again that, although he felt at the time it was right to go, it wasn't, and that he would always regret it. The whole evening was emotionally charged, with the smoke filled room, the wine and the food failing to bring any light to Irving Scholar's darkest moment in football. I knew he didn't want to sell. He didn't want me to keep on telling him precisely what he already knew. But I was the only person who had lived through this nightmare with him, who had experienced first hand the night when he thought his life was threatened by some madman, and who had put up with so much for so long, that it had all brought him to his knees. Who could blame him for wanting out? I couldn't blame him for that, I told him. Surely, it made sense to sell, get out of the madhouse, and let someone else have a go? He knew his time was up, but he couldn't come to terms with it.

I reminded him of the battle to acquire the club in the first place, how he had out-manoeuvred the old board, to buy up shareholders' voting rights, to ensure he had a foot hold in the club. No one would have more heart and soul in the club, no matter who bought it now or in the future.

Irving desperately wanted me to tell him it was the right thing to do. Eventually, I did. Just to console him. But deep down, I knew he could turn it around if he had the energy and/or the inclination. I sensed he had neither. He was drained, and he feared the club he loved so much was drowning. He no longer felt he was the man to pull them out of the mire with the determination to take it forward. It had been such a hard slog to get to this point. He knew it might be years ahead of struggle, and it was a really tough call.

Irving will never concede that I was right. What he didn't know at the time was that his associate and former friend, Paul Bobroff, was under financial pressure to sell his shares. Bobroff was made bankrupt in 2006, having failed in a number of subsequent ventures.

More significantly, to this day, Irving tells me the truth about what really happened behind the scenes during that contentious period, and he swears that the extent of the crisis was greatly exaggerated. He was deeply hurt by what he describes as "lies" that the club was on the precipice of going bust. He never believed that was the case, or that the problems were insurmountable. He argues very formidably that the facts didn't support the "spin" put about by his enemies.

What a shame that such a genuine football man was hounded out. Many people who get involved in football, often from afar, think that it's easy; it isn't. Irving is living proof that even a deep affection for the club doesn't guarantee it will all go smoothly.

Irving Scholar was an outstanding chairman. He understood a manager's mind set and their problems. He shared their desire for a successful team, as the priority for the club. He shared the supporters' desire for a winning, successful team that could bring back the glory, glory days. His heart was in the right place. Now, you cannot say that about some of the owners of Premier League clubs today, can you?

The 'will-he-won't-he' sell Gascoigne scenario alienated his support, but the fans didn't know the truth, and it's my hope that detailing much of what really went on behind the scenes will make them understand where Irving was coming from, and where he was going.

In an exclusive interview, Scholar recalled how he tried to tip off Alan Sugar that Venables had no intention of remaining as manager; that he was plotting to quit the dug out for a more lofty position in the boardroom. Sugar was convinced Venables was unfit to do this and he was equally adamant that he would not allow the manager to move into the board room. Scholar reveals that had he known Venables would have been allowed to become chief executive he would not have sold out to Sugar!

"Just prior to the takeover I spoke with Alan Sugar on the phone and we agreed to meet one to one and I was going to warn him what Terry Venables was like. The day of the meeting I got a message from a friend that Venables had found out and was going to be there. I rang Sugar and told him it was off but wanted his confirmation about what Venables' role was going to be should he take over. He assured me that he would continue as manager and came out with the phrase that caused trouble when *Behind Closed Doors* was published, 'Venables thinks he's an entrepreneur but I don't'. Had I known that Venables was leaving the dressing room, I would never have sold to Sugar and he would have known that. I wanted him to continue as manager, because that was what the fans wanted, I knew he would have lasted maybe another season; two maximum if I had stayed with him, but the fans believed in him. He's too clever by half and knew that in the end, all managers reach their sell by date, unlike CEO's or directors.

"In September 1994 I watched Spurs at Leicester and sat next to Nat Solomon in the director's box. In 1991 he had been completely seduced and won over by Venables and was totally convinced that he was vital going forwards. At Leicester Solomon said to me during the game 'I am sorry Irving, but had I known what he was really like, I would never have made that decision. I apologise'. At least he was honest about making a bad judgment.

"When I met Sugar in the South of France in the summer of 1993 just before the court case, I asked him what he would have done about Venables had Spurs won the FA Cup again in 1993 instead of losing to Arsenal in the second semi-final between the two clubs at Wembley. 'I think I've got big balls, but they ain't that big' he said, and that from the supposed hard man in the boardroom! So Football *is* all about results after all, even morality takes a back seat."

It took Irving some time to recover from the traumas of Spurs and being forced to walk away from the one thing above all else he treasured the most. Irving tried his hand at football club ownership again, consulting me before he took the plunge with Nottingham Forest. He missed the day to day involvement with football, but it was always destined to end in tears at Nottingham Forest, as any club would always be second best for a man who

> **"A lot of nonsense was written in the papers at the time, and indeed consistently since, that the club was bankrupt and heading for receivership, that it couldn't pay its way. It was factually all not true, and, of course, we ended that season winning the FA Cup."**

had, and still has, Spurs in his blood. He had his moments at Forest, appointing Dave Bassett, who got the promoted club straight back into the Premiership, and then appointing Paul Hart to revamp the youth policy. Spurs bought three players developed through the Forest academy, Michael Dawson who captained Spurs, Andy Reid, and Jermaine Jenas, who left Forest as a 19-year-old in 2002 and spent three years at Newcastle before joining Spurs in 2005 for an eight-year career at the Lane. Irving also revitalised the Spurs youth system in his time at the North London club, bringing through Sol Campbell and Nicky Barmby, after earlier giving Keith Burkinshaw a totally unexpected £250,000-a-year budget.

Reflecting on his time as chairman, my chief memory is of my incessant questions and begging him to allow me to publish some of the 'off the record' stories he told me about, but despite this the former chairman and I have remained true friends and he is still a confidante many years after he ended his involvement with football. His biographer, Mihir Bose, called him "the Martin Peters of the board room", reflecting Sir Alf Ramsey's comment about his midfielder being ten years ahead of his time. In his biography *Behind Closed Doors*, this is what Irving had to say about me...

"The only journalist I was close to was Harry Harris. He had been on the local paper in Tottenham and shared my deep love for the club. Almost from the beginning we got on very well. Harry, by this time, was the chief football writer of the *Daily Mirror*, which meant that like all Maxwell employees, he was at the beck and call of Captain Bob. How Harry balanced Maxwell's dictates with his own journalistic needs is a story that he must tell one day himself, but all I can say is that, despite everything I went through with Maxwell and others, my friendship with Harry remained unimpaired. If anything, I came away appreciating how well he understood my own, and Tottenham's, predicament."

Irving has kept his counsel since leaving the club; but the former chairman and one of the most influential figures in the club's recent history, discussed his beloved Tottenham with me for

Down Memory Lane.

In the near 60 years I have followed the club and been privileged to have an inside track through the scope of my job, one of the men who fashioned the modern game and the modern Spurs, is someone who wants to say the least but has the most to say.

So, when I approached Irving at his home in Monaco for the first edition of this book, I convinced him he owed it to himself to have his say and put the record straight on a few sensitive issues.

"When I left Spurs in 1991 the club, and indeed the entire game, was ready to take a big step forward," he told me, "it was a very important time for Spurs. We had been working on the formation of the Premier League for years together with my great friends Peter Robinson of Liverpool and Martin Edwards of Manchester United. I went to many meetings and, together with David Dein, we were among those pushing for it.

"It had been a long, hard season in 1991 but we had come out at the end of it with everything sorted out, and we were ready to go forward and prepared for European competition.

"A lot of nonsense was written in the papers at the time, and indeed consistently since, that the club was bankrupt and heading for receivership, that it couldn't pay its way. It was factually all not true, and, of course, we ended that season winning the FA Cup. Firstly if that had been the case, which it wasn't, I can assure you I would have put in every penny I had in to avoid it. Our biggest problem was persuading the Bank to give us a 12 month overdraft facility instead of month to month; they didn't throw it around then like the confetti of recent years.

"Finally in late May, shortly after the FA Cup final, the terms of a new 12 month facility were finally agreed and all the paperwork signed off by Nat Solomon, the chairman of the PLC. The club, as always, was running smoothly and profitably. End of nightmare, end of problems, no more sleepless nights, shackles off, freedom to go forward... unhindered. Let's get back to what the business is supposed to be about and what we do best, winning football matches!

> **"You cannot blame somebody who knows nothing about something for making mistakes... he [Sugar] once appeared on *Football Focus* and confessed, 'My regime was not successful', and he said as much when he left the club."**

"Spurs were one of the big five clubs at the time, they were in Europe, which they hadn't been since before the UEFA ban on English clubs following the horrific tragedy at the European Cup final of 1985 staged at the Heysel Stadium in Belgium.

"We had finished third the season before but it was only the top two that qualified that year and new money was about to flow into the club from the recently announced Premier League. The club was set right for the big step forward with football finally on the "up", after all the horror stories of the past eight years.

"The game was heading for change, and for the better, all our painstaking efforts were about to pay off. Tottenham should have played a major part in that new beginning, they would have been part of the new dawn had things naturally moved forward in the right direction but the right decisions weren't being taken on important issues."

He continued: "I remember in late 1990 attending a lunch at The Savoy Hotel at the invitation of Jeff Randall, then business editor of the *Sunday Times* who had gathered a few heads of Industry to talk about their sphere of business. When it came to my turn, I painted a picture of where I felt football was heading and how things were likely to change dramatically over the next few years.

"Television was clearly going to play a formidable role and Sky, which was facing its own very major financial problems at the time, was likely to use pay per view to drive themselves forward. Basically they were going to copy the model of Canal Plus in France which had launched itself on the back of football, by buying the exclusive rights and becoming the most successful Pay-TV broadcaster in Europe at the time. Open mouthed surprise was an understatement from those around the table, I think they thought I was from Planet Loony.

"Several years later, when Rupert Murdoch tried to buy Manchester United, Jeff Randall rang me as soon as the bid became public and asked me if I remembered the lunch at The Savoy. He then told me that he had never forgotten it, even though he thought at the time I was off my trolley, but it was so vivid a picture it was virtually what had happened with the formation of the Premier League and that when a major player such as Murdoch is bidding it was final confirmation that it had to be taken very seriously and was no longer just a rich man's toy. He apologised profusely for thinking I was crackers and said he was going to write his column that weekend and tell the story of the lunch and all the prophesies that came true. Well he is a West Ham fan, what can you expect!

"When Manchester United were valued at £100m on the Stock Market you just knew that people who really didn't have a great interest in football would start paying attention to it. They probably thought that if someone like Martin Edwards could do it, so could they. What they hadn't taken on board was that Martin had been brought up in it and his father, Louis, had been chairman before him for many years and first joined the board immediately following the Munich air crash in 1958.

"Back in 1984 I had been approached to buy 10% of Manchester United for £300,000. Whilst being an obviously good long term investment and cheap at the time, I just felt I couldn't, on principle, invest. It just didn't feel right that the chairman of Spurs could be a decent-sized shareholder in another club. There were no football rules at the time stopping me, but in my mind it wasn't the right thing to do. A short time after I declined, someone approached me and asked me if they should buy them at the same price and I greatly encouraged them to go ahead and they did, finally selling them, when the company was sold to the Glazers. Wise investment."

Then Irving discusses his successor: Alan Sugar, Sir Alan Sugar or is it Lord Sugar? Scholar never mentions him by name…

"You cannot blame somebody who knows nothing about something for making mistakes. In football, as in life, no one gets it right all the time. Everyone is always going to make mistakes. He is the first to admit he knew nothing about the sport. In fact he once appeared on *Football Focus* and confessed, 'My regime was not successful', and he said as much when he left the club. He appeared on *Match of the Day* and when he looked back he confessed that 'we didn't do it'. Well, it doesn't take a genius to work that one out!

"Let's be fair to the past two owners; they have spent considerable sums in the transfer market. But my philosophy has always been, it is not what you spend, it's what you spend it on that counts. Everyone signs players even down to non-League where it may be for a dozen tracksuits, but he who makes the fewest mistakes wins."

Irving was very much a hands-on owner and chairman but, he stressed, "I never told any of my managers which players to buy, but there were times that I would play devil's advocate, that I would want to know more about the players and would ask pertinent questions. It was just a friendly chat and my view was that I only wanted the manager to buy the right player for Spurs and wanted him to be sure in his own mind that he was making the right choices. No manager ever resented that line of conversation. In fact I think it helped them make up their own minds.

"Look, it's easy sitting on the couch on TV criticising without any of the responsibility. Look how many failed managers sit there picking out all the faults, pointing to which players should be playing and why others shouldn't, showing exactly where everything is going wrong. No manager ever had to pick a team in a television studio; if they were that good how is it that they aren't looking after one of the top clubs instead of pontificating on everyone else's failings? How often have they had to appoint a manager? It's much tougher than it looks, believe me, so it's not so easy to apportion blame."

Scholar took enormous pride in his own achievements. "Don't forget that every manager I worked with finished in the top three at one time whilst one ended up fourth and that was Keith Burkinshaw, his best finish. After I left it took Tottenham another eight years to get back into Europe, now that's not very good by the club's standards. But I am not knocking Sugar." Well, at long last the name of the Lord finally passed Scholar's lips.

Selection of the manager is always key. He is the man who dictates the areas of the team that need strengthening. Scholar

> **It must still rankle with Spurs supporters that the genius of Dennis Bergkamp, who loved Spurs and who had pictures of Glenn Hoddle on his wall as a kid, ended up at Arsenal when all he wanted to do was to play for Spurs.**

continued: "One of the keys is to give the manager time and understanding, to give him the help that he needs, understand his problems. It's easy to moan and groan and tell everyone you want to come in the top four, who doesn't? When players are on the floor who is there to lift them... the manager. When the manager is on the floor, whose job is it to lift the manager... the chairman. He needs to put a consoling arm around the manager; encourage, listen, understand. When the chairman's head is on the floor, who consoles him... tough! No one, the buck stops there. But it's the manager who gets the sack normally once the crowd start singing 'sack the board'. Yet, it's the chairman's job to try to run the club smoothly, to keep everyone on their toes, to get the best out of them.

"But it's an old chestnut of mine - whoever is doing the job of chairman must have a feel for it, a passion for the club, a passion for football. Alan Sugar has a feel for electronics that is why he has been so successful in that field. Football is different, it's special, and no one can quite put their finger on what makes a good chairman. For me it is a real feeling for the club. Football is the peoples' business. Unfortunately, this is not just common to Spurs, it happens at many clubs, the men who run the club don't understand it's the peoples' club, it's their business as well."

One of Scholar's big problems was the amount of pressure he put himself under when events both on and off the field were not going as well as he had hoped. He felt personally responsible. The years in charge took its toll as he lived the job day and night. He always wanted to buy the best players. He would always do all he could, and possibly more, to keep a player he wanted to stay. He always put the club first at all times.

He reflected on how the club lost Sol Campbell on a free transfer to Arsenal.

"The club allowed Sol Campbell to run down his contract and walk out on a Bosman free. Daniel Levy had taken over about seven months before and I know they tried to persuade him to stay, but Sugar had the best opportunity to keep him. Sol Campbell should not have gone. Life is all about timing and picking the right moment to sit down with him and agree a new contract and ensure he signed it. That time was immediately after the 1999 League Cup final win, when he still had over two years left on his contract.

"Sol went up to lift the cup and he was as high as a kite. All you needed to do was to put an arm around his shoulder and invite him for talks over lunch the very next day. For me, contracts in football are an art form. You must never allow any player that you really want to keep come anywhere near the end of his contract. I always tried to be one step ahead. It is a really bad sign when players want to leave, it creates the wrong atmosphere. Of course, top players were sold when I was chairman, but we always replaced them and improved.

"When Chris Waddle left the club in the summer of 1989, lots of people were upset, me included. But we got on with the job and ended the following season in third place and won the FA Cup the year after. I had players crying their eyes out in my office when they had to leave, although I am not going to say which ones."

It must still rankle with Spurs supporters that the genius of Dennis Bergkamp, who loved Spurs and who had pictures of Glenn Hoddle on his wall as a kid, ended up at Arsenal when all he wanted to do was to play for Spurs. "Sugar had the chance to spend his money on a player like Bergkamp but his manager didn't want him!" Scholar reveals. "Bergkamp was desperate to sign for Spurs, so desperate that in the cab on the way to Highbury to sign for Arsenal, his agent was calling Sugar begging him to sign Bergkamp - I know that for a fact as Bergkamp's agent told me.

"There was a missed opportunity if ever there was one. But then again, it's easy to criticise, as I have already said, so I am not going to point a finger at Gerry Francis for not wanting Bergkamp, when even the best managers, like Sir Alex, have bought some duds in the past.

"The trouble was that Alan Sugar openly admitted he knew nothing about the football industry, but he would not accept he was wrong until it was far too late. Even Alan knows it, and at least he has had the gumption to admit it. He's now doing what he really likes, being recognised from *The Apprentice*, he needs that. The big problem for Spurs was that Sugar was not a football man and he even told me so. It was 1993, he had been in charge at Spurs for two years, and he was surprised to see me at Anfield, as a guest of the Liverpool club. Spurs had signed Jason Dozzell and the fee was being settled by a tribunal. I asked Sugar what he expected to pay. He said, 'what are you asking me for, I know more about pickled herrings than I know about football...' I was so taken aback my mouth must have dropped open. I was stunned!"

One time, Scholar bumped into Sugar's son Daniel, "Daniel shocked me when he said, 'Never mind that so-called Dream Team of my dad and Terry Venables, the real Dream Team would have been my dad and you!' With that he walked off. You could say I was taken aback."

Returning to his early days as chairman, Irving said: "When I first joined, practically the first thing I discussed with Keith Burkinshaw was how we could invest in the youth set up and produce our own. We set out to create a competitive youth system and we did. Since then I don't know what's happened. How Gary Mabbutt was allowed to leave the club is a disgrace, I would have had him in the youth set up from the day he retired to learn the ropes and progress from there. Waddle would have been back too, he had a very good eye for a player, but the game has changed in the same way as life has; it has an uncanny

knack of mirroring life. It has also gone from, what Danny Blanchflower called the Glory Game to the Money Game. It has been overdone and I am disappointed that clubs haven't shared a little bit of their newly found wealth with the fans, in at least trying to avoid hiking the prices every season."

Irving Scholar has never received the recognition his tenure as Spurs chairman deserves. He was one of the game's greatest innovators: the first to take a UK club to the Stock Exchange to be listed as a PLC, the first to have TV advertising for the games, the first to seek and find more global merchandising deals, and appointed architect Bill Jenkins to prepare the master plan for the modern White Hart Lane, although, of course, the new Lane is now a global market leader.

He was a leading light in the development of the modern game, along with his close friend the Arsenal vice-chairman David Dein, he helped smash the TV cartel which had artificially held back revenues to the game, and he was one of the architects of the formation of the breakaway Premier League in the days when a breakaway was not as loathsome as it is today with the proposed breakaway European Super League, and Scholar advocated that the new Premier League should retain its links to the Football league and the rest of the pyramid and gained FA approval.

Despite his wealth and status, Irving Scholar was not aloof and on a Saturday you would even find him in the Spurs shop selling the products himself in an effort to make his ideas work. His encyclopaedic knowledge of the game was legendary and he always loved a Spurs quiz because invariably he knew all the answers and would win!

The Gazza Phenomenon

Gazza is a hero to me and every other Spurs fan who loved watching him dribble into the opponent's box, getting down to the by-line, turning and dribbling his way back out of the box past the same defenders, before turning again to face the goal, and shooting into the corner. Such invention and impishness endeared him to the Spurs faithful right from the start. Irving Scholar wanted to buy Gascoigne from Newcastle, but knew there was strong opposition from Manchester United. Irving told me how he made it his personal mission to persuade the Geordie to come to London and play for his beloved Tottenham.

How every Spurs fan rejoiced when he fired that long range free-kick over David Seaman's head in the FA Cup semi-final. It was so sad to see Gazza wound up like a man possessed when he came out for the Wembley final against Nottingham Forest a month later when he inflicted that horrendous knee injury upon himself with that ludicrous flying tackle on Gary Charles. Gazza was never quite the same force after that.

A measure of my admiration for his talents is that when I received my first PC at the Mirror offices and had to use a password for the first time, I chose G-A-Z-Z-A, and used it throughout my 18 year stay there.

I invented the phrase Gazzamania. Mel Stein was his agent, friend, minder and advisor for more than a decade. I know Mel exceptionally well. Stein wrote Gazza's first of many autobiographies and in it said, "*The Sun* started Gazzamania officially with their constant use of the phrase, but Harry Harris in the *Mirror*, had probably been responsible for coining the phrase almost a year before. All *The Sun* was doing, as it did so often, was reflecting opinion."

I first noticed Gazza when he turned out for England's Under-20s in the annual Toulon Tournament. During this tournament you noticed, not just his extraordinary talents, but his sheer cheekiness. The stadium was rudimentary at best, it had concrete seats and one side was open to the motorway with a wire mesh and stretch of grass between the players and the traffic. After scoring a spectacular goal, Gazza ran across to the side line looking out on the passing cars to begin his celebrations to an imaginary crowd!

Back at the team hotel, where a handful of Fleet Street's more junior journalists had gathered for a daily briefing with the manager, Gazza didn't simply look out of his window above us, but decided to urinate down in our direction. Literally taking the piss out of the press!

At the airport, the players wandered off in groups to board the little buses to take you to the plane. Not Gazza. He got lost, and ended up on the bus full of journalists and assorted FA officials. He was a bag of laughs, always smiling, and you sensed here was a boy in love with the game and loving every minute of it. No one imagined he would turn into a man with such dark moods and deep personal problems.

I recall telling Bobby Robson to pick him ahead of the final friendlies before Italia '90, but the England manager told me that Gazza was "daft as a brush" suggesting he couldn't be trusted. I am convinced Bobby listened to what I had to say, and although he wouldn't admit it, picked Gazza because of it. We can all recall his tears in the semi-finals and how close England came to glory.

I had many trips to Rome to watch Paul play for Lazio, when he wasn't injured that is, but I never wanted him to ever leave Spurs and I know how much Irving fought to keep him. Such was Scholar's desperation that he accepted my advice to tempt Robert Maxwell, my boss at the *Mirror* at that time, to buy Spurs instead of the Sugar-Venables partnership that I sensed would come to grief. Gazza was so close to Venables, it was always going to be impossible to gain Gazza's support for the Maxwell move. Yet, when Maxwell made his pitch to buy Spurs, 'Captain Bob' wanted to have his picture taken with Gazza.

Stein wrote, "On 9th September, the morning after the Derby game, the headlines were not so much about Paul's hat-trick as Robert Maxwell's bid for Tottenham. Paul's reaction was immediate, 'I'm not playing for that fat bastard. If he takes over then I'm off.' He knew the way Maxwell, when owner of Derby, had treated Arthur Cox and believed football was an ego trip rather than a passion to him, and wanted no part of it. Stein added: "Harry Harris of the *Daily Mirror* phoned me on behalf of his newspaper's proprietor to ask if there was any chance of a photo of Gazza with Maxwell if the deal went through. 'No chance,' was the reply."

Stein continued, "Maxwell was still playing his own game, and whilst no formal proposal had been made, he was still using the *Mirror* to sway public opinion in his favour by its campaign to keep Gazza, as a national treasure, in the country of his birth. Harry Harris, chief football writer of the *Mirror*, was recalled from abroad." Mel was referring to how I was summoned from Malaysia, the last port of call for a summer England tour in 1991, to help Cap'n Bob orchestrate his final pitch to buy Spurs.

Maxwell would also lean heavily on my inside track on events inside White Hart Lane with my close friendship with Irving Scholar and how best to keep the FA and Football League at bay because of his son's ownership of Oxford United and his own control of Derby County.

It was my idea to focus on Gazza, whom Venables had lined up for a move to Lazio. And, I am sure, Maxwell's pitch to keep their star player had resonance with Spurs fans, who were devastated that he had to be sold off to pay off the debts. It nearly worked, but Sugar won the day, which was probably for the best in the long run given the later revelations about Maxwell's plundering of the Mirror's pension funds.

Like Irving Scholar, I was desperate for Gazza to stay, and would have done everything in my power to assist Irving in his quest to balance the books so Gazza could stay at the Lane but it wasn't to be.

Manager Terry Venables was a beleaguered man and badly in need of some encouragement and it continued to be supplied in the competition in which Spurs had excelled over the years, the FA Cup. Spurs were drawn at home to Brian Horton's Oxford United, the club so much linked to the Maxwell family, who had already disposed of Chelsea at Stamford Bridge with a convincing 3-1 scoreline, but now they came across Gascoigne in irresistible mood as he scored twice and made the other two in a thrilling 4-2 fourth round success at the Lane. It was a performance that had Venables purring, "You cannot compare him to any player from the past. He has Dave Mackay's attitude, a hunger for the game. He has that upper-body strength that helped make Maradona a great player."

Gazza was helping to build his own reputation as Spurs FA Cup run continued with a 2-1 win at Fratton Park against Portsmouth on 16th February 1991 with another outstanding virtuoso performance and two more goals that took Spurs into the quarter-finals, where they would face Notts County. Spurs duly beat Notts County in the quarter-final as expected - 2-1 with goals from Nayim and almost inevitably Gazza again - to set up a semi-final date with Arsenal. For the first time, a semi-final was to be staged at Wembley, a controversial decision at the time. Gazza recovered from a double hernia operation and had successfully come through a test on the injury against Norwich four days before the big Wembley date. With the team's form erratic and the club in crisis off the field, Arsenal, sailing serenely towards the title, were clear favourites to beat Spurs and reach the final. But Venables' decision to risk him proved momentous.

Gazza's free-kick in the first few minutes remains one of the outstanding goals ever seen at Wembley, old or new, and he also contributed to the second, scored by Lineker. Venables could hardly contain his delight about the way Gazza's free-kick put Spurs in control of the match. "It must be one of the best ever seen at Wembley", he said, "It is easy to bend a ball without pace but to bend it with power and accuracy is very special, especially from 35 yards." Alan Smith pulled a goal back before half-time but Spurs were in control even though Gazza was replaced halfway through the second half by Nayim. With Arsenal taking risks Lineker was able to score his second of the match to wrap up a memorable 3-1 win.

By the time of the final Lazio already had negotiated terms to buy Gazza while the price of the new shares was set at 70p, just over half the amount that had been offered and 21p less than the price at which they were suspended. Just 11 days before the final there were more meetings with Venables pushing for a sale and leaseback deal. Scholar had been advised it would need a package worth £2m plus salary to keep Gazza at Spurs. Scholar was highly suspicious as to whether the money really existed despite Venables' persistent assurances that it did.

In Cup final week, Venables' obsession to take control continued as he prepared his team against Brian Clough's Nottingham Forest. He wanted a deal sealed before Wembley. Gazza's future was also on the agenda before the final. Stein asked Scholar if the club was in a position to present a package to keep the player, to guarantee him a minimum £2m net after tax over the first year plus a hefty annual salary of £1.3m a year,

> "Gazza's free-kick in the first few minutes remains one of the outstanding goals ever seen at Wembley, old or new and he also contributed to the second, scored by Lineker. Venables could hardly contain his delight about the way Gazza's free-kick put Spurs in control of the match. 'It must be one of the best ever seen at Wembley!'"

plus extras such as bonuses and appearance-related add-ons. Scholar had to at least match the Lazio signing-on fee for there to be any chance of negotiations to continue. Scholar told him the chances were virtually nil. It was the eve of the final, and Scholar knew he had lost his battle to keep Gazza.

Spurs board was anxious for Gazza to sign for Lazio that morning; if Gazza was injured in the final it could jeopardise the big deal that would stabilise Spurs' finances. The stakes couldn't have been higher; the drama of the entire situation could not have been more intense.

While the players were in the Royal Lancaster Hotel, the day before the final, Scholar took a call, at 4.30pm, from a mutual friend of both Venables and himself to say the Spurs manager had the money in place. Scholar made one last gesture; he said that he was prepared to deal at 80p a share... but if Venables could guarantee to keep Gascoigne he could have the club at 70p a share. Scholar was ready to drop £270,000 for his stake to keep Gazza.

The mutual friend, Sir Philip Green, went to report back to Venables at the team hotel and the lawyers and advisors got to work on preparing the agreement. Scholar came to join me and some friends for a drink while keeping in constant touch with his own solicitor, Peter Robinson. By 10pm there was a hitch. Still no agreement. Venables was seeking "certain comforts from the Midland Bank", and as they were conditional, Venables' hopes that he would lead out his team at Wembley as the new owner of the club, could not be fulfilled.

Venables had made his own representations to Stein in an effort to keep Gazza, and to convince him to go to Italy later in his career. While Venables' mind was in a state of turmoil, Brian Clough took the week off! His side were firm favourites with Stuart Pearce, Des Walker and Gary Charles at the back, and Roy Keane in midfield. But Spurs had Gazza, whose goals against Oxford, Portsmouth, Notts County and Arsenal, had brought them to within touching distance of glory on the field with the future of their star player still top of the agenda. Clough commented, "I have not seen much of him actually, but I think he has a lot of talent and I've asked our coach driver, if he sees him in the Wembley tunnel, to run him down."

When Gazza was lining up for the presentation to the Prince and Princess of Wales and the Duke and Duchess of York, it was clear that he was once again hyped up. Perhaps more so than usual, and this surfaced in the opening minutes with a dreadful challenge on Garry Parker for which he should have been cautioned. A few minutes later, as Gary Charles supported his attack on the edge of the Spurs box, Gazza again lunged in crazily, his leg outstretched, a desperate dangerous challenge which should have brought an instant red card, but referee Roger Milford awarded a free-kick. The real damage had not been inflicted on Charles, but on Gazza himself. And if that was not bad enough, Stuart Pearce then drove the resulting free-kick beyond Erik Thorstvedt to put Forest ahead. As Spurs restarted the game from the centre spot, so Gazza collapsed and had to be stretchered off, his final finished after 15 minutes..

Gazza's enforced departure initially left the Spurs team, which was lucky not to be down to 10 men, in a depressed state. Gary Crosby missed a glorious chance to increase Forest's lead, but Eric the Viking made the save and when Lineker found himself one-on-one with Mark Crossley, he was dragged down. Penalty given. Lineker took the kick himself but Crossley flung himself to his left and touched it away for a corner.

Seven minutes into the second half, Spurs took control. A move began by Nayim and carried on by Paul Allen provided Paul Stewart with the opportunity to drive the ball across Crossley for the equaliser. From then on Spurs revelled in the Wembley atmosphere, but couldn't find the winner. When the whistle went for the end of normal time, Venables was quickly in

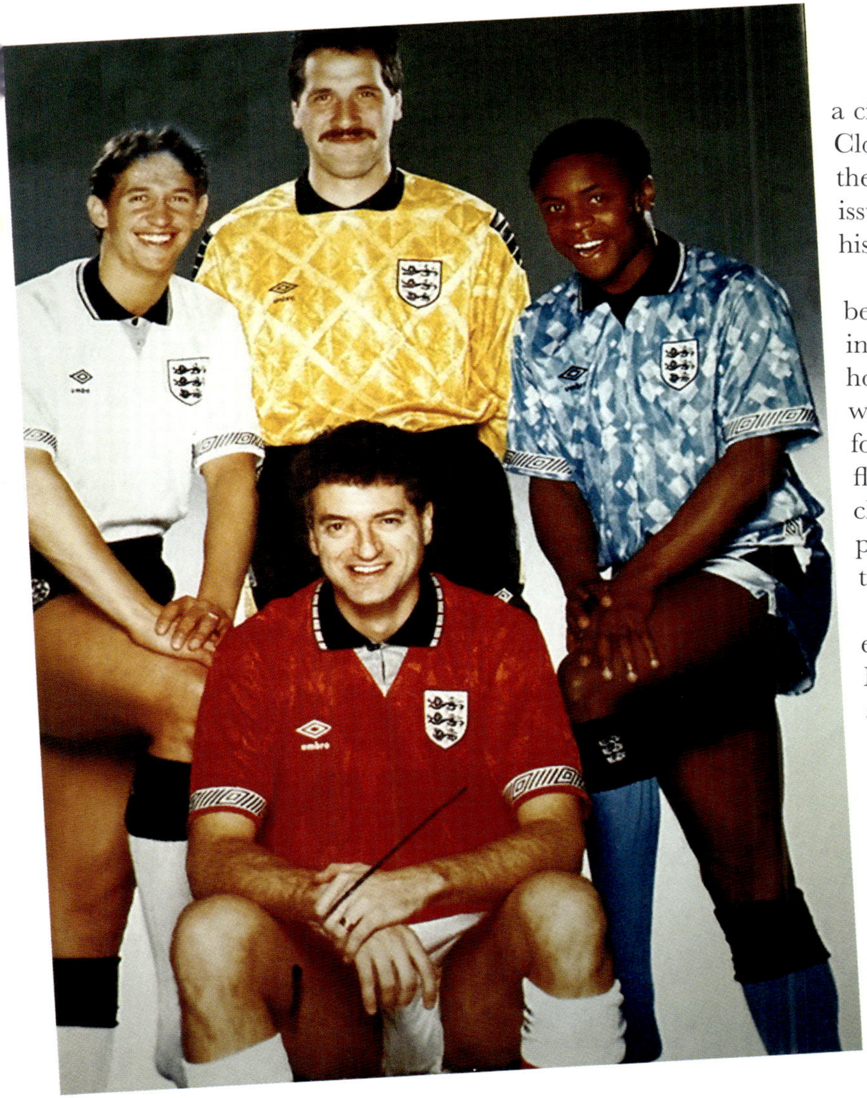

At the height of his fame Paul Gascoigne was notoriously unreliable, so when The Mirror *organised a photo-shoot ahead of the 1990 World Cup I had my doubts that Gazza would show up. When he failed to show the Sports Editor thought it would be fun if I stood in for him!*

a circle with his players with instructions and encouragement. Clough, in contrast, never moved from his seat except to pass the time of day with a policeman. He left his coaching staff to issue the orders and this was surely an error of judgement on his part.

Clough had his own unique way of going about his job, believing his aloofness scared his players and frightened them into action. This time it didn't work out. Spurs continued to hold the initiative in the extra half hour, but the goal that won the FA Cup for them was a cruel stroke of misfortune for England's centre-half Des Walker. A Nayim corner kick, flicked on by Stewart, was heading towards Gary Mabbutt, charging in behind the Forest defenders. Walker sensed his presence, went to intercept but succeeded only in deflecting the ball past his own keeper.

Proud Tottenham lifted the FA Cup - without Gazza who ended the day in hospital. For Venables, it was his first major English trophy. While the celebrations continued that night and the next day around Haringey Town Hall, thoughts were spared for Gazza, who was undergoing surgery on his right knee, a career-threatening injury to his anterior cruciate ligament. Venables revealed at the time, "The boy is pleased for the lads but is devastated by his injury and by missing most of what was the biggest game of his life."

Venables was destined never to win another domestic trophy, and Gazza was destined never to be quite the player he was at his peak.

With the contest about to hot up between Maxwell and Sugar for control, Scholar felt more confident than at any other time that it might be possible to keep Gazza at Spurs. Scholar felt this opened up the possibility of Spurs forcing Gazza to honour his existing contract. Scholar recalled in his book *Behind Closed Doors*, "I had just walked

THE ITALIAN PURSUIT OF GAZZA ... Mirror Sport catalogues the chase for England's most gifted player

GOODBYE GAZZA

£8m

PAUL Gascoigne will sign for Lazio today in an £8m deal

Spurs ace *WILL* sign for Lazio today

PAUL GASCOIGNE signs for Lazio of Italy today for a world record £8 million that will leave Spurs and their supporters shattered.

EXCLUSIVE

By HARRY HARRIS

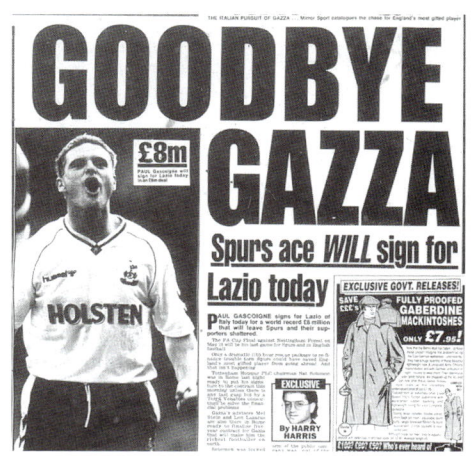

into the room when Nat (Solomon) came running over to me, holding a piece of paper. He said, 'Irving, look at this'. It was a proposal by Terry Venables and Alan Sugar, but Nat was pointing to a clause in the proposal and I read it with absolute incredulity. It said that the Sugar-Venables offer was conditional on the sale of Paul for a figure of not less than £4.5m. After I had recovered from my shock I started laughing. For months now there had been any number of stories in the press as to how keen Terry was to keep Gascoigne at White Hart Lane, how if he was allowed to take over the club Gascoigne would actually remain at White Hart Lane, and he would do everything in his power to make sure he did. I was painted as the villain of the piece, the man who said he wanted to keep Gascoigne was secretly planning to sell him. In contrast Maxwell had made it clear to Nat that he would be very unhappy if Gascoigne were sold."

Given the catalogue of injuries suffered by Gazza after 1991, including a shattered knee cap after a nightclub incident, perhaps Tottenham did well to sell him when they did. As Alan Sugar recalls, "I'm still shocked when I recall the sale of Paul Gascoigne to Lazio. Gazza's injury in the 1991 Cup Final had seen me decide to step in but the transfer was still going to be worth £5.5million. But during his rehabilitation he damaged his knee again, putting the whole healing process back several weeks. Terry Venables explained to me that a very well-connected Italian called Gino Santini was going to broker the deal to see whether we could get Lazio to pay us even though Gazza hadn't recovered. Gino turned out to be a restaurateur in Kensington who spoke Italian and had helped Mark Hateley move to AC Milan. However he was absolutely useless in the negotiation on this matter. It was handled in the most unprofessional manner, with stupid suggestions such as: 'Insurance policies will cover Gascoigne's recovery and provide a warranty to Lazio.' Why would anyone in their right mind pay us £5.5m when the player was still injured, without any medical evidence he was fit to play? Despite this, Eddie Ashby convinced Venables he would find an insurance company who would cover the risk, came up with a Mickey Mouse insurance policy and ran up a bill with a broker. The offer put forward was so ridiculous Lazio laughed at it. In the end Lazio sent over a medical team to examine Gascoigne at the end of his rehabilitation and approved him fit to play. They then paid up. In the meantime, Santini had slung in a bill for £200,000 which we paid into a Swiss bank account. There was nothing I could do about it other than demand that he send us a proper invoice."

One of my favourite pictures is of Gazza and Paul Stewart in the background during one of my many meetings with Pelé. At the fair were giant photos of England players, Paul Gascoigne and John Barnes and it was a photo opportunity that I couldn't resist as Pelé had been discussing the virtues of both players during my breakfast interview. Pelé thought Gazza was exceptionally gifted but despaired about his life style.

A Gazza Semi-Final Memory

I was expecting a phone call with confirmation of a meet up with Paul Gascoigne to illustrate a *Soccer Skills With Gazza* book. I had been expecting this phone call since January, it was now December, but then everyone wanted Gascoigne. He was in constant demand not only from Spurs autograph hunters, but every club worldwide who were trying to sign the new football world star.

So when the phone rang and I picked it up I was, as the saying goes in football, 'over the moon' because it was the voice of Roddy Bloomfield on the other end of the line. Roddy was the commissioning editor for Stanley Pauls and the much talked about *Paul Gascoigne Soccer Skills Book* had a starting date! "Paul it's finally on. We have tied Gazza down. It's Sunday next week, then the following Wednesday. It's a 10am start at Wembley stadium. I have just put the phone down but not before Gazza said 'Tell my neighbour Trevillion to bring stacks of pencils!'"

I arrived early on the Sunday morning, but not before Gazza. He was already on the Wembley grass and one of the many balls surrounding him flew my way. Knowing Gazza well, I had already ducked as a ball flew over my head and from that moment on he continued to do magical things with the footballs that took my breath away as I was busy with the pencil.

I didn't realise it then but this was a

moment in time. As Gazza lined up eight footballs in and around the penalty box 25 yards out and said "Name a top corner Paul", "Top right" I replied and that was exactly where the ball ended up between the crossbar and the goalposts. "Top right again" I said, and it was repeated. "Top left" I shouted, and the same result. Gazza continued and each of the five balls at his feet ended exactly in the top corner I shouted out.

A letter from Mel Stein, Gazza's business manager, confirmed the many pencil drawings I had captured at Wembley which were signed off by Gazza would be in the soccer skills book.

Tottenham started on an FA Cup run which resulted in a dream semi-final against Arsenal, with the demand for tickets so great it would be the first FA Cup Semi-Final to be played at Wembley. I was there and just five minutes into the game Tottenham were awarded a free kick outside the penalty box. But not 25 yards… 35 yards from goal. Gary Lineker and Paul Stewart put their hands in the air, but Gazza being Gazza decided on a Wembley repeat and the ball flew past the Arsenal and England Goalkeeper David Seaman into the top right hand corner, ending up in the back of the net. Spurs went on to win the game 3-1 and then lift the FA Cup at Wembley. Both Gascoigne and I enjoyed a champagne drink out of the FA Cup as we both flicked through the pages of the SOCCER SKILLS WITH GAZZA book…what a memory!

PT

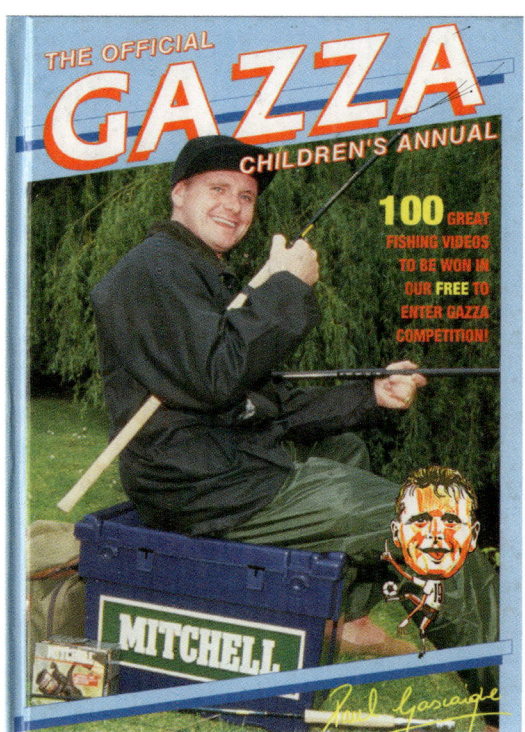

Gazza became a huge and marketable star after his starring role in the 1990 World Cup, here is a small sample of the products with which he was associated to which I leant my art.

PETER KIRKLEY'S WORD (YOUTH DEVELOPMENT OFFICER AT NEWCASTLE) WAS ENOUGH FOR NEWCASTLE TO SIGN YOUNG GAZZA - THEY BECAME FIRM FRIENDS.

WARNING PENCIL SMUDGE EASILY

GAZZA'S 'SHIRLEY TEMPLE' MOP OF HAIR, MADE HIM STAND OUT IN HIS FIRST TEAM PICTURE IN THE NEWCASTLE SQUAD, 1985-86.

17 YEARS OLD

WARNING PENCIL SMUDGE EASILY

ROUGH SKETCH NOT TO LEAVE STUDIO

GAZZA WAS NO SOCCER DUNCE, WHEN IT CAME TO DRIBBLING ROUND THE CONES. BUT HE WOULD PRETEND TO BE ONE IN TRAINING.

WARNING PENCIL SMUDGE EASILY

ROUGH SKETCH NOT TO LEAVE STUDIO

ON GAZZA'S RETURN FROM THE WORLD CUP, OVER 500,000 PEOPLE WERE THERE TO GREET THE ENGLAND TEAM. GASCOIGNE WAS HANDED A PAIR OF FALSE BOOBS AND TRIED THEM ON FOR A LAUGH.

WARNING PENCIL SMUDGE EASILY

GAZZA'S LAST KICK IN A SPURS SHIRT - NOT THE BALL - BUT FOREST'S GARY CHARLES.
FA CUP FINAL 1991.

WARNING PENCIL SMUDGE EASILY

Gary Lineker

The greatest English striker of his era became a star by scoring ten goals in two World Cups and helped Spurs win the FA Cup but he was soon sold for a relatively small fee in 1992 that caused outrage among supporters and caused a breach between Spurs 'Dream Team' owners: Sugar and Venables.

I interviewed Gary at Heathrow Airport before he boarded the plane for Nagoya for his first visit to the home of his J League club, Grampus Eight, having agreed a highly lucrative deal, his final contract as a footballer.

Three chief football writers, myself included, through Gary's agent Jon Holmes, had arranged to accompany the striker and his "bad toe" to Japan and when British Airways discovered that we were being welcomed by Lineker and his agent, we were upgraded to first class and it was quite an experience. The first class cabin was virtually empty apart from Lineker and his entourage which had now swelled to include our small media group.

The media had a lot of time for Lineker. He always made himself available, he was articulate, and had a charming, disarming smile. He was clearly destined to become a media star in his own right once he finished playing and indeed he has fulfilled that ambition more than he could have ever imagined. So much of that is down to his highly efficient and well connected agent, Jon Holmes.

One of the world's greatest violinists, Nigel Kennedy, a mad Villa fan, stayed at the Forte Village during Italia '90 where I got to know him very well and we ended up playing doubles together against Gary Lineker and Ron Atkinson on Centre Court in front of a handful of on-lookers. Big Ron was devastating at the net, where he didn't have to run too far, but not too hot on his ground shots. Gary, ever the natural athlete, was by far the best of a very average bunch and just about carried Big Ron over the victory line!

It was my investigations into Gary's manager at the Lane, Terry Venables, that led me to probe deeply into his move to Grampus Eight. Although Lineker played on at the Lane until the end of the 1991-92 season, the move to Japan had been agreed much earlier, and was one of the main issues that led to the fall out between Sugar and Venables.

The sale of Lineker formed part of the contents of my book, *Venables — The Inside Story*, co-written with Steve Curry. While Steve concentrated on the life and times of Venables, the player, manager and multi-faceted personality, my part of the book focussed on his transfer dealings and business enterprises. Let me make it perfectly plain from the outset that not at the time, nor now, am I in any way suggesting that Gary did anything untoward, or knew of anything untoward in his transfer to Grampus Eight. My investigations at the time were into the fall-out between Sugar and Venables and the fact that Lineker's transfer was a catalyst for their fall out. I did not investigate Lineker or insinuate that he had any knowledge that his move was behind the acrimonious break down of the working relationship between chairman and chief executive.

Here is my interpretation of the Lineker sale as chronicled in the Venables book,

"England captain, superstar, Mr Clean, and still one of the world's top goalscorers, yet Gary Lineker was sold off for just £850,000! When Lineker and Gascoigne returned to Tottenham after Italia 90, after England had narrowly missed out on the World Cup final, beaten by eventual champions Germany on penalties in the semi-finals, their value on the transfer market soared. The then Spurs chairman Irving Scholar rejected a near £5m offer for Lineker from Torino; £3.5m in cash plus a Yugoslav striker valued at between £1m and £1.5m. Gascoigne was priceless. Scholar felt, even though Lineker would be 30 in November 1990, he was worth keeping - and made his views plain to Jon Holmes."

In the chapter about Lineker, Scholar was quoted as saying, "Jon Holmes went to Italy for talks and Lineker himself indicated that he would be interested in a move to Italy if the club were agreeable. I was not agreeable and, to be fair to Terry, he too was annoyed with Holmes.

"I told Holmes that he had no right to negotiate in Italy without the club's permission. Lineker was under contract and he would have to honour it. I have a lot of sympathy with players in this country because salaries are so vastly higher abroad, and it is hard to stand in their way. But Lineker had already made his pile from a move abroad with Barcelona, so I did not have so much sympathy. Gary and Terry were always very close, but I didn't sense that Gary turned against me because I had blocked a move to Italy. Once I had put my foot down that was the end of the matter, we never discussed it again."

Scholar and Venables did meet the Torino go-between, who was a friend of Venables, and he suggested that if they would pay £5m for Lineker that would enable him to go to Derby and get Mark Wright and Dean Saunders. Torino, however, were not prepared to bid more than £3.5m. Holmes went to Italy to speak to the club, but Scholar was adamant the deal would not go through unless he got his price.

In the book, I went on to observe, "Sugar was unaware of Lineker's valuation in 1990, only a year before an agreement was made prior to the 1991-92 season to sell him to Grampus Eight for just £850,000 at the end of the year. Venables' argument was that Lineker had reached the wrong side of 30 and had two years left on his Spurs contract at the time the deal was made. He considered it a good arrangement, but Sugar was deeply disappointed that Tottenham received such a small sum.

The reason for Sugar's reaction was that, in his second meeting to buy the club, his prospective partner Venables had told him that Lineker would fetch £4m. Once the pair were running the club, Sugar questioned why Spurs had got only £850,000, referring to their original conversation about Lineker. Venables explained that, given Lineker's age, he was unlikely to fetch much more than £1m on the transfer market. Lineker, personally, would stand to make £4m in salary and signing on fees – but not Spurs."

The plot thickened as I continued to relate the inside track on the Lineker transfer, "Sugar describes this as one of the 'misunderstandings' that began to creep into his relationship with Venables. Sugar relied on Venables' footballing knowledge, being a novice to the game, but would no longer make such a mistake. His suspicions about Venables' ability had increased, perhaps justifiably, as £850,000 was certainly cheap for Lineker, when an earlier £2m offer from Blackburn Rovers had been rejected.

Sugar was further concerned because a fee of £1m had been mentioned but Venables explained that the 'balance' was made up by Lineker waiving a cash payment of £166,666 as the final part of his signing on fee that was due on 1st August 1992. However as Lineker had asked for a move, Spurs would not have been liable to pay it anyway.

To be balanced and fair, I put forward Venables' point of view as to why it made sense to him to sell off his star striker at what seemed such a give away price, "Venables was pleased with the deal he made with Japanese club Grampus Eight because he got cash up front and kept Lineker for another year before he moved on with his age approaching 32. Indeed, had he insisted that Lineker saw out the final year of his contract, to the end of 1992-93, Tottenham would have received nothing for the sale. But, as a result of the Lineker transaction, Sugar insisted that Venables kept him informed in future of all major transfer dealings."

It was clear that the details of the Lineker "transaction" were beginning to leak out, as I pointed out again in my book, "Spurs intended to keep the details of the deal with the Japanese club under wraps for the entire season, no doubt not wanting to risk the wrath of the fans so soon after the departure of Gascoigne. But the news leaked to the press, and so it became public.

The Lineker issue formed part of the court hearings between Sugar and Venables. On 10th June, 1993, Venables' QC, Mr Mann, pointed out how Sugar's affidavit gave the impression that "Mr Venables' integrity has been questioned. We are, ourselves, questioning Mr Sugar's integrity." Claim and counter claim - and Lineker at the centre of the storm.

Sugar mentioned in his affidavit how Venables led him to expect over £1m, but in the end the club received £850,000. Sugar wanted direct access to those in Japan who facilitated the transfer deal, and thought that would be relatively simple because of his contacts in that country through his Amstrad company.

Sugar wanted to reassure himself that the full sum Grampus Eight was paying to sign Lineker was being disclosed.

As I wrote in the book, "The implication from Sugar was that some money was being paid to a third party, a suggestion that infuriated the Venables camp."

For Venables' part, he pointed out that Tottenham had signed Lineker for £1.2m, so "he was obviously worth considerably less aged 31. The effect of that transaction was that Tottenham were getting their money back for him. The alternative would have been to have let him serve out his contract and get nothing at the end. It is absolutely incredible that Mr Sugar should state that his faith in my business acumen has declined as a result of this purchase."

Jon Holmes backed Venables' understanding of the situation. He, too, rubbished Sugar's estimate for Lineker of £4m. He also criticised Sugar's fears that the Grampus Eight agent, Christian Flood, was hiding something from Tottenham. Like Sugar, Flood had plenty of experience in dealing with the Japanese, having negotiated tours of the country by Margaret Thatcher.

Another important fact, to justify the transfer, was that Lineker wanted to make the move and if he was kept on against his will then his motivation at Tottenham would have been sure to decline (where have we heard that one before? Oh yes... Berbatov and Keane). Sugar's lawyer was quick to state that there was no question mark against either Lineker or Holmes in their dealings with Grampus Eight.

I concluded in the book, "That accounts for Lineker's and Holmes' positions, but not all the facts of the deal emerged in court. Flood and his Japanese partner Yoshio Aoyama were approached by Grampus Eight, backed by Toyota, and given a sum with which to negotiate a deal to sign Lineker, with the money to be split between Lineker and Tottenham. Although the precise sum is confidential, it is in the region of £5m. For concluding the deal, Flood and Aoyama received a commission of £100,000 plus the lucrative rights to market Lineker's Japanese deals in England. All payments, other than the commission, went direct from Grampus Eight to Tottenham or Lineker and his agent. It was Flood who initiated the deal because he understood how popular Lineker would be in Japan. He remains convinced that both parties got as good a deal as was possible given the sum of money available.

"Therefore we can see how, within the first few months of the Venables-Sugar partnership being set up, there had been three big money transfer deals, involving Gascoigne, Gordon Durie and Lineker in which Venables had tried to minimise the role of Sugar in the negotiations even insisting that he did not get involved. Yet each of the deals disappointed Sugar in one way or another, giving rise to his concerns about Venables' business acumen. Had Venables involved Sugar more closely there would have been less chance for misunderstanding and suspicion."

HH

My Footballing Friend Gary Lineker

Every time I've met Gary Lineker I've always received a very warm and friendly welcome and found that, providing the question is on football, he always has an answer, and he never acts the superstar. He is very honest and will tell you he is not a naturally gifted footballer in the same way as 'Gazza', Maradona or Glenn Hoddle. "They are the gifted ones and I haven't got that many tricks or footballing skills when on the ball. I've always had to work hard and I mean VERY HARD at improving my football ability but I have always had an eye for GOAL and I mean ALWAYS. In one season as a schoolboy I smashed in over 160 goals.

"I practiced hour after hour running with the ball at my feet with my chin lifted up resting on an imaginary shelf and eventually I was able to let my feet be my eyes on the ball as I surveyed the entire field looking for a teammate free in space to pass the ball to or space to run into with the ball and hurt the opposition.

"I also practiced endless hours with a teammate knocking long high balls into the penalty box until I could tell the instant the ball left my team-mate's foot by checking on the ball's trajectory where it would land and I would race to collect it. FOOTBALL was always my NUMBER ONE love and I was determined not only to play for a league club but also to represent England. Ability is one thing, but above all you have to believe in yourself. IT'S THE UNSHAKEABLE SELF BELIEF THAT TURNS AMBITION INTO REALITY."

THE SECRET OF BEING FIRST IN THE BOX

"The secret of being first in the box is not to follow the ball in, but to anticipate before the cross is made where it's going. Defenders watch the ball more than they watch their opponents, but because they are generally bigger and stronger than attackers, you will, if you follow the cross into the box, nearly always be beaten to it by the defender.

"I never wait until the cross has been made, but race into a particular SPACE where I believe the ball will go. Whenever I make a success of such a move and put the ball in the net, people will say 'Lineker was in the right place at the right time'. But the truth is, I will have made twenty or more runs into those spaces. It's when the ball arrives at the same time and I put it in the net, the defenders and the fans notice me. It's all about getting there, free in space every time a goal chance presents itself."

MY SECRET DREAM GOAL

"For my secret dream goal I would have my old mate Peter Shilton in goal for the other side. Shilton's team are on the attack and I've raced back to help out in defence. I am on the goal line as their striker shoots. I block it and control the ball on the line, saving what would have been a certain goal. Then I dribble the ball up-field, performing three 'NUTMEGS' along the way. Then I'm in a ONE ON ONE with Shilts, so I nutmeg Shilts and the ball rolls through his legs towards the unguarded goal. I nip round him as he makes a backward dive. TOO LATE. Then I race forward with the ball, I stop, standing with my foot on the ball on the goal line. I then wait for Shilts to get up then turn and I back heel the ball into the goal.

JUST SEEING THE LOOK ON SHILTS FACE WOULD MAKE IT THE PERFECT DREAM GOAL!

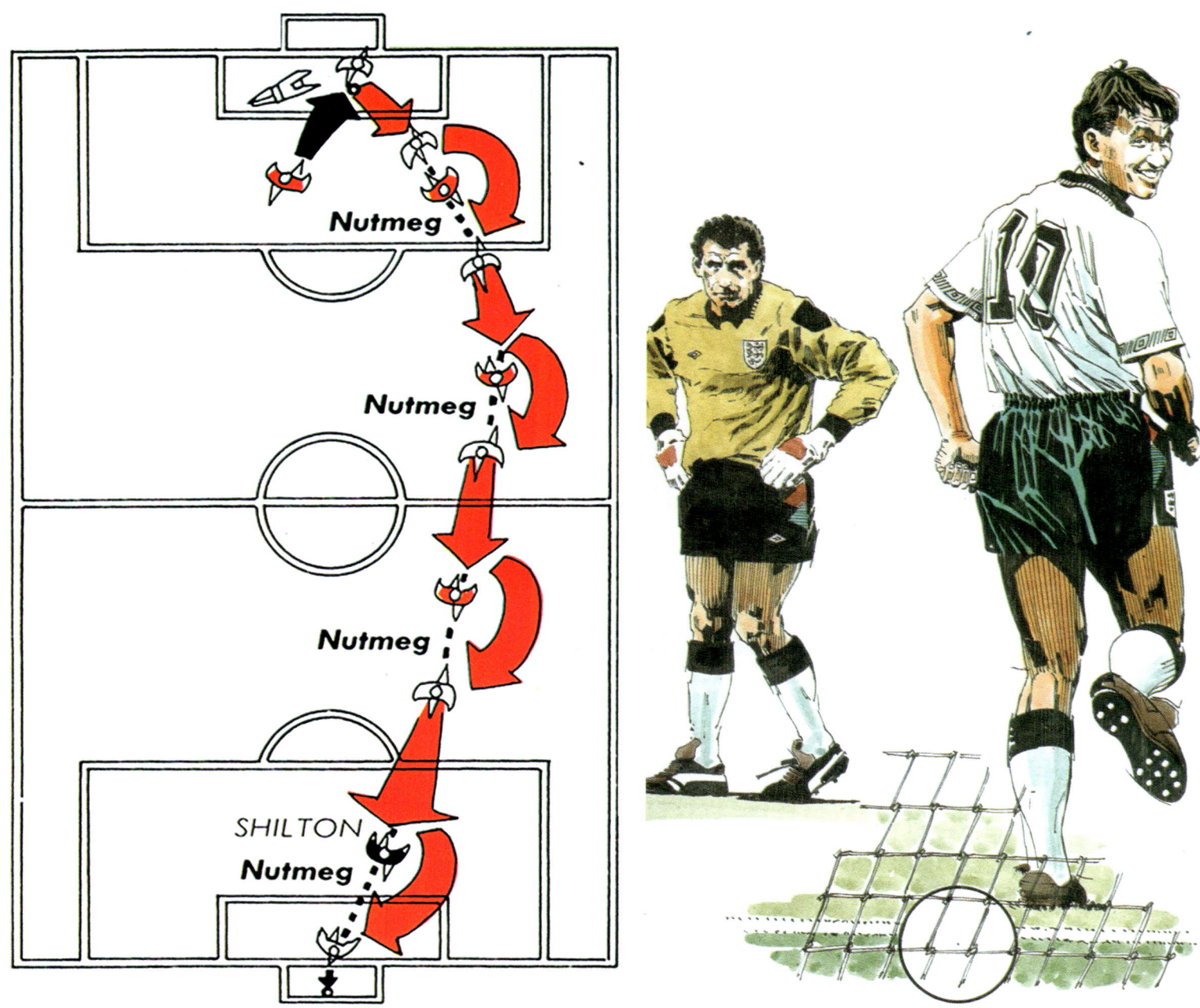

Lineker's Low Down On Shooting...

Many football fans believe the most embarrassing thing to happen in football is when an opponent knocks the ball through a player's legs and then runs round him and collects it. This was never my thinking. The most embarrassing thing I have always believed is when a good goal chance presents itself and you sky the ball well over the bar. I could count on one hand the times I sent a goal chance over the bar during a season and that includes international matches.

Shooting is by far the most important part of a striker's job. I've always concentrated on keeping the ball LOW. The only certain way to achieve this is to ensure the KNEE of the kicking foot is OVER the ball when you strike it. Then follow through in the direction of the ball adding power to the shot.

Never attempt for maximum power when striking the ball. Hit it too hard and there is every chance you will mis-hit it.

KNEE OVER BALL

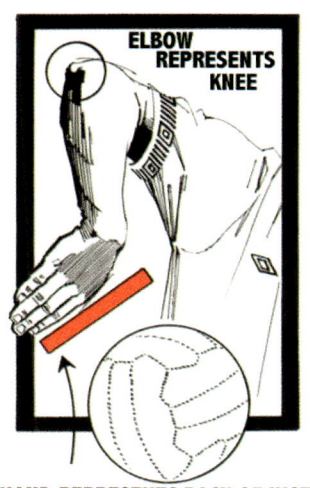

ELBOW REPRESENTS KNEE

HAND REPRESENTS BACK OF INSTEP

Grant Curran

I have supported Spurs for 35 years; my first game was against Nottingham Forest, 30th December 1989, which unfortunately we lost 3-2. I first met the Spurs players in the car park of their home ground on Saturday 10th March 1990 before the game against Charlton Athletic. Tottenham won 3-0 and the goal scorers were Lineker, Polston and Howells.

The players in the photographs are:

Paul Gascoigne - before and after! - I met Paul again at Spelthorne Leisure Centre on Saturday 24th February 2024 for *An Evening with Gazza*. I showed him the photo of us in 1990 which he signed and had my picture taken again with him some 30 odd years later.

Gary Lineker; Gary Mabbutt; Erik Thorstvedt (which he signed for me at a later date); David Howells; Paul Walsh; Paul Allen and Vinny Samways

I met Peter Shreeves at a football presentation and he also took a training session for my football team.

I also met Paul Miller, Tony Galvin and Mark Falco at a La Royale event near Tottenham stadium. Later that same day I met Gary Lineker at Spelthorne Leisure Centre in Staines as he was reopening the centre.

I am a Business Development Director in the AV industry. I still play football, as a goalkeeper for Vets Football team Windlesham FC, I am a former Brentford youth team goalkeeper, and also a member of a grass court tennis club in Windsor.

Terry Venables

Terry Venables arrived from Barcelona at a difficult time for the club both financially and on the pitch. He galvanised the team and led them to third place behind perennial champions Liverpool in 1989-90 and signed quality players such as Paul Gascoigne and Gary Lineker. The two prominent and exciting England players would have made a formidable force with Chris Waddle, but the Geordie had been sold to Marseille in 1989, the same summer as Lineker arrived. In 1990 all three players would star in England's World Cup adventure in Italy and return as national heroes as football leapt from the back page to the front page, from sport to celebrity, from the remnants of a working class sport to a future where footballers become multi-millionaires with all the trappings that go with it. The real disconnect between the ordinary fans and the sport began, and the corporate interest in the sport was about to explode.

Despite these star names and all that glamour at the Lane, despite Venables' success in guiding Spurs to victory in the 1991 FA Cup, the club remained in financial peril, although then chairman Irving Scholar always insisted that the financial issues were manageable. Eventually Venables brought in Alan Sugar, after numerous failed attempts to find a viable and acceptable financial backer, to devise a rescue plan, but their falling out brought further stress to the club with court issues and supporter opinion split.

In the dug out there is no doubt that Terry Venables was a genius, and I have repeatedly stated that fact in numerous interviews about his status in the game, and how much his ability as a manager was ultimately tarnished by his antics in the boardroom. Equally there can be no denying that he was a flawed businessman. After my expose in the *Daily Mirror*, it was clear that there would be charges of inappropriate business practices levelled against him. One headline didn't beat about the bush labelling the former Barça boss "El Till".

As a player Spurs fans had booed Venables soon after he arrived at the Lane from London rivals Chelsea in 1966, despite his reputation of being one of the brightest young players of his generation, but I was too young to fully appreciate why. I regarded Venables as a skilful new star but even someone as young as I was could differentiate between Venables and his predecessors in the Spurs midfield who were such colossi of their era that it was tough for someone new to fit in. Above all he just didn't seem to raise his own standards from his outstanding career at Chelsea. It was a demanding role to fill the shoes of players such as John White who had gone before him. Yet he was part of the Spurs team that beat Chelsea at Wembley in the first all-London FA Cup final the following year. That was also my first final, so I have nothing but fond memories of an exciting day out.

Venables left the Lane after a short spell filled with personal torment, and I never really, as a Spurs fan, followed his career much after that. It never crossed my mind that he would play such a significant part in my career as a journalist.

From a professional point of view, of course, Venables and I seemed to be joined at the hip! A lot of people felt that I had a vendetta against him when he was at loggerheads with Sugar. He certainly thought so after my investigation into his private business affairs and his sporting business practices during his time as chief executive at Spurs. My investigations into Venables though brought me into contact with some fascinating characters. One of them was TV journalist Martin Bashir, who would later become synonymous with coercing Princess Diana into a notorious TV interview just 12 months before her untimely death. My first contact with Martin was as a rival. Unknown to me, he was heading up his own TV documentary with the BBC investigating Venables. At the same time I had already been employed as a consultant by Roy Ackerman at independent TV documentary makers, Diverse, to make a special on Venables for Channel 4's *Dispatches* programme. After a couple of months it became apparent that *Dispatches* were in a race to screen the Venables story on TV ahead of *Panorama*, where Bashir was working on the same story. *Dispatches* was screened first, a week ahead of *Panorama*, and while their documentary was highly acclaimed, no doubt because it appeared on the BBC, I always felt that the *Dispatches* programme had come closest to unravelling the complexities of business interests and practices inside Spurs. Afterwards I became very close to Martin and got to know him well. We often talked about collaborating on a number of other football-related exposes, but never quite found the right subject. Martin was working as a freelancer for the BBC at the time, and was very ambitious and, of course, his documentaries on Princess Di and then Michael Jackson brought him global recognition and prominence which eventually manifested itself into a lucrative contract to work in the States.

Not just Venables, but all of his close associates, came under scrutiny in my *Mirror* investigation, and some who were friends and close contacts prior to it became instant enemies at first, although they mellowed as the years went by.

Frank McLintock former Double-winning captain of Spurs' great rivals Arsenal, was one, I knew Frank well; he was a highly articulate player and manager and went on to be a very good pundit on BBC radio, but when he became an agent linked to the Venables saga my relationship with him deteriorated. Frank took great exception to being drawn into this controversy and felt he had been victimised by me in the *Mirror* articles. We didn't speak for some considerable time, but to Frank's credit, he has since appreciated that I was doing my job, that I had got all my facts right, and we have spoken since, although they could not be described as deep or meaningful conversations.

Venables, dubbed El Tel by the tabloids during his successful spell as Barcelona's coach, was labelled "El Till" in one of the hardest

hitting back page headlines in my series of exposes. The five-year Premier League enquiry team handed over their extensive files to the FA. Graham Kelly was the chief executive of the FA at the time and he welcomed my offer to deliver files in a big black case, marked with a huge *Mirror* logo, on our investigations into irregular payments and dodgy invoices in football. Graham seemed keen enough and sincere in his desire to clean up the game. We were pictured together outside the FA at Lancaster Gate and he promised to act upon our findings. We reported his interview at great length. The FA did not push the boat out in this area and it took allegations by then Luton manager Mike Newell in early 2006 to finally spark a proper investigation into transfer dealings.

The DTI declined to pursue the matter of Venables' financial affairs in the criminal courts. A number of cases against celebrities of this nature brought by the DTI had failed in front of starstruck juries, so they wisely opted for a civil action against Venables instead. However, when the charges were made in the civil court, they referred to them as "criminal" charges. Venables was found guilty in the civil courts and banned by the DTI for seven years from serving as a company director. That ban expired in January 2005.

*

The general perception at the time was that I was anti-Venables. Worse, that I had a personal vendetta against him. Nothing could be further from the truth. Yet Venables clearly believed it, and I had problems from a section of Spurs fans whipped up by the propaganda. It was even reported in some papers that Venables had, in fact, issued legal proceedings against me or was about to do so, and that the whole issue he had with me and the *Mirror* would end up in the High Court but he didn't actually issue a writ until the very last minute. Libel actions can be brought up to three years after the event of an article being published. On the last possible day inside the three year limit his lawyers dispatched a messenger to deliver the writ, which I would need to accept personally for it to take effect. The messenger somehow got through security at the *Mirror*, reached the third floor editorial offices where I would normally be found and asked for directions to my desk. Now, came the crunch, he had to find me and hand over the legal documents personally which I would then pass on to the legal department to handle. Fortunately that was a rare day off for me and Terry's lawyers clearly hadn't realised that football writers, and indeed most journalists in general, do not work nine to five and tend not to keep regular working hours.

It may be a huge surprise that my declared opinion of Venables as a football manager is not prejudiced by my investigations into his business dealings; I believe he is an outstanding coach. I thought he did a marvellous job with Barcelona and England, and that he wasn't that bad as a Spurs manager. It was only when he became Chief Executive that he bit off far more than he could chew. In fact, I admired his abilities as a manager and coach so much that I recommended him to the FA to replace poor old Graham Taylor. Following Taylor's disastrous reign, FA Chairman Graham Kelly made an audacious decision to come down from his Ivory Tower and canvas the views of a select group of journalists about his successor. We were invited into Graham's hotel room when we were covering an England game. Unanimously we agreed that Venables was the right choice, strictly on his prowess as a coach,

The late Steve Curry and I held the book launch for
Venables - The Inside Story *at a Sports Bar owned by former Tottenham boss Terry Neill near the Mirror offices.*

as someone who would be able to galvanise the players into a team. Venables was, indeed, appointed England coach and had a good tournament when England hosted the European Championship in 1996, although it can be argued that he had a fortuitous tournament too, and that the highlight, the thrashing of Holland, was against a nation on a downward spiral. Perhaps so, but Venables succeeded in bringing the nation to its feet singing 'Football's Coming Home' and were unlucky to lose to the Germans in the semis… again.

Long after the dust had settled on my investigations into Venables, it seemed our paths were still destined to cross. We dined at the same Indian restaurant early in 2006, the Bombay Brasserie near Gloucester Road tube station. As I walked past his table, his jaw dropped open and all he could manage was one of his usual cheeky smiles. "Not stalking you, Terry!" I said cheerily as I walked on. Yes, I can forgive Terry for thinking I was stalking him because this was not the first time we had bumped into each other outside of our usual football meeting places. One of the funniest was when Terry was strolling along in the sunshine, outside the five star La Manga hotel, oblivious to all around him as he concentrated on a business deal he was hatching on his mobile phone. El Tel was back on his Spanish beat putting into place the final part of his master plan to construct a La Manga-style resort that specialised in coaching young players. My sources had told me that Tel wanted to import poor African kids with outstanding promise and develop them into future stars, and then have part-ownership in them to sell onto elite European clubs. Naturally, my chances of discussing this grand scheme with Terry were zero considering our history. Although I knew in advance of Venables' mission in Spain, it was sheer coincidence that I just also happened to be spending some time in the resort. Suddenly our paths crossed outside the hotel and there was no way I could avoid him. Linda and I were walking towards the hotel entrance, and I hoped he might continue his conversation and not notice us. But Terry turned and caught my eye. His voice stopped, his jaw dropped, and off he dashed cutting short his mobile phone conversation for fear I might overhear. "Don't worry, Terry, I'm not stalking you," I said again. Venables, to his credit, smiled, unable to speak as he was making a hasty exit.

My battle to uncover the truth at Tottenham left deep scars. It was one of the reasons my love affair with Spurs, and with football

in general, took a nasty turn for the worse. You have to recall how temperatures had been raised to boiling point by the Venables-Sugar war. Alan Sugar was vilified as he walked to court, his car pelted with rotten eggs, and he suffered personal abuse. Venables was hugely popular with the masses, Sugar was painted as the villain. Anyone siding with Sugar was instantly branded as a traitor to the Spurs cause. It wasn't that I sided with Sugar but I must confess, it certainly looked that way. I had my concerns, but as a journalist, my objective was to view the facts. As a fan, I was torn. In my opinion Sugar was in the right, but the fans also had a point; they wanted him to spend even more cash on players, while Alan knew that it was prudent to balance the books and he refused to gamble with the club's long term financial security.

I was also in the privileged position of having the inside track on Sugar's thoughts, whereas the fans were largely in the dark — all they could see was a successful Spurs manager being sidelined by a ruthless capitalist who admitted that he had no knowledge of the game. While I could publish most things, I could do so only providing I had the evidence. It was tough enough even *with* the evidence with Venables' lawyers threatening legal action; their purpose was to slow me down, or stop me completely, rather than actually really wanting to fight a legal action in court. Some of my best friends, those closest to me for many years, suddenly turned on me. At first they tried to persuade me to back off, but it soon became nasty.

One of my greatest pleasures had been to stroll along the route towards the Lane, relishing another match and all the thrills and twists and turns the afternoon's entertainment might bring. It would be followed by listening to the managers in the main press conference, and then hanging around to catch an interview with the odd player who felt inclined to stop for a chat with the media. It provided a wonderfully rounded account of the game, which provided the basis on which to write a match report. This whole experience was soured by the level of abuse I would suffer at the hands of fans, although I must say it was a tiny section of the Spurs support who had turned against me. Fans who recognised me from appearances on Sky, more so than my postage stamp sized by-line picture in the *Mirror*, screamed abuse at me, or more menacingly sidled alongside me to whisper dire threats for maintaining my stance against Venables. I started out

My investigation into Venables business practices were specifically mentioned in the House of Commons by Labour MP (and Arsenal fan) Kate Hoey.

that inspired me, nor was it something I could enjoy any more. Therefore, when the chance emerged with the Express Group in 2000, I left the *Mirror* to write a column with the Daily and Sunday *Express* titles without having to cover the games. The 'Ahead of the Game' column was investigative and news led which meant I could work from home. I became the first football writer who did not actually go to games, which certainly threw my colleagues. However, I went to far more games than my rivals imagined, but instead of rubbing shoulders with them in the press box, I was in the more influential sections of the grounds, either in the director's box, or with the leading sponsors in their executive boxes. Believe me, I gained far more insight there than ever I did in the press room, where most of the gossip came from journalists about fellow journalists!

It took me a while to regain my enthusiasm for football, and for Spurs in particular and the Sugar era has long since passed. Since Lord Sugar, as he is now, sold his shares very little has been seen of him at Tottenham aside from very infrequent appearances at home games, and Spurs fans have come to change their opinion of Sugar as the years have rolled by. They no longer seem to have such partisan views with regards to he and Venables. However, the Spurs supporters still mistrust Sugar's motives for being involved with "their" club and they will never be won over to the reason he held back in the transfer market as a prudent financial policy. Football fans want to see new signings and they feel that is what Tottenham lacked in the 1990s. In retrospect, it is easy to criticise Sugar for riding to Spurs' rescue to raise his own profile. He was knighted and made a Lord for his business acumen and for what he has done for the country taking that business abroad. However it can be argued that he shot to real fame because of his involvement with Spurs.

As for Venables - a statement from the Department of Trade and Industry reached a settlement with him when he agreed to be banned from any directorship, or virtually any other relationship with a commercial operation, for seven years. Accepting 19 charges of serious misconduct, all of which he had strenuously denied for the previous four years, Venables also agreed to pay half a million pounds of the DTI's costs. Three weeks earlier Venables' friend

by trying to explain my stance with anyone who did not raise the debate beyond acceptable politeness but it was to no avail. Few of the pro-Venables mob wanted to listen to my view that while I admired Terry as a coach, as a businessman his practices needed to be exposed in the public interest and that it was up to everyone to make up their own minds.

The Venables-Sugar saga soured my love affair with Spurs to such an extent that it put the thought in my mind that there would come a time, long before retirement, when I would seek a life change, that continuing "on-the-road" was no longer something

> **"Fans who recognised me... screamed abuse at me, or more menacingly sidled alongside me to whisper dire threats for maintaining my stance against Venables."**

and business partner, Eddie Ashby, completed a four month prison sentence for breach of the bankruptcy laws.

Martin Bashir described El Tel as a "loveable rogue" in the English tradition of Arthur Daley in *Minder*. Yet Bashir himself was later caught out in the way he secured his global exclusive interview with Princess Diana, and Venables clung to Bashir's dubious conduct as an excuse that his *Panorama* programme on him might also have been put together with bogus methods. The fact that I had put together a documentary in opposition to *Panorama* that had reached the same conclusions as Bashir's from impeccable sources seemed to elude El Tel.

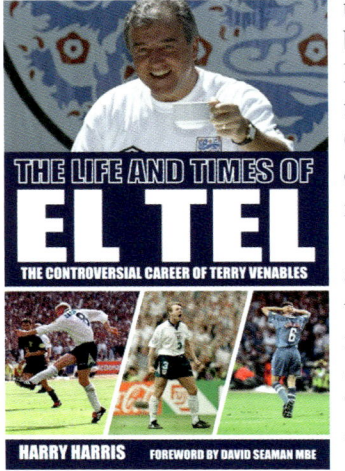

What is undeniable is that Venables had charm, charisma and a character that drew people in, and that extended to the vast majority of the media. Despite being successfully investigated for dubious business practises, Venables was one of the managerial greats, achieving success at both club and international level. England's Euro '96 performance earned him national acclaim, but he walked away at the end of the tournament to fight the legal battle that emerged in the wake of his time at Spurs.

Terry had built his coaching reputation in early spells with Crystal Palace and Queens Park Rangers, having played for both clubs in the latter part of a career, that saw him earn honours at every single level for England. His playing career began at Chelsea where he came through the junior ranks, he made over 200 appearances in midfield and helped the Blues to victory in the 1965 League Cup. After six seasons at Stamford Bridge Terry moved to Tottenham where he spent three years before moving back west to join QPR, and then south to join Palace.

Having retired as a player, Terry took on the manager's job at Selhurst Park, succeeding Malcolm Allison, and guided the club into the top flight as champions of Division Two, in the 1978-79 season. He then returned to take charge at QPR, and took the Superhoops to the FA Cup final in 1982, and to the Second Division title the following season. His success in charge of two London clubs attracted the interest of a number of clubs in England and Europe, and in 1984 he became the manager of Spanish giants Barcelona, then in something of a slump. Terry won the La Liga title (the club's first since 1974) in his first season and his incredible success and popularity earned him the nickname 'El Tel'. With English clubs banned from European competition he also lured some of Britain's best players to Catalonia during his three-year spell in Spain with the acquisition of the likes of Mark Hughes, Gary Lineker and Steve Archibald. His success continued the following season as he won the League Cup but his reign in Spain never quite recovered from Barcelona's failure to beat Steaua Bucharest in the European Cup final in Seville. Before 70,000 Catalans they couldn't score in normal time or extra time and then missed all their penalties in the resulting shoot-out and lost it 2-0.

After Spurs and England, Terry enjoyed spells at Portsmouth and a return to Crystal Palace, as well as a short period in charge of the Australian national team, who were desperately unlucky not to qualify for their first World Cup in 1998 under him. Two years later Terry got his first taste of life in the FA Carling Premiership and it was very much at the sharp end with Middlesbrough, alongside Bryan Robson. His remit was to save the club from another quick return to Division One, and once more he was ultimately successful. Terry decided his business interests and media work could not allow him the time to take up a permanent role on Teeside, and he continued to work as a pundit on ITV, particularly during the 2002 World Cup.

Venables was appointed manager of Leeds United on July 8, 2002. After his spell at Leeds, he returned to the international scene with England assisting Steve McClaren. When Terry retired from football he ran a boutique hotel in Spain with his wife and latterly there have been rumours of ill health and possible dementia.

Terry's death in November 2023 was marked fondly before Tottenham's home game against Aston Villa with the players wearing black armbands and a minute's silence. Venables was a complex character for sure, but his Spurs team between 1989-1991 was superb to watch with Gascoigne, Lineker and Mabbutt taking Tottenham to their last FA Cup triumph.

HH

David Buchler

DAVID BUCHLER has witnessed some of the biggest board meetings and most important decisions Tottenham Hotspur has ever made. For the first time he tells the inside story of how close the club came to going bust, how the Receiver arrived at the club, and how a split board finally opted to sell Gazza to save the club - and how close Robert Maxwell came to pipping Alan Sugar to become the next owner! Here, the former vice chairman reveals the truth behind a tumultuous period in the club's history.

"I have been fortunate to be involved with Tottenham Hotspur as Chief Executive and Vice Chairman on two different occasions. My first introduction to the Board was during the latter part of 1990 when the club was facing difficulties with their bankers, Midland Bank, over a £10million overdraft. I advised the Board on insolvency matters and when Nat Solomon became Chairman at the beginning of 1991, I became Chief Executive and Vice Chairman. I remember my first meeting with Midland Bank, meeting Stephen Adamson, a Partner of Ernst & Young and a friend, who was introduced to me by Midland Bank as their Receiver and Manager. Luckily, because our personal relationship was good, and Midland Bank knew me and respected me, the discussions relating to the reduction in the £10m overdraft quickly became cordial and not confrontational. This helped me find a solution to what otherwise was a difficult problem. In the end the solution was to sell Paul Gascoigne as he was the only asset the club had that came anywhere near the £10m bank debt.

"The overdraft had hit £10m, but you would really laugh today to think that the club nearly went under for that small amount as it's now worth £4 billion!

"The sale was not a simple process; the Board was split with one half recognising that the sale of Gazza for £10m to Lazio was the solution to the club's problems and the other half recognising that losing him would severely affect the team's success. The majority shareholder, Irving Scholar, was very much on the side of saving the club, and to that end he appointed Nat Solomon as chairman, and Nat and I had to work together to find a solution, but Irving was adamant it would not be at the expense of selling

BUCHLER PHILLIPS

the team's most prized footballer. He made it clear, "I do not want to sell Gazza". Irving took control of the club with Paul Bobroff, who was a financier and very much in favour of the sale of Gazza for purely financial reasons. He knew that realising his value was the only way of avoiding the appointment of an insolvency practitioner as Receiver and Manager. That had become a real possibility, that the Bank would appoint a Receiver to take control of the running of the club.

"It even reached the critical stage that at one meeting Brian Clair, the Midland Bank director in charge of matters relating to Spurs £10m overdraft, had attended with the purpose of recovering the loan and he introduced to the Board Stephen Adamson. Eventually, Nat persuaded Irving that it was the club or Gazza but he couldn't have both and Irving had to save the club and agree the sale of the player he wanted to keep the most.

"Of course, everyone wanted to keep Gazza, what a character! We all have our favourite Gazza story, so here's mine. Paul had been ruled out of a game in 1991 with a groin injury. I arrived at the club with my girlfriend at the time, a stunning blonde bombshell, and as we got into the lift to go to the fourth-floor directors lounge, all of a sudden this hand appeared to prise open the lift door. Gazza got into the lift just before the doors were closing… My girlfriend knew he couldn't play because of a groin injury, so she said, 'Oh Mr Gascoigne, how is your groin?' The door opened at the third floor where Gazza exited; he turned round to her and said, '….all the better for seeing you, lass!' She didn't respond, she was quite posh and gobsmacked!

"The club eventually agreed to his sale but in the Cup Final against Nottingham Forest in 1991 Gascoigne was badly injured which opened up the possibility that, despite a signed contract with Lazio, the sale might not be completed. After a worrying period, the sale eventually went ahead resolving the club's difficult financial position.

"During the course of the sale of Tottenham Hotspur many aspiring buyers came forward, but none seemed to have the funds necessary to buy the club. Tony Berry's only reaction to these people was "show me the money". It was only when Robert Maxwell and Alan Sugar put their names forward that the club felt at last that there was some financial credibility. I met with them both and had dinner at Harry's Bar with Robert Maxwell. It was a surreal experience; bizarre, extraordinary. On the table next to us was Princess Diana. It was that sort of evening. Maxwell was a very good speaker, and an incredible personality. He was clearly interested but already owned Oxford United and the League refused him permission to own two different clubs. After a long discussion he eventually left the restaurant as he had another appointment, saying on his departure, 'I really want to buy the club, I just need to sort out the League.' He was so serious that he added, 'I want you to phone me if there is any news - I know we can do great things together.' He provided me with six different telephone numbers including that of his homes in New York and London, his boat and his aeroplane to name just a few!

"Did I think Robert Maxwell was a viable buyer? Yes, I did. He didn't think it would be a problem for him sorting out the £10m overdraft with the Midland Bank given his assets at that time, and that level of debt wouldn't stop him joining the club or paying off the debt, if necessary, very quickly, and he wanted to keep Gazza.

"Later, I joined with Daniel Levy in 2001 to buy the club back from Alan Sugar. Again, I became Chief Executive and Vice Chairman until Daniel took over directly as Chief Executive in 2003. The manager when we took over was George Graham who had been appointed by Alan Sugar, even though he was a previous long-term manager and legendary player for Arsenal. Despite being very personable whenever I saw him at the training ground, he took me aside one day and said, 'now then laddy, when you want to come down to the training ground again just telephone me first.' Bearing in mind I was Chief Executive I found this a rather unnecessary burden. In the meantime, we had discussed the constant bad press reports being leaked and agreed that this should stop. However, it didn't and when I found out that he was the source, I asked him eventually to leave the club. As a result of a number of discussions Glenn Hoddle was appointed in his place.

"I'm always asked my opinions of Alan Sugar, and it surprises people when I say that I liked him. He is very much the character in life as you see on TV; a bit grumpy, and can be difficult, but he has a very good heart, and he only wanted the best for the club.

"Daniel Levy gets a bad press, but he is extraordinary, very intelligent, and he is like a dog with a bone, but he has done an exceptional job at the club. The training ground is beyond brilliant, the stadium is something else, as good as you get anywhere in the world. Both are unbelievable achievements. In years to come, you will look back, and say, 'Wow, did he really do that?'

"Of course, he has excelled off the field, but on it there could have been more silverware, however, I am convinced that it will eventually come, particularly under Ange Postecoglou, the new manager. Daniel has tried, he has brought in some world class managers, and he has spent as much if not more than the biggest clubs, so he can hardly be at fault for the failures of those managers. I don't have the answer why there hasn't been silverware, but it will come.

"As for what he has done with the club, in my opinion he has made it worth as much as £4 billion. We know there have been suitors who want to buy Spurs from America to the Middle East, but an offer of £3.25billion would not be of interest to Daniel, he would want to see something starting with a 4. I believe that Spurs are now a long way ahead of Manchester United and Chelsea, with a stadium that can host football and NFL, and that is why Daniel can see the club's value being in excess of £4billion. Although Joe Lewis is the majority shareholder, I believe it will be Daniel's decision whether to sell or not, and I don't think he

© *Adam Duke Photography for Mayfair Times*

particularly wants to sell having brought the club to this level in this new super stadium, but if there is a realistic offer that matches his valuation then I think the club could be sold."

 **BUCHLER PHILLIPS**

Alan Sugar

Tony Blair was charming. He enquired about the state of the game and portrayed a genuine affection for football when my wife Linda and I were introduced to him at Alan Sugar's 50th birthday bash.

As you would expect from the Sugars, it was a grand affair organised by Alan's lovely wife Anne, his family and his trusted aide and PR guru, Nick Hewer, at the rather swanky Reform Club in the West End. Although the PM didn't stay for dinner, no doubt with affairs of state to concern him, he did put in an impressive appearance during the lavish evening.

The event had been a closely guarded secret, kept from Alan to maximise the impact of a "This is Your Life" red book presentation, which made for wonderful theatre with a packed audience of close family and friends. Michael Aspel was there to present the red book, and apparently, Michael was ticked off by his TV bosses for taking part in the stunt. But it went down well on the night, if not with the powers that be at Television Centre.

Sugar, who later became Sir Alan in 2000 and Lord Sugar in 2009, enjoyed enormous profile as Spurs chairman, elevating him beyond the pigeon hole of a mere industrialist/entrepreneur. But with it came grief in equal measures to any pleasure and kudos he might have got from winning the League Cup at Wembley. If anything the downside was ultra turbulent, and I always felt that he was relieved to have got out of the game after a relatively short period.

Apart from the nightmare scenario of taking on Terry Venables, of continually switching managers, and his personal conflict with numerous players, Sugar was always needled by the accusation that he was reluctant to put his hand in his pocket for player purchases.

Former QPR maverick turned media motor-mouth, Rodney Marsh, was one particular thorn in his side on Sky TV, until he was kicked off after making a distasteful joke about the Asian tsunami disaster in 2005 on their *You're On Sky Sports* programme. Alan felt Rodney was not fully conversant with all the facts and

misunderstood his motives. To be fair, Rodney was only repeating what the majority of Tottenham fans felt of the chairman during Sugar's reign — that their chairman could have spent more in the transfer market than he did, an accusation that wasn't supported by facts.

My advice to Alan at that time was not to sue Rodney, as he threatened to, but to fight back with some juicy quotes in my column. Sorry if that sounds like biased advice but it was genuine. He always suspected that I had an ulterior motive, which may have been true to a point, but equally I never let down a good friend or contact, and would always try to advise them on the best course of action. It never pays to sue, as it often takes a year or more to get to court, by which time the issues are long forgotten, and Sugar, for example, has failed to get his point across when he needed to most.

The only problem was that Alan was a stickler for getting his comments precisely as he wanted them. It was hard work to get the article I wanted. He would like to paw over his comments, so I would fax him the article (yes fax in those days!), he would then "go into one" blasting down the phone that I was crap at my job and hadn't written it the way he wanted, and had changed his comments or put them in the wrong place. Phew, it was time consuming to get it the way he wanted it, in return for a hard hitting article that would make people sit up and take notice the following morning, but it was worth it as the "piece" would often be quoted the next morning on TV and radio for maximum impact. That was the way to hit back, and invariably it worked a treat.

It is only since Alan sold up and has become ennobled, that the Spurs faithful have come to appreciate him more. The passage of time has allowed for a recognition of the contributions he made to stabilising the club's finances. In fact, under Sugar, Spurs' level of expenditure on player purchases were far higher than most people were prepared to give him credit for. Accusations of being a miser were little more than an irritant compared to the main event; the court room battles with Terry Venables.

When Venables first lured Sugar into buying Spurs, the battle lines were drawn in the PR arena, with Venables convincing Sugar that I should be *persona non grata* for a variety of reasons. Venables had clearly put the knife in, and that was no huge surprise, as he knew how close I had been to Irving Scholar when he was manager, and how much he had to be careful when it came to his personal views about me. No longer. He was off the leash, and anxious for revenge. He took it alright, and as quickly as he could. So Alan Sugar had a preconceived idea about me, provided by his new ally Venables. Then, when they fell out, I was the journalist Sugar came to for help.

Alan invited my sports editor Keith Fisher and I to his Chigwell home to meet Nick Hewer and himself. I had made the initial approach through Nick and Alan was persuaded to give me an interview. However it seemed I wasn't to be trusted on my own, and so Nick suggested that my sports editor should attend the meeting so that Alan could set the parameters of the interview and the head of department would be on the spot to agree them. This, of course, suited me, because the worst case scenario would be for me to agree something with Alan, only to be overruled by the sports editor, and that would have been a recipe for disaster. I had been nagging Nick for some time saying that I thought it would be in Alan's best interests to comment on Terry Venables, following his enforced exit from Spurs for financial dodgy dealings.

In the midst of the storm caused by my revelations, the club was threatened with having 12 league points deducted and being banned from the following season's FA Cup, although in the end both penalties were suspended. As the supporters' anger grew, Alan, as chairman, took enormous flak as Venables had been hugely popular with the fans, due largely to the style of play he had brought to the team as manager and the success of that 1991 FA Cup win.

Of course it was also in my best interests to pull off such an exclusive interview. What a coup that turned out to be. But there was no point in trying it on with someone as streetwise and astute as Alan Sugar or his vastly experienced media advisor. So, it was a genuinely mutually beneficial exercise to get together. Nick Hewer could see it. So he took the risk and organised it.

Sugar took us into his office at his home and the interview turned out just as Keith and I thought it would - wall to wall sensationalism. Keith recognised the newsworthiness of the interview, and could hardly contain himself as we left for the nearest pub to plan the next day's paper. Keith contacted the office and instructed his back room team to clear the decks for his back three pages. No mobiles or computers in those days. Just my notebook and pen, and the wall mounted phone in the pub. If anyone wanted to use the phone, of course, we had to let them. Keith decided which stories he wanted and I got onto the phone, went through to the copy takers to ad lib the lot.

The *Mirror*'s sports pages inside spread headline was "I Feel Like The Man Who Killed Bambi" as Sugar explained why he had no choice other than to rid the club of Venables and why he was painted as the ogre, even though he knew he was taking the correct course of action.

*

In his memoirs Sugar referred to the Bambi analogy and explained how he bought the club in the first place. "Friday 14 May 1993. The day I sacked Terry Venables, the day my son Daniel told me that this time I really had caused World War Three. Never mind Bambi's mum - I was the man who'd shot Bambi! I don't want to portray myself as a fanatical Tottenham supporter, but most people tend to follow one football club - and Spurs was my club, from when my dad and Uncle Jack used to take me. Around 1991 I couldn't help but read about a load of aggravation going on with Spurs' finances and how it was on the verge of bankruptcy and being shut down. To this day I don't know what possessed me, but the Monday after the FA Cup Final I put out a call to Venables. My vision of Venables at the time was of a chirpy chappy, a shrewd lad. I told his adviser, Eddie Ashby, I was prepared to go ahead on the basis that Terry put up his £3million. I would then match it. The essence of the deal was that Venables, as chief executive, would look after the football side of things, while I would oversee the business side and finances. That was supposed to be the dream ticket. But the problems soon started. I'd gone away on holiday straight after the Charity Shield and told Ashby we didn't have the money to buy Gordon Durie from Chelsea. By the time I got back Venables had gone ahead with the transfer without my permission. I reminded him that I'd given my personal assurance to Midland Bank there would be no spending on players because of the £11m debt we'd inherited. Venables seemed to be oblivious to this. He buried his head in the sand like an ostrich.

"As chief executive, Venables was totally out of his depth. He knew nothing about the commercial side of business. He didn't have a clue about things like Stock Exchange requirements, accounting, cash flow or marketing. I was getting very concerned. On many occasions, at board meetings, Venables would make some totally stupid comment. So much for the so-called dream team. Peter Shreeves was asked to leave as manager after the first season and Venables took over, jointly appointing Doug Livermore and Ray Clemence to assist him. It came to a head after a tournament which I'd had to beg Sky to cover to meet the contract. Venables was convinced the deal was lining my own pocket. From that moment on I decided this arrangement with Venables was not going to work. It seemed the man loved to have an enemy, that he was not happy unless he had a fight of some kind on his hands and now I was the enemy he had to fend off. I wanted to give Venables a clean way out of the situation. I'd offer him his £3m back and pay off the remainder of his outstanding contract. Venables arrogantly believed he would be able to out-ride my challenge.

"The date of the board meeting was set but the evening before, at the annual FWA Footballer of the Year Dinner, Venables and his associates leaked his imminent dismissal. As we arrived for the board meeting, the forecourt of the club was packed with press, cameramen and fans, all screaming for my head. On my casting vote as chairman, Venables was officially fired there and then. By 6pm that night, a judge had reinstated Venables. We had a disaster on our hands and by the time I'd got home there was a protest group outside my house. Of course we went to the High Court in the Strand. There were huge crowds standing outside, screaming my name, snarling abuse at me and calling me 'Judas', spitting on me and my wife, Ann. When we finally got to court, Venables' barrister stood up and started to read out the section of my witness statement about Brian Clough taking a bung over the Teddy Sheringham deal. The media went bananas about the Clough bung allegations. Venables had shot himself in the foot. The judge called a halt to proceedings halfway through the second day. I was advised to exit the courtroom through his chambers and out the back entrance and to have my vehicle standing by. When the court reconvened, the judge read out his decision and upheld the firing of Venables. A few days later, Venables told the media he was going to continue his fight against me. After a lot of twists and turns, Venables finally threw in the towel. Businessman Philip Green called me to let me know that Venables was prepared to sell his shares to me for £3m. But winning the battle was not the end. I realised things could potentially get worse."

*

I still enjoy a healthy professional relationship Teddy Sheringham, which is all to his credit as Teddy became the unwitting focus for my investigation into bungs during the Alan Sugar era, following his £1.1m move from Forest to Spurs in 1993. Brian Clough had insisted on a bung to smooth the deal and Terry Venables was willing to pay it. Forest's 'bag man' was Clough's assistant manager Ronnie Fenton, who spent part of the money on his daughter's wedding reception. That bung formed the central part of my investigations for the *Mirror* that made headline news virtually on a daily basis for some time. My favourite part of the story was how it all came to light — Alan Sugar had spotted an invoice and in all innocence inquired why VAT had not been added, which, in due course it was, but while the paperwork was being revised, it meant that the £50,000 in cash had to be returned to the White Hart Lane offices. The money was stashed in a safe and forgotten about, it was far too hot to handle, until it was spotted about a year later! Teddy gave evidence to the Premier League enquiry at the time yet by the time the enquiry had concluded, both Clough and Fenton had retired from active involvement in the game, and in any case, there really wasn't a will on behalf of the Premier

League to press charges as Lord Stevens enquiry team flagged many potential dodgy deals but failed to find the smoking gun to prosecute conclusively.

In his fascinating book *What You See is What You Get*, Sugar recalled: "One match-day, Terry Venables uncharacteristically came into the boardroom and asked to speak to me. He told me he was interested in a player at Nottingham Forest by the name of Teddy Sheringham, but there was a problem because, as Venables put it: 'Cloughie wants a bung'. I told him I wasn't interested in listening to anything involving corruption and bungs. I'd heard it went on in football, but I told him it was absolutely and totally out of the question. Spurs would have no part in anything like that. He immediately said: 'Sure, yeah, that's what I thought you'd say, but I was just checking it out with you, just letting you know. I mean, Teddy's a great player, but that's how it is – Cloughie wants a bung'. As far as I was concerned, the matter was closed but over the next couple of weeks, there was constant discussion about the acquisition of Sheringham and how the transfer was being delayed. The next thing I heard on the Sheringham transfer was that an agent, ex-player Frank McLintock, had handled the deal which Eddie Ashby claimed was now done. Venables had agreed to pay McLintock a £50,000 fee for arranging the transfer of the player to us. With the transaction about to take place, I received a phone call from Colin Sandy (the finance director I'd appointed) who told me that he'd been instructed by Ashby to go down to the bank and withdraw £50,000 in cash to pay McLintock. I told him this was absolutely ridiculous. If McLintock was an agent, he should simply send his bill to us and we'd pay it in the normal way — by cheque. Colin said he'd explained this to Ashby, but that Venables had insisted he went down to the bank now to get the money. I told Colin he was absolutely not allowed to do it and that he should go back and tell Ashby to tell Venables that if we had to pay McLintock a fee, we wanted an invoice showing VAT. A few hours later Colin called to say that McLintock had agreed to issue an invoice to the club for his services for the transfer of Sheringham, but was paid in cash. I found out afterwards that Ashby had instructed one of the club's accountants to go down to the bank and withdraw £58,750 in cash and the money was given to McLintock to settle his bill."

When Sugar discovered the extent of the behind-the-scenes

financial shenanigans and board room plots, he knew he had to fire El Tel. This was the basis of the 'Bambi' interview. I had been reporting in the *Mirror* how Venables had cheated Spurs out of £400,000: the bungs to Clough, the false invoices and how the club was now threatened with having 12 League points deducted and being banned from the following season's FA Cup. In the end, with the FA being threatened with legal action by Sugar by his lawyers at Herbert Smith, Graham Kelly capitulated and the penalties were suspended. Yet despite these facts, supporters sided with their managerial hero who had just delivered the FA Cup, and as their anger intensified it was directed at the club chairman and owner and, eventually, yours truly.

*

Following the success of the 'Bambi' interview, Alan and Nick trusted me, and from then on our relationship grew and we socialised regularly throughout his reign at Spurs. He was a generous host and every season, when Spurs were at home to

Chelsea, he invited my wife, Linda and her dad to the director's box for a lavish lunch and the best seats in the house while I slummed it down below in the press box!

Although Alan confessed to be clueless about the game, he proved to be a transformative figure in football. Perhaps his biggest coup was securing the football rights for his pals at Sky, as he explains, "Initially I never attended the regular Premier League chairmen's meetings, as I was told they were just discussing fixtures, until I was told that a very important vote on television rights was going to take place. Up until then, rights for English top-flight football were held by ITV who broadcast *The Big Match Live* on Sunday afternoons. They were paying around £4m per season to the league for the rights. A small nucleus of clubs comprising Arsenal, Manchester United and Liverpool seemed to attract most of the television coverage. They were closely involved with ITV and wanted to keep the next round of negotiations with them. Rick Parry, the Premier League's chief executive, quite rightly insisted that a proper tender process should be followed. This was no longer going to be a closed shop or a foregone conclusion. I turned up at the Royal Lancaster Hotel. As we entered the room Trevor East, an ITV executive, was handing out pieces of paper to the chairmen. This was a last-minute dirty trick. I, of course, wanted BSkyB to succeed, so I went to the public phone cubicles opposite the meeting room and called their chief executive, Sam Chisholm, telling him ITV were trying to pull a fast one. Little did I know this call would go down in the annals of football history as the phone call that irrevocably altered the history of sport and media in Britain. Sam told me ITV had somehow found out the details of BSkyB's bid and wanted to top it. I told him: 'There's only one way to clinch the deal. Make your final bid £60m per season and blow them out of the water.' When the deal came up I declared a conflict of interests saying that Tottenham would abstain but most of the clubs objected and despite objections from Arsenal and Manchester United the meeting agreed that Tottenham should indeed be allowed to vote. I was disappointed by all the sniping going on when discussing whether Spurs should be allowed to vote or not and I could see agendas forming. The big clubs were trying to bully the rest and it seemed clear that they wanted to line their own pockets by favouring ITV. After a couple of hours' discussion, the motion was put to the room as to whether we should accept BSkyB or ITV's offer. BSkyB got the deal. Ironically, they won it by one vote - clearly Spurs being allowed to vote *was* important. The ITV people were furious."

Ossie Returns

At the end of their playing careers, Ricky Villa had returned to his homeland to finish his career and buy a ranch, while Ossie Ardiles played under David Pleat before moving into management. After a successful stint with Swindon Town, followed by spells at Newcastle and West Brom, Ossie was welcomed "home" as manager of his beloved Tott-ing-ham. Ossie took on the challenge that Glenn Hoddle had, wisely in my view, shied away from. Glenn had opted to sign up for Ken Bates at Stamford Bridge at the time, but a phone call from Alan Sugar nearly scuppered Ken's plans and Hoddle's move to the Bridge where he was destined to start the Chelsea revolution with the signings of Ruud Gullit and Mark Hughes.

At that same 'Bambi' interview where my then sports editor Keith Fisher and I had discussed Sugar's fight with Terry Venables for control of Tottenham, I suggested that Glenn Hoddle was the man to take over from Venables. Sugar loved the idea and when Keith and I popped round the corner to a pub to file my interview, I also contacted Glenn to tell him about the Spurs job. Glenn said he would come back to me after he gave it some thought overnight and I relayed the message back to the chairman.

The next morning Glenn said how tempting it was, but there were two major problems which he found insurmountable. Firstly, he had already given a commitment to Ken Bates and didn't feel he was able to break it even if he wanted to, which I took to mean he probably had already signed a contract and secondly, he didn't feel the time was right to become Spurs manager, no matter how tempting, even though he thought he was destined to return to the Lane as their manager at some point.

It must have crossed Glenn's mind that the chance might never come again but he felt, instinctively, that it would be far too "political" to be the one taking over from Venables after all the problems with the fans and the war with Sugar. The supporters and press had largely sided with Venables in the High Court battle with Sugar and I believe Glenn made the right call at the time.

So, having seen one club legend turn the chance of a lifetime down, Alan Sugar turned to another. Ossie Ardiles' love-affair with Spurs continues to this day as he remains part of the furniture as a highly-respected Global Ambassador for the club and has a high profile on every match day at the glittering new stadium. He made 311 appearances and scored 25 goals for Tottenham between 1978 and 1988, helping win the FA Cup twice as well as the UEFA Cup to become one of the club's all-time greats.

In July 1989 he was appointed manager of Swindon Town and began to transform their style of play, leading the club to their highest-ever league finish but despite winning the second division play-offs in 1990, the club were denied a place in the First Division due to financial irregularities. The following season he was instructed to sell players because of the financial crisis and before long Ardiles was offered the job at Newcastle United, however his spell at St. James Park was a disaster with the club languishing at the foot of the Second Division table when he was sacked. Ossie moved on to Third Division West Brom guiding them to promotion with a 3-0 play-off victory over Port Vale at Wembley, after which the inevitable happened; he was offered the manager's job at the Lane in 1993 in what would prove to be a roller-coaster ride.

Under Alan Sugar the club splashed the cash on World Cup stars Jürgen Klinsmann, Illi Dumitrescu and Gheorghe Popescu, as the manager embarked on a gung-ho policy of five attacking players; they were a joy to watch when it came off, a defensive disaster when it didn't. For strikers like Teddy Sheringham it was a pleasure to be involved in such an attacking team, but it exposed defenders who were not up to the task. The team were far too inconsistent and finished 15th. Ossie's last game in charge came a few months into the following season, with Spurs rooted to the bottom of the league, Sugar sacked him, and appointed Gerry Francis.

In the words of Sugar, from his autobiography, *What You See Is What You Get*, a League Cup defeat at Notts County was Ossie's undoing. It was that evening in the directors' lounge at Meadow Lane that Sugar and the other directors present decided that he would have to go. On the Sunday after the win over West Ham Ardiles was summoned to Sugar's house where he was told he would have to leave.

In his autobiography, *Ossie's Dream*, Ardiles describes this as, "the hardest thing that's happened to me in my life. The blackest time, after the Malvinas aftermath, was my departure from Tottenham. My life changed completely after that. Tottenham is my home, my family, my everything. I sincerely believe, have always believed, that I was destined to manage Tottenham. There is a way of being that we share a footballing identity that both I and the club have. I've always known that if I was asked to manage Barcelona, Real Madrid, any legendary club or Tottenham, I would choose Tottenham every time. Without hesitation. I was born to play for Tottenham and to manage Tottenham. So when I did get to manage Tottenham it was quite literally a dream come true."

Being sacked hit Ardiles hard but he knew it was coming. "The season had started well with wins against Sheffield Wednesday and Everton, but as it progressed there were a few results that weren't exactly good for us and the whole five forwards issue was aired again. Perhaps I was too stubborn…"

Ossie was loyal to his assistant Steve Perryman. With my personal relationship with Ossie and the chairman, I did all I could to save him from the axe. I suggested to Sugar that bringing in a defensive coach of the calibre of Don Howe might help. Don was up for it. Ossie's 'Famous Five' were sensational going forward but defensively there were too many gaps, they were left wide open too often. Howe would close those gaps. Sugar went for the plan, Ossie thought about, but said that was Perryman's job and he would not go for it.

"The key match, the one I got sacked after, was against Notts County in the Coca-Cola Cup. The night of 26 October 1994 was wet, dark and cold – horrible. When we arrived at Meadow Lane with Tottenham and all its stars I remember feeling that it was a recipe for disaster, We had already conceded two goals in the first half when Dumitrescu got sent off. We were down to ten men. We lost the tie 3–0. I think of it as my black night. I knew my time was up."

After Tottenham beat West Ham the following Saturday at least Ardiles left on a high. He was called to the Chairman's house the next day. "Alan Sugar fired me (although he never actually said 'You're fired'). I genuinely think he was sorry. He had to do it, in a sense. He felt a change was necessary. The fires had been quashed, the squad was superlative, and he thought another manager could pick the baton up and run with it."

Ossie thinks that, in hindsight, he should not have gone to Spurs when he did. It was a very difficult time at the club and he feels he would have been better to have waited. He admits that being sacked from Spurs was very hard for him and it has taken him a very long time to get over it. "I've never quite got over the hurt of how things turned out. I spent years not going back to the club at all. Not once, for many years. Now I go to games and feel closer to the place again, but until very recently if you asked me when did I finally get over all the disappointment I would honestly have to say, 'Oh, any day now…' I am over it now, and really feel part of the Tottenham family again."

Ardiles is a Tottenham legend and, along with Ricky Villa, is always given a warm welcome by supporters and is a global ambassador. Ossie will always be loved by Spurs fans.

Since managing Spurs, he has also had managerial spells in Croatia, Mexico, Japan, Israel, Argentina and Paraguay. He has won a number of awards in management which include winning the Nabisco Cup with Shimizu in 1996, the Tokai Cup with Shimizu S-Pulse in 1996 and 1998 as well as the Emperor's Cup in 2005 with Tokyo Verdy 1969. He was also named J. League Manager of the Year in 1998.

Jürgen Klinsmann

Following the acrimonious departure of Venables, German World Cup winner Jürgen Klinsmann had the ability and profile to inspire a much-needed Spurs revolution. Klinsmann, like Dennis Bergkamp, had failed in Italy and with Monaco, but was an inspiration when he first arrived at Spurs in the summer of 1994.

During the 1990 World Cup Jürgen was the golden boy of German football. I and a handful of other English journalists, interviewed him ahead of England's epic clash in the semi- finals of the 1990 World Cup, turning up at the German team hotel before one of English football's biggest ever games. When he came out of the lift to conduct the interview agreed by him and set up through the German FA's communications department, he wanted to know which of the English writers was from the *Mirror*.

He looked me straight in the eye and said, "Ah, you're the one I am supposed to worry about!" It was hard to tell whether he was deadly serious or taking the mickey. "Not at all", I told him but he didn't look assured. Someone had obviously tipped him off about me! But then he broke into a wry smile. He was certainly as assured off the pitch as he was on it, dealing with the Fleet Street hounds in perfect English, interlaced with some wise-cracking and some more smiles. He had charmed us all. You came away warming to him even more.

A few years later when he turned up on Alan Sugar's yacht and ended up signing for Spurs, I thought it was a tremendous coup, not just for the North London club, but for English football in general, even though he had been experiencing a goal-drought during his spell at Monaco. I still considered Klinsmann to be one of the most charismatic goal scorers in world football at that time and a wonderful addition to the growing list of Category A players beginning to turn up in English football.

Klinsmann was such a captivating new addition to the Premiership scene that I decided to write a diary of his first season at White Hart Lane, detailing his life on and off the field that surrounded his high profile first season. It was certainly an uplifting experience, even if somewhat unexpected for a German to sign for a predominately Jewish club, with a Jewish chairman, and a high percentage of Jewish support. A certain section of the fans still do, after all, call themselves 'Yids'.

Jürgen showed he had a sense of humour when he "dived" in a unique goal scoring celebration that captivated the nation when he scored on his debut in the first game of the season at Sheffield Wednesday. It was Jürgen's way of mocking the critics who for years had taunted him as a player who dived. Compared to some in the English game at the moment, that accusation looks laughable now.

However, I saw a more calculating side to Jürgen's character. All my efforts to seek his approval for the book, maybe for him to endorse it in some way, perhaps write a foreword, came to nothing. In frustration I opted for the direct approach and the next time I was at White Hart Lane I hung around the entrance area where the players pass by from the dressing rooms to the stairway taking them to the players lounge. It was the perfect vantage point for reporters hoping for a quote or two, if one of the players was prepared to take a few minutes of his time to stop and chat. Most suspected the reporters by this time, and even if they did stop to be interviewed, were cautious about what they said.

I asked Jürgen if he would stop for a chat, and he was happy to do so while he thought it was an interview for a newspaper which would provide him with an opportunity to project his image. He was one of the few footballers of his generation who knew that any publicity was good publicity and that if you co-operated with the media and made sure you were in control with your answers, the vast majority of the time he would be generating positive publicity for himself. However, he was most reluctant to continue the conversation as soon as I mentioned the book, even though I explained that the publishers were happy to make a contribution to one of his favourite charities and for him to see it before it went to print, to show him that it was going to be an upbeat celebration of his first season with Spurs.

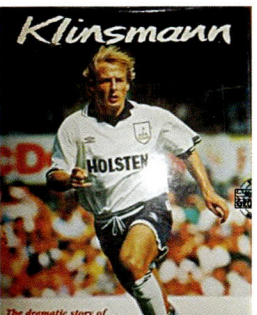

Only later did it dawn on me that one of his reasons for his reticence was that he didn't plan to hang around too long and had known that he might be heading off to a bigger club for more money. I don't know, maybe I had misjudged him.

Perhaps he was protective of his own image and was not interested in any unauthorised book. However, my gut instinct told me, judging by my conversation, that his annoyance was because he was not in control of something that was a commercial issue using his image, even though there was an aspect of it that was for charity.

As I have always said, as a journalist it is imperative to try to keep your personal allegiance to a club distinct from your working environment, in other words to be unbiased. I didn't hold it against Klinsmann being difficult about the book project as I voted for him as Footballer of the Year, an honour which he won. But just before he received the award at the prestigious Football Writers Association annual dinner at the Royal Lancaster Hotel, it was announced that he was quitting Spurs and heading off to another country. No wonder Sugar threw his Klinsmann shirt in the bin in a very high profile fit of pique on TV.

Sugar told me the inside story of how he had been misled by Klinsmann and his entourage. He told me how Jürgen and his agent had been in his Chigwell home discussing how best to persuade the star striker, and now Spurs talisman, to stay on, but it became clear that even though the player told the chairman he was happy at the club, he would be invoking a clause in his contract which gave him a way out if he wasn't... well, happy!

Sugar felt bitterly let down. In his desperation to lure Klinsmann to Tottenham in the first place, he had given away far too much in the contract details. A "happy" clause was something that was far too weighted in the player's direction. He could have contested it, but there's no point keeping a player who wants to go, and he was not in the mood to make him too much of an extravagant offer to persuade him to stay, considering he felt the player owed him because he had rescued him from his gloom in French football and Spurs had helped resurrect his career.

So after one season in which he scored 29 League and Cup goals and been voted England's Footballer of the Year he was off. Nobody expected to see him in a Spurs shirt ever again, but remarkably two and a half years later that is exactly what happened. By the middle of the 1997-98 season Spurs were struggling with relegation a real possibility but Jürgen returned to the Lane and crashed in nine League goals in 15 appearances, including four in a 6-2 win at Wimbledon, to guarantee their safety before bowing out the following week with a stunning long range goal in a 1-1 draw against Southampton in the last match of the season.

Gerry Francis

Fate intervened as I heard a shout outside my local Waitrose here in Sunningdale. "Harry!" In the front seat of a parked car sat Gerry Francis. When I told him I was in the advanced stages of writing a book on Spurs we agreed to have a more detailed chat. Gerry wanted to put into perspective his fascinating, if brief, reign as Spurs manager. But first he revealed his deep rooted affiliation to Spurs, dating back to the early 1960s and memories of the great traditions and the glory days under Bill Nicholson.

"As a kid my earliest memories were watching Spurs on the old black and white television when they played Dukla Prague in the snow. The two teams making the most impact in the early 1960s were Spurs and Burnley and I was fascinated by both clubs, but more so with Spurs and they were the team for me at that early age, I could rattle off all the names then, and still can today; Jones, White, Mackay, Marchi when he came into the team, Maurice Norman, Smith, Dyson, Baker, Brown, Blanchflower... and then Jimmy Greaves coming to the club and replacing Les Allen.

"If I had to pick a player out of that lot, the one I admired most as a kid, it would have to be Cliff Jones, and those diving headers, I was in awe of such a small winger able to gain such heights and power with those far post headers. Jones on one wing, Dyson on the other, it was a wonderfully attacking team. Whenever I watched England my boyhood hero was Bobby Charlton, I looked up to him maybe because I was a midfield player. I got to know Dave Mackay quite well later on, as a manager against him, and it was such a privilege to have so many discussions with Bill Nicholson and Alf Ramsey

"My dad played professionally for Brentford, so Brentford and QPR were also teams that I followed, but Tottenham and Burnley were the teams were always in the news. Spurs were winning the FA Cup two years in a row and I supported Spurs because of what was going on at the time, while Brentford were in the Third

Division, and it wasn't quite the same compared with Spurs who were one of the best teams in Europe.

"So in the early 1960s, Spurs thrilled me, then England won the World Cup in 1966, and not long after that I was being called up into the England team by Alf Ramsey. Then I go on to manage Spurs and get to meet the great Bill Nicholson and to work with him..."

So we come onto the three year reign of Gerry Francis as Spurs manager which lasted three years and four days to be precise between November 1994 and November 1997 . I remember that period well. I was reporting on the *Daily Mirror*, Alan Sugar was the chairman, the politics of the club had taken over from the football and I had an inside track into the thought process of the chairman and what he thought of Gerry. Sugar actually liked him a lot but the fans never quite took to him. Maybe the supporters wanted someone more flamboyant with a greater emphasis on individuals, but the mind can play tricks, because it was nowhere near as bad as you might have thought at the time. And history has proved it was much better than what was to follow.

Gerry's Tottenham Hotspur actually finished above Arsenal in the league in 1995 in an era when the Gunners celebrated plenty of trophies. George Graham was dismissed as Arsenal manager in February of that season and Stewart Houston, put in temporary charge. He was replaced by Bruce Rioch in the summer and a year later Arsene Wenger was appointed manager at Highbury and the rest is history.

The Tottenham team back then was: Ian Walker, Dean Austin, Colin Calderwood, Gary Mabbutt, Justin Edinburgh, Ronnie Rosenthal, Darren Anderton, David Howells, Nick Barmby, Jürgen Klinsmann and Teddy Sheringham. From one of the world's greatest goalscorers to one of the most injury prone.

When Francis took over from Ossie as manager, Tottenham were effectively in the bottom four because of the points deduction for financial irregularities and were banned from the FA Cup. By April they had been reprieved, had brushed aside the eventual champions, Blackburn Rovers, in exhilarating style, but lost in the FA Cup semi-final to Everton at Elland Road and finished seventh in the league.

Sugar's highly successful TV series *The Apprentice* has the well known catch phrase "You're Fired" and when chairman of Spurs, he had a reputation for firing his managers. Gerry tells me, "I wanted to talk to you about my time at Spurs because it does rile me when I still see some articles saying that I was sacked at Tottenham. I was never sacked, and that is a poor indictment of Alan Sugar to suggest that he sacked me as he spent a lot of time trying to talk me out of leaving. We actually got on very well. There are two sides to Alan Sugar, the side everyone sees and the side you're not able to see, but I was able to see it. He is one of the best chairmen I have worked with. He would make decisions, and make them quickly, it was a simple 'yes' or 'no', very little messing around, but at least you knew where you were with him. Yes, of course we had our rows, arguments, and disagreements, but we worked together."

So why did he walk out? "Lots of reasons. It's quite complicated. Spurs, at that time, were very much a political club, and as far as I can see, nothing much has changed! There was still the Terry versus Alan saga, the media sided with either Venables or Sugar. Terry was the England manager, there was the points deduction, the ban from the FA Cup, the Jürgen situation. There was no money to spend in the first year. Perhaps one of the big reasons was that, after what I did for the club, I didn't think I was appreciated. I always felt sometimes, had I been at any other club in the country, I would be treated like a god for what I achieved.

"Sometimes I felt I was under pressure not only to win, but to win in a certain style, and it is not always possible. That has been one of the reasons why Spurs have never been able to sustain a really good league run. Yet, I'm the only manager to have finished as top London club in the Premiership with two different teams (Tottenham and Queens Park Rangers). The Premier League wrote to me a while ago to point out that record, as they were compiling some sort of quiz. I managed the best two league positions in over a decade until Martin Jol finished twice in the top five. I had the best record in the first 50 games going back to Arthur Rowe in 1949. The biggest problem with doing well is to reproduce it when you are under pressure. The expectation becomes tough and people were causing the team a lot of problems."

Francis, considered one of the brightest young managers in England at the time, was more pragmatic. "I would hear things on the radio, that it was boring to win 1-0. Supporters would say,

'We would rather have lost 4-3', as was the case under Ossie. The attitude at Tottenham appeared to say, 'Well it's not our day today, we will try next week'. I wanted (my team) to roll our sleeves up, because they can't stop us working and fighting for a result. But 1-0 was a result, a good result for a coach, but it was not reflected in the minds of the fans who sometimes weren't that impressed with four wins on the trot if it was 1-0 wins, they wanted more goals, more excitement, to win with style and that is not always possible."

From a promising beginning, the team's progress stalled and things turned sour. Come the summer, Jürgen Klinsmann left for Germany, Nick Barmby fled north and Gheorghe Popescu moved to Barcelona. And some supporters, for whom panache remained as valuable as points, became more demanding, yearning for the kamikaze style adopted by Ardiles, who had installed Klinsmann as the star of the fondly-remembered "famous five" attacking diamond (the others were Sheringham, Barmby, Dumitrescu and Anderton).

Gerry recalls, "We had our moments, though. An FA Cup quarter-final at Anfield where we won 2-1 and I am convinced that, had I had Sol Campbell, Darren Anderton and Justin Edinburgh, we would have won the semi-final against Everton, who, mind you, went on to beat Manchester United in the final.

"I had beaten United at Old Trafford 4-1 when I was manager at QPR and finished fourth in the league. We had such a good run up until Christmas that we hardly conceded a goal. But after that first year, they all seemed to go; Jürgen, Dumitrescu, Barmby. I didn't know Jürgen had a clause in his contract that allowed him to walk away. That summer I had to build a completely new team. We bought Chris Armstrong, who in the end cost £4.5m."

A lot has been made about Spurs turning their backs on Dennis Bergkamp, the one player above all others who transformed a dour Arsenal under Graham, the authentic 1-0 specialists, into the prototype side under Wenger. Yet Gerry tells me his side of the Bergkamp saga, "I had Jürgen and Teddy, a fantastic partnership and then Chris and Teddy, and I believe Chris and Teddy scored more goals than Jürgen and Teddy. You know Chris Armstrong and Teddy formed a great partnership and it was such a shame for Chris that he broke his ankle and he was never quite the same player. I don't believe for one minute that Alan Sugar would have spent the amount of money Arsenal did on Bergkamp, we would have struggled financially to have pulled off that deal.

"But I had Teddy Sheringham and Bergkamp was identical, they played in exactly the same position and performed the same function within the team. They both liked to drop off into that 'hole' behind the striker. Yes Dennis was an exceptional player but so too was Teddy and he scored more Premier League goals. How would I have accommodated both of them in the same team? Alan Sugar made a statement at the time, shortly after Arsenal signed Bergkamp, that they had paid a ludicrous amount of money for him. Yes, Alan was saying what everybody else was thinking, but it didn't do me any favours, it only put me under more pressure."

Three years after taking charge Francis stepped down after a 4-0 defeat away to Liverpool. He doubted that it was the right decision and Sugar implored him to change his mind. "I never finished below halfway, my worst position was 10th and that was mainly because we had such a lot of injuries that season. But for the first two seasons we were as good as anybody outside the top four. I went to Spurs without signing any contract, I only shook hands, and that was good enough for me. People said I was mad, but contracts didn't worry me at the time and never have done, but in the last year I was there I did actually sign a contract. I didn't get a pay off because I wasn't sacked."

Francis did, though, sign Ledley King as a teenager. "We had to be on our strictest behaviour because of previous financial activities and had lost quite a few good kids. Alan rang me up and said, 'You have to sign Ledley'. I called him later and said that Ledley had gone to Manchester United. He went mad, and I said, 'It's okay, we signed him'. Ledley was talented, quick, strong, good on the ball. He reminded me of Sol Campbell."

Francis lost to Arsenal just once in seven derbies, winning 1-0 against George Graham's side at White Hart Lane early in his Spurs reign. "My first taste of the derby was electric, a frenetic game, a feeling that you never want to finish. We were mentally strong, and it's getting that psychological strength that Tottenham need to adopt now. Like Arsene Wenger, George Graham was winning things. I didn't have the luxury of the money that Martin Jol had available. Tottenham's consistency has always been their inconsistency since 1961."

Teddy Sheringham formally requested to leave Tottenham on

Gerry's wedding day! On the first day of his honeymoon he flew back to Heathrow to try to sign Eyal Berkovic, only for the deal to collapse. Sugar put a fax machine in Francis' honeymoon suite so he could keep in touch and, despite his early departure, Jürgen Klinsmann still calls Francis about once a month for advice.

Christian Gross

When pressure from fans and media drove Gerry Francis to resign as Tottenham boss in November 1997, a disappointed Sugar bitterly quipped that, what with fancy-dan foreign coaches suddenly being all the rage, his manager would have had a much fairer public hearing if he'd changed his name to Geraldo Francisco. However that theory was quickly disproved. For although Francis faced flak, it was never as fierce as that fired at his Swiss replacement, Christian Gross, who, from the moment he arrived at White Hart Lane, was targeted for abuse and ridiculed in the press for nothing more than his broken English.

Before Sugar hired Gross I was so convinced that Sven-Goran Eriksson was the right manager at the right time for Spurs, that I almost begged him to employ the Swede. With hindsight, some might argue it was a blessing in disguise that the move that I initiated fell through. Although Sven had a tough time as Manchester City boss later, he had a decent spell as England coach, reaching two World Cup quarter-finals in 2002 and 2006 and the quarter-finals of the Euros in 2004. But at the time I recommended Sven to Sugar he was at the peak of his powers, and his reputation within European circles was at its height.

I was waiting outside the gates of England's training ground at Bisham Abbey with the rest of the media pack awaiting entry to the usual format of events prior to an England match when my mobile rang. It was an old friend, Bryan King, whose wife comes from Scandinavia, where he lived and worked and had become somewhat of an expert on football in that part of Europe. He wondered how Spurs were getting on in their search for a new coach and I told him that they couldn't find the right candidate, and that Sugar was at a loss.

"How about Sven-Goran Eriksson?" ventured Bryan. What a great idea, I thought, but I didn't think for one moment that Eriksson would come to England. I was sure he had much bigger fish swimming around him in Europe to want to consider England. Sven had been highly successful in Sweden, Portugal and Italy, although he had only managed to win one League title, and was rather unfairly dubbed the "nearly man". Instead of the negativity that came with him from Italian football, all I had heard was glowing, positivity surrounding his laid back managerial style.

When I suggested to Bryan there was little to no chance of luring Eriksson to Spurs, he quickly put me right. "Oh yes, he would be tempted", continued Bryan, "I know him well, and I have spoken to him recently and he would love to come to England. Do you think Spurs would be keen?"

Immediately I contacted Sugar. Naturally enough, the Spurs chairman hadn't heard of him and suggested he would make some enquiries about Eriksson and his CV and come back to me. The next day he called back and told me that he had consulted with people at his club and elsewhere and that Eriksson was not for Spurs.

So instead Spurs fans were treated to the unique management style of Christian Gross who arrived at Heathrow and took the tube, waving his underground ticket for the photographers. It wasn't long before most people hoped he had taken the precaution of buying a return!

The media campaign against him was sustained throughout a 10-month tenure that saw the words "Christian Gross" become synonymous with "clueless continental". Yet although he was dismissed in September 1998, Gross actually did a respectable job despite being regularly undermined, steering the club to 14th place before a poor start to the 1998-99 season did for him. He went on to have success back in his native Switzerland with FC Basle and in 2016 won the Saudi Arabian League with Al-Ahli.

*

Des Bulpin was on Gerry Francis' coaching staff at Tottenham and Peter Crouch was struggling as a first-year YTS trainee, all finesse and no brawn, when Bulpin told Crouch that one day he would play up front for England.

Tottenham would allow Crouch to leave in 2000, unconvinced that he would make the grade. Yet Gerry stood by Crouch throughout his growing pains and when he left QPR with Francis for Tottenham in 1994, he encouraged his new club to take the youngster across London. "When we first got Peter at QPR, he was outstanding on the floor, he had a brain and technique but he just couldn't run," said Bulpin. "But I knew that once Peter got his strength he would be good in the air and become a player. People make mistakes with kids by letting them go before they develop physically. At 17, the weak boy can become just as strong as the others."

Bulpin recalls the taunts that Crouch endured. The other boys would call him "Stick" and Crouch, introverted and conscious of his height, would hunch himself over in an attempt to blend in. Having taken him to Tottenham, the efforts to bulk him up began in earnest. "I gave him a load of milk, yoghurt, porridge, currants and raisins, told him to put it all in a blender and drink it wherever he went," said Bulpin. "I don't think he liked it. Then, there was the weights programme we put him on."

When Crouch left Spurs, Francis and Bulpin took him back to QPR in a £60,000 deal where he scored 12 goals in 2000-01. Global recognition has since followed after spells with Stoke, Liverpool and 42 caps and 22 goals for England. Bulpin recalls, "A lot of people were talking about Defoe at the time; I think he was at Charlton, it was just before he moved to West Ham and people were talking about him like they had done with Michael Owen. I'd seen Defoe play and he was very quick, a perfect foil for Peter, in a little-and-large partnership."

Crouch returned to Spurs when Harry Redknapp was manager and earned a lasting place in the fans hearts when he scored the goal in a 1-0 win at Manchester City on 5th May 2010 that brought Champions League football to Spurs for the first time.

George Graham

When Alan Sugar opted to hire a former Gooner to take the reigns at White Hart Lane, I never thought it would work and told him so. Spurs had had an "Arsenal man" in charge before with Terry Neill in the 1970s and that hadn't ended well at all... but George Graham! Well, that was about the worst moment of all. Not only had he won the double with them as a player but he had brought back the glory years to Highbury in the late 1980s winning two league titles.

Known as "Stroller" as a player, Graham had a reputation as a ladies man and a rebel, who was once sent home by Tommy Docherty at Chelsea along with a group of the stars of that era for misbehaving in Blackpool in 1965, an incident that Chelsea fans still claim cost them the league title. Ironically Graham the manager was the archetypal disciplinarian who fell from grace at Arsenal when he was sacked for his part in a bungs scandal.

When Graham later popped up as Spurs manager, I felt it was a bizarre choice for Sugar and told him so at the time. I had the effrontery to disagree with him and this is an important point. Steve Perryman says in his extremely hard hitting piece this book that he felt Sugar had surrounded himself with "Yes" men and that he felt "his" club was crying out for someone with Sugar's ear to tell him when he was getting it wrong. Steve thought I had sufficient influence to be in that position. For many years Perryman had harboured the belief that I was one of Sugar's "Yes" men, when, in reality, it was the opposite.

When Sugar rang me to tell me he had definitely appointed Graham as his manager, I told him that while he had appointed an outstanding manager, one of the finest of his generation, he was the wrong man for Tottenham. I made the point that he was appointing a man who would never be taken to the hearts of Spurs supporters and it would all end in tears. If he won the league title,

> When Sugar rang me to tell me he had definitely appointed Graham as his manager, I told him that while he had appointed an outstanding manager, one of the finest of his generation, he was the wrong man for Tottenham.

which I knew he couldn't given Spurs position back then, then I might reconsider my opinion but the warning was made right from the start, and I never wavered from that view. Sugar, as is his nature, became very defensive about it (as defensive as Graham's Arsenal back five), and, although to a degree, he shared my reservations deep down, he explained how he had left it to the so-called 'professionals' on his board and the overwhelming recommendation had been to go for Graham.

Of course, Graham did win Sir Alan his sole trophy as Spurs chairman, the League Cup in 1999, but eventually, inevitably, he was on his way out and as usual I got the blame for Graham's sacking.

As it turned out, I did play a role in Graham's dismissal, but purely an unwitting one as I was merely doing my job in pursuit of a good story. I had noticed Graham on the ITV local 6 o'clock news programme *London Tonight* complaining about his budget, or lack of it, and the fact that he couldn't spend as much money in the transfer market as he had wanted on the new players he was telling the world were necessary to take the club forward.

Now, this was like a red rag to a bull to Sugar. No one at the time, maybe apart from the big three or four clubs, were spending more than Tottenham and yet the chairman had been savagely criticised by Spurs fans, and in turn by the media, for not spending enough. I knew it would hit a raw nerve and pursued the matter, tracking down David Buchler, the club's executive vice-chairman, for an official reaction. It proved to be a pretty powerful one and was clearly the prelude to a confrontation between George and the board that would see only one winner!

Buchler might never have responded publicly so quickly, perhaps not at all, if I hadn't been successful in tracking him down. An article in the *Sunday Telegraph* analysing how Graham came to get the sack by Colin Malam was spot-on, as he wrote, "The strangest thing about the whole affair is the rather implausible explanation Buchler gave for the appearance in the *Mirror* on Friday — the day every other newspaper eagerly carried Graham's complaint about a 'limited budget' — of an exclusive story quoting the executive vice-chairman as telling the manager to shut up."

According to Buchler, it came about quite by chance... "It so happened that when I came out of a meeting on Thursday night at about 6pm", he explained, "I put my phone on to ring my wife. I pressed the green button and, instead of getting my wife, Harry Harris, the *Mirror* chief football writer, had just phoned in. He asked me if I knew about Graham's remarks. I said 'no' and added that it was not the sort of thing I wanted to have discussed in the press. I really didn't think that the press should know about the intricacies of a meeting."

Now, that didn't just happen by coincidence. I must have rung Buchler's mobile a hundred times that evening, maybe even more, determined that I would get hold of him, knowing the fragile position of Graham at that time, and the extreme

sensitivity of his remarks. Colin Malam pointed out that to publicly express concern about having a limited transfer budget is an old managerial trick to prise more cash out of the board, but not at Tottenham, and not at that time. Graham knew the score, it was as if he was pressing the self-destruct button. If he was taking some kind of calculated risk, then it backfired on him spectacularly.

So just three weeks before the 2001 FA Cup semi-final against Arsenal at Old Trafford, Graham was sacked when Buchler called him in the next day for an explanation of his comments. Did I play a part in Graham's sacking? Colin Malam seems to think so, and I am not going to argue with such an esteemed football writer.

One of the most contentious internal squabbles Sugar endured during his time at the club concerned the defection of Sol Campbell to Arsenal on a free transfer. I have known Sol since he was a boy at Spurs and always admired his determination, speed and solid defending, and I got to know him even better whenever the England squads assembled for major tournaments.

Sky Andrew, his agent, wanted some balanced media coverage at the time of Sol's move to Arsenal, as his client was going through a torrid time with the Tottenham fans, which was hardly surprising. I was only too willing to help. Sky is one of the few agents who I trust unequivocally. Equally, he trusts me. He knows he can confide in me and I won't let him down.

Sol really wanted to move from Spurs to better himself, something that he could hardly say in public, as Spurs fans would

Sol really wanted to move from Spurs to better himself... he desperately wanted to play Champions League football... and with all due respect to Spurs, he couldn't have done that at White Hart Lane back then. Now, as a Spurs fan, that is hard to take...

have wanted to crucify him. As it was, they hated him for moving to their bitter rivals but he desperately wanted to play Champions League football, to test himself at the highest level, and with all due respect to Spurs, he couldn't have done that at White Hart Lane back then.

Now, as a Spurs fan, that is hard to take, and that is what made them genuinely angry. Yet they were angry as much with the way the club was going, rather than angry with Sol himself. For Sol, the Judas chants, and the hatred, was something I was surprised he was prepared to put up with. Equally, no one is irreplaceable, not even the mighty Sol, and there were such huge hopes for Ledley King, who had all the attributes to become as good as Sol, perhaps even better, for both club and indeed country, so what a shame his career was blighted by a succession of serious injuries.

HH

Daniel Levy

I had many business-related dealings with Daniel Levy long before he became Spurs chairman, and maybe I can take the credit for pushing him towards making a big investment in the North London club. Together with Alan Green, the chief football commentator at Radio 5 Live for many years, I had dinner with Daniel and his then secretary Tracy, soon to become Mrs Levy, to discuss an internet project that Alan and I had started up called *Voice of Football*.

The four of us ate at an Italian restaurant that Daniel and Tracy frequented quite close to their offices. Tracy is a big Spurs fan and over dinner I tried to persuade Daniel to increase ENIC's portfolio of European football clubs with the purchase of Spurs. I was persistent, if nothing else, in trying to convince him that it would prove to be the right move, and I could sense Tracy was most definitely up for the idea. He wasn't too keen at the time, but I must have sowed the seed as he eventually made Lord Sugar, as he now is, several offers before one was finally accepted, becoming chairman of Spurs in February 2001, the month he turned 39, and taking over the day-to-day running of the club in October. My hunch is that Tracy liked what I had to say and that gave her the extra encouragement to push Daniel into the deal.

However Daniel was not the only potential owner of Spurs with whom I had discussions. Surprisingly, one of them was a fellow journalist, *Daily Mail* columnist Richard Littlejohn. He's a lifelong Spurs fan and I know he was more than interested in mounting a consortium to buy out Sir Alan Sugar at the time. I know Patrick Barclay thought he would have made an interesting independent chairman of the Football Association before the appointment of Lord Triesman of Tottenham, so why not a journalist as part-owner of a football club?

Another potential owner of Spurs would have been Robert Earl, but he chose to help out his old pal Bill Kenwright at Everton. The London-born owner of Planet Hollywood was once tipped to buy Spurs before Sir Alan Sugar took control. I met Robert at the Sofitel Hotel in London recently and after a long chat I know his allegiance to Spurs remains intact, although he was totally committed to the Everton cause while still involved at Goodison Park.

Sir Philip Green, the then high-flying boss of Arcadia, and one of the country's richest men who was later discredited following the collapse of British Home Stores, was a go-between in some of football's biggest deals. His behind the scenes activities are known to only a handful of insiders in the game. Sir Philip helped out Kenwright by bringing Earl onboard at Goodison Park as an investor, at a time when Kenwright was experiencing great difficulties with his former shareholder at the club. At Green's prompting, Earl bought out the previous shareholder and between them they took 51 percent of the club. He also acted as a go-between in arranging Wayne Rooney's transfer from Everton to Manchester United, where he was well connected with Sir Alex

Ferguson and his trusted agent Pini Zahavi.

Even back then Levy had ambitious plans for a new 60,000-seater super sleek stadium with all its additional income that it can generate. The battle to get the stadium plans off the drawing board and into reality took years and while that saga was being played out, Levy was busy hiring and firing managers as success proved so elusive.

Since Levy took control at the Lane the managers position has been little more than temporary with George Graham, Glenn Hoddle, Jacques Santini, Martin Jol, Juande Ramos, Harry Redknapp, Andre Villas-Boas, Tim Sherwood, Mauricio Pochettino, Jose Mourinho, Nuno Espirito Santo, Antonio Conte and Ange Postecoglou appointed - that's 14 full time managers in 22 years! He has also appointed caretaker managers on 6 more occasions.

This turnover of managers and their coaches was pinpointed by Glenn Hoddle, the first of those managers who Levy fired, as the root cause of Spurs' failure to establish themselves among the elite. "There has been a lack of continuity at Tottenham. They have not built. When you are building a house, you start with strong foundations and Tottenham have not done that." Glenn believed Martin Jol didn't get the time he needed and he also thought that Juande Ramos should have been given the chance to finish the job. Yet Levy believed the club could have been relegated had they stuck with Jol. Speaking after taking some testing questions from Spurs shareholders at the club's first Extraordinary General Meeting after the Jol sacking, he claimed Spurs were on a downward spiral under the Dutchman who had "lost the confidence" of his squad, adding, "We wanted Martin to succeed. The outside publicity was unfortunate but, in the end, it comes down to results. You can't have a situation where everybody is talking about finishing in the top four and then being in the bottom three. You cannot afford to take the risk that you may end up in a very, very bad situation. No club is too big to be relegated. We just weren't winning at all and you could look at the players, and there was a point when I think Martin had lost the confidence of the players. That happens in football." Levy refused to apologise for the way he sacked Jol, insisting the Dutchman never said sorry to him for applying for other jobs behind his back. Levy went on the record saying that Jol spoke to Newcastle and Ajax Amsterdam, while he was in charge of Spurs, adding, "People say I should apologise, but I don't hear anyone talking about Martin going for two jobs while he was here. No one has had a go at him. Have I got an apology? We are in the football business and I completely understand that he went to talk to club X while he was still here, that's just the way it is."

So, out with Jol, and in with Ramos. Yet, after all the fuss and bad publicity in prising Ramos from Seville, it wasn't destined to last very long. Nor did it last long for Villas-Boas, or Sherwood after him. Mauricio Pochettino looked to be the man to take Tottenham to the summit, and he did very briefly, but he was fired 6 months after reaching a Champions League final and replaced by Jose Mourinho, a serial winner everywhere else, who was sacked just days before the 2021 League Cup Final. Nuno Espirito Santo, fresh from great success at Wolves, was sacked within months and his replacement Antonio Conte succeeded only in falling out with players and inflicting a very un-Spurs approach to the game on the club's supporters, boring most of us to tears.

Yet Daniel clearly has clearly done his homework on his latest appointment. Ange Postecoglou has been a real breath of fresh air. His attacking style chimes precisely with the way Spurs fans want to see their team play - he has a clear commitment to score goals. It is to be hoped he gets the time to grow deep roots at Tottenham and leave a lasting legacy.

HH

Juande Ramos

The Last Trophy

Carling did their best to make the 2008 League Cup final, the fans' final. Their motives were good, their marketing strategy spot on. The problem is that the game had already headed off towards the corporate sector, slowly at first, and rapidly over the years. Roy Keane predicted this with his "prawn sandwich" comments in the 90s. That's not to say that Carling shouldn't have attempted to address that situation. It's all credit to their marketing department and PR advisors Hill and Knowlton trying to make it more of a fans final.

For a start, more ordinary tickets are designated to the club's supporters for the League Cup than the FA Cup, and that's how it should be. But the FA have a much more global problem in satisfying everyone connected with their vast organisation. There is less of that problem for the Football League. Paradoxically, my wife Linda and I were in the exclusive hospitality area designated for the Football League dignitaries, and some selected media. The corporate sector at Wembley has taken some deserved stick for preferring to continue with their food and drink after half-time rather than allowing supporters to take their seats, leaving gaping holes in the stands which have been caught on TV. This is not conducive to persuading everyone that this is still the people's game.

I have seen the gradual move to corporatism over the years, and more recently the lightning change towards the corporate sector throughout the game, not just at Wembley. This is one of the reasons Spurs needed a brand new stadium to cater for more executive boxes and corporate areas.

Just because I took up Carling's invitation via Hill and Knowlton doesn't necessarily make me an elitist football fan. But let's face it as you get older and wiser, who would turn down the

comfort and luxury that goes with being on such a Grade A guest list?

While the dress code suggested was smart casual, many of those in the official sector wore the shirts and scarves of their team, supposedly such attire was off limits but it showed a degree of flexibility, and there was no hardship to discover such a partisan section of the hospitality group. Of course it was tough for me to celebrate too strongly, as my delight at Spurs' success, over Chelsea came at a cost; Linda's misery. My son Simon and his Spurs supporting friend attended, courtesy of more strings pulled to obtain the tickets, and they were delighted when we met up with them afterwards outside the stadium in the North London drizzle.

Spurs' unexpected victory 2-1 over Chelsea at Wembley sent expectations soaring, but instead of building on that success, it all went, well, a little bit Spursy. A £77m summer spending spree yielded only two points from their first five Premier League matches of the following season, leaving Spurs bottom of the table after their worst start to a campaign since 1955.

Chris Waddle worried that the Carling Cup triumph raised hopes to an unrealistic level. The former England winger observed at the time, "The Carling Cup came too

soon for Spurs, because it meant that expectations grew out of proportion. Spurs have always been a great cup side, but the fans see other teams challenging for the title or a Champions League place, and think that is where Spurs should be. Cup competitions are the best bet for the clubs. It is not easy to get into the top four". Waddle made his observation just before Juande Ramos was sacked as the bad run of results extended into October and thought that the manager should be judged at the end of the season.

Waddle was critical of the system that contrived to work against Ramos, as he explained, "You cannot have players coming into the club who Ramos does not want. You do not want to be a puppet, so he should be in charge of team selection and player recruitment."

Ex-Spurs defender Chris Hughton was in temporary charge at Newcastle United at this time. Chris spent 13 years as a player and 14 as a coach at Spurs, and had been No. 2 to Ramos' predecessor Martin Jol before he walked out of White Hart Lane for the last time after 27 years service to the club, sacked along with the Dutchman. Hughton was in charge of first team affairs immediately after Kevin Keegan left Newcastle, with the club's hugely unpopular owner Mike Ashley desperate to sell up after seeing the fans turn on him. Hughton was working alongside Jol when Spurs signed Jenas from Newcastle and the England midfielder admitted he was surprised by Tottenham's lack of progress since their Carling Cup win.

Jenas said at the time, "The Carling Cup was a benchmark for us, and we wanted to take that into the new season, but it hasn't happened. We definitely didn't envisage being bottom of the league after five games. Some very influential players have left, like Keane and Berbatov, but it is a matter of us gelling. Going forward, we just don't seem to be clicking."

The only bright spots at the start of the 2008-09 season was a 2-1 home win over Wisla Krakow in the first leg of the first round of the UEFA Cup on 18th September and a 2-1 third round Carling Cup win at Newcastle six days later. A 1-1 draw in Poland against Wisla Krakow secured their place in the UEFA Cup group stage, but that draw came during a run of three straight league defeats to Portsmouth (0-2), Hull City (0-1) and Stoke City (1-2). Spurs opened their group campaign with a 2-0 defeat at Udinese

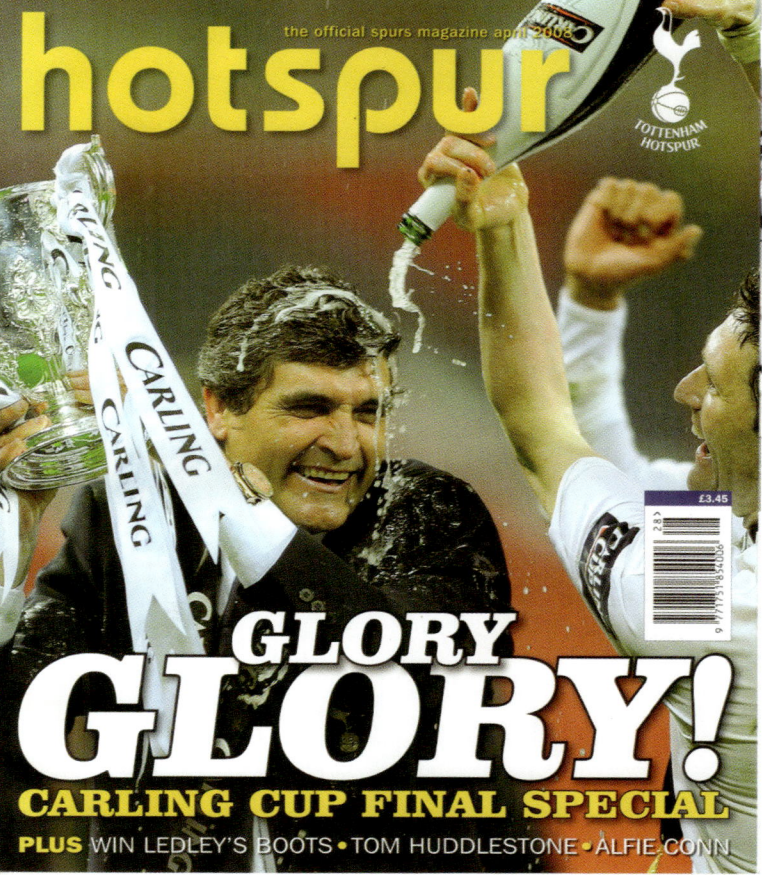

on 23rd October and two days later Ramos was sacked. The Carling Cup win over Newcastle had ramifications for two former popular Spurs players too. Chris Hughton had been managing Newcastle on a caretaker basis since Kevin Keegan had resigned at the beginning of September, but Newcastle had lost all four matches they had played under the former Spurs defender. After losing to Hull, West Ham, Spurs and Blackburn Rovers, another former Spurs defender, the late Joe Kinnear, at that time 61, was appointed interim manager by Mike Ashley.

I was due to discuss the possibility of Terry Venables becoming their new boss on BBC Newcastle radio, but the debate became defunct after Ashley failed to persuade Venables to take over on a temporary basis.

So a month before Ramos left Spurs, Kinnear was installed at St James' Park, typically cracking a joke when he was unveiled. "I am being linked with the 'Cockney mafia' - they forget I was born in Ireland and played for Ireland all my life. So be it. I have come here to do the best I possibly can because I know it's a short contract. I know what is stored around the corner for me, if you like. But sod it, so what? If I can come and do a really good job here, who knows where it is going to lead?"

Kinnear had not managed a club since resigning as Nottingham Forest boss in December 2004. He made his name at Wimbledon until he was forced to take two years out of the game after suffering a heart attack in 1999. Born in Dublin Joe had moved to Watford when he was seven years old and there was not a trace of Irish in his accent. He joined Spurs as an amateur in August 1963 after playing for St Albans City and turned professional in 1965 and went on to make more than 200 appearances. He made his debut at right-back against West Ham in April 1966, and his international debut for Ireland a year later against Turkey. He played 26 times for his country up until 1975.

Joe played in the 2-1 FA Cup final win over Chelsea, and was part of the team that beat Aston Villa 2-0 to land the League Cup in 1971. He also won a UEFA Cup medal when Spurs beat Wolves over two legs in 1972, and a year later when they lifted the League Cup again beating Norwich 1-0. In 1975 Joe left Spurs for Brighton and retired as a player aged 30 in 1976.

After five years abroad managing in Dubai with former Spurs

team-mate Dave Mackay and heading India's national side, he rejoined Mackay at Doncaster in 1977. He became manager when Mackay switched to Birmingham, but a takeover saw him lose his job to Billy Bremner. Bobby Gould recommended him for a job as reserve team coach at Wimbledon on £15,000 a year. Dons owner Sam Hammam later said he liked him so much when he first met him he gave him an instant £2,000 pay rise when he joined in 1991. Kinnear was highly successful at Wimbledon, then the bad boys of English football, as he kept the club in the top half of the Premier League for most of his 7 year reign and guided the club to semi-finals of both cup competitions in 1997. Joe also turned down the chance to replace Jack Charlton as Republic of Ireland manager because they didn't offer him enough money. A heart attack in March 1999 led to his eventual replacement as Dons manager and the club were relegated within a season. Joe, a dear friend, died in April 2024. He will be sadly missed.

So while two hugely popular former Spurs players were caught up in the turmoil at 19th-placed Newcastle, who eventually were relegated at the end of that season after Alan Shearer replaced Kinnear, two other former Spurs players were making life difficult for Spurs, the only team below Newcastle in the table. Jermain Defoe and Peter Crouch both scored against Spurs in Portsmouth's 2-0 victory over Ramos' tottering Hotspurs at Fratton Park which left Spurs with only two points from their six league games as the club made their worst start for 53 years.

Ramos was the target from some angry Spurs fans at Portsmouth, but, asked after the game if he had the confidence of his chairman and board, the Spaniard said, "Absolutely. We speak regularly and everyone is aware of our delicate position." Some Spurs supporters were unhappy with Ramos when he substituted Roman Pavlyuchenko with Darren Bent after 73 minutes. The move kept the visitors with just one recognised striker on the pitch, despite having to chase the game. "Whether I survive is something for the chairman and the board to decide but I'm not hurt (by the fans' abuse)," added Ramos. "What hurts is not winning matches."

Spurs were then the only club without a Premier League victory. They had twice as many points at the same stage the previous season, yet that got Martin Jol the sack and led to the appointment of Ramos. To add to Ramos' discomfort, Jol was now in charge at Hamburg, who led the Bundesliga in Germany.

The manner of Tottenham's defeat heaped humiliation on Ramos. Portsmouth had conceded 10 goals in their previous two matches, losing 6-0 at Manchester City in the league and 4-0 to Chelsea in the Carling Cup, and although no-one knew it at the time, that win over Spurs was their second to last victory before Harry Redknapp left Portsmouth for Spurs a month later. Before that though, the name of Terry Venables re-appears in our story.

After qualifying for the group stage of the UEFA Cup following their second leg draw in Poland, Spurs were due to play Hull at White Hart Lane on Sunday, 5th October, with the *News of the World* carrying a report that morning that Spurs were lining up a return to the Lane for none other than El Tel. Coincidently I had been booked by Radio 5 Live for a morning review of the Sunday papers and a look ahead to the fixtures.

Part of the review of the press was Martin Jol's comments in the *Sunday Times* that the club had lost its identity, and it was a point that was sure to raise a fascinating debate not just about Spurs but a number of other clubs. The point I made on Radio 5, was that, for Spurs fans, a heavy dose of nostalgia would help ease the pain of the present predicament. Could it get worse? It could. Spurs lost at home to Hull that afternoon to register the club's worst start since 1912... the year the Titanic went down. The same afternoon Kinnear's Newcastle side, 2-0 down at Goodison Park, fought back for a valiant and unexpected 2-2 draw lifting Newcastle to 18th.

Crouch and Defoe scored for Portsmouth again that weekend in a 2-1 win over Stoke who slipped to 19th. Spurs were well and truly rooted to the foot of the Premier League with just two points from their opening seven games with Ramos coming up to his first year at the club. The curtain was about to fall on Ramos... and Stoke were the club that helped bring it down. My Spurs supporting pal Barry sent me a flood of texts with the latest Spurs jokes, all revolving around three points and not being

Could it possibly get any worse? Oh yes it could: Stoke City 2 Tottenham Hotspur 1... Everything that could go wrong for Spurs did go wrong that afternoon... It was the worst start in Spurs history.

able to beat anyone.

Jol, a year after being sacked, was still keeping an eye on events at the Lane and felt strongly that Spurs should not sack his replacement so soon after his own departure. "They've changed the team but have done it with good intentions as they want to be better. They need to get good results, but it will take time, and unfortunately in England you don't get time. I was unhappy to leave Spurs. It wasn't to be and I've moved on. Yes, they won the Carling Cup after I left, but that was my team and my players. Now the team is different. I did well for a couple of seasons, the sun was always shining, it was a great atmosphere at the club and the players did well.

"The only person who was always complaining was Berbatov. They said to me he wants to leave because of you, but I don't think it was because of me. He proved me right and left anyway. I wish them all the best as they are a big club with over a million supporters and they were great to me. I pity the fans because they are the best in England."

Could it possibly get any worse? Oh yes it could, and it did at the Britannia Stadium in the Potteries on Sunday, 19th October: Stoke City 2 Tottenham Hotspur 1. Gareth Bale saw red after 19 minutes for a foul on Tom Soares and Danny Higginbotham scored from the ensuing penalty before Darren Bent poked home an equaliser for 10-men Spurs six minutes later. But after the break Spurs' fight-back disintegrated as Rory Delap tapped in to make it 2-1 eight minutes into the second half before Ricardo Fuller struck both posts with a penalty and Delap hit the bar. Spurs were then reduced to nine men late in an 11-minute period of injury time when Michael Dawson, who came on as a 77th minute substitute, was sent off for a tackle on Mamady Sidibe.

Everything that could go wrong for Spurs did go wrong that afternoon. The long injury time period was necessary after Croatian defender Vedran Corluka was badly hurt after being caught on his chin by the knee of his own keeper, Heurelho Gomes. He eventually left the field on a stretcher wearing an oxygen mask and was taken to hospital. Spurs were looking like an emergency case themselves. They had played eight, won none, drawn two and lost six. No team with two points from their first eight league games had survived relegation in the Premier League. It was the worst start in Spurs history.

Juande Ramos looked back on his first days as Spurs manager in a fascinating article in *The Guardian* which provided a shocking insight into the way the club had been run. When he and his staff walked into the dining room at the training ground they asked each other "where's the wedding?"

"Incredible," Ramos said, shaking his head, "it was like a wedding buffet: cakes, pastries, sauces — and that was what they ate regularly. Honestly, and I say this with no bitterness at all, there were players who were... fat." he laughs, "they were sedentary."

He elaborated: "A sportsman's physical condition has to be impeccable: your body is your living. A runner is like this. You can't live like the man on the street who's had dessert or cake. If you eat a cake, you're putting in diesel; a sportsman's got to run off super. A sportsman who makes, say, £6m and drinks and smokes and eats, it makes no sense at all. A lad who's 22, 23 and has cash might think: 'This guy's not telling me what to eat'. We train not far from a McDonald's and we'd see them in there eating hamburgers, drinking Coke but you explain and they understand. 'This is your ideal weight, the percentage of body fat.' I can't go to their houses to watch them eating but we could train morning and afternoon and weigh them. If you're not in shape, you don't play and with work the team started improving."

At Sevilla, Ramos won five trophies but he was never given any credence or recognition as a manager in the Premier League. However he insisted that, "At White Hart Lane they'll have good memories: the last title that Spurs won was with me, so I guess they'll remember me fondly." Unfortunately, they probably can't remember him much at all!

"We hadn't beaten Arsenal for years and we won 5-1. We won the Carling Cup, everyone's really happy… " And then? "I was sacked. Levy had an easy explanation: 'No, the thing is, the coach doesn't get it, the players are hungry, they don't eat, he doesn't understand …' When we won the Carling Cup I understood and then I don't understand any more! They sacked a manager they'd given a four-year contract to. So they say: 'He didn't understand!'"

He counters the view held at the time that he had little or no relationship with the players. "My relationship with them was excellent," Ramos said, "you know who it was bad with? [David] Bentley."

He has a bit more to complain about: "The year before

"In my opinion, the problem isn't selling him and Keane, it's not replacing them. So we were left with Bent and Campbell... We couldn't beat anyone. We couldn't have scored if we'd used a rainbow as the goalposts."

they'd signed Darren Bent for £17m. They sell Robbie Keane and Berbatov because they want Bent to play, so they left us with Darren Bent and Frazier Campbell. Without strikers!" And Roman Pavlyuchenko? "Yes but he was new to England, didn't understand and hardly played — and not just under me. I'm sure that if Levy had known what would happen he would have either not sold Berbatov or signed a replacement. But he wanted Bent to play and Bent had a brilliant pre-season, so Levy thinks: 'We've got the players. Bent scored 12 or 13 during pre-season. That's the worst thing that could happen!' So Levy says: 'This guy [Berbatov] out, this guy [Keane] out… Berbatov didn't want to stay. Against Middlesbrough he said: 'No, no, I'm not playing.' I understood. It's more honourable to say 'I don't want to play' than to go out and not even try. If he stays and he's pissed off, he's pissed off all year. In my opinion, the problem isn't selling him and Keane, it's not replacing them.

"I wanted Samuel Eto'o and David Villa. Eto'o wanted too much in wages. We negotiated with Villa, when he was one of the world's best. Levy's a hard negotiator and in the end it didn't happen. So we were left with Bent and Campbell. We couldn't beat anyone. We couldn't have scored if we'd used a rainbow as the goalposts."

Ramos could see that Gareth Bale was going to be very good but the Welshman spent eight months injured. He also speaks highly of Jermaine Jenas who "always offered tactical solutions", describes Tom Huddlestone as like "a bear" with a "scandalously good touch" and calls Jonathan Woodgate a "very good, intelligent player". But Woodgate, as with Ledley King, was injury prone and Michael Dawson was "still just a kid". He remembers: "We could only use King in important games: he didn't train, which was a pity. He was so talented. Even at 50%, he was the leader but, sadly, you can't fight for the titles like that. So, eight weeks into the season — I'm out! Then what happens? In December they spent £51m to rectify the mistake. Defoe, Keane, Kaboul, Palacios. 'No, the manager doesn't understand… it's the coach, that silly little Spaniard who hasn't got a clue…' I took the blame but they had to spend £51m to sort it out. The honourable thing Levy did was sack [director of football Damien] Comolli too: if he'd truly blamed the signings on me, Comolli would have continued but the whole structure changed. He knew but when it came to the [message to] the press and fans, it was the manager's fault. They know they ruined the team when they sold two strikers and left me none."

The Spaniard admits he also made mistakes. "Of course. I shouldn't have accepted some decisions that weren't mine. I can't think of a specific thing I'd change but the responsibility for the team is mine, absolutely. I accepted Comolli's players, who I hadn't proposed. That was a mistake." Perhaps he should have refused to work with Comolli? "With hindsight that might have been the right thing to do."

Ramos added: "Spurs works as a business. That's legitimate and I'm sure the model's built with the right intentions. They think the economic model enables the sporting model to function but that's not always true. Levy makes a £17m investment [Bent] but has two better players in the way. They have to remove obstacles so the investment plays. In economic terms, fine. In sporting terms it turned out to be a disaster.

"Spurs spend a lot of money but only sign players who are 20 or 22 because they're thinking of future sales. Bale, for example, or Modric: I advised Spurs to sign him. He's a great player but you still need patience; it doesn't happen immediately. The idea is: sign players, see if they take off, sell and reinvest. Fine but are you trying to win money or titles? The criteria at Manchester United, Manchester City, Chelsea is that the sporting side is the priority. If City sign Navas or Negredo, they don't look at the player's age; they look at his performances.

"Spurs aren't going to win the league. Economically, it works well but in sporting terms maybe it needs retuning. You can't demand something that doesn't fit the reality."

> "Spurs works as a business. That's legitimate and I'm sure the model's built with the right intentions. They think the economic model enables the sporting model to function but that's not always true. Levy makes a £17m investment but has two better players in the way. They have to remove obstacles so the investment plays. In economic terms, fine. In sporting terms it turned out to be a disaster."

When 'Arry Met Harry

Harry Redknapp and I share the natural affinity of being typical Londoners, a bit of jack the lad, cockney rebels, at least that is how much of the country perceive those of us from the East End where we both grew up. We have had quite an up and down relationship, mostly up at the moment I should note, but we have crossed swords on occasions when 'Arry didn't approve of some of my hard-hitting investigative stories in the *Mirror*, but our mutual friend and agent Jon Smith brought us back together when he agreed to be one of my many guests when I presented a TV programme.

Harry had his moments as Spurs boss, and some of the football was a joy to watch with the likes of Gareth Bale rampaging down the wing and scoring some sensation goals that earned him the recognition of Real Madrid. Yet Daniel Levy aborted his plan to offer Harry a new contract when it was clear he would have deserted Spurs to become England manager, and he was close, but not quite close enough, to the big job and burned his bridges at the Lane as a result.

Harry eventually reinvented himself as the Housewives Choice winner of *I'm a Celebrity Get Me Out of Here* as the nation fell in love with his endearing love-affair with his wife Sandra.

When Redknapp took the Spurs job he immediately said, with typical cheeky Cockney humour, "I thought it was a wind-up at first" and in one quick sentence he won over the Spurs fans. Not since Terry Venables had the club had an English boss with such quick witted one-liners in a familiar cockney accent — Harry has a wicked, cheeky smile and quickly had the fans and media eating out of his hands.

The 'King of the Jungle' never quite made it as 'King of England' as the manager of the national team, but he was welcomed to the Lane with open arms when, following a defeat at Stoke and the subsequent loss at Udinese four days later, it was announced on Saturday 25th October that Juande Ramos's reign at Spurs was over. Immediately after that news, and before Redknapp's appointment, I was being interviewed on Radio Five Live and asked for my reaction to the Spaniard's dismissal.

"Predictable", I replied adding, "and, Harry Redknapp is the new manager of Spurs!" Even though 'Arry's appointment had not yet been officially announced.

The show was broadcast from Manchester, and the presenter, who was unfamiliar to me, was indignant that I should be so confident in suggesting that Redknapp had been appointed the new manager. "Who have you been talking to? What are your sources? How can you be sure?"

Usually, during my media interviews, I try to be circumspect because my newspaper column would be appearing the next day. But after I left the *Daily Express*, my TV and radio appearances increased and the need for such caution no longer existed. So, it must have come as a shock that I was not holding back and that radio presenter was the recipient of one of my "exclusives". While I declined to reveal my sources on air, despite being challenged to do so, I mentioned the fact that I was writing the first edition of another Spurs book, and that it didn't take a lot of research as events at the Lane had become so predictable.

Tottenham Hotspur joined the Football League from the Southern League in 1908 - the same year that they moved to White Hart Lane. Exactly 100 years later Spurs suffered their worst start taking two points from a possible 24. *The Guardian* and *The Sun* ran pages of jokes after the 2-1 defeat at Stoke on 19th October 2008 left Spurs with the unwanted record of the worst start to a league campaign in the club's history. My mobile was overloaded with text messages, or rather text jokes but really it was no joke being a Spurs fan then.

The jokes finally stopped when Daniel Levy summoned up Harry Houdini who inspired them to their first win of the season against Bolton and then stunned the Emirates crowd with that astonishing 4-4 comeback against Arsenal a few days later.

Having prolonged the agony of Martin Jol as a "dead man walking", it was apparent that Ramos was dead in the water after the humiliating defeat at Stoke, followed by the 2-0 loss in the UEFA Cup in Italy a few days later. According to my sources the Spurs board felt the performance against Udinese was the final straw, that the manager's run-ins with players such as David Bentley and comments about a losing mentality from Jonathan Woodgate, caused a dramatic U-turn in the attitude of the players which was evident by performances on the pitch. My feedback was the players were no longer were playing for their manager.

The call immediately went out to Redknapp, who opted to quit Pompey before the club was sold and he might be replaced by the new owners seeking another foreign option, and it was clear he would not say no to Spurs as he had done when he was offered the job when Jol was still in charge.

In the days and even hours leading up to the sacking of Ramos the club's legends lined up to give their views. One of the most pertinent came from Steve Perryman. The former skipper was going through agonies watching their relegation battle unfold. Perryman blamed the Spurs board for the management structure they imposed on Ramos, with sporting director Damian Comolli having a huge say in player recruitment. Perryman said, "When I was a player at Spurs there was a base of home-grown people there. What the club stands for now is increasingly difficult to see. Everyone seems to be just passing through. Tottenham is not the same club I knew. It's Hollywood. It's not real. We were not passing through. I did 19 years at Spurs. We had a depth of feeling about the place. We had our cobblers kicked by the supporters when we did badly, we were lifted on their shoulders when we did well. But any club that devalues the power of the manager is walking on thin ice. I don't know if the manager is going to be good enough or not. That has not been proven either way yet, though there are certainly doubts now. But you have to appoint a manager you believe in, and follow it up. Don't water him down or attack him from above. I saw all that go on when Ossie Ardiles was undermined as manager. I've been through all that crap. Bill Nicholson was the right man. You could not possibly question him. Get the right manager and then back him.

"The manager has to be the man. The success must be the manager's, the failure, his. That's why he picks the team, that's why he buys the players, he makes the substitutions. Fighting relegation is dark. They were dark days in 1977. There is never any let-up. You are depressed, you are down, negative, not confident. You are expecting bad things to happen. You need strong people to drive through it and we did not have them then. I hope there is integrity at Tottenham to do the right thing. The right thing might mean making the hard decision to get rid of someone. Or it might mean to keep them. You can never say they are too good to go down. We went down in 1977. It happens."

On arrival Harry admitted he couldn't turn down the opportunity. Shrewdly, Redknapp laced his comments at that time with a touch of Tottenham tradition, references to Bill Nicholson, and icons of their real glory days. "It's a big opportunity to manage a big club before I retire. I am a big follower of the history of the game and Tottenham have been a great club over the years. I followed Tottenham, I trained there as a kid so I know the history of the club. People think I was a West Ham fan as a kid because I love that club, but it was Spurs I used to go and watch, they were the team I supported. Now I've been given an opportunity that I've waited for all my life. Since I started as a manager, I've always craved working for a big club, a club with heritage and style, that's what Spurs have got. I want to put them back where they belong, up there with Arsenal.".

Redknapp recalled telling Nicholson that he was a right-winger who did not score goals when he came for a trial at the age of 11. Nicholson replied that Stanley Matthews was similar, but that Redknapp probably didn't have the same ability. Redknapp said, "He was one of the all-time great managers."

Nothing would endear Redknapp more to the Spurs fans than the belief he was returning to his roots, even if they were really only partial. He went on, "It is a big, big, club. It is a club that has massively underachieved this year - to be sitting there with two points and, let's be honest, in a real desperate situation, a relegation battle. There's a lot of quality players there that obviously haven't done as well as they should have done. You don't end up with two points from eight games if you're doing what you should be doing. So they need to start performing as I know they can. Whether it's confidence or whatever, it's up to me to go in and try to get the best out of them players."

'Arry came to Spurs as a winner, having led Portsmouth to victory in the FA Cup final against Cardiff City only five months earlier, their first major success since winning back-to-back League titles in 1949 and 1950 and their first FA Cup triumph since 1939. "I had a great time at Portsmouth and we had an unbelievably, successful time over the six years I was there. But Tottenham made a fantastic offer to Portsmouth and it was difficult" he reflected, "It was a lot of money - I think £5m, crazy money really. Of course it's tough to turn my back on Pompey because I loved it there and I'm leaving behind some great friends. But how often do you get the chance to manage Spurs?

"When anybody says Spurs, I think of Bill Nicholson and the great Double winning team of the 1960s. They played with style and that's what I want to bring back. It was a hard decision but Portsmouth have picked up £5m in compensation and I reckon that's a world record transfer fee for a manager! I hope that helps heal a bit of the pain they'll be feeling and I think they'll understand my reasons for leaving. I spoke to Clive Allen, who is Spurs through and through, and he just said, 'Harry, go for it, it's what you've been waiting for all your life.' And he's dead right, a fantastic club with a magnificent history, how could I say no?"

The enforced sale of strikers Berbatov, Keane, and Defoe in such a short space of time had left Juande Ramos struggling to

> "Associated so closely with West Ham, it was refreshing for Spurs fans to appreciate how much the club was actually in his blood. As a kid he trained with Spurs, met the club's greatest legend, Bill Nicholson, and rubbed shoulders with the likes of Dave Mackay, John White, Danny Blanchflower and Cliff Jones."

fill the void. So, out went Ramos and in came Redknapp; from a succession of foreign bosses to one as English as pie and mash and as East End as jellied eels. Associated so closely with West Ham, it was refreshing for Spurs fans to appreciate how much the club was actually in his blood. As a kid he trained with Spurs, met the club's greatest legend, Bill Nicholson, and rubbed shoulders with the likes of Dave Mackay, John White, Danny Blanchflower and Cliff Jones. Perhaps, he's even half Jewish! Who knew? But then Harry went and almost spoilt it all when he confessed, "I was an Arsenal fan!" Oh no, can't be. Well, no need to panic. He truly had a deep and meaningful relationship with the Tottenham traditions.

Of course, the Hammers are in his soul, after all he played for the East London club and managed them too. Arsenal are in his heart, because his dad supported the Gunners and took him to Highbury as a kid, but Spurs formed much of the fabric of an impressionable young footballer.

Harry is passionate about everything, "My dad was Arsenal mad", recalled Harry as he took his own trip down memory lane with me at the time when he was appointed Spurs manager, "and as a mad Arsenal fan he took me along to watch them, so Arsenal were the team I supported as a kid. But when I was 11, and playing for East London Schools, Spurs scout Dickie Walker spotted me playing at the Old Den against Wandsworth Boys, came over to my dad and said, 'Hello, I'm Dickie Walker the Spurs scout, your son has what it takes.' Dickie asked to see my dad for a chat and I ended up the next four years at Spurs training on Tuesdays and Thursdays. Tony Marchi took the kids and Bill Nicholson had time for us boys and that's where I first met him. During the school holidays I would train at Cheshunt where I first came into contact with the likes of Dave Mackay and Danny Blanchflower. I ended up following all their games, especially the European midweek ties which were something special in those days when Spurs played against sides like Gornik and Bobby Smith terrorised opposing goalkeepers the only way Bobby Smith could. I ended up at West Ham and people think they are my club

and in many ways they are. I was playing with Bobby Moore at the age of 15, but now Spurs are 1000 percent my club."

In his first game in charge Redknapp instantly delivered what Tottenham wanted all season – a 2-0 win over Bolton. Roman Pavlyuchenko scored after 17 minutes and Darren Bent grabbed the second from the spot 14 minutes from the end. They were still bottom but made up ground on the other strugglers and crucially had a morale-boosting first league win of the season, at the ninth attempt. Ramos' hasty departure came too quick for the club to change the match day programme, so fans were given a chance to read the Spaniard's final notes. "If you believed everything that was being speculated on then your perception of the club would be far removed from the reality," he wrote. The reality was Ramos already back in Spain (pitching up at Real Madrid a few months later) and Redknapp was in the dugout, even though reserve team coach Clive Allen picked the team for that first game.

Redknapp was unveiled to the Spurs fans before kick off. The encouraging sign for Redknapp was skipper Ledley King being available, four days after playing in the defeat to Udinese. It was the first time he had been ready for games in such quick succession since the start of the season when he played against Sunderland and Chelsea in August.

As expected of a team with a new manager, there was an extra zip. Luka Modric had struggled to make an impact since his £16.5m signing from Dinamo Zagreb in the summer, but he was given a free role behind the striker and resembled a new player. David Bentley was back in the team after being dropped for Ramos' final game against Udinese following an outspoken assessment on Spurs' start to the season. The fans sang, "Harry Redknapp's blue and white army," after watching two players who struggled under Ramos combining to set up Pavlyuchenko's opening goal against Bolton.

Redknapp remarked, "I've taken over clubs before where I look at it and think how do we get out of this one, but there is real quality in this group of players. You look through and there are international players. You look at the quality and they shouldn't be where they are, but two points in eight games is an amazingly bad start. We have to start working as hard as we did today for each other, picking up points, playing as we did. They passed the ball with real quality which I was really impressed with."

Redknapp insisted he alone was going to pick which players came to the Lane. "I wouldn't let anyone else pick my players. I will pick the players we sign and if the chairman can deliver them, then great. I'm not going to ask him to buy Ronaldo for me. There'll be some players out there in January who we'll bring in. I'll just deal with the chairman. There will be no sporting director or director of football. The last word on players has to be with the manager. At Portsmouth, Peter Storrie did all the deals but it was my choice on picking the players. If people are giving you players you do not fancy, it is impossible." Tottenham fans made it clear they would welcome Jermain Defoe back by chanting his name within 10 minutes of the Bolton match starting. Defoe duly returned to Spurs from Portsmouth in the January. In his second match back he scored in a 1-1 draw... against Portsmouth.

The Bolton match was one thing, but 'Arry's second match three days into the job was an altogether tougher task - an away match at Arsenal, yet a rejuvenated Spurs produced an incredible performance to come away with a heart-stopping 4-4 draw.

"It was a real old-fashioned slugging match," Harry enthused, "we went for it and then they went for it. We conceded sloppy goals but we never gave up, we showed a never-say-die attitude and came back brilliantly. It was a fantastic performance and a great result in the end."

The extraordinary display at the Emirates provided further encouragement, Redknapp even suggested he had never experienced a match like it in his entire 25-year coaching career, "It's been a difficult week, leaving home at 5.30 in the morning and not getting home until nine, but this makes it all worth it. It really was an amazing game of football to be involved in. We gave away some bad goals, from set-pieces too, even though we worked hard on that in training. We need to stop giving away goals like that, especially as one of them was straight after we pulled it back to 3-2. But the boys have been fantastic, there's a real spirit there, a determination. They are jumping for joy in the dressing room."

Spurs opened the scoring in the 13th minute with former Gunner David Bentley beating goalkeeper Manuel Almunia with a superb 40-yard volleyed lob. Surely, goal of the season! Jermaine Jenas, who scored Spurs' third in the 89th minute, hailed Redknapp's immediate impact. "Harry is great motivationally," he said. "The lads have done him a favour by reacting to it. It showed complete team spirit and togetherness. We always believed. We just showed that never-give-in spirit. Any team who comes to the Emirates and gets a result has done well but given the circumstances, this is just brilliant."

Redknapp's arrival coincided with Tottenham confirming their intention to build a new 60,000-capacity stadium next to White Hart Lane. Spurs announced the Northumberland Development Project at the same time as their financial results in June 2008. Speaking about the need to sell naming rights, Levy said at the time, "Unfortunately it's a function of modern day finance - absolutely there will have to be naming rights on the stadium. It's going to be a new stadium so it won't be White Hart Lane. If we want things to progress, things have to change. The stadium will have no impact on our transfer policy."

The board had no alternative but to demolish the old ground and build a new one, but despite their complicated involvement with the Olympic Stadium in Stratford, now West Ham's new home, there was a real belief they had to remain in the Haringey area. "With a waiting list for season tickets of over 22,000 and club membership levels of over 70,000, our need for an increased capacity stadium has been clear for all to see for some time," said Levy. "Having reviewed our stadium options it was clear that there were a limited number of alternative sites to our current location. Following discussions with council bodies, the London Development Agency, Transport for London and local and central government officials, redeveloping the existing site emerged as the most viable route. We have spent five years buying and taking options over property around the current stadium site to enable us to either develop locally or to gain the critical mass to achieve a substantial site sale as a contribution to relocation. To date this includes almost 60 separate property transactions, including 40 residential and potentially 160 commercial properties at a commitment of £44m."

Meanwhile Harry Redknapp was concerned with more down to earth matters and quickly made himself popular with the players by putting tomato ketchup back on the tables of the dining room at the Tottenham training complex. In addition to his basic £3m salary, he agreed a very lucrative bonus system, close to £1m for

maintaining the White Hart Lane outfit's Premier League status, which he did, and was on additional bonuses for winning the domestic cups and getting Spurs into the Champions League.

The domestic honours never came, but Champions League football duly arrived in 2010-11 with Spurs making it back to Europe's elite competition for the first time since they reached the semi-finals of the old European Cup in 1961-62.

Levy's words at the time were also somewhat prophetic in terms of where Spurs were in 2008 when Harry arrived and where they are now. Although Harry left the club in 2012, Levy's ambitions were fulfilled by Harry. Levy had said at the time: "Champions League football is obviously something this club strives for eventually but it is very difficult to break into the Big Four. The hope is that Harry is here for the long term and will help us achieve it. In Harry, I believe we now have the right manager and one the players do respect. Now the players have to show the club and the fans what they can do. Can we make a Big Four become a Big Five? That is certainly possible."

By taking Spurs into the Champions League Harry transformed the club. Peter Crouch, who had returned to Spurs under Redknapp, earned a lasting place in the fans hearts when he scored the vital goal in a 1-0 win at Manchester City on 5th May 2010 that brought Champions League football to Spurs for the first time. Their past glories still make Spurs a big name in European football. Within the decade Tottenham had reached the Champions League final and become an established part of the 'Top Six' having qualified regularly for the elite European tournament, and it all began under Harry Redknapp. The years of mid-table obscurity were over.

Yet to be critical, while Harry was a great motivator and believer in good football, he bought a lot of ready-made players with minimal, if any, sell on value, such as Peter Crouch, Alan Hutton and Ricardo Rocha. These players didn't have sufficient quality to consistently qualify for the Champions League or compete at the sharp end of that tournament, something the club required to make sense of their business plan in raising the funds for the new stadium or attracting new investors to help with such a massive task. Instead it would take bank loans similar to the mortgage Arsenal took out over 25 years to move from Highbury to The Emirates, to underpin the building of the new Lane.

Yet there were some magical moments under Harry as he guided Tottenham into the Champions League for the first time and oversaw progress to the last 16. Spurs topped their group ahead of holders Inter Milan before defeating AC Milan over two legs to reach the quarter-finals. Finally, this looked like a team that could take the club forward and get the fans dreaming.

Redknapp had signed five new players in the January 2009 transfer window, bringing back Jermain Defoe from his old club Portsmouth for £15.75m and Honduran midfielder Wilson Palacios from Wigan for £12m. Long-serving Chelsea keeper Carlo Cudicini also joined on a free transfer, former Spurs player Pascal Chimbonda returned to the Lane from Sunderland for a fee in the region of £3m and Robbie Keane who, like Chimbonda and Defoe, had only left Spurs within the last year, re-joined after an unsuccessful spell at Liverpool for an initial fee of £12m.

In the second half of the season, Spurs moved up the League after a significant improvement in form. In March 2009, Redknapp led Spurs into the Carling Cup final as holders but lost on penalties to Manchester United after a goalless draw at Wembley. Spurs eventually finished eighth in the Premier League with 51 points, narrowly missing out on a Europa League place.

Harry made significant alterations to the squad in the summer of 2009. Striker Darren Bent was sold to Sunderland for an initial fee of £10m, while midfielder Didier Zokora departed for Seville for £7.75m. England striker Peter Crouch returned to the Lane and a long-standing Redknapp favourite, Croatia midfielder Niko Kranjcar, joined him from Portsmouth for £9m and £2m respectively, while defender Sebastien Bassong arrived from Newcastle United for £8m.

In his first full campaign with the club, Redknapp guided Spurs to their most successful Premier League season. Beginning with four consecutive League wins, Spurs went on to finish in fourth place with 70 points, gaining the chance to qualify for the Champions League through the following season's playoffs. 'Arry won the Premier League Manager of the Year award, only the second manager to do so in a season when his side did not win the title, and Spurs looked as though they could achieve something special.

On 13th July 2010, it was confirmed that Spurs had extended his contract until the end of the 2012-13 season. On 25th August

2010, Spurs confirmed their position in the Champions League group stages by overturning a 3-2 first-leg deficit to defeat Swiss team Young Boys 4-0 at the Lane in the Champions League play-off second leg.

At last Spurs were really back in the big time of European football. After a surprising run to the quarter-finals, they were knocked out in April 2011, after a 5–0 aggregate defeat to Real Madrid. Spurs ended the season fifth with 62 points. Although it was not enough to secure a second year of Champions League football, Redknapp's team qualified for the Europa League.

In 2011-12 he continued to reshape the side, signing 40-year-old goalkeeper Brad Friedel, after his contract expired with Aston Villa. He also made a season-long loan move for former Arsenal striker, Emmanuel Adebayor. On transfer deadline day, he signed midfielder Scott Parker from West Ham United and went on to win the Manager of the Month award for both September and November.

Yet despite leading Tottenham to their second fourth-placed finish in three years and missing out on Champions League qualification only due to Chelsea winning the competition, Redknapp was sacked by Spurs on 13th June 2012. It was widely reported at the time he left because the Board felt he was hopeful of the England job. Whatever the real reason, Harry left Spurs but also left an indelible mark by taking the club back into the highest echelons of the European game. For that at least, Spurs fans owe him their appreciation.

As a fan I have been so fortunate that my job as a football reporter has given me enviable access to the team I love. There has been so much to marvel at on the pitch through the decades but it is the action off the field that I, unlike so many other fans, have also been part of. In the end of course, it proved something of a false dawn as so often happens at Spurs. 'Arry did lay the foundations of Spurs considerable improvements, but although he took the club into the Champions League for the first time, both Bale and Modric were tempted away to Real Madrid, and 'Arry never brought a trophy to the Lane.

Despite that, it still seemed as though he was set for a long stay in the manager's chair but once he was linked with the England job in 2012 it was the beginning of the end. However, it was fun while it lasted.

Spurs provided Redknapp with a platform that could, finally, elevate him to be a candidate for the England job provided he made a big enough success of turning around Spurs' fortunes. He did enough to be under consideration, but the big job eluded him, and he lost his job at the Lane as a result. Redknapp was in the frame as England manager when Steve McClaren was sacked. Personally, I never thought he was on the FA's short-list. My FA contacts assured me that he wasn't. Redknapp was not convinced either, despite the media hype at the time. However, there was a momentum growing in the media, where 'Arry, like Venables, was hugely popular. Redknapp felt his arrest at that time scuppered any chance he might have had of fulfilling that particular dream. The City of London police came knocking at Redknapp's door just after 6am on 28th November 2007, less than a year before his appointment as Spurs boss. After fraud officers investigating alleged corruption in football raided his Dorset retreat, the then-Portsmouth manager condemned the heavy-handed approach. His wife, Sandra, was described as "absolutely petrified". At the time Ladbrokes had put Redknapp at 9/2 to succeed McClaren as England manager. The night after the raids, he had slipped to 10/1.

It wasn't the easiest question to field, yet typically Harry refused to shirk it. "Yeah, you're right, I do have an image problem but that's because people don't know me. They think I'm a Jack the Lad, but that image couldn't be further from the truth. I have been married 40 years, and Sandra and I just love the quiet life. There is nothing flash about me, even though people think I live in a big house on Sandbanks, but I spend every spare minute of my life with the wife, or walking the dogs on the beach. People think I spend all my life ducking and diving, but that couldn't be further from the truth. I live a very quiet, probably even boring, life." 'Arry doesn't seem to have any deep lying psychological hang-up about being overlooked for the England job, or even that he is wrongly perceived to be something he is sure is not the real him.

As an investigative journalist, I scrutinised the peculiar betting patterns when he returned to Fratton Park from arch rivals Southampton. The FA investigated, but apart from indicting a minor player, nothing much came of it. Redknapp called me once at home for a long chat. He wanted to get it off his chest, he wanted to let me know that he was innocent and felt he was victimised. It was an impassioned 30-minute conversation. I have got to hand it to him, he was never abusive, he never accused me of victimising him, but he felt that my *Daily Express* column at that time was concentrating far too much on this aspect. Perhaps he had a point, I told him. I had a meaningful chat with my then sports editor Bill Bradshaw, a seasoned campaigner, who himself was Sports Journalist of the Year at the *Sunday People* for his investigations into Swindon Town. We both felt that my column had made its point. We called a truce. And again, to be fair to Redknapp, he agreed to appear on my World Cup TV and radio shows during the 2006 tournament in Germany. His appearance was facilitated by his agents Jon

> "Yeah, you're right, I do have an image problem but that's because people don't know me. They think I'm a Jack the Lad, but that image couldn't be further from the truth. I have been married 40 years, and Sandra and I just love the quiet life."

and Phil Smith who wisely wanted to end hostilities. Unfortunately, four months later Redknapp was pictured outside FA headquarters in Soho Square by *The Sun* where he was being questioned for a second time about the betting patterns on him returning to Pompey. Bill Bradshaw called; with Redknapp back in the headlines my sports editor wanted an update. I rang Redknapp's private mobile several times, and left several apologetic messages, my point being that I had to break our agreement to no longer mention him in my column because he had suddenly become newsworthy again.

Yet when he became Spurs manager, by chance, I was working with Barratt Southern Division and one of the builder's directors, Julian Jones, had been in touch with Harry. I suggested to Julian that it might be worth mentioning my involvement with Barratt and whether Harry might want to renew acquaintances. Could he forgive and forget one more time?

To my astonishment, Harry agreed to take my call. I asked him why? He said, "You know me, I never hold a grudge, life is too short." He accepted that I was doing my job, and, in reality, I had never actually accused him of anything. I was reporting the accusations being made by others. I told him I hoped he would succeed in managing "my club", and asked him if he would cooperate with the *Down Memory Lane* project and he agreed.

Jermain Defoe
A Remarkable Life On and Off the Field.

It was a privilege to have been part of the documentary, *Defoe: For the Love of the Game*, which highlights his 325 career goals, most of them scored at the Lane, his humble roots in Beckton, east London and his friendship with Bradley Lowery. Defoe speaks of his special bond with Bradley and their 'genuine love' in a new film about his life. The 41-year-old former England star tells of the first time he met the football mascot while playing for Sunderland in September 2016. The film features interviews with his former mentor at West Ham, Harry Redknapp, England team-mates Peter Crouch and Joe Cole, Gus Poyet, ex-Charlton boss Alan Curbishley and his devoted mum, Sandra.

Defoe says "it is not just about football" as he recounts his time with Bradley, who died aged six from neuroblastoma, a rare form of cancer, in July 2017. "With Bradley, the way he looked at me, I have never experienced anything like that before. In football, people want to get close to you and sometimes you have to put your guard up. But with Bradley, all he wanted was to meet me. It was genuine love." Bradley's mum Gemma told how Jermain visited her son in hospital while he was undergoing treatment as they developed a special bond, which remained until her son's tragic death.

His moving and heartfelt relationship with Bradley has come to define him as a player and man. Defoe's dad, Jimmy Defoe, died aged just 47 in 2012 after a long battle with throat cancer, on the eve of Euro 2012. The striker left the England camp in Poland but returned in time to play at the tournament. His half-brother Jade, died at the age of just 26 following an assault in Leytonstone in 2009. The father-of-three fractured his skull and suffered brain damage after being punched by Christopher Farley, who was jailed for three years. Director James Ross said: "As a Spurs fan, working with a legend like Jermain was a dream come true. But though I knew his goals on the pitch, I never expected that by asking him to trace his roots and his career, it would reveal such a complex tale of love, loss, trauma and redemption off the pitch."

Produced by Zig Zag Productions with CEO Danny Fenton producing, the film looks at Defoe's life on and off the field. Fenton added; "Telling Jermain's story has been an absolute privilege. The film is a raw and honest account of a man with an undisputed talent who has managed to shine on the field while dealing with unbelievable heartache and pain. As Jermain says, 'there is more to life than kicking a ball'."

Defoe began his career with Charlton Athletic, joining their youth team aged 14, before he moved to West Ham United aged 16, making first-team debut in 2000. After a season-long loan spell at Bournemouth 2000–01, he established himself in the West Ham line-up. After relegation in 2003, Defoe joined Spurs for £7m in January 2004 and made his England debut against Sweden the following month, the first of 57 caps, collecting 20 goals. He excelled at White Hart Lane, netting 64 goals in 176 games during his first spell lasting four years and 79 in 186 during his second. In between he spent a season-and-a-half with Portsmouth. His second Spurs spell featured Champions League football before he rounded off his career with Toronto in MLS,

Sunderland, Bournemouth and Rangers.

Defoe represented England at the 2010 World Cup and Euro 2012. He was appointed an OBE in the 2018 Queen's Birthday Honours for services to his charity, the Jermain Defoe Foundation. Defoe is now an academy coach at Tottenham, and he holds nothing back in the film. As well as his personal tragedies, he delves into the murky world of tabloid journalism - and that's where the producers saw my role, to explain why he became a target.

Defoe talks about 'love rat' tabloid headlines that scarred his life at the time they were published, but at the time, he had no idea why his private life had been targeted. In the film I explain in detail how, at the peak of Defoe's scoring exploits, football had been turning away from the back pages to make the front page and the gossip columns as the sport had turned players into celebrities. Editors thought that if salacious tittle-tattle about the private lives of the likes of Gazza would sell newspapers, then all were fair game for gossip and lurid headlines.

In an exclusive interview for my book *Red Card to Racism*, Jermain said: "I've got great memories of Bradley in my head but it wasn't easy seeing someone that you love suffer like that, especially a young kid, where he didn't really understand what was going on and you have to remain positive." Defoe's foundation was launched in 2010 after a hurricane in St Lucia, the Caribbean island his grandparents came from. The charity hopes to open a home for abused and vulnerable children there and the foundation had expanded to help children in Dominica and the UK.

Defoe's right arm bears a tattoo 'hard work and dedication' and his union, the PFA, believe he is a great ambassador. His brother Jade died from head injuries sustained after he was attacked in the street, he lost his grandparents at around the same time and in 2012 his father died of cancer and a cousin died in an accident at a swimming pool. Defoe becoming the ambassador of the E18HTEEN project – endorsed and supported by the PFA among others – which helped mentor kids between the ages of 16 and 19, who either had been, or were, in care. Such was the success of the project, whose primary objective was to get those in care into training, education, apprenticeships and full-time employment, that it won the London Beyond Sport Award.

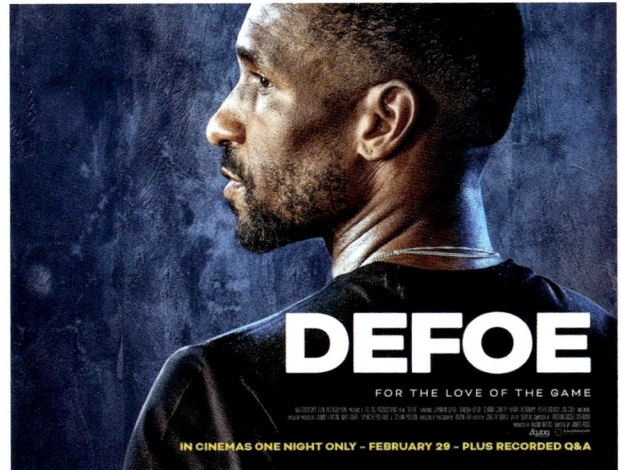

Jermain added that he felt "blessed and humbled" at the honour, and called it his biggest achievement to date. "It's at the top because I feel like this is something completely different. I am proud of it to be honest. It's important to just give back and try and help others."

Jermain has been an ambassador for the Prince's Trust, one of the PFA's long-standing partners, providing opportunities for young people who need that extra support in life to gain employment, education or training. And he launched his own Foundation three years ago, focussing on helping the homeless and vulnerable from the island of St Lucia in the Caribbean, his ancestral home.

In an interview for PFA's *Tribute* magazine, he commented: "I came from East London, a massive family and I just remember clearly when I was younger playing in a park with my mates and I don't feel like I've changed in any way. You have to acknowledge you're blessed where you've been to, where you've come from and to be able do something that was my dream. When you're in a position like I am now, it's important to give back. It's all very well saying it, but it's doing something for the community. I know how important it is to the kids, they love it. I remember being at a local club in the East End, we were told that a professional player would come to do the presentations and the night before, you couldn't sleep. We had Kevin Campbell of Arsenal one year and though I was a huge Ian Wright fan, it was incredible to see Campbell in the flesh and be able to hear him speak. Little things like that, to understand the feeling I had. If you [as a player] just turn up for an hour, it's unbelievable.

"I lost my brother in 2009 and I spoke to some of the people at Tottenham and we came up with an idea of doing my own thing. We thought of eighteen, my special number. We wanted to help get kids who were in foster care, kids on the street, kids without families to have a better life and we came up with the E18HTEEN project. One day Sky TV came to film a session we had with the kids and I sat at the top of the class, Geoff Shreeves [the lead Sky TV interviewer] asking me a few questions. There was a group of 10 who were about 17-18 years of age and he said I should stop talking and let's hear from the kids. He asked them what they thought of me and they said 'he's changed my life.' You don't ever expect anyone to say that.

"They made the point that 'you're in this privileged position, why would you give us time?'" says Defoe. "They said they would be on the streets if it wasn't for the positive message I had. I got emotional. I started to cry a little. It meant an incredible amount to me. You think that going out on a Saturday afternoon and scoring the winning goal is the greatest feeling ever but this is on another level, isn't it?

"I'm old school mentality. With my family background I realise it's important to give back, to go into the community. These are the people who pay your wages. I did an interview with a few games left of the season at Sunderland, we talked about pressure and I said 'I don't think a lot of players realise but staying in the Premier League, so many people keep their jobs at the football club'. There's a lot of pressure on your shoulders but the reality is if you go out and work hard and do what you should do, that's your job."

Jermain commented on the issue of racism in my interview when he told me: "I played for England against Spain in a friendly at the Bernabéu in 2004 and it was well documented that me, Ashley Cole and Shaun Wright-Phillips were among the black players who received monkey chants. It was a huge international match and it shocked me that this was happening. But that was probably the last time I experienced any kind of racism, and every year it seems to be improving. Maybe I've been lucky but I haven't experienced much of it directly towards me. I've obviously heard stories, especially from years ago. John Barnes came into the England camp once to give us a talk about what it had been like for him in his early Watford days but since then massive steps have been made in this country and I believe things are heading in the right direction. Attitudes are changing on and off the pitch and people are trying to get it out of the game completely. Racism and discrimination shouldn't be happening anywhere, whether that is sport or society in general.

"I can't speak highly enough of Kick It Out and all the initiatives they have put in place over the last 25 plus years. Kick It Out has been so important to this country. All the things they have done over the years, show people they are serious and that whatever goes on – or used to go on – will not be tolerated. Football is such a powerful tool. It brings people together. It unites them, educates them and helps break down boundaries. We saw that with the World Cup in Russia and we see it every weekend around the country. It can have a huge impact on making sure discrimination is no longer part of our society, and that is what Kick It Out have been working hard to achieve over the last 25 years. Over the years, I have seen so many players get involved in Kick It Out's projects.

"Footballers are role models and when we go into schools it is a chance to help educate young people, to show them what is right and what is wrong. The kids we are speaking to are the next generation and we have the opportunity to help mould their views and beliefs. Twenty-five years is a huge achievement. In the nicest possible way, you would hope that there isn't a need for Kick It Out in another 25 years but who knows?"

Andre Vilas-Boas, Tim Sherwood, and (almost) the return of Glenn Hoddle

On 3rd July 2012 former Chelsea manager Andre Villas-Boas became head coach, signing a three-year deal. He made an impressive start becoming the first Tottenham manager to win at Old Trafford in 23 years following an incredible 3-2 victory. His first North London derby on 17th November 2012 at the Emirates saw Spurs take the lead early on through former Gunner Emmanuel Adebayor before the Togolese striker was sent off just eight minutes later, and Tottenham eventually lost 5–2.

AVB earned his first piece of Spurs silverware when he won the Manager-of-the Month award for December, picking up vital points to pursue their top four ambitions. Impressive wins away at Fulham, Aston Villa, and Sunderland, along with home wins against Swansea and Reading, left Tottenham in third place going into the New Year. One set back was a tough trip to Goodison Park, where Spurs were leading up until the 90th minute, before two late goals in as many minutes, snatched victory away.

In February 2013 he guided Tottenham into the last 16 of the Europa League after a last minute goal from Mousa Dembele, secured a 1–1 draw against Olympique Lyonnais at the Stade Gerland. Spurs won the tie 3–2 on aggregate, after a 2–1 win at home the previous week. Following a 3–2 away win at the Hammers, a third win from three Premier League matches that month, AVB was awarded the Manager-of-the-Month award for February, along with Gareth Bale who picked up the Player of the Month award.

On the final day of the Premier League season, Tottenham sat a point behind Arsenal, knowing that in order to qualify for the Champions League they would need a win and hope that Arsenal would either draw or lose. Spurs secured a late dramatic 1-0 win against Sunderland thanks to a sensational strike by Bale, but their victory was marred by Arsenal's 1-0 win at Newcastle. Even though Tottenham finished a point behind the Champions League playoff spot, they set a new club record with 72 points. This was also the highest points tally ever achieved by any club in the Premier League to not finish in the top four. It was impressive stuff which looked to vindicate AVB as the Boy Wonder. Surely he was the long-awaited Messiah. But it proved to be a false dawn.

In the close season the wheels started to come off when AVB claimed he was approached by Paris St Germain and Real Madrid to fill their managerial vacancies. He insisted that he had rejected these offers to remain with Spurs for a second successive season, something which he had not previously done as a manager.

Following the sale of Gareth Bale to Real Madrid for a world record fee of £85.3m, AVB brought in defensive midfielder Etienne Capoue, midfielder Paulinho and striker Roberto Soldado, the versatile Nacer Chadli, ball-playing defender Vlad Chiriches, winger Erik Lamela, and play-maker Christian Eriksen. Of these signings only Eriksen became a fixture in the team and was the only really big success resulting from the sale of Bale. Meanwhile AVB sold Tom Huddlestone, Clint Dempsey, Steven Caulker, and Scott Parker.

It was little surprise then that on 16th December 2013 Tottenham announced that AVB had left the club "by mutual consent." The dismissal came with Spurs lying seventh in the Premier League and having won all six of their Europa League group games, but followed a series of disappointing domestic league results that included a 6–0 defeat at Manchester City and a 5-0 home defeat to Brendan Rodger's high-flying Liverpool. Vilas-Boas left with the highest percentage of league wins of any

Then when Fleet Street came to a close, I moved into digital and online with ESPN and BT Sport and Glenn returned from Spain after nearly five years running his Academy over there and we joined forces. H&H Sports Media Ltd was born in my kitchen over coffee and biscuits. Of course its one of my little jokes when I explain that while Glenn Hoddle thinks "H & H" stands for Hoddle & Harris, it's really Harris & Hoddle. That joke has worn a bit thin from over-use. Having vastly over-played that line, I can no longer use it. I make no excuse for repeating it here but it is the last time, I promise.

'H & H' had two grand-plan ideas. One was the Football 30 Legends, the other was zapsportz.com, an online news and comment channel. Zapsportz was a "news with attitude" platform which kept my hand in with breaking stories, at the same time as running things like a prediction challenge with some of our readers joining in, notably Simon from my local Sunningdale Waitrose, until he moved on to Camberley, but he still posted his predictions on Zapsportz! It was a market leader of its time, but such ideas quickly fade without intensive investment.

Glenn had managed Spurs from April 2001 until September 2003 and with the club always so dear to his heart, there would never come a time when he wouldn't answer the call to help them out. That call seemed to arrive with the demise of AVB in December 2013 and the elevation of Sherwood from the Academy where good young talent was emerging. Glenn's last job had been at Wolves in 2006 and in the time since he had spent nearly five years running an academy in Spain rescuing players kicked out far too early from their clubs in this country, and re-inventing them, some very successfully, back into the system.

manager in the club's Premier League era but that figure should not mask the poor quality of his purchases in the transfer market.

*

Following the departure of AVB, Tim Sherwood put up a good case for promotion from within having done such an impressive job at Academy level, while a return to the dug out for Glenn Hoddle was rumoured. Again, life was coming full circle as Glenn was one of those who featured prominently in my formative days as a novice football reporter, writing his autobiography, then following his fortunes in Monaco on a professional basis.

In his quest to find a long term replacement, Daniel Levy had nipped over to Amsterdam and had an agreement in principle to hire Louis Van Gaal, quite a coup at the time, but he wasn't in a position to take the job until his commitments with the Dutch national team after the World Cup in Brazil were over. So Glenn was asked by Levy if he would consider coming to the club's aid until the end of the season, a prospect which Glenn was warming to.

Speaking on Sky Sports at the time, he said: "Do I want the job? Well I've had the job there once. Tottenham Hotspur, you know I supported them when I was eight years of age. I went there at 12, left there at 28. Went back and managed. It's in my blood. It's in my bones. If I was offered the job, yes I would want to go back, even if it was for the sake of the club. Tim is in pole position here."

By that point Sherwood was in charge of the side in a caretaker capacity and also made it publicly clear he wanted a permanent position with the club. Hoddle's Sky Sports interview continued: "If he gets a good win today, and he moves on, and the club decides that whatever is right for the football club, and if they felt that they wanted me to go in until the end of the season or wanted something else long term, I would be prepared to do that because I love the club."

Hoddle insisted that he would be willing to work for Daniel again, even though Levy had sacked him a decade earlier. "They've not offered me the job, so it's all speculation, it's all a bit of media hype. It's a different club completely this time. I think I had a squad that was ageing at the time, we were bringing free transfers in, we brought Teddy Sheringham and Gus Poyet in on free transfers. This isn't the same scenario at this club at the moment. It's a completely different scenario to that. I think there's a way forward."

Glenn and Daniel did get together and for a short period, behind the scenes, it looked as though it would happen. As you might expect, being so closely linked with Glenn in our projects, I was living the moment with him, albeit in strictest confidence - not even an exclusive on Zapsportz!

One day Glenn was watching Sky Sports News by chance in the morning and spotted the yellow ticker tape announcement that Sherwood had been given a two-year contract, it came as a big shock, as deep down he really did want a second crack at managing Spurs. I spotted the news break too, and was straight on the phone. Glenn was not in the best of moods, as you'd expect. It was a shame as I think he would have made a much better fist of it second time around, as he had matured and that would have given him a far better chance than first time around. Glenn didn't want to return to management with any other club but he would never say no to Spurs, or indeed England, if the chance came round again.

Through my association with then FA Chairman time Greg Dyke, I facilitated a meeting between the two which eventually led to Glenn being one of the highest profile 'signings' to Dyke's FA think tank on the future of the England team. So from being totally on the outside as far as the FA were concerned, he was suddenly back as an accepted authority in his field. In addition I had the greatest pleasure of facilitating Glenn's move to ITV to become an authoritative voice on England, the Champions League and Europa League. He was the first pundit to hold contracts with ITV and Sky, and then ITV and BT Sport.

I don't think he had itchy feet, but he admitted that he wanted to "dip my toe back in the water" when he got the call from Harry Redknapp to join QPR's coaching staff during the 2014-15 campaign. It didn't last the season though, as Harry left, hobbling on a bad knee. Of course Glenn left shortly afterwards, even though Harry recommended Glenn to take charge as manager. Glenn resumed concentrating on his punditry and also kept a close eye on the emergence of some promising new talent coming through at the Lane, just as he himself had done some 40 years ago.

In the event Tim Sherwood guided Spurs to sixth in the table in 2013-14 but was sacked quickly afterwards.

HH

Mauricio Pochettino

Ossie always told me: "In Poch We Trust". The Argentine connection was strong within the managers inner circle with Mauricio Pochettino fully aware of Ossie and Ricky's history at the club, but more so their value in winning the World Cup for their country in 1978. Ossie was a confidante of the manager and also someone the manager sought advice from with such vast knowledge and experience.

After he was sacked from the Spurs job Ossie paid tribute saying that Mauricio had, "Put us in the elite of world football". His five-year tenure came to an end when a statement from chairman Daniel Levy confirmed his departure, the shock decision arriving off the back of a poor start to the domestic season less than six months after the Argentine had guided Spurs to their first ever Champions League final.

"One glorious chapter in our club history has come to an end today," Ardiles wrote on Twitter. "From my part I would like to say a big, big thank you to Mauricio for everything he has done for our club. These 5 years have been a roller-coaster of a ride. In extremely difficult circumstances, leaving our beloved White Hart Lane - who can forget The Finale? - playing at Wembley, etc., Mauricio put us in the elite of world football. We owe him so many memories. Where to start? With him we learned to 'believe'. Everybody at Spurs owes him so much. It was such a pleasure to arrive in the training ground and witness the camaraderie, the atmosphere there. From everybody. From my personal point of view, life gave me a wonderful present. Unique. His friendship. The friendship of a wonderful, principled man that would last forever. Mauricio, my friend, have a very good and deserved rest and come back to football (football needs people like you) revitalised, refreshed and, of course, we meet again... On behalf of everybody at Spurs (and I know I talk for everybody)... THANK YOU! And of course, COYS!"

It is a measure of Pochettino's success that ever since his departure Spurs fans have hankered for his return, although maybe not so much now that Big Ange has brought back a brand of football the fans crave.

Photographs from Ossie Ardiles' 70th birthday celebration showed Poch alongside a host of club legends but by then he had already departed for Paris Saint Germain with no one quite believing it wouldn't eventually be The Bridge! Pochettino shared photographs with Ardiles and Villa at the event, one of which was captioned: 'celebrating life with legends'. Another photograph from the event saw Pochettino, Ardiles and Villa alongside a number of other Tottenham heroes from down the years, including Garth Crooks and captain Steve Perryman. Sharing them on social media, Pochettino accompanied it with the customary 'COYS' acronym.

Poch guided Spurs to fifth in his first season and reached the League Cup final, which was lost 2-0 to Chelsea, perhaps a portent to come in that, despite all the fantastic football, Poch's teams always seemed to lose the biggest games. In 2015-16 Spurs were in genuine title contention against surprise eventual champions Leicester City but contrived to finished third behind Arsenal on the final day of the season. Yet the progress he had made was recognised with a new contract from Daniel Levy at the end of the season and a change of role from 'head coach' to 'manager'. Spurs finished a distant runner-up to Chelsea in 2016-17, yet it still represented the club's highest finish since the days of Bill Nicholson during their last season at the old White Hart Lane, however Spurs didn't make it out of their Champions League group, lost in the fourth round of the League Cup at Anfield and in the FA Cup semi-finals to Chelsea.

2017-18 saw Spurs relocate to Wembley for the season. They finished third behind the two Manchester clubs, were knocked out at the semi-final stage of the FA Cup at 'home' by Manchester United, despite Dele Alli giving them the lead, and made little progress in either the League Cup or Champions League. Yet the following season saw Poch's Spurs at their peak, as they embarked on an incredible run in the Champions League.

After losing their first two games in the competition to Inter Milan and Barcelona and drawing the third away at PSV Eindhoven, Tottenham somehow qualified from the group following two narrow victories against PSV and Inter before a 1-1 draw in the Nou Camp helped edge out the Italians on goals scored. After a comfortable 4-0 aggregate win over Borussia Dortmund in the Round of 16, Spurs drew Manchester City in the quarter-finals. The home leg saw a late goal from Son give Poch a precious 1-0 lead but the game in Manchester was crazy - the score was 2-2 after just 11 minutes before City took control and appeared to be home and dry as they led 4-2 on the night (and 4-3 on aggregate) after an hour. Yet all of that only set the scene for a finale that featured a controversial goal that was allowed by Llorente (that appeared to come off his hand) and a last minute winner from Aguero that was belatedly disallowed for offside after Guardiola had raced down the touchline in celebration. Instead, Spurs somehow marched into the semi-final on goal difference.

The semis saw Tottenham paired with Ajax and this time the Dutch masters appeared to have taken control of the tie in the first leg in London as they took a 1-0 lead back to Amsterdam, which they then added to with first half goals in the second leg from De Ligt and Ziyech. Tottenham looked finished at 3-0 down on aggregate as the home crowd sang the Bob Marley anthem 'Three Little Birds' but it was Spurs fans who should have been thinking 'every little thing is gonna be alright' as Lucas Moura produced a stunning second half hat-trick, sliding home an incredible winner six minutes into injury time, to squeeze through on away goals again.

After that the final in the Wanda Metropolitano in Madrid was something of a let down; a penalty was given for handball against Sissoko in the first minute of the game which Mo Salah converted and while Spurs, with a half-fit Harry Kane up front, enjoyed plenty of the ball, they created very few chances. A late Divock Origi goal secured Liverpool their sixth European Cup and many critics felt that the hero of Amsterdam, Lucas Moura, should have started the game instead of coming on after 66 minutes.

Nevertheless from the outside Poch seemed to have the world at his feet. He'd guided Tottenham into the biggest club match in the world and secured another top four finish in the league. Yet the following season started with just three wins in 12 Premier League games, a shock defeat on penalties in the League Cup to Colchester and the biggest set-back, and one from which the Argentinian would not recover, a 7-2 home defeat to eventual European champions Bayern Munich, made worse by four of the German goals coming from former Arsenal man, Serge Gnabry.

On 19 November 2019 Pochettino was sacked by Levy with the club sitting 14th in the table, the chairman citing 'extremely disappointing' domestic results. Poch's final goodbye to his Spurs squad was a hastily scribbled message on a club tactics board. With no time to say his farewells face-to-face, he wrote: "Big thanks to you all! We can't to (sic) say goodbye.... you will always be in our hearts", with his signature at the bottom. The image was tweeted by his assistant Jesus Perez, a poignant end to a reign that had begun with the club in something of a crisis.

Named Tottenham boss on 28 May, 2014, having taken Southampton to their best-ever finish in the Premier League, Daniel Levy made what would prove to be an inspired appointment after the sacking of Tim Sherwood. When he took over the club had managed just two top-four finishes in 22 Premier League seasons. In a little over five years he transformed the club to regular visitors to the knock-out stages of the Champions League, masterminding the end of St Totteringham's Day as Spurs finally finished above Arsenal in 2017 after 22 years beneath them in the table. It wasn't just the improvement that left an impression, but the style he brought to the team, the energetic high-pressing, all action style by increasing the fitness levels that had Tottenham fans believing he would bring back the 'Glory, Glory' days when the club had a reputation as one of the most entertaining teams in the country.

Pochettino's record in the north London derby wasn't amazing; in all competitions he won four of 13, drew six, lost three, with only one of those victories away from home — a 2-0 win in the League Cup quarter-final. Nevertheless he took Tottenham from a mid table team into top four regulars; after finishing fifth in his debut season the club qualified for the Champions League in each of the next four seasons finishing third, runner-up, third and fourth.

His record remains impressive, even without a trophy to show for it; Pochettino became the first opposition manager to beat Pep Guardiola in England when Tottenham defeated Manchester City 2-0 in October 2016, while his tally of 382 Premier League points ranked behind only Manchester City (446), Liverpool (404) and Chelsea (398) over the course of his reign.

'Poch' may have paid the price for a poor start to the season but he is recognised as one of the most forward-thinking and progressive Tottenham managers for guiding Spurs to the Champions League final which assured the Argentine of his place in the club's history. He became only the third man to lead the club out in a major European final. He took charge of 293 games in all competitions, which ranks him fourth in the club's all-time list. Only Bill Nicholson (832), Peter McWilliam (505), and Keith Burkinshaw (431) have been in charge longer and only the legendary Nicholson (55) led them in more European games than Pochettino (53).

When Pochettino suggested before the Champions League final that winning that trophy might prompt him to leave the club, it seemed to many that the beginning of the end was closer than anyone expected. Arguably, perhaps he might wish he had left whatever the result of the final! During the calendar year of 2019 Spurs showed relegation form. No Premier League side had lost more matches in all competitions than Pochettino's (18). Spurs last lost more games in a calendar year in 2008, when they suffered 19 defeats during spells under Juande Ramos and Harry Redknapp. A dismal away record was the main issue, their last away league win came in January when they scraped an injury-time victory against a Fulham side destined for relegation. They also lost more points from winning positions than any other Premier League side (12), bringing into question the players' motivation.

Tottenham's tally of 14 points was their lowest after 12 games of a Premier League season in 11 years, and for a club in such a swish new stadium with so many England and international stars, this was a huge let down. Little wonder Levy said results had been "extremely disappointing" and the manager paid the price, but there had also been simmering tensions behind the scenes. The media were full of conspiracy theories. For example that back in July, as players returned for pre-season training, Pochettino wanted to install fixed cameras on the training pitches to record sessions, only for Levy to refuse to pay the £80,000 cost. The manager offered to pay, only for Levy to refuse permission to buy them.

Then Levy accepted £10m from Amazon to record a fly-on-the-wall documentary series documenting the club's season. As part of the agreement, fixed cameras were installed in Pochettino's office, they were not dissimilar to those he had requested to film training sessions! Managers generally consider their office to be a personal sanctuary.

The manager was the head of the playing department, and all requests related to first team matters to Levy go through the club's head of football operations, Rebecca Caplehorn, who sits above five heads of department, of which Pochettino was just one. Her remit was to run the club on a daily basis and communicate messages between department heads and Levy. A key part of her role was to deal with recruitment and contract renewals for players and staff alongside the Spurs chairman. After the Champions League final, Pochettino wanted to sell players he knew had no intention of playing who could walk away for nothing at the end of the season, such as Eriksen, Vertonghen and Alderweireld. He wanted to raise funds to reinvest in rebuilding the squad. But Levy and Caplehorn decided all three were to remain, even if it meant losing them for free.

The negativity caused by such big influences within the dressing having such a big desire to leave had a toxic effect on the manager's reliance on squad unity. There were supposed to be clear-the-air talks with Levy in August but the season started calamitously with a 3-0 defeat at Brighton followed by a 7-2

humiliation at home to Bayern Munich at the start of October. Spurs had won just twice in the Champions League (both against Red Star Belgrade) as it seemed the club were preparing for his departure with the final route to an exit being the substantial compensation. The 1-1 home draw against Sheffield United before the international break proved to be the manager's final game and Levy initially enquired about the then Leicester boss Brendan Rodgers but was told prising him away from the King Power Stadium would be impossible. Spurs then turned to Julian Nagelsmann, but were told RB Leipzig's impressive rising young manager would be too hard to land having only just moved clubs in the summer and, with no Premier League experience it would be asking a lot for him to hit the ground running at a time of a mini crisis with some fans fearing relegation. So perhaps that it was inevitable that preliminary soundings were taken with the unemployed and readily available Jose Mourinho. Eddie Howe was another name considered as the best young English manager option but had not as yet handled the big name stars and was again deemed too much of a risk. It soon became clear that Mourinho had been holding out for the Spurs job as he rejected a number of alternative approaches and bided his time working as a Sky sports pundit. The media had predicted that Pochettino would go into the clash with West Ham under even greater pressure than the under-fire Hammers boss Manuel Pellegrini but time was on Levy's side to sort out compensation issues and install Mourinho during the international break.

The arrival of Mourinho seemed, at the time, to be a sure fire short fix for a trophy or two. Gary Neville believed the relationship between Mourinho and Levy was "a marriage of convenience". The decision to appoint Mourinho seemed an uncharacteristic call by Levy's standards, according to the Sky Sports pundit, whose views are notoriously controversial and generate so much media reaction. For Neville it was a simple equation; Mourinho's desire to return to the Premier League and the chairman's urgent need to keep players like Harry Kane. "If you'd said Levy would hire a manager of Mourinho's stature, that would stand up to him, I would have said not in a million years. For me this is absolutely a bridge for Levy and Mourinho. Mourinho needed to be back in the Premier League and establish himself. He wanted to be back in London. This is a marriage of convenience. Levy is not stupid enough to expose himself to a £25m hit if achievements are not made. They are using each other. It's a hard, cold conversation between two men. Jose wants to be back at the elite level winning a trophy, and Levy needs to keep the players he's got. The contract will be that detailed around what he has to do, and ultimately both of them would have protected themselves."

While much has been written about Mourinho, in fact I've written four books about him myself, there is still an enigma whether is a hero or a villain. Levy presided over a near £1billion super stadium, rated one of the best in the world, yet still kept the club's finances under control and oversaw a team that reached the Champions League Final under Pochettino and another top four finish; he will be regarded as a mastermind. Levy is the longest serving chairman in the Premier League, who rarely gives interviews and shuns publicity, however he was sacked ten managers, and as Mourinho's career had played out elsewhere, it was inevitable that at some stage he will be sacking No. 11!

The Tottenham Hotspur Stadium

Daniel Levy's Greatest Achievement

Born in Essex, Daniel's father, Barry Levy, was the owner of a clothing retail business Mr Byrite (later re-branded as Blue Inc). The company was founded by Abraham Levy and began trading as A. Levy & Sons. They had a hat shop in Stratford, east London. The company traded via a number of brands, chiefly as Mr Byrite, a chain of discount stores selling menswear. The company expanded rapidly in the 1980s and was then run by the three children of Barrie Levy – Jonathan, Robert and Daniel.

Daniel studied Economics and Land Economy at Sidney Sussex College, Cambridge, and graduated in 1985 with a First Class Honours Degree. He was appointed to the Spurs Board in December 2000 and is currently the longest serving Chairman of any Premier League club. He is also Managing Director of the ENIC Group of companies, a sports, entertainment and media group, a position he has held since 1995. A lifelong Spurs supporter, he attended his first match at the Lane against QPR in the 1960s but when I met him in the late 1990s, he confessed that he wasn't one of those all consuming passionate regulars.

Levy was also a director of Glasgow Rangers, in which ENIC held a significant stake until 2004. In November 2017, he was named CEO of the Year at the Football Business Awards. Much has been made of the club's massive financial commitment to the new stadium being responsible for seemingly capped players salaries, and conservatism in the transfer market.

Back in the summer of 2018 the *Evening Standard* conducted a question and answer with Donna Maria-Cullen, perceived as Levy's 'right hand women' on the board.

London Evening Standard: Are Spurs being restricted in the transfer market because of the club's move into their brand new stadium?

Donna Maria-Cullen: "No, no. That is a misconception. Daniel works closely with the managers. He identifies targets, works to get them and we are no different to other clubs in occasionally not being able to acquire who might be top of your list. Sometimes there's a degree of frustration [from Daniel] at how much is written that isn't accurate. But Daniel is so focused on delivering for this club. And that's why any of us who work around him think the criticism is grossly unfair."

Donna argued that "money doesn't guarantee you success" as she explained: "We've had seasons when we've brought eight players and it's not been right. What's key is we've still got so many young players. I remember years ago looking at our Under-16s, U17s and U18s and knowing a golden generation was coming through. They were the Harry Kanes and Harry Winks. We've still got young players. You saw Luke Amos play this week. The potential is still there, so why would you necessarily need to look so much further?"

When asked if the £850m bill for the new stadium was impacting on transfers, Cullen said: "Not necessarily. The whole notion of us moving to an increased capacity is to collect the greater revenues from match day that other top-six clubs have been enjoying for many more years than ourselves."

Levy was passionate about the new stadium, and immensely proud when it finally opened after months of delay which played a heavy toll on his stress levels but a measure of that pride came through when he and a host of Tottenham academy players buried a time capsule filled with 'artefacts that capture the passions of

White Hart Lane' at the club's new stadium. The capsule will be on view through a glass cover in the West Atrium section of the stadium and will form part of the stadium tour route that will become open to fans. Levy said: 'We are at a significant point in the club's history as we embark on our next chapter and prepare to enter a new home that will be enjoyed by future generations and our community for years to come. It is vitally important that we, as custodians of this great club, capture this moment in time and give future generations of players and supporters an insight into our thoughts and hopes during this exciting era. I am delighted that we were joined by members of our academy teams for this historic moment and hope that they are here in 50 years' time to open the capsule."

Publicly at least, Mauricio Pochettino backed his chairman when the stress was at its height. When there was anger from fans over delays to the near £1 billion project, Pochettino said: "The chairman is suffering a lot. He is so tired about work. The last few months he didn't sleep because he is trying to deliver the stadium. I think people don't realise the magnitude of the project and how difficult it is to manage. Everyone is disappointed because we are still not playing there but the day we move everyone is going to realise how massive the project was and how good the facilities are. It doesn't just depend on him. When you build something, you depend on many companies. I think it's more than 20 that are working there. It's so, so difficult. That is why he needs to feel the love from the fans and the club. He is working so hard, too hard, to leave a legacy for ever. And I think that's fantastic."

Pochettino, meanwhile, laughed off rumours of interest from Real Madrid. "I prefer that newspapers talk about things like this than, 'Tottenham is going to sack me', or 'people are tired of me'. I don't get bored (with the speculation) but he (Levy) maybe is worried," joked Pochettino. "He suffers because he's jealous about me! It's normal, no? He's a very jealous person."

How times change? And oh so quickly. When Pochettino was coveted by Manchester United, and the media was full of stories about a potential move to Old Trafford, former manager Tim Sherwood made this observation on the Sky Sports Debate show, in mid-December 2018. "Daniel Levy will be worried because it's Manchester United, any other club in the Premier League, forget about it. I don't think he will go. I think he is halfway through building something very special. Daniel will dismiss it. You could give £200million at this present moment in time for Pochettino, Daniel Levy will turn that down."

Pochettino's relationship with his chairman was the subject of enormous debate with continuous conspiracy theories that all was not well behind the scenes when it came to the manager's vision of recruitment, once culminating in Pochettino stating that he was the "coach not the manager". At another time Pochettino was far more reflective when he said, "I speak to him a lot, we talk a lot, we have very good communication. We don't always agree but, of course, that is normal. He is a person with a lot of experience managing this type of project and we are football people trying to advise on the decision on football. That means sometimes we agree and sometimes we don't agree. But after, when the decision is made, we are so strong in the delivery of it which shows it is best for the club."

Levy had sacked managers before when they were under performing, and there might have been a small degree of sympathy for their exit by the fans. This time it was vastly different. He knew that the hysteria over the sacking of such a popular manager as Pochettino would vanish overnight with the appointment of someone so high profile and a serial trophy winner as Mourinho. Pochettino called for Levy to "be brave, take risks and work in a different way" after the final game of last season — widely interpreted as a plea for the chairman to release the financial shackles. Pochettino signed a five-year deal soon after, suggesting he had been placated with promises of money to spend.

Yet while Levy is the public face of Spurs, the actual owner is Joe Lewis, and he is the man who makes all the major decisions. Lewis's best mate is Tiger Woods, who has called Joe "my business mentor" in the past. Each year, when he's not injured, Tiger takes part in Joe's Tavistock Cup competition in Florida, held on two of Joe's developments in Orlando called the Isleworth and Lake Nona. When Tiger Woods had his infamous 2009 low-

> **Levy was passionate about the new stadium, and immensely proud when it finally opened after months of delay which played a heavy toll on his stress levels**

speed car accident, it was at Joe's Isleworth complex, where the golfer has a home. Joe, who also owns property in Argentina and Bulgaria, lived next door to 007 legend Sean Connery, who he was reportedly close to. South African golfer Ernie Els is another pal, and the pair are said to regularly dine together. Joe plays off a 14 handicap and has practised with Woods and Els in the past.

The East End-born self-made billionaire had a new 321 foot-long, £112m masterpiece of a yacht delivered from famous shipyard Abeking and Rasmussen in Lemwerder in 2017, the vessel took nearly three years to build. Nicknamed "The Boxer" because of his sporting namesake, Lewis is a true cockney who was born within the sound of the St. Mary-le-Bow church bells in 1937. Thought to have been raised in a flat above the Roman Arms pub, Joe left school at 15-years-old to work in his family's cafe as a waiter earning £6 a week, later establishing businesses in London's West End under the name Tavistock Banqueting, he opened restaurants including the Northumberland Grand, which was the first fancy dress-themed eatery in London aimed at tourists.

He developed the Beefeater, the Cockney, the Caledonian and the Hanover Grand, and managed his first super club called The Talk of the Town in the 60s, where Frank Sinatra, Diana Ross and Tom Jones performed. At the Hanover Grand, Joe gave The Nolans their first ever live show and gave Planet Hollywood and Hard Rock founder Robert Earl his first job. He also moved into the world of tourist shops, selling souvenirs and laying on bus tours of London for tourists and dropping them off at his restaurants. He sold the business in 1979 for £30m and moved to the Bahamas as a tax exile. He set up home in Nassau, the capital of the islands and entered the world of currency trading, accumulating tens of millions, gambling on stock.

In September 1992 he became a billionaire, in part to one shrewd investment on Black Wednesday, teaming up with investor George Soros believing the Pound was overvalued and would collapse as Britain attempted to align it with other Euro countries. He bet on the Pound crashing out of the European Exchange Rate Mechanism and as it did so he became a billionaire overnight. He repeated the ploy many years later betting successfully against the Mexican peso.

Joe has been married twice, his first wife, Esther Browne, who he met at his greasy spoon, now lives in Ireland. They had two children, Vivienne and Charlie, before they divorced. Joe then married his former assistant Jane, they don't have any children.

In May 2013, Spurs went on a trip to the Bahamas and were welcomed on board the super yacht by host Joe. Michael Dawson, who was skipper at the time, said: "I had never met him before, so it was nice to go over there and a great experience. What a really nice guy. And that yacht is unreal! But he's just a normal guy. You could chat to him about anything. He tunes into all the games, he loves it. We just sat there chatting. He made us feel so welcome over there. It was relaxed. A lot of team-bonding together. It helps to be able to put a face to the person investing so much in this club he wants to be successful. He's always watching. He knows what goes on. He would remember every game, every little thing."

The Bedi Family

At the age of 5 I started supporting Spurs because of my elder brother, Rahul (above). They have become my life and now they have become my family's life as well; I have five daughters - Nikita, Shania, Rhianna, Shivani and Tara pictured here with me at the Champions League final in 2019 - and a son, Yash, (middle top) and my wife Laura (top right) and they are all Spurs season ticket holders and go home and away. I even have grandchilden now who love Tottenham, so it's in our blood!

As a teenager I queued up at 4am for a ticket for the 1981 FA Cup Final replay and managed to get a pair for me and my brother, who couldn't make it as he was studying for his accountancy exams. He was the clever one!

That night was magical - my mum dropped us off at Wembley and my brother bought me a flag walking down Wembley Way. We watched an incredible game that went back and forth and top it all off I was behind the goal for Ricardo Villa's amazing goal, later voted the best of all time at Wembley. I was so lucky to meet Ricky and Ossie later in life, what legends!

Pictures of my family and I with Tottenham stars past and present

When I was 15 I should have been studying for my mock exams but instead I went to Oxford Street to play in the arcade. Next to the arcade was a car park and when I came out of the arcade Glenn Hoddle and Ray Clemence were walking out. Glenn Hoddle! My hero! I said "hello" and asked for his autograph but I didn't have a pen. I went into a shop for a pen and paper and chased them down Regent Street where they went into Aquasqutum to get their suits fitted for the FA Cup final and I met nearly the whole team.

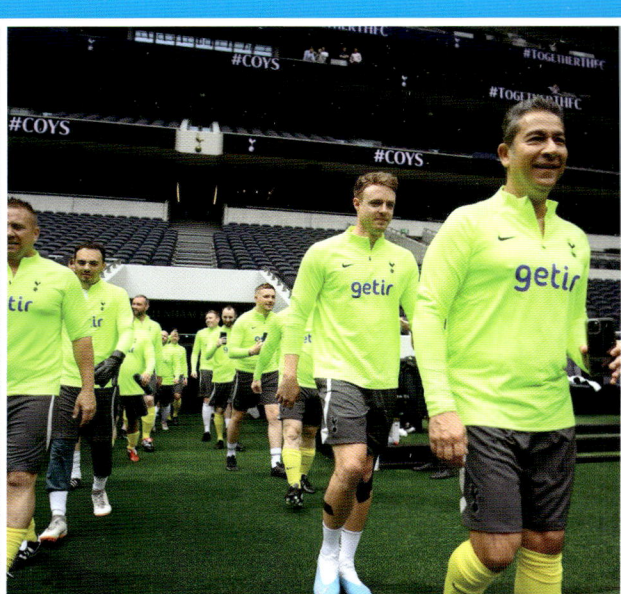

My daughters have appeared in adverts on the Spurs website, they have been mascots for Tottenham and England and two of my daughters were ball girls for the club. Top Left: The girls treated me to a VIP tour of the stadium for Fathers Day - My dream come true! I got the opportunity to play at White Hart Lane new stadium, what a great experience;. Facing page (top right) my son Yash and his kids - we are all Tottenham mad!

Congratulations to proud grandfather Ashwin Bedi on the arrival of his beautiful grandchild **AYLA**, the newest member to the Spurs Family.

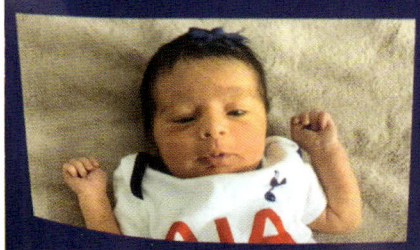

Jose Mourinho
The Not So Special One At Spurs!

Many outsiders assumed that, for a club without a League title since 1961 and whose last trophy was the 2008 League Cup, a move for serial-winner Jose Mourinho would be cause for celebration, with the very strong likelihood of Tottenham ending that silverware drought, given that Jose had won a major trophy at every club bar União de Leiria, the tiny club where he began his managerial career.

However many Spurs fans questioned Daniel Levy's decision to fire Mauricio Pochettino and replace him with 'The Special One' claiming that the club were looking for short term glory rather than building a team fit to grace their brand new stadium in the long term.

During his four and a half years Pochettino had transformed Tottenham and seemed to have got rid of the 'Spursy' stigma that had afflicted the club for decades by recruiting or promoting a super-fit looking squad. Poch's high pressing game brought new energy to the football as he turned Spurs into an entertaining Top 4 outfit capable of winning anywhere; yet silverware still eluded the club as they lost the 2015 League Cup final to Chelsea and were beaten by Liverpool in the 2019 Champions League Final. They also finished second in the Premier League in 2017 behind shock winners Leicester City. Suddenly, in the wake of an incredible but ultimately disappointing Champions League campaign, it all went pear-shaped very quickly and the 'Spursy' stigma was back; a lack of fighting spirit hastening the end for the popular Argentine. Some felt the squad had been listening to the same voice for far too long and it was time for a change.

By November 2019 Mourinho, a regular on Sky Sports football coverage, was getting itchy feet and was eager to restart work at his eighth club. For a born winner like Jose, pontificating about the shortcomings of others was never going to entertain him for long. Quite simply, he's too good to be a pundit.

Mourinho's honours read like a who's who of the biggest trophies in club football. Besides two Champions Leagues, two UEFA Cups, three Premier League titles, a La Liga title and a Serie A title, he won the main domestic cup competition in all four of the countries in which he has managed and three League Cups in England. He is also the only manager to have won both the Champions League and the UEFA Cup more than once - winning both with Porto, the former with Inter and the latter with Manchester United. At the time of his appointment he had more honours than his new club by 20 trophies to 17!

By November 2019 he had managed 14 complete seasons and he had only finished outside the top three of the league in which he is managing once, so it was a compelling CV that Daniel Levy brought to Spurs. The only time he has left a club in a position lower than sixth was when Chelsea sacked him in 2016 with the side 16th. His win percentage across his entire career was an impressive 64.8%, picking up a coveted 2.15 points per game on average.

In the Premier League, he had won 61.9% of his matches.

Only four managers had taken charge of 50 or more games in the competition could better his 2.10 points per game - Manchester City boss Pep Guardiola (2.39), former United manager Sir Alex Ferguson (2.16), ex-Chelsea boss Antonio Conte (2.14) and Jürgen Klopp of Liverpool (2.12). For reference, Pochettino's points-per-game average was 1.79.

When Mourinho first breezed into English football fresh from a Champions League triumph with unfancied Porto, he seemed to be a breath of fresh air. His first news conference at Chelsea in 2004 set the tone as he proclaimed himself 'The Special One'. In the multitude of books I've written about him since I described him as a modern day Brian Clough: abrasive, arrogant, but a genius as a motivator of star players, a brilliant tactician, and a serial winner. All these ingredients made him popular in west London during a first spell in which his Chelsea team dominated the league for two seasons, setting a new record points total in the process. Rivals grudgingly admired his ability to back up the press conference talk on the pitch and, but for Luis Garcia's 'ghost goal' at Anfield, he would have led them to a Champions League final. Yet by the end of his first spell at Stamford Bridge unsavoury incidents intertwined with his winning mentality had soured his relationship with the neutral fan; now you either love him or hate him. It is a pattern that has continued wherever he has managed. The big question for Spurs fans was whether he could retain all the good ingredients and dispense with the bad. Could he stick around at a club for longer than three seasons?

Fifteen years on from that startling entrance his growing army of critics at the time of his arrival at Spurs, many of them in the media, claimed he was no longer the same force. For a start, his own brand of football was no longer in vogue. Chelsea were built on incredibly solid foundations, his 2005 title winners conceding just 15 goals in 38 games. Their defence was so good that opponents knew that going a goal down was tantamount to losing the game. Yet 15 seasons later and the Premier League had been transformed by the possession football of Klopp and Guardiola at the top of the league. Teams no longer felt safe parking the bus

In turning to "one of the most successful managers in football"... Daniel Levy appointed the most talked about manager in world football. Some wags have even claimed that the Spurs manager was now bigger than the club he joined!

and, as Mourinho had discovered during his spell at Old Trafford, the fans don't want to pay to watch 1-0 wins and goalless draws. With higher ticket prices comes a different clientele and they want to be entertained.

Yet, despite all the negativity that surrounded him at United, Jose still won two trophies in two full seasons and then claimed that finishing second in the Premier League in 2018-19 points, behind a record-breaking Manchester City team, was his greatest managerial achievement! Well that was Mourinho at his most obtuse, as he claimed it was an incredible feat of management because of all the factors working against him and the squad he had to work with, although supporters would claim he brought a lot of it on himself with some highly questionable signings and terrible man-management. In particular signing the likes of Romelu Lukaku and Paul Pogba for world record fees, neither of whom led United anywhere close to challenging for the league title.

His critics will point to the bible of the modern game, 'statistics'. They indicated that his powers were on the wane, as his win percentage (53.8%) and points-per-game ratio (1.89) at United were the lowest of his managerial career since his first job at Leiria in the Portuguese Liga between July 2001 and January 2002.

Yet remarkably that points-per-game number was exactly the same as that achieved by Pochettino during the same period at Tottenham, and while the majority of United fans were glad to see the back of Jose, there was an outpouring of weeping and wailing when Pochettino was shown the door! It just goes to show the difference the style of football can make.

There were more stats which indicated his decline: since leaving Real Madrid in the summer of 2013, Mourinho had won 58.6% of competitive games and 56.8% of league matches. From the start of his managerial career at Benfica to the end of his spell at Madrid, he had won 67.6% of competitive fixtures and 70.8% of league games. However, the stats can equally be used to show that Mourinho could still be management's main man, he was the go to boss if you wanted to win major trophies, a rare talent in this day and age.

Mourinho remains the fastest manager to reach both 50 and 100 wins in Premier League history. However his 50th win with United came in his 92nd game. His total of 176 Premier League points with United was fewer than four other teams during his time at Old Trafford, including Tottenham! Mourinho's United side scored fewer goals than all of their main rivals during this time – 151, a disturbing 83 goals fewer than that scored by Manchester City during the same period, a statistic which goes some way to explaining his dismissal in December 2018.

In turning to "one of the most successful managers in football" who "has won honours at every club he has coached", Daniel Levy appointed the most talked about manager in world football. Some wags have even claimed that the Spurs manager was now bigger than the club he joined, as evidenced by his first press conference which was over-flowing with media from all corners of the globe. And, while Jose's record at United was a concern, it was still the exception rather than the rule; perhaps the Old Trafford club was too big and the tradition too strong, even for Jose. Now at Tottenham, where fans were more accepting if he brought them some glory, he might get a little more leeway.

Mourinho arrived with a compelling track record of starting strongly with clubs, and always seems to deliver in his first season, but it is rare for him to move into a club in mid season without the benefit of preparing his players for the season ahead and perhaps recruiting new ones.

Mourinho won 11 of his first 16 league games to win the Portuguese title in his debut season with Porto and lost just once en route to guiding Chelsea to the Premier League title in his first season in England. He suffered only four defeats in his first successful Serie A campaign with Inter and failed to win only nine of 38 matches in his first La Liga season at Real Madrid.

By the end of his predecessor's reign, Tottenham's Enfield HQ had become a rather miserable place to work, made worse by Pochettino's crankiness, according to sources close to the players, which usually means the players' agents. By contrast it was being suggested that Mourinho's arrival had lightened the mood. He was fully involved in training sessions and the players, in turn, felt his enthusiasm and it was immediately rubbing off on them and

the evidence was visible on the field with improved results.

Mourinho shared jokes with his players and staff at their training complex, engaged in regular individual discussions with his players, and his engaging personality, at least the one he usually brings to a new club, encouraged a squad who appeared to be going flat in the last throws of Pochettino's time. New assistant head coach Joao Sacramento's sessions were said to be refreshing and engaging, and it always helps when a new manager kicks off a new regime with a winning start.

Spurs fans might not have liked the appointment of a former Chelsea manager, but the arrival of a serial winner should have signalled success but it wasn't long before he was shown the door, his tenure becoming as toxic as it had at Manchester United as Daniel Levy fired him just days before a League Cup final at Wembley.

Mourinho also found it tougher than he imagined to turn around the club's fortunes on the field. One of Mourinho's priorities was to work closely with the then 23-year-old Dele Alli, to attempt to rekindle the spark that took him from lowly MK Dons to goalscoring Premier League sensation in a matter of months. The conversation between Alli and his new boss inevitably made headline news.

Mourinho asked Alli: "Are you Dele or Dele's brother?"
He replied: "I am Dele."
Mourinho told him: "Okay, so play like Dele."
Mourinho knew he had the potential to become the top class player he once was, but had completely lost that edge to his game.

In a press conference Mourinho said: "I already spoke with him. I think he is potentially a fantastic player!"

Yet, after scoring three goals in three games early in Mourinho's reign, Alli made just 7 more Premier League starts in the 2020-21 season and 8 the season after. In January 2022 he moved to Everton but made just 13 appearances before being loaned out to Besiktas in August 2022. Far from motivating Alli, Jose could do nothing to halt his slide into footballing obscurity.

The Alli situation was typical of Mourinho's reign. The PR sounded great but the reality was different. In the final assessment Mourinho's reign at Tottenham only seemed to reinforce the claims of his critics. In his first season he took the club to a respectable sixth place during a campaign blighted by Covid-19. Tottenham reached the last 16 of the Champions League but exited with a whimper to RB Leipzig (0-4), they lost to Norwich City on penalties in the fifth round of the FA Cup and fell at the first hurdle by the same method to bogey team Colchester United in the League Cup.

The following season began with a bang – a record-breaking 6-1 win at an empty Old Trafford that appeared to indicate huge progress, while a 2-0 win in the North London in December took Tottenham to the top of the league. Unfortunately that was as good as the 2020-21 season got as Spurs slid down the table to finish seventh. An incredible 4-5 extra time defeat at Everton in round five of the FA Cup represented a set back but by that time Tottenham had already booked their place at Wembley for the League Cup final, having disposed of Leyton Orient (via a Covid-19 walkover), Chelsea (on penalties), Stoke City (3-1) and Brentford (2-0). The final was delayed until 25th April to allow some fans to attend but Jose was sacked just four days before and Ryan Mason took charge. Tottenham predictably lost the game 1-0 to Manchester City.

Tottenham Hotspur were the first club Jose had managed where he had not won a trophy since he left União de Leiria in 2002. In May 2021 Jose was appointed manager of Roma and won the club its first trophy in 11 years by lifting the UEFA Conference League. It completed a unique hat-trick as became the first manager to win all three major European club competitions.

"He's One Of Our Own"
The Harry Kane Phenomenon

Jimmy Greaves remains my all time favourite player. I watched him as a fan in the 60s and we have all probably seen the re-runs of his goal against Manchester United when he seemed to dribble past their entire side before rounding the keeper to score. Greaves scoring record appeared untouchable, but now this generation has its own hero etched into Lilywhite folklore. Incredibly, the player once described as a 'one-season wonder' is now an England captain who has scaled the dizzy landmark set by the legendary Greaves and funnily enough he was born in Leytonstone just 20 minutes from Greaves' birthplace!

Harry Kane has been responsible for a few spectacular strikes down the years but the vast majority of the goals that helped him surpass Greaves' record at Tottenham were from close range with that mix of running and anticipation which is the hallmark of the great striker. Kane and Greaves were both fine exponents of the Art of Goalscoring. Greaves was a vastly different forward in style and technique to Kane - he was quick, elegant, could dribble and would score sublime solo efforts. His friend and author, Norman Giller, called him "Messi with bells on". Both strikers redefined their position in their own right. Greaves as the modern English forward of his time, Kane as a goalscorer who is also his side's chief creator, winning the Premier League Playmaker of the Season prize in 2020-21 for his 14 assists.

In setting records for club and country Kane surpassed two other great Spurs strikers - Gary Lineker and Jimmy Greaves. Greaves' record as the all-time leading scorer in the English top flight will surely remain elusive - an incredible 357 goals achieved during spells with Chelsea, Tottenham and West Ham, especially now that Harry has departed for the Bundesliga.

Greaves began his career at Chelsea, and played for AC Milan, before becoming a Spurs legend, while Kane is regarded by the fans as "One of Our Own", until he finally left for Bayern Munich around the same age that Glenn Hoddle departed for Monaco, and the supporters respected both players' decisions and still regard them as Spurs through and through.

Sky Sports pundit Graeme Souness, who started his career at Spurs, felt that his old club always had a chance of a top four finish simply because Kane was in the team, "You don't have to play well to win games because you have goals. He is Mr Goals."

The night Kane equalled Greaves record, Jamie Carragher insisted he will go down as Spurs greatest ever player. After Kane's 266th strike for the club against Fulham, Carragher, speaking on Sky Sports, branded Kane as 'one of the greats' while praising his consistency over the years. "Year after year he delivers", Carragher began. "We see him every year getting 25-30 goals a season." Gary Neville compared Kane to Alan Shearer, whose Premier League goal scoring record of 260 goals was being chased down by the forward before he retires. "He is the most reliable of finishers", Neville said, "Alan Shearer was an unbelievable finisher, and the thing for me was his mentality, and I think Kane has that same mentality. That is the biggest compliment I can give."

In the first half Kane had just 13 touches - eight fewer than anyone else - yet he still tipped a tight game with one moment of magic. Craven Cottage was the 33rd different ground where Kane had scored a Premier League goal. Only Andy Cole (37), Frank Lampard and Wayne Rooney (both 34) have netted at more stadiums. Kane scored 24 goals from outside the box - only Kevin De Bruyne (25) has more since Kane's debut.

Harry Kane hit the back of the net at a relentless rate since first breaking into the Spurs side under Tim Sherwood at the end of the 2013-14 season. His record breaking 266 goals came in 415 games, Greaves reached that figure in just 379 Spurs appearances, having arrived in north London as one of the game's most revered strikers on the back of a short and miserable

If Greaves' goalscoring legacy is one of a forward blessed with outstanding natural talent, Kane's will be the reward of perseverance, resilience and graft.

- yet still prolific - spell at AC Milan where he scored nine goals in just 13 games, including the winner in the Milan derby. Greaves had already scored 124 times in 157 top-flight games for Chelsea before his short-lived Italian experiment, and picked up where he left off for Bill Nicholson's double-winning Tottenham side, scoring a hat-trick on his debut after completing a £99,000 move that rescued him from the San Siro after he had fallen out with Milan's manager. Greaves went on to score 30 goals in 31 games for Tottenham as they retained the FA Cup and 44 in 49 the following season as they became the first British club to win a European trophy, beating Atletico Madrid 5-1 in Rotterdam to lift the Cup Winners' Cup, Jimmy scoring a brace. Greaves was the goalscorer supreme in this period, although following the arrival of another Italian exile, Denis Law, at Manchester United he soon found himself out-shot as the exuberant Scot hit 46 goals in just 42 games including six hat-tricks!

Having earned his Spurs debut in a Europa League qualifier against Hearts in 2011, the gangly youth product won a penalty only to see it saved. He finally got off the mark in a Tottenham shirt in the same competition against Shamrock Rovers a few months later, but humbling yet educational loan spells at Millwall, Norwich and Leicester all followed before Kane seized his big break under Sherwood.

Former Spurs striker Les Ferdinand, who worked alongside Sherwood with the club's under-21s, likened Kane's movement to Teddy Sheringham and said he struck the ball like Alan Shearer, while Sherwood saw a player outperforming then-club record signing Roberto Soldado in training. "Harry wanted to get to the top, and nothing was going to stop him achieving that because of the ability, desire and mentality he possesses," said Sherwood. "He needed to work on sharpening his feet up around the box, so we spent a lot of time doing sessions where he had to move his feet a little bit quicker, open the space and shoot off both sides. But he also had that knack of being aware of players around him, and the intelligence to slide people in. He could see a pass and he could execute it."

When Mauricio Pochettino arrived that summer, however, he felt Kane was not ready for first-team football, instead reverting to Soldado and Emmanuel Adebayor. After failing to make the bench against West Brom, Kane went to see the Argentine and his coaching staff and was met by reams of video analysis showing the 20-year-old where he needed to improve to earn the new boss's trust.

By November, after a hat-trick against Asteras Tripoli - and a stint in goal - Pochettino placed his faith in Kane and the young forward responded by scoring a free-kick the manager credits with "saving" his career and allowing him time to implement his project at Tottenham.

Kane's 90th-minute deflected winner at Aston Villa off the bench was the first of 21 Premier League goals for the youngster that season which also included iconic doubles against Chelsea and Arsenal. He scored 31 times in all competitions on his way to being voted the PFA Young Player of the Year. The goals have flowed ever since. Three Premier League Golden Boots, to complement the one he won at the 2018 World Cup with England, and a five-time entrant in the PFA Premier League Team of the Year. "Harry Kane is a special player in the history of the club," said Jose Mourinho while Tottenham manager. "He will beat every possible record."

He scored all sorts of goals for Spurs. Most came with his right foot, quite a few from his weaker side, many have been headers. He mostly scored inside the box, including numerous penalties, yet quite a few from outside it.

"Just a one-season wonder," the away end chanted at Craven Cottage as Kane moved alongside Greaves with a reliably clinical winner against Fulham; his 199th Premier League goal on his 300th appearance in the competition for Spurs. "To get the goal and equal the record was a nice feeling," Kane told BBC Sport in typically understated fashion, thinking instead about another chance he saw saved that would have broken it. Gary Lineker commented: "What an incredible achievement for Harry Kane to equal the great Jimmy Greaves as all-time top scorer for Tottenham. And, yes, before you start, I know he's not won anything. Also, that fact doesn't make him any the less of a footballer."

Steve Perryman added: "Harry deserves all the accolades he gets because his focus and professionalism off the pitch has made him the history maker he is today. Liverpool's academy director Alex Inglethorpe, who was my reserve centre forward at Watford, was a youth team coach at Spurs. He worked with

Harry and says he's never met anyone with such a competitive spirit. You don't see that in his face: he's cool. But he's competitive with himself. And that competitive spirit drove him to practise, practise, practise. Alex used to be quite picky about collecting all the balls after training. But they were always two balls short. It annoyed him because he suspected the players were hiding them. Then he'd look out of his office in the afternoon and Harry and his group would be out there doing a skill drills with the balls they had hidden. And it wasn't like you want to go out and shout at them because that's what you want them to do. That's what Harry has always done: just kept improving season by season until now, when he's even surpassed Jimmy's record."

Kane moved ahead of Greaves to become Tottenham's all-time top scorer netting his 267th goal for the club as they beat Manchester City. He reached the landmark with a low finish which secured a 1-0 win and took him to 200 Premier League goals in 304 matches. The enormity of the moment wasn't lost on Kane, who wheeled away in celebration, taking time to compose himself before appearing to wave to family members in the crowd. The strike also happened to be his 200th in the Premier League. It was met by a rapturous reception by the Tottenham supporters, all rising to acknowledge the magnificent achievement.

Greaves' record has stood for over 50 years, having left Tottenham in 1970 for West Ham. Acknowledging the moment, Tottenham flashed up a silhouette of Kane celebrating with the words 'Congratulations Harry' emblazoned across the big screens. The screens then displayed the words: 'Harry Kane, Tottenham Hotspur all-time record goalscorer.' There was an element of irony in Kane securing the achievement against City, the club he almost joined in the summer of 2021 - with only Daniel Levy's stubbornness in the face of Pep Guardiola's desire to land the England captain preventing the move.

Guardiola commented after the game, "Big congratulations, he deserves it, he is an exceptional player — on behalf of Manchester City I congratulate him."

Shearer led the praise for Kane after the striker achieved two milestones. Shortly after Kane scored, Shearer posted a picture of himself and Rooney accompanied by the caption: 'Congratulations @HKane passing the great Jimmy Greaves record at @SpursOfficial. Also @WayneRooney and I were wondering where you've been! Well done on joining the 200 @ Premierleague club.'

Shearer, whose only major honour was the 1994-95 Premier League title with Blackburn Rovers, turned down the chance to join Manchester United (and sure fire trophies) in 1996, moving to his boyhood club Newcastle instead, where he played out the rest of his career. Kane had spent his whole career at Spurs, excluding loan spells, after coming through their academy, before that move to Munich. Shearer told BBC Radio 5 Live: "There is not one minute of any day I look back at my career and say I wish had gone to Manchester United because I would have won medals. Harry has the Tottenham record and will have a statue, will get the England record and probably a statue at Wembley and a good chance at the Premier League record. They are his medals. I can see why he would take the decision to stay at Tottenham. He already has greatness around him and if he doesn't win a trophy I don't think will bother him at all. He is the only one who can answer it, if he can say 'I'm the happiest guy alive, I have all the records, I might not have a trophy, but I'm happy'.

Sky cameras showed Kane in a phone conversation with Antonio Conte after the game in the changing room. His manager was in Italy after surgery to remove his gallbladder. Conte told Kane, "You make me proud," with the Spurs coach confirming he was feeling fine after surgery. Kane added: "He was congratulating me for the achievement and said he was proud of all the boys. It's not easy when you don't have your coach there. We're all happy the surgery went well and he's recovering well but whenever you don't have your coach there it's never easy."

Harry also recalled his first Spurs goal, "It was a Danny Rose cross, Andros (Townsend) headed it back and I kind of swivelled and hit it through the legs. It was a special feeling just to be playing for Tottenham at that age and to score. I can remember it like it was yesterday and that was 11 years ago. Time goes quick, there's been a lot of ups and downs along the way but I'm just extremely grateful to a lot of people to still be here, performing and scoring goals. Scoring a goal never gets old. It's one of the greatest feelings I can ever feel. Special memories to score the first one and now to be here on 267. When you look at the names who have been here, to overtake Jimmy Greaves – one of the greatest to play the game – I'm extremely grateful. The years go by so quick so I try to take it all in. Not sure I've done that yet but my friends and family were here so it was a special time to do it. It's hard to put into words and I'm so glad it came in a win. We worked so hard to keep a clean sheet. It was so special to do it in front of the fans is a moment I will never forget. There has been so much talk about it in the last couple of weeks and to do it in such a big game is even more special. It is a great feeling. When I started playing regularly it wasn't even in my imagination to score 200 Premier League goals and I have a few more years left so hopefully there are more to come. [Jimmy Greaves] is a complete hero, one of the best strikers to play the game so to be in that conversation is special. And to overtake him is a huge moment for me."

Of the goal itself, he said, "Just a magical moment and I was so desperate to do it with a win as well. I wanted to win so bad. Once we went 1-0 up it was just about keeping a clean sheet. Especially being here at home in front of the fans. To do it in a big game against one of the best teams in the world, it's a special feeling."

Kane also spoke about reaching 200 Premier League goals. "It's a great feeling. Tim Sherwood gave me my first start and I was so desperate to make an impression. To score and win that, that was just the start and a lot of hard work between that game with Mauricio and all the coaches, so just a magical feeling. I saw Alan [Shearer, record Premier League scorer] earlier in the week. I'm sure he'll be watching but not sure if he'll be happy or not! I've got plenty of goals to come, I'm feeling good. Alan has set the record to beat. I'll see if I can beat it."

This was a goal he will recall without much effort. As for the rest he needs a little nudge to bring them back to life. Asked if he could remember all 267 goals he said, "Don't put me on the spot but if you told me the game, I could probably tell you the type of goal. Every goal was special in its own way. It's been an amazing journey. I've been here since I was 11 years old. Eighteen years of my life, a lot of hard work and dedication. I'm extremely proud to represent this club, to score 267 goals for them and 200 Premier League goals. It's something I'll never take for granted. I've just got to keep it going, try and score as many as I can and see what happens. Of course it's there in the back of my mind. It's definitely there to be broken. I'm feeling good and feeling fit so we'll see what happens. "

Pressed for some of his favourites, Kane picked two against Arsenal to clinch a thrilling 2-1 comeback win, at the old White Hart Lane, eight years ago. "My first North London derby, the header and the one I bent in from the left, post and in," he said. "Those two stick in my memory for sure. There's been some good ones over the years but that one against City was right up there, just the atmosphere and the occasion. It was a special goal and a special night and to get the three points. We were playing one of the best teams in the league, a really important game. As a striker you always dream about scoring winners so it was just the perfect night."

Little more than a month before his double against Arsenal, on New Year's Day 2015, there were two more to cherish in a 5-3 victory against Chelsea. "That was an important game. Chelsea at the time were one of the best teams in Europe, and top of the league. I'd done well before then and scored goals against other teams, but hadn't done it against a big team yet. Not just those goals but the whole performance was one of my best performances in a Spurs shirt and that just gave me the confidence I needed to know I could do it against any team on any stage. I feel like that was the moment when I thought, 'OK, I'm here to stay'. I just had to make sure I kept working hard. That's what I've tried to do. Trying to be consistent, perform every year, and improve every year. I'm only 29 and I feel like there's still room for more improvement and trying to get better and that's what I'll keep trying to do for the rest of my career. I feel like my brain is probably my strongest asset as a player and the more games I play the more experience I get and that only gets stronger so I'm in a good place. It's really pleasing for me and for the team as well."

Kane was honoured by his club with a special trophy after becoming the club's record goalscorer. Ahead of the match against West Ham at the Tottenham Hotspur Stadium, Kane was greeted on the pitch by Greaves' widow Irene and daughter Mitzi Robinson, who presented him with the award along with another Spurs legend Ledley King. The trophy depicts a Nike boot worn by Kane placed on a plinth that lists all 267 of his goals scored by opponent and date in chronological order. Kane later walked out on to the pitch for the London derby with his two daughters Ivy and Vivienne, who both wore shirts with the name 'Daddy' on the back and with the number 267 to mark his record feat. Spurs supporters paid tribute with one end of the ground unveiling a crowd motif reading 'HARRY'.

Moving above Rooney was not Kane's only landmark - he overtook Duncan Ferguson to become the first player to score 10 headed goals in a single Premier League campaign. It was also his 100th home goal in the Premier League - making him just the fourth player to reach that tally for a single club after Rooney (101 for Manchester United), Sergio Aguero (106 for City) and Thierry Henry (120 for Arsenal). His 26 goals in 35 league games in 2022-23 - his third-highest in a single campaign - came during a turbulent season for Tottenham, which featured the end of Antonio Conte's tenure and the later departure of interim boss Cristian Stellini.

*

It all began for Kane as a six-year-old for Ridgeway Rovers, a youth club based in north-east London that also produced David Beckham. He turned up for their annual trials with a brief stint as a goalkeeper! Dave Bricknell, Ridgeway coach at the time, said: "This six-year-old boy turns up at Loughton Rugby Club, and we're doing a little shooting session, and I ask for a lad who can go in goal. This little boy puts his hand up and says: 'I'll go in goal.' So we give him some gloves, and he performs heroics - makes some fantastic saves. I think, yes, I've got a goalkeeper here - because goalkeepers are very hard to find, particularly at six. They do it for five seconds and they want to be a centre-forward. Then I get told he's not a goalkeeper, he's on the pitch. So I think ok, and I stick him on the pitch. And he's scoring loads of goals, on a very long pitch as well, so he ends up being our striker." For two years, Kane couldn't stop scoring for Ridgeway Rovers – earning him a move into Arsenal's youth set-up. Bricknell said: "He could see a pass, he could play. He was very, very good at an early age. He could strike a ball like an 11-year-old even at the age of six. But Harry's best attribute was his great self-belief. He had good touch, but his main attribute was that he had major confidence in himself. He would score lots of goals, but if it went wide and he didn't score, he wouldn't worry about it - he'd just go and get his next chance and try to score again."

Luke Robinson, Kane's former school friend and Ridgeway team-mate, said: "He had a great sense of humour, we always had a laugh, but he was always driven. He used to keep himself to himself, he had his goals. Anywhere from 30 yards, he knew where the goal was. I remember we were in the London Cup and were losing 5-1, Harry scored five and we went through."

Harry was released by Arsenal at 10 despite being second top scorer behind Benik Afobe - and was then turned down by Watford. At 11, he was given a chance at his local club Tottenham and with his school team at Chingford Foundation. "Aged 11 Harry was technically very gifted, with a great first touch, and a very clever player; he always knew where to go, right from an early stage," says Mark Leadon, Kane's PE teacher. "He was also a very good cricketer - he opened the bowling from year seven to 10 and batted at four or five. But he loved his football. He was never a prima donna, and he would always put a shift in. Some students think they're better than others, but not him. Yet what came through more than anything else was his determination to succeed. He's always wanted to make a mark - and from a very early age you could see how driven he was."

From 11 to 17, Kane progressed through Tottenham's youth set-up until he was loaned to League One Leyton Orient in January 2011. During that time, he signed scholarship terms with Spurs on his 16th birthday. Alex Inglethorpe, formerly Tottenham youth team coach, said: "When I joined Spurs as under-18 coach, Harry was 13. Part of my remit was to work with the under-14s, so every Wednesday evening we'd get together. I'd like to say he was the gold medallist in the group and that we'd all spot he was going to be the fantastic player - but I'd be lying. He probably wasn't even on the podium. He had a lovely technique - an ability to pass and receive and shoot - but if there was something that endeared him to you it was that he was very low maintenance. It became fairly evident when Harry became a scholar that he was someone who could finish. He wasn't great with his head and he wasn't great on his left side, but he was his own best coach. That boy at 13, who didn't have everything, taught himself an awful lot more in those five years that followed. He was very aware of what he didn't have and very aware of what might stop him - and he was very determined to make that right."

He spent the next four seasons on loan in the lower leagues at Leyton Orient, Millwall, Norwich and then Leicester, finally earning his big chance with Tottenham at the age of 21. In his first loan spell at Leyton Orient he scored five in nine starts. "Harry was not like other Premier League players, where you feel they're going to come in 'Billy Big Time', a bit of a Charlie boy," says former Orient team-mate Scott McGleish. "He wanted the experience of learning what I call men's football. He could play the 18s and the 21s, but he wanted to learn - and from the word go he was ready to fight for his place. In training, he was willing to learn from everybody, and even more importantly willing to just knuckle down and work hard. You could see in training and subsequently the matches that he had ability and a desire to go further, but you're still looking like a young 17-year-old: very slight, still needing to physically develop, not the quickest but technically excellent."

He joined Championship team Millwall in January 2012 in the midst of a relegation dog-fight. Millwall's then veteran defender Alan Dunne remembers a moment in training that stood out. "It was a copycat of Marco van Basten's goal at Euro '88," he said. "It was probably the best goal I've seen in training in my time. If I'd scored a goal like that, I would have run off waving my shirt around my head, but it didn't faze him. It was like it was expected. I've seen a lot players come to the Den and freeze, because within five minutes they're being called names that they've never heard before and they can't cope with that pressure. Harry had that in the back of his head, because it's always spoken about when young players come in. But it didn't faze him - he was a focused lad, he was confident in his ability. It was a challenge to him, and a challenge that he rose to."

"I used to sit next to Harry in the changing room," says former Millwall defender Darren Ward. "After training every day, he used to sit on his spot and just stay there. You're thinking, 'What's he doing? What's he looking at?' He wouldn't move for a while. One day someone asked him, 'What are you doing Harry?' And he said: 'I'm just thinking about what I could improve on in training, how it went, what went right, what didn't'. Whenever I looked at him after training, he'd be sitting there, going over it in his head. That is a player who takes care of his football. He means business. And he was doing that at 18. That's incredible."

After scoring nine goals in 26 starts, Kane was voted the club's young player of the season having helped saved them from relegation. "If there's one word to describe his finishing, it was immaculate," said Dunne. "People say immaculate isn't really a football word, but he would find each bottom corner the same time, every time. No scuffs. It wasn't top corners, it was bottom corner, bottom corner, bottom corner." Ward added: "Did I think he would break into the Tottenham first team, yes, but to be one of the top three strikers in the world? I don't think anyone would have expected that. I don't think you would have said he'd be where he is now."

Another two loan spells followed, one cut short by injury at Norwich at the start of the 2012-13 season, before spending the second part of the campaign at Leicester, mostly on the bench with Jamie Vardy. He then spent that summer with England at the Under-20 World Cup, scoring once as the Three Lions were knocked out at the group stage. Peter Taylor, England under-20 coach in that summer of 2013, said: "The impression I got was firstly what a nice boy you are, and secondly that you're not going to have regrets at the end of your career, because you're going to give it everything you have to be a player. I've dealt with League One and League Two players, and you have to keep reminding them about things. Harry you only had to tell once. He's a very intelligent player."

In July 2013 Swindon Town spent a week of pre-season in Portugal's Algarve and played a couple of fixtures against a Tottenham XI made up mostly of young players. Ward had just joined Swindon from Millwall, and in the tunnel before one of the friendlies spotted his former team-mate Kane. An informal relationship with Spurs had seen a handful of young players arrive on loan, with Grant Hall, Ryan Mason and Alex Pritchard all set to spend 2013-14 at the Wiltshire club. Rumour had it Kane would follow. "Wardy, they want me to go on loan again," Kane confided before adding, "I want to stay here. I'm good enough to get in this first team." For most of the 2013-14 season, though, Kane continued to struggle to make a meaningful first-team impact at Tottenham. His breakthrough finally came on 7 April 2014, just three months shy of his 21st birthday. Andre Villas-Boas had been sacked, replaced by former youth coach Tim Sherwood, and Kane got his Premier League debut - scoring against Sunderland. "It didn't feel a gamble at all to give Harry that start. It was almost overdue to be honest," says Sherwood. "Roberto Soldado was in front of him in the team, and nobody wanted Roberto to do well more than me, but every single day in training Harry was outperforming him. I was the biggest believer Harry Kane ever had, because I used to think he was a mix between Teddy Sheringham and Alan Shearer, both players I played with. It's a big accolade, but I think it's the right one."

Three in three games followed his Sunderland strike by scoring against West Bromwich Albion and Fulham, as he ended the season as first-choice striker. "You have to have the bravery of Tim Sherwood and Les Ferdinand to put him in the team ahead of Soldado, who was a Spain international at the time," says Chris Ramsey, the Queens Park Rangers technical director who was Tottenham's head of player development at the time. "It showed the confidence the club had in him. When we took charge, there was talk of him going back on loan, and he said, 'No, I'm not going. I don't want to go'. He backed himself, knowing that we rated him, and that if he kept on doing what he was doing - and the first team at that time weren't doing what they needed to do - that we'd play him."

The following season Kane, who represented England at all age groups, had hit 29 goals by the end of March in the 2014-15 season, he earned his first senior England call-up as he was named in Roy Hodgson's squad to face Lithuania. It took him just 79 seconds, three touches and one header to mark his international debut with a goal. "One thing Harry's got that's the same with all the great players — the Messi's and Ronaldo's — he wants to play, because he wants to score," says Ramsey. "I definitely would have said he was good enough to play in the Premier League, good enough to play for England, but good enough to become the phenomenon that he has? I can't say I would have predicted that. But if anybody had the will to become world class, I definitely would have said it was him."

Kane's international career could also be prolonged by the lack of a natural successor.

Reflecting on the record before that Ukraine game, Harry said: "It's been a magical few days after the amazing result the other night. A lot of messages from friends and family and ex-players. Tom Brady reached out. A lot of ex players Wazza (Rooney), Beckham, all the English legends. It's been a whirlwind few days. I've been trying to settle down as this one's really important. We need to get this one out of the way then we can enjoy it. It will be a special night. I will have my wife and kids with me walking out to have a picture. We've got an important game so I'm trying not to think about it too much." Kane proudly walked out with his two small girls as mascots, to receive the Golden Boot for breaking the England record, and was joined by his wife and son for a family picture with the award.

Wayne Rooney declined the invitation to award Kane with the Golden Boot. The FA approached the former England captain Rooney, but the DC United head coach could not make the trip to England due to his commitments with the MLS side. FA chair

"When we took charge, there was talk of him going back on loan, and he said, 'No, I'm not going. I don't want to go'. He backed himself, knowing that we rated him, and that if he kept on doing what he was doing - and the first team at that time weren't doing what they needed to do - that we'd play him."

DANIEL RAMSEY
Former Tottenham Head of Player Development

"I used to sit next to Harry in the changing room. After training every day, he used to sit on his spot and just stay there. You're thinking, 'What's he doing? What's he looking at?' He wouldn't move for a while. One day someone asked him, 'What are you doing Harry?' And he said: 'I'm just thinking about what I could improve on in training, how it went, what went right, what didn't'. That is a player who takes care of his football. He means business. And he was doing that at 18. That's incredible."

DARREN WARD
Team-mate at Millwall

Debbie Hewitt made the presentation just before kick-off. Kane received the award alongside his wife, Katie, and three children Ivy, Vivienne and Louis.

Naturally Kane collected his obligatory goal, his 54th, as England ran out comfortable 2-0 winners to top the group and ease their way towards Euro qualification as one of the favourites to win it. Kane, though, had "a big decision to make" about his career, according to a previous England skipper Steven Gerrard. "I've been there myself, where you're thinking 'is my team good enough to get me the medals? Am I going to get out of my career what I want to get?'"

Six and a half years separated Rooney and Kane breaking the England goals record. It will be much longer for Kane's eventual successor, if indeed there will be one. Kane could reach 100 caps and 100 goals for his country, every chance of putting the record unreachable."Knowing Harry, it's not something that will go to his head," added Rooney. "He will kick on and, in fact, I believe that when he stops playing he will leave the England record in a place where it will be very difficult for someone else to break it. He wants to be like Poland's Robert Lewandowski, a goal machine who is still at the very top in his mid-thirties, and he has it in him to make that happen. I think Harry will finish with an England goals total well into the 70s."

Kane believes 100 goals for his country "is not out of the question". "Getting 100 will be tough for sure, but I never count out anything. I am still young - I am 29, I am still fit and strong. I want to play for England for as long as I can." At the time this book went to press he stood on 62 goals for his country. A century doesn't feel so far away.

In 2023, Harry finally made the much-anticipated move away from Spurs however Daniel Levy, aware of the excellence of Kane and his value to any Premier League rivals, had rebuffed offers from both Manchester clubs and agreed to sell him to Bayern Munich. Once in Germany, the goals flowed faster than the Rhine with Kane scoring 25 in just 21 appearances in all competitions by the mid-winter break, although the team honours he had hoped for continued to elude him. With the Bundesliga record standing at the 41 hit by his predecessor Lewandowski in 2020-21, it seems that Harry might be a record-breaker in Germany as well!

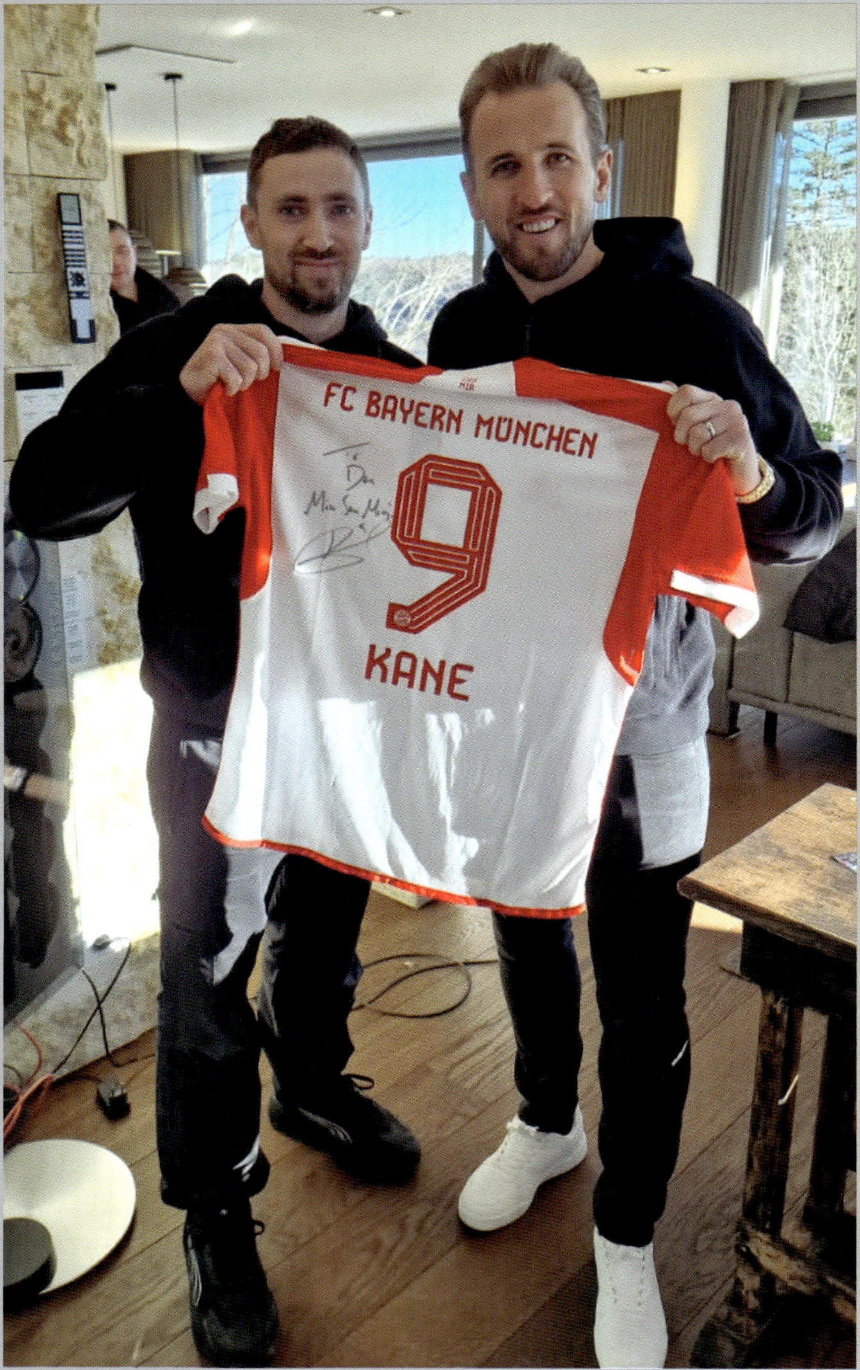
FC BAYERN MÜNCHEN
9
KANE

FC BAYERN MÜNCHEN
9
KANE

premier

premier

ICON

HUGO
premier
relocation

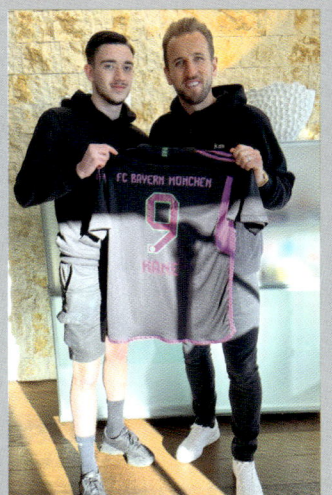

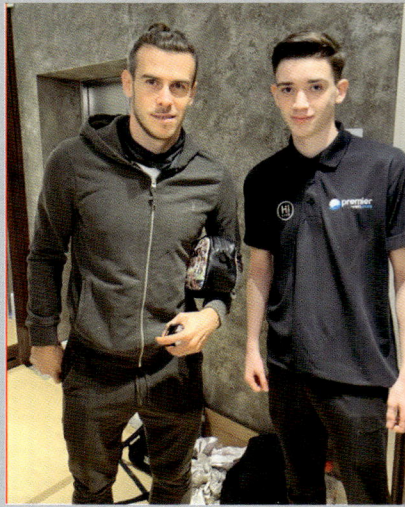

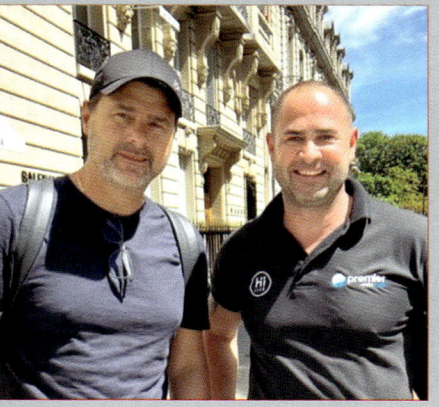

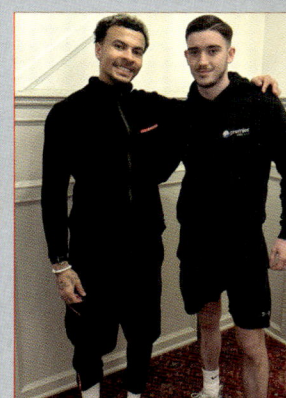

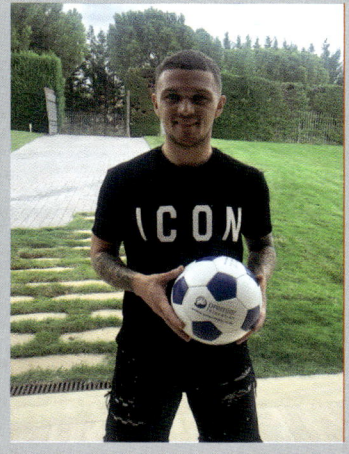

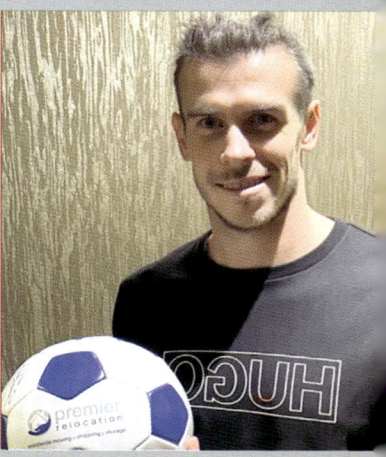

Harry Kane admitted that his first few months in Munich away from his wife and kids 'wasn't easy' but the England captain feels Germany is like home now. Kane spent the first five months living in a £10,000-a-night suite at the luxury Vier Jahreszeiten Kempinski Hotel in Munich but all that luxury didn't heal the heartache of being separated from his family making the move more difficult. Eventually, his wife Katie and their four children Ivy, Vivienne, Louis and Henry moved over from London. And the men who brought the Kane family together are Andy Wells and Vlad Piskia who run Premier Relocation.

Andy, Vlad and his team are the movers for elite sportsmen and celebrities, and they masterminded Kane and his family's move into what has been widely reported in the media as a £30m hilltop mansion in an area dubbed the 'Beverley Hills of Bavaria.' The *Mirror* reported his new home comes complete with a spa, sundeck, views of the River Isar and a garden on the edge of a forest. But you won't find the guys from Premier Relocation 'leaking' any information; they know before anyone who is moving during the transfer windows, and have been approached often by the media to spill the beans, but they never have and never will. In fact they are so trusted within the industry that they have now signed a three-year contract with the Professional Footballers Association.

Despite the settling in period, Kane made a sensational start to life at Bayern, scoring 28 goals in his first 27 matches. "It wasn't easy, the first four or five months being in the hotel and being away from the family," Kane told PA news. "That was difficult, so I was proud of the way I was still able to perform on the pitch in those circumstances. We've had a good winter break and everyone came back with me, the kids are in school, we have got the house. Month by month it starts to feel more like home, you meet parents at school, my wife is meeting new friends and you just start to meet new people and see new things. Everyone has been fantastic, all the fans here, the club have been great and trying to make me welcome and so far it is nothing but praise for everyone here."

Kane told *The Guardian* his family are embracing Bavarian life and go skiing in the Alps at weekends. His children are picking up the German language quicker than he is, despite his best efforts in class. "I've started German lessons and have these at least once or twice a week. I want to fit in as much as possible and learning the language is important and I'm willing to try. The Bayern fans are great, I hear them chanting lots of songs throughout the matches."

The winter weather means he has been unable to play much of his beloved golf: "Since the snow hit us we have been struggling, I don't think the courses open here until March so I have been hitting the golf simulator a little bit and trying to stay in a decent shape for now. That is one thing I am looking forward to, I am starting to feel at home with the family, the kids are in school so the next step is to start finding the golf courses when I get some alone time with friends."

After firmly establishing itself as the movers of choice among the pre-eminent and prestigious elite of the football world, Premier Relocation have now partnered with the PFA to provide moving services to all their members. Offering a whole suite of relocation services specially tailored to the Industry, Premier Football Relocation can already count some of the most high-profile managers and players among its clients.

Commenting on the new PFA collaboration, Andy at Premier Relocation said: "It's a privilege to work with the players. There's a lot of paper work involved in what we do but we're specially placed to help members through that process. We take the pressure off players and their families, and work to get them settled and set up as quickly as possible in their new homes."

Premier Relocation is a leading home moving company, providing global services in household removals and storage. The team's services also include pet relocation, car transportation and customs formalities. All PFA members have access to a 10% discount on all booked services and a special introductory deal offers a Samsung Airdresser worth over £2,000 for the first 25 full household moves booked.

Ange Postecoglou

When Spurs appointed Ange Postecoglou as their new manager on a four-year contract, some Spurs fans wondered if he was the Australian Ted Lasso but what happened next was nothing short of a minor miracle. Following the misery of life under successive managers Jose Mourinho, Nuno Espirito Santo and the ailing Antonio Conte, followed quickly by the saga that led to the sale of Harry Kane, spirits among the supporters were load and, initially at least, there was scepticism about how this Fair Dinkum Aussie would perform. Yet Big Ange proved an instant hit and led the club to their best ever start to a Premier League season as they topped the table after 10 games and briefly looked title contenders.

Postecoglou become the first manager to begin his career in England with a hat-trick of Premier League manager of the month awards, he was the first to claim the first three monthly awards from the start of any Premier League season as Spurs won against Luton, Fulham and Crystal Palace in October, earning recognition for their manager. His side won eight games from 11, drawing two before a home defeat to Chelsea which, strangely, only seemed to increase supporters' affection for the new manager Only Conte, Guardiola and Klopp had previously won the Manager of the Month award in three consecutive months.

The 57-year-old left Celtic after winning successive Scottish Premiership titles in his two seasons in charge, but apart from a reputation of being the right guy for the job, he was little known inside Europe's big leagues where he hadn't managed. He was Spurs' fourth permanent manager since Mauricio Pochettino led them to the Champions League final in 2018-19.

"We are excited to have Ange join us," said Daniel Levy on the appointment in the summer of 2023. "Ange brings a positive mentality and a fast, attacking style of play. He has a strong track record of developing players and an understanding of the importance of the link from the academy — everything that is important to our club."

Spurs had been searching for a new manager since Conte's departure in March with Cristian Stellini and then Ryan Mason taking charge on an interim basis. Postecoglou, the first Australian to manage in the Premier League, arrived at Tottenham after winning a domestic treble in Scotland, where he claimed five of the six trophies available to Celtic during his two campaigns with the club. He is one of only five managers, along with Jock Stein, Martin O'Neill, Brendan Rodgers and Neil Lennon, to secure a domestic clean sweep with Celtic."It has been a pleasure working with Ange, a great football manager and a good man. He has served the club with such energy and determination and delivered a phenomenal level of success," Celtic chief executive Michael Nicholson said. "Of course, we wanted Ange to stay at Celtic and while there is real disappointment we are losing him, he has decided he wants to look at a new challenge, which we respect."

Spurs spent 10 weeks searching for Conte's successor, with Julian Nagelsmann, Luis Enrique, Arne Slot, Graham Potter, Julen Lopetegui, Brendan Rodgers and former boss Pochettino all linked with the role at some point. Since the 2019 Champions League final defeat, Spurs had managed just one top-four finish in the subsequent four seasons.

Postecoglou took over Celtic in the summer of 2021 after they had finished the previous season 25 points behind champions Rangers. When he arrived chief executive Peter Lawwell had been replaced by Dominic McKay, Nick Hammond stepped down as head of football operations and long-serving captain Scott Brown left to join Aberdeen. Levy was also searching for a new sporting director following the exit of Fabio Paratici, who resigned after losing his appeal against a 30-month ban from football, while club captain Harry Kane was destined to leave following a protracted courtship from Bayern Munich - so the Aussie was seen as someone equipped to steady the ship and deliver a winning mentality to a new group of players.

Postecoglou's playing career was spent in Australia, primarily with South Melbourne, where he played under Ferenc Puskas, the legendary Hungarian to whom he attributes his coaching philosophy. He began management in 1996 with South Melbourne before winning back-to-back A-League titles with Brisbane Roar between 2009 and 2012. After a season with Melbourne Victory he became manager of Australia in 2013 and guided his country to the 2014 World Cup as well as victory in the 2015 Asian Cup. In Japan, with Yokohama F Marinos, he ended the club's 15-year wait for a J-League title in 2019.

Big Ange changed the mentality at Spurs virtually overnight delivering attacking, flair football, in the tradition of Spurs in their "glory, glory" days. But the whirlwind unbeaten start came to an incredible end when they were reduced to nine men yet still went on the attack! Eventually it ended in a 4-1 defeat to Chelsea that crushed Postecoglou's chances of matching Pep Guardiola's record of four consecutive manger of the awards, yet the Australian's response to criticism of this gung-ho approach was to state, "This is who we are, mate".

Spurs were applauded for the spirit and character, but they were responsible for their own derby downfall having lost their starting centre-backs before half-time, one through injury, the other red carded, Ange had to bring on Eric Dier and shift a full-back inside. Despite his numbers decreasing further with a second red, he continued with his high line defending.

The following week, stoppage-time goals from Pablo Sarabia and Mario Lemina saw Wolves produce a stunning late comeback to beat a depleted Tottenham 2-1 at Molineux as Big Ange suffered the aftermath of red cards and key injuries. The damage from Spurs' stunning defeat at home to Chelsea was laid bare at Molineux, with the manager forced into four changes thanks to the suspensions of Cristian Romero and Destiny Udogie and the long-term injuries to James Maddison and Micky van de Ven. At first it looked as though the absences of those key players wouldn't affect Spurs, who raced ahead inside three minutes thanks to Brennan Johnson's first goal for the club but that was as good it got before Sarabia volleyed a leveller past Guglielmo Vicario in the 91st minute with Lemina plundering the winner in the 97th minute. Spurs looked to be passing that test during the opening exchanges, with Pierre-Emile Hojbjerg, Emerson Royal, Eric Dier and

Ben Davies slotting into the team and Johnson putting his side ahead from Pedro Porro's low pass. But Spurs took more than 40 minutes to register their next shot and only remained level thanks to Vicario's sharp low save from Lemina, while Davies bailed out Dier's mistake by blocking Rayan Ait-Nouri's dangerous effort.

Spurs second straight defeat meant they missed the chance to replace Manchester City at the top of the Premier League. Life had been plain sailing for Postecoglou until the wheels came off inside a week after Spurs set the pace at the top of the Premier League remaining unbeaten in their first 10 games.

Postecoglou admitted Spurs lacked fluency due to the changes: "We started well but we could have been a little bit more positive and aggressive with the ball. We made so many changes so we're not going to get the same sort of fluency. The second half I thought wasn't too bad. Maybe because we were winning the game and a lot of those guys haven't played that many games, there was a bit of self-preservation - just get through to the end. It's understandable."

Asked about the mood in the Spurs dressing room after back-to-back defeats, the manager said: "Disappointed, obviously. It's part of the pain in football. You've just got to take it. I can't fault the players' effort or their commitment. It was always going to be a tough game and we couldn't hold out."

This display exposed the lack of depth in Spurs' squad that everyone knew existed. Without Maddison, Spurs lacked creativity, Dier looked shaky. The authority of Romero and, in particular, Van de Ven was sorely missing.

Spurs were still in the top four - more than anyone expected at this stage - and the progress under Postecoglou is undeniable. But this was a reality check for anyone who believed Tottenham had the depth to maintain their imperious start throughout a gruelling season.

*

ON THE EVE OF SPURS' Premier League game against treble-winners Manchester City at the Etihad, Pep Guardiola declared that Ange Postecoglou "makes football a better place". Tottenham had been the last team to lose their unbeaten record in the 2023/24 season as Big Ange broke a record winning the first three Manager of the Month awards of the season. As they faced a defining game at champions Manchester City, following another sobering 2-1 defeat at home to Aston Villa that allowed the visitors to climb above them into fourth, Ange told the media he would not move away from the principles that had taken him so far in the game and enthused football fans all over the world.

For Guardiola there was no doubt he felt Ange Postecoglou would transform Spurs. Even in his short time in charge, even in the games where they didn't win, Pep was a fan of the new Spurs style, "I am impressed at many things they do - the chances they create, aggression in all departments. He came here with nothing and within a few months already you can recognise Spurs as his team. Every team that plays with desire and determination comes from the manager. He has done this in the past in Japan and in Glasgow with Celtic. He makes football a better place - a person like Ange. I enjoy watching them play and the approach they have. The impact he has made has been quick and really good."

Pep recalled his first meeting with him in Japan during a pre-season tour when the Australian was Yokohama manager. "I saw clips of his team play and immediately I thought 'wow', there were things in there I really liked. I told my players we are going to face a good team. We won because we had better players, but I realised that though this was the first time I met him I would see him again. And since then I have followed him and in a short time he is here. So dynamic. It happened at Glasgow and now here [Tottenham]. I know they lost the last few games but did you see who they played? I see a lot of similarities when they were winning. Football is like that sometimes, two red [cards] against Chelsea, bad moments, but the dynamic is always positive."

Injuries to James Maddison and Michael van de Ven, plus suspensions to the likes of Argentine World Cup winner Cristian Romero, left Spurs vulnerable, and while it was inevitable they would dip without a squad with the depth of City, the manager refused to change his philosophy. Guardiola admired the "courage" of Postecoglou's style and enjoyed watching Spurs. "I think all the Spurs fans and the people in England can admit that his impact has been quick and really good," the Spaniard added. He anticipated that Big Ange would go for it despite his depleted team, "I encourage the fans to come to the stadium because they will have fun."

As for Spurs being contenders… even when they launched their unbeaten run, that was always going to be difficult to maintain, "It is a more difficult competition to win in every season. I have said that many times before. Every season is getting better, with more teams involved [in the title race], so every single game is difficult. Spurs is a fantastic team. Yes, they have important absences, but I saw the first 20 minutes against Aston Villa. They created a lot of chances, so they are really good for football."

Big Ange was fully aware of Spurs' rich history, none more so than having two great World Cup superstars Ossie Ardiles and Ricky Villa. The Australian admitted, "I am still like a kid half the time. I got introduced to Ossie Ardiles and I was buzzing, mate. Even in Australia he had a massive impact. When I got the job here one of my two best mates said I had to meet Ardiles and Villa. So I have ticked half of that off, yeh."

Ange had always wanted to test himself in the Premier League; it was a long wait until his big break. "We were obsessed with English and Scottish football," Postecoglou says, "the big matches were marked on our calendars. When you love football in Australia there is a big commitment because [matches kick-off at] two in the morning. My early FA Cup Final memory was 1974 and Liverpool against Newcastle. Then 1975 would have been West Ham and Fulham. All these things stay with you. I remember Trevor Brooking scoring [in 1980] and I remember Alan Taylor scoring [in 1975]. Villa scoring for Tottenham. It was something that took us away from our existence. We were a migrant family trying to adjust to life in a country where they loved sports we didn't understand. As a kid it was easier for me to understand cricket but my dad had lived in Australia for 50 years and still didn't understand it for the life of him! I took him to the MCG in Melbourne one day and he lasted until lunch. Chris Tavare was batting so maybe it was understandable! Not a great choice by me…

"But because we were struggling with so many things, the football was great. We understood it. Dad understood it. Everything we experienced with my family or friends in terms of football made a massive impact on us."

Spurs had finished the previous season in a post-Antonio Conte vacuum. With Harry Kane leaving, Postecoglou was lured from Celtic after a domestic treble but optimism was in short supply. However the fans were immediately struck by Big Ange's fearless style, playing at speed, on the front foot, entertaining. As his CV suggested, he was a winner, but also a throw back to Spurs' traditions of attacking football at its best.

"I certainly feel very comfortable with it [Spurs' history], mate. Its origins, its history, how it looks at itself. I really felt that if I came in and made the kind of impact I really wanted to, it would resonate with the people who really love this football club because historically that's what it's been based on. I try to create football teams that make an impact. But what does that mean? In our game, you have to win things otherwise it's not sustainable. But it's also teams that make an impact because the way they play, the memories they leave. That's my goal here, you know?"

A goal up at home to Chelsea in early November, Tottenham were top of the table and looked likely to stay there, and remain the only unbeaten team, but a red card for Romero, plus the penalty he conceded, changed everything as things started to unravel. Down to nine men in the second half, Big Ange chose not to hang on. Instead they tried to press Chelsea high up, something English football fans have never seen before in such circumstances. Inevitably they were punished with three late goals but does the boss have any regrets? "I don't know any other way. In the broad church of football philosophies, I have stayed really strict to one religion. I went into a library of football books and got stuck on one section that was about attacking football. It's the only space I feel comfortable. If you asked me to set up a team to get a point by playing defensive football I could probably do it but I wouldn't have anywhere near the conviction as if you asked me to try and win 3-0. I actually understand what people are saying about that night. If I was on the outside I would be saying the same thing. But this is the test for me isn't it? The amount of times I hear managers saying, 'I would like to play this way but I don't have the players…' I just think: 'Just do it mate…'".

Before the game with Villa he tried to halt successive defeats he confessed: "All eyes are on me now. The scrutiny will come but more importantly the players will see and the staff will see that I am not changing. Yes we have players missing. But we are gonna go out there whether it will be Villa or Manchester City and we are gonna play our football."

When Ange first spoke to Daniel Levy, he warned the Spurs owner that the changes he would make would look 'scary'. He explains, "Well the scary bit may now be coming, you know. When I said that I meant that when you want to change the course of what you do then actual change is really important. Too many people want change but don't really want to do anything about it. I meant we were gonna make some major decisions around staff, around players, around how we play, how we train, how we behave and whenever change is that drastic its gonna upset the equilibrium of some people. We have had a great start which has helped us accelerate certain things. But perversely this now is the bit I love. It tests me as a person. It tests my belief. What's he gonna do under the harsh spotlight of the Premier League? Let's find out."

Postecoglou bucks the trend as he doesn't take his coaching staff from club to club. He arrives alone and starts interviewing. Of his motivation he says, "I never used it as a drive to prove people wrong but I did get frustrated because I knew, with the all the work I had done and the experience I had, that I deserved an opportunity and really the only reason I wasn't getting one was because I was Australian. People were dismissive about my success. I didn't think it was fair because whatever competition you win, it's still a competition right? You still gotta be the first team. Even Celtic gets dismissed a bit. So I enjoy the fact I am here because hopefully it breaks some stereotypes and lets people open their minds. I am not here because of my playing career, my profile or my connections. I am here because of my work. I still feel like an outsider but maybe that's a bit of a protection I have put there for myself. It's a space I feel comfortable in. I think I am different. I certainly am when I look at Premier League managers but I don't mind that. I don't think it means people are disrespectful towards me. What I do want to do is show I am worthy of this level. If this was a disaster or Celtic hadn't worked out, to open the door for another Australian would have been very difficult. All the frustrations I have felt would have effectively passed on to another three generations. So there is a burden there, you know, but you are hoping now that people will look at things differently."

A Robbie Williams classic has already been rewritten in his honour while Spurs fan Sir Kenneth Branagh invited him to the theatre. He accepted. He says he doesn't do small talk, or get too close to his players. "I don't take that other stuff too seriously. Rod Stewart used to love me too [at Celtic] but now he's asked for his wine back! So I know it's fleeting. It doesn't really permeate my home life. I am still a dad, I am still a husband, somebody's mate and that doesn't ever change. I can sit here with you two and talk about football all day but we go out there in the foyer and you start talking to me about what I did yesterday and I will start to get really uncomfortable. It's not me. With the players and staff I don't spend a lot of one on one time with them but that doesn't mean there is not a connection there. It wouldn't work if they didn't feel connected to me but how I show that is probably different to many. We have so many people here. My goal is to make every single one of them feel valued so I try and get across as many as possible. But if I had coffee with every single one of them I would do nothing else but have coffee. Most of the chats I have with the players are as a group. Of course players can come to me with issues. It's just that I won't be sitting down with them and asking how their day was. I have to make decisions and some of them are hard. It's human nature that if I like one person more than someone else then I ask: 'Why am I making this decision?' but because I have the same relationship with everyone, I make these decisions on the basis of what's best. I don't have anything nagging on my conscience. The key is that the players know this is who I am as a person. I am not putting this on. So they can live with that."

Ange's father, Jim, died in 2018. When he finally got his move to Celtic, he was able to suggest to his wife Georgia that he had finally made it. He didn't get to do that with his dad. "All that stuff we used to watch together in the middle of the night. Father and son. So just to see me out there now. Yeh, he would be proud but he would have been giving me clips round the ear, mate, for doing things wrong because that was his way of complimenting me. But it's not lost. One of my best mates lost his dad recently. We are at that age. The only words of comfort I can give is that I see my father in me. I look in the mirror and see him. That's his expression or I say something and I know it's him talking. We carry them with us. I have no doubt about that. He's on the

Jacqui Hall

**When I left The Sun in 2007 after 36 years service, I was presented with a Tottenham Hotspur signed ball and something that I will always treasure, a signed Spurs shirt by The Master, Jimmy Greaves.
As you can see, I've had it framed.**

Harry K, Harry H, now here's Harry B...Harry Bowler (pictured), son of a famous Berkshire gardener, is outside the stadium before a Guns & Roses concert. As a big Spurs fan Harry also enjoys the diverse events that now take place at the new £1billion super stadium. The Tottenham Hotspur stadium is multi-use with a unique, dividing retractable grass surface enabling the staging of a variety of major events in addition to Spurs matches, including NFL, boxing, rugby and concerts - creating recurring sources of revenue for the club to reinvest in its football activities.

Spurs are now the highest revenue-generating football club in London, eighth in the world, according to new figures from Deloitte for the 2022/23 campaign. The home of Tottenham Hotspur Football is the largest club stadium in London with a capacity of 62,850. The club are a money-making machine generating £5m every home game due to their new super stadium. Daniel Levy has excelled from a business point of view. With the venue hosting music concerts, NFL games, and boxing, the club's revenue soared and with Financial Fair Play regulations becoming increasingly strict, Spurs are in a strong position to continue operating without fear of punishment.

DAVID BOWLER LANDSCAPES

Tottenham manager Ange Postecoglou insisted: "It helps and it's a credit to the club we got ourselves in that position, but that's not what clubs are measured by. They're measured by other things." By that he means silverware.

The stadium is designed to maximise the supporter experience and brings fans closer to the pitch than at any comparable size stadium in the UK - distances from the front row to the touchline range from just 4.9 metres to 7.9 metres. The 17,500-seat, single-tier South Stand is the largest in the UK and stands at more than 34 metres in height - on top of which sits the famous golden cockerel.

Over 60 food and drink outlets across the stadium are inspired by London's vibrant street food scene, offering supporters a wide range of choice, including plant-based options throughout. Highlights include The Market Place in the South Stand, featuring Europe's longest bar - The Goal Line. With the addition of Visitor Attractions, including Stadium Tours and The Dare Skywalk, and world-class Conference & Events facilities, Tottenham Hotspur Stadium brings nearly two million visitors to N17 every year and a £344m annual boost to the local economy in one of London's most deprived areas. Spurs is Premier League's greenest club and the stadium is powered by 100% renewable energy, with a zero waste-to-landfill policy, a reusable beer cup scheme and a wide range of public transport options.

journey but it would have been nice to give him a bit of a glimpse of what his boy became…".

On Spurs going forward, Ange was realistic, "If we are gonna grow and be the team we want to then we will have to expose ourselves and we exposed ourselves that night against Chelsea. Part of me felt a perverse pride because it showed these players are 'all in'. Now it's up to me to show them the way forward and I will. The beauty of it is that I had nine men out there who totally believe in something. For me that's the biggest part of the battle. That's gold.'

*

Big Ange stuck to 'his way in the religion of football' after waiting throughout the international break. In his interview with the It's All Kicking Off podcast, he said: "The scrutiny will come but internally, the players and the staff will see I'm not changing. This is who we are going to be. Yes we're under demand, yes we are going to have some key players missing but we are going to go out there, and we're going to play our football. [Against Chelsea I thought] I've got nine men out there who totally believe in something and for me that's gold because that's the biggest part of the battle. Being ourselves, playing our football, we can still get to where we want to."

Asked what would have happened if his side went down to eight, he joked: "I think I said after the game, 'if we were down to five we'd still have a go' - well there's no point defending with five is there, you've got no chance!" Ange added that he "couldn't be happier" with his players despite a few defeats and the end of the honeymoon period. Defeat to Aston Villa left Spurs contemplating three consecutive defeats before a trip to champions Manchester City. A lack of clinical finishing was the primary factor that let them down. After the game Postecoglou admitted, "Obviously it's not great when you're going through a run like this and we're obviously down in numbers. But, again, the players who were out there today — I couldn't be happier with the way they approached the game."

For the big test of the season at the Etihad, he was excited to welcome Bissouma back but wanted his team to improve their discipline. The former Brighton man had served a one-match ban for five yellow cards before the halfway point of the season. The summer signing had enjoyed a superb start to the new campaign but played only three times since being sent off for two bookings at Luton in early October while Romero and Udogie saw red against Chelsea. "Really pleased to get 'Biss' back. He is such an important part of our set-up with the way he plays in that role," Postecoglou said. "If you look at the first third of the season, from a results' perspective I reckon we are still on the positive side of the ledger. Performance-wise, I still think we are on the positive side of the ledger, even though we've had some disappointments, but an area we need to improve is discipline. He is part of that. That has let us down in this first half of the year. Not just in terms of cards, but being really focused in our approach and these are the things we need to learn as a team. I am sure 'Biss' probably feels himself a bit frustrated with the fact he had such a great start and now it's been disrupted, but great to have him back, particularly against a team like City. He is going to be really important for us. It is a lesson for him and us as a group. If you want things to run a bit more smoothly, you have to be really disciplined in your approach and really focused in what you do. Hopefully he comes out of this knowing for him to maintain becoming a really important part of our team, he needs to have that discipline and focus."

Tottenham had no reason to fear going to City despite a lengthy list of absentees, as the club boasted an excellent record against the Premier League champions, albeit previously playing in a pragmatic way, and Postecoglou knew his different attacking approach was questioned. "That's not a bad thing," claimed the Spurs boss, "that's a good thing. We need to be scrutinised. I need to be scrutinised, I need to be questioned. That's what tests my resolve. I ain't gong to change, but bring it on. It doesn't just test me, it tests the players, it tests the club. How resolved are we about doing this? Look at all the top teams, they've all been through the process, through the tough times. They've all got questioned, they've all got scrutinised, they've all had criticism. How did they handle it, the ones that are through the other side? The ones who handled it differently, where are they now? I have a real strong belief in what I do and where the team is heading and I'm just not going to waver from it. There's a reason I'm sitting here and the reason is the end game is not to beat City. If that's the end game, that's been done. It's a hell of an achievement to knock them off, absolutely, but it's not why I'm here. I'm not trying to set up a team to beat Manchester City, I'm trying to set up a team to be successful. I'm sure the players are thinking, "Is this really going to work against Man City?" and those are justifiable questions that they need to asked. My role is to show them this is still the way forward for us as a group if we're ever going to bridge that gap to being a successful side. I don't feel like it's at a point where I'm losing people. Even internally people will always ask those questions, 'Can you do this?' 'Are you able to continue playing this way?' 'Is it working or is it not working?' When I lay my head at night, I just believe in it. I get up the next day thinking I feel strongly about it. Maybe I'll end up in a heap, mate. I don't know, because there are no guarantees but my gut tells me that I won't. I enjoy it."

The game itself was fun, but not for the faint-hearted for either set of fans. Dejan Kulusevski's 90th-minute header denied City victory in a breathless six-goal thriller at the Etihad. City thought they had won it nine minutes from time when Grealish turned home Haaland's cross for his first goal since April following some awful defending from Spurs but Tottenham snatched a point from a match that ended in controversy as referee Simon Hooper blew for a foul on Haaland, who had already shrugged off Emerson Royal's tackle and chipped a pass to Grealish which seemed to set the England man clear. Haaland was still complaining long after the final whistle and responded to something said from the Tottenham bench before furiously marching down the tunnel. Yet it was fitting both sides got something out of such an entertaining game. By half-time, there were three goals, two shots that hit the woodwork, 14 shots and 10 corners. At the final whistle, there had been six goals, 26 shots, 18 corners.

Son scored at both ends within the first ten minutes, opening the scoring from a typical Spurs break and beating Ederson with a shot that the City keeper will feel he should have saved. Three minutes later he deflected a free kick into his own goal via his knee. City poured forward for the remainder of the first half as Spurs attempted to play out from the back, Haaland missed at least two gilt-edged chances but the home side would live to rue the fact that only Phil Foden had the composure in front of goal to add a second before the break, finishing off a slick City attack.

The second half began with City closing Spurs' attempts at playing out from the back but gradually Spurs came back into the game as City dropped off. When Giovani Lo Celso curled an equaliser past Ederson to pull Tottenham level midway through the second half it was no more than the visitors deserved but Bissouma was swiftly punished for losing possession close to the Spurs area as Foden fed Haaland, who delivered a low cross for Grealish to convert for what appeared to be the winner. However Kulusevski's late intervention, a mix of head and shoulder sending the ball in off the bar, ensured Tottenham avoided a record fourth successive Premier League defeat, with Postecoglou's side fifth on 27 points, three behind champions City, who dropped to third.

Despite the controversy over the late refereeing decision to halt the game having initially waved play on, City manager Guardiola underlined his admiration for the visitors, "We make this sport better when both teams want to do it, football is a nice game".

Postecoglou agreed: "We promised goals and we delivered. It was entertaining. I want to beat them but you can appreciate what a fantastic team they are."

Only a week earlier Roy Keane had labelled Tottenham's third successive defeat "Spursy" after they had squandered so many chances in their home defeat to Aston Villa. Yet Kulusevski's header suggested there was character in the Tottenham squad. "To be fair to this group, I think they have shown that," said Postecoglou, as he considered his team's spirit. "The last three games has masked that a bit, but I don't think it has been a question of character. We are going through a tough period in terms of personnel, players having to play in positions they are not familiar with and me not wanting to compromise. But if you can get through these periods by staying true to what you are working on, you'll come out stronger irrespective of the knocks you take along the way. If nothing else, a day like today gives the players more belief in themselves."

With so many book launches, having written 90 books, its important to have a nice smile. While not quite in the Jürgen Klopp or Firmino league of pearly whites, my local Sunningdale dentists do a great job on my nashers, as you can see.

Dr Rajit Singh Panesar and Dr Dharmesh Barot are also regulars at the book launches in the area as you can see from the variety of pictures.

They have enjoyed the company of Glenn Hoddle even though Rajit is an Aston Villa fan, and thrilled by the way his team have been performing this season, while Dharmesh follows Manchester United.

It must be like pulling teeth watching United these days, but Dharmesh specialises in implants and if the new owners at Old Trafford want to add some bite in their team, they know where to come!

Spurs All-Time Greatest Teams

As chosen by the authors and Spurs Legends

Harry Harris

Jennings

Knowles   Mackay   Gough   Bale

Ardiles   Hoddle   Gazza

Jones   Greaves   Kane

Subs Burgess, Lineker, Klinsmann, Ginola, Mullery, Modric

"Jennings is better than Yashin, Greaves is better than Eusebio, and we will give you a thrashing!"

The old songs seemed so much more imaginative than some of those today and far less vile. And as for the longevity of the reputations of Greaves and Jennings, they have lasted the test of time. So, too, have quite a few others among the incredible galaxy of superstars that have worn the Cockerel on their shirts.

It is therefore no surprise that Paul and myself, who both go back in time more than most, should pick the same names in attack, midfield and in goal. However we differ when it comes to defence, particularly in central defence. Here there have been a profusion of big bold stoppers, gifted ball players and the variety makes it tough to make a choice.

I see Paul and many others went for Maurice Norman or Mike England, or indeed both of them together, and who can blame anyone for picking such dominating forces of nature.

Few, however, picked out Richard Gough who for me was dominant in the air, especially as he was 'just' 6ft tall and not a giants. but he was a warrior, a leader and a massive influenced off the pitch as well as on it, while alongside him I went for Dave Mackay.

It is simply impossible not to select the world class talents of Gazza, Hoddle and Ardiles in midfield, so where is the holding player, although back in the day there were wing halves. Mackay had the fierce competitive spirit that he could step up from the back into the midfield to offer that vital protection.

I can see why Kyle Walker is a compelling choice at full back for his sheer pace, while Sol Campbell and Ledley King had that pace in the middle as well. Personally, I loved watching Gareth Bale when he started out as full back and he would be the classic attacking wing back. Bill Nicholson told me the best player he ever saw in the Lilywhite shirt was Ronnie Burgess, but it's hard for me to judge as I never saw him play, but who wouldn't take the word of the club's greatest ever manager, so I have at least named him among the subs, where I have also gone with the creativity of Modric and the flair of Ginola as well as the authority and charisma of Jurgen Klinsmann.

Paul Trevillion

	Jennings	
Walker	Perryman	Norman
Hoddle	Mackay	Ardiles
	Gascoigne	
Jones	Greaves	Kane

SUBS: Ted Ditchburn, Gary Lineker, John White, Ledley King, Ron Henry

Every time I used to walk down what is now Bill Nicholson Way, in the days of the Double winning '60s side and the Double FA Cup winners, I always believed the Cockerel on top of the clock was crowing. But times have changed. We now have VAR. Players – and Grealish of Manchester City started the trend – play in 'ankle socks' and the salary of some of the elite players is eye watering!

Today I can touch the cockerel but I can still hear the words

of Danny Blanchflower "The game is about glory, winning in style. Not boring the other team to death." But Tottenham Hotspur will always be my club and my great friend Jimmy Greaves always said to me "I played in London for Chelsea and I played for West Ham, but Tottenham was always my club". If Jimmy was alive and playing today, he would be a multi-millionaire… so very different from the days when he wore the cockerel on his shirt.

I look back over 87 years of watching Tottenham Hotspur and I can see Arthur Rowe doing battle with Everton's Dixie Dean, watch Ted Ditchburn fly through the air and catch a Jackie Milburn rocket. I can watch Alf Ramsey, Ron Burgess, Bill Nicholson… the list of the superstars who have played for Tottenham is endless, so I apologise to all those Tottenham players who I have left out in my All-Time Spurs XI. The truth is, I could have picked at least ten teams over those 87 years without repeating one name TWICE.

COME ON YOU SPURS!!!

And then sing along with me…

"Oh, Their Name Is Tottenham Hotspur They're The Best Team In The Land.
They Play The Finest Football And Their Spirit Is So Grand.
They'll Win The Cup, They'll Win The League Of That There Is No Doubt,
That's Why You'll Hear Us Tottenham Fans So Very Proudly Sing -
Play Up You Hotspurs And Bring Us Glory,
You're The Finest Football Team Throughout The Land
Tottenham Rejoices With Happy Voices
You're The Finest Football Team Throughout The Land!"

And I still sing that Tottenham song …Very Loudly!

Harry Kane ranks as English football all time greatest goalscorer, but maybe not the scorer of the greatest ever goals, but certainly world class, a term often over used on players not really worthy of such lofty praise. Harry, though, is world class, as he is proving in his first season with Bayern Munich and indeed as he has proved as captain of England.

Spurs have been fortunate to boast some of the world's greatest ever goalscorers from Jimmy Greaves to Jurgen Klinsmann, from Gary Lineker to Bobby Smith all very different in their styles and goalscoring prowess.

How would Spurs own legends rate as the clubs greatest striker and indeed their greatest ever players I asked them to name their Greatest Spurs team? Kane, Greaves, Hoddle, Ardiles, Gascoigne, Mackay, and Jennings, are (almost) unanimously selected, while Bales, Jones and Blanchflower are in most selections of the Greatest Top Ten or the Greatest Team selections.

Glenn Hoddle

One glaring omission for Glenn... himself! "You can't pick yourself" he explained.

Jennings
Walker   Campbell   King
Mackay
Gazza   Ardiles   Gazza   Son
Greaves   Kane

Subs: Clemence, Gough, Perryman, Blanchflower, Waddle, Chivers.

Paul Miller

Paul 'Maxie' Miller is one of the most active of Spurs legends and until recently he would have picked the great 'G-men' to lead the all time greatest Spurs attack, but Gilly has now been relegated to a place among Maxie's seven subs to accommodate Kane. Maxie tells me: "We selected our greatest eleven Spurs team a few years back. Here's mine with only one change Kane for Gilzean!" He added: "I'm only going on players I saw play or played with."

Jennings

Perryman   England   Mackay   Knowles

Ardiles   Hoddle   Gazza

Jones   Greaves   Kane

Subs: Clemence, Gilzean, Klinsmann, Ginola, King, Mullery, Peters

I reminded 'Maxie' that he had played, albeit the one game, alongside Diego Maradona. He retorted: "He's the best ever!"

John Gorman

John Gorman was one of Spurs best-ever left backs, but rarely if ever appears in the greatest teams. He went on to become Glenn Hoddle's assistant manager with the England team, which was a 'first', the first Scotsman to coach the England national side.
Here is his considered team selection:

Jennings

Perryman   Mackay   England   Knowles

Ardiles   Hoddle   Bale

Son   Greaves   Kane

Subs: Ray Clemence, Garry Mabbutt, Phil Beal, James Maddison, John White, Martin Chivers, Paul Gascoigne.

Not a bad team!

Tony Galvin

Tony's choices were "based on players I have watched regularly or played with".

                                    Jennings

Mabbutt   **Perryman**   **Mackay**

Hoddle   **Eriksen**   **Ardiles**

                                  Gascoigne

Greaves   **Son**

                                      Kane

As for Pat Jennings, he was assured the No 1 shirt in an all-time eleven but, typical of the gentle giant who avoided controversy and shied away from media attention, he told me: "I don't pick teams, never have done, too many greats to choose between." I responded: "Not to worry. You are my number 1. And everyone else's. Great drawings of you by Trevillion. Hope you can make the book launch."

Lord Sugar

The former chairman picked two lists. First, Greatest Players: Jimmy Greaves, Pat Jennings, Ledley King, Harry Kane, Glenn Hoddle, Danny Blanchflower, Gareth Bale, Dave Mackay, Paul Gascoigne, Cliff Jones and secondly, Greatest Team.

                                    Jennings

Walker   **Mackay**   **Gough**   **Bale**

Hoddle   **Blanchflower**   **Gazza**   **Ardiles**

                Greaves   **Kane**

Subs: Ted Ditchburn, Bobby Smith, Ossie Ardiles

Ramon Vega

Jennings

Romero Mabbutt Vertonghen

Ginola Eriksen Modric Bale

Son Greaves Kane

Subs: Lloris, Teddy, Chivers, Ardiles, Perryman.

David Pleat

Brown

Baker Norman Henry

Blanchflower Mackay

Jones Smith Allen Dyson White

Subs: Modric, Greaves, Clive Allen, Hoddle - Manager: D. Pleat

Teddy Sheringham

TOP TEN PLAYERS

Greaves; Kane; Hoddle; Ardiles; Klinsmann ; Anderton; Bale; King ; Jennings; Modric

Acknowledgements

To my wife Lorraine Trevillion, a special 'thank you' for your support and assistance in researching and collating the Trevillion Spurs art which appears in this book. To Donna-Maria Cullen, Executive Director at Tottenham Hotspur — thank you for answering every email I send relating to Tottenham Hotspur with the positive spirit of Spurs! To Peter Willis, my personal manager and friend of 60 years whose knowledge of the 1960/61 Double team is second to none. To lifelong Spurs fan Derek Kelly and our unforgettable visit to Blenheim Palace at which we mostly talked 'Tottenham Hotspur'! And last, but by no means least Ashley Shaw of Empire Publications who has worked tirelessly, devotedly and inspirationally on producing the book.

My thanks to all of those who have supported the book: David Buchler (Katerina @ Buchler Phillips), John Ferguson (Audacia Capital), Vlad Piskia and Andy Wells (Premier Relocation), Ashwin Bedi (VDC Group), Paul Dyer (Laithwaites), Alex Garland (Planet Hollywood), John Grimsdell, Jaqueline Hall and Grant Curran.